NOT the ISRAEL MY PARENTS PROMISED ME

Also by Harvey Pekar

Harvey Pekar's Cleveland (with art by Joseph Remnant)

The Beats (with Ed Piskor, Paul Buhle, et al.)

Students for a Democratic Society (with Paul Buhle and art by Gary Dumm)

The Quitter (with art by Dean Haspiel)

Our Cancer Year (with Joyce Brabner and art by Frank Stack)

American Splendor and

More American Splendor: The Life and Times of Harvey Pekar

Also by JT Waldman

Megillat Esther

NOT the ISRAEL MY PARENTS PROMISED ME

Harvey Pekar
and
JT Waldman

Epilogue written by Joyce Brabner

Lettering by Charles Pritchett

A Novel Graphic from Hill and Wang

A division of Farrar, Straus and Giroux • New York

For Harvey Pekar (1939—2010)

—JTW

For Dana and Asi (who we called Uri), because we promised

—Harvey and Joyce

Hill and Wang

A division of Farrar, Straus and Giroux

18 West 18th Street, New York 10011

Text copyright © 2012 by Harvey Pekar and JT Waldman

Illustrations copyright © 2012 by JT Waldman

Published in 2012 by Hill and Wang

First paperback edition, 2014

The Library of Congress has cataloged the hardcover edition as follows:

Pekar, Harvey.

Not the Israel my parents promised me / Harvey Pekar and JT Waldman.

p. cm.

ISBN 978-0-8090-7404-4

1. Pekar, Harvey—Political and social views—Comic books, strips, etc.   2. Jews—United
States—Attitudes toward Israel—Comic books, strips, etc.   3. Jews—History—Comic
books, strips, etc.   4. Judaism—History—Comic books, strips, etc.   5. Graphic novels.
I. Waldman, JT.   II. Title.

DS132 .P45 2012

956.94—dc23

2011047024

Paperback ISBN: 978-0-8090-7404-4

www.fsgbooks.com

www.twitter.com/fsgbooks • www.facebook.com/fsgbooks

P1

NOT the ISRAEL MY PARENTS PROMISED ME

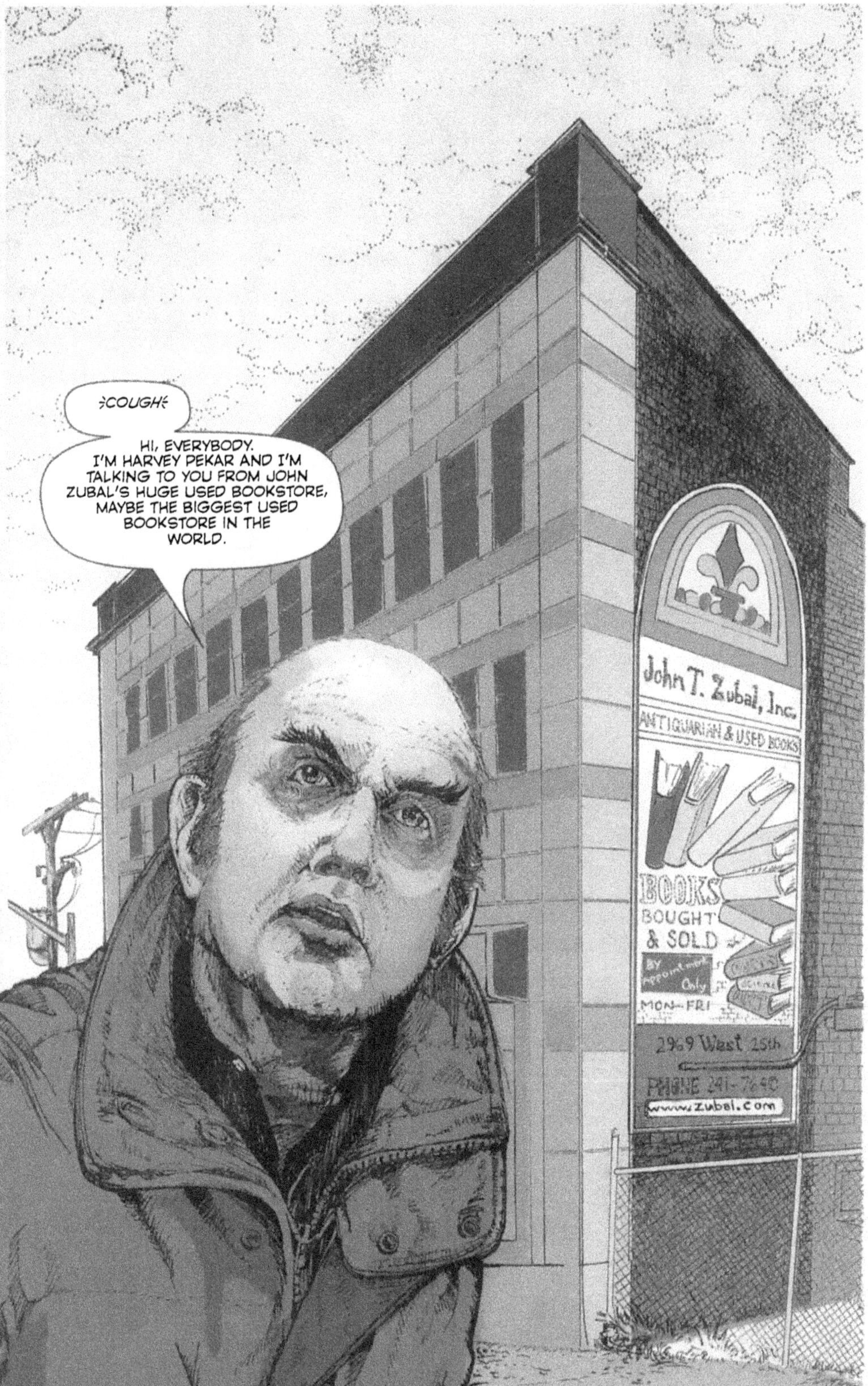
COUGH
HI, EVERYBODY. I'M HARVEY PEKAR AND I'M TALKING TO YOU FROM JOHN ZUBAL'S HUGE USED BOOKSTORE, MAYBE THE BIGGEST USED BOOKSTORE IN THE WORLD.
John T. Zubal, Inc.
ANTIQUARIAN & USED BOOKS
BOOKS BOUGHT & SOLD
By appointment Only
MON-FRI
2969 West 25th
PHONE 241-7640
www.zubal.com

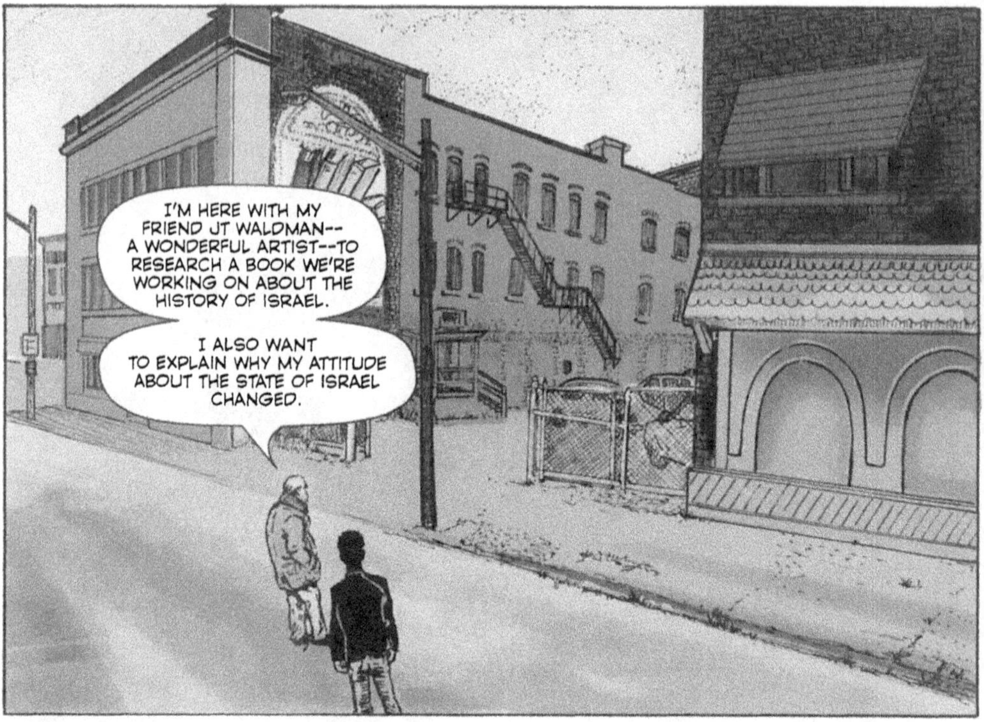
I'M HERE WITH MY FRIEND JT WALDMAN-- A WONDERFUL ARTIST--TO RESEARCH A BOOK WE'RE WORKING ON ABOUT THE HISTORY OF ISRAEL.
I ALSO WANT TO EXPLAIN WHY MY ATTITUDE ABOUT THE STATE OF ISRAEL CHANGED.

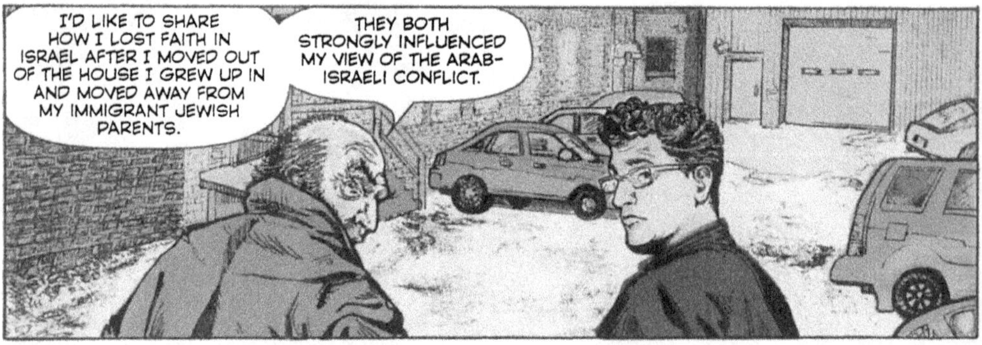
I'D LIKE TO SHARE HOW I LOST FAITH IN ISRAEL AFTER I MOVED OUT OF THE HOUSE I GREW UP IN AND MOVED AWAY FROM MY IMMIGRANT JEWISH PARENTS.
THEY BOTH STRONGLY INFLUENCED MY VIEW OF THE ARAB-ISRAELI CONFLICT.

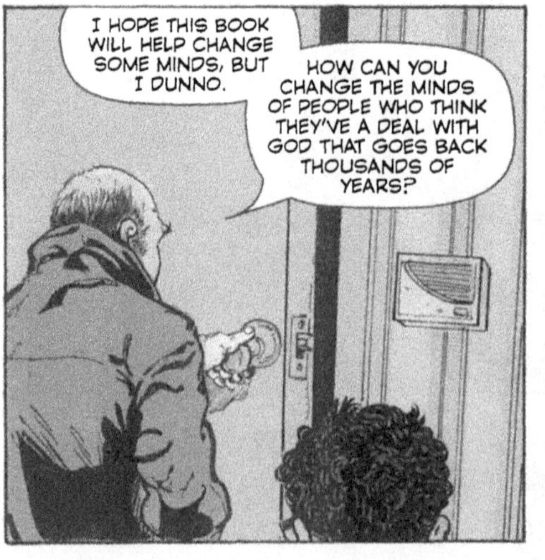
I HOPE THIS BOOK WILL HELP CHANGE SOME MINDS, BUT I DUNNO.
HOW CAN YOU CHANGE THE MINDS OF PEOPLE WHO THINK THEY'VE A DEAL WITH GOD THAT GOES BACK THOUSANDS OF YEARS?

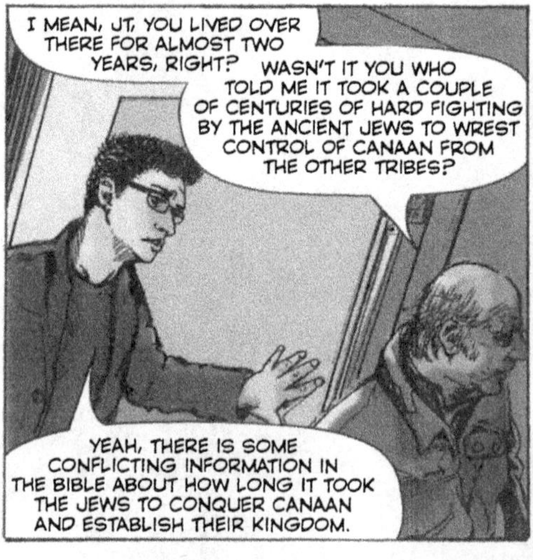
I MEAN, JT, YOU LIVED OVER THERE FOR ALMOST TWO YEARS, RIGHT?
WASN'T IT YOU WHO TOLD ME IT TOOK A COUPLE OF CENTURIES OF HARD FIGHTING BY THE ANCIENT JEWS TO WREST CONTROL OF CANAAN FROM THE OTHER TRIBES?
YEAH, THERE IS SOME CONFLICTING INFORMATION IN THE BIBLE ABOUT HOW LONG IT TOOK THE JEWS TO CONQUER CANAAN AND ESTABLISH THEIR KINGDOM.

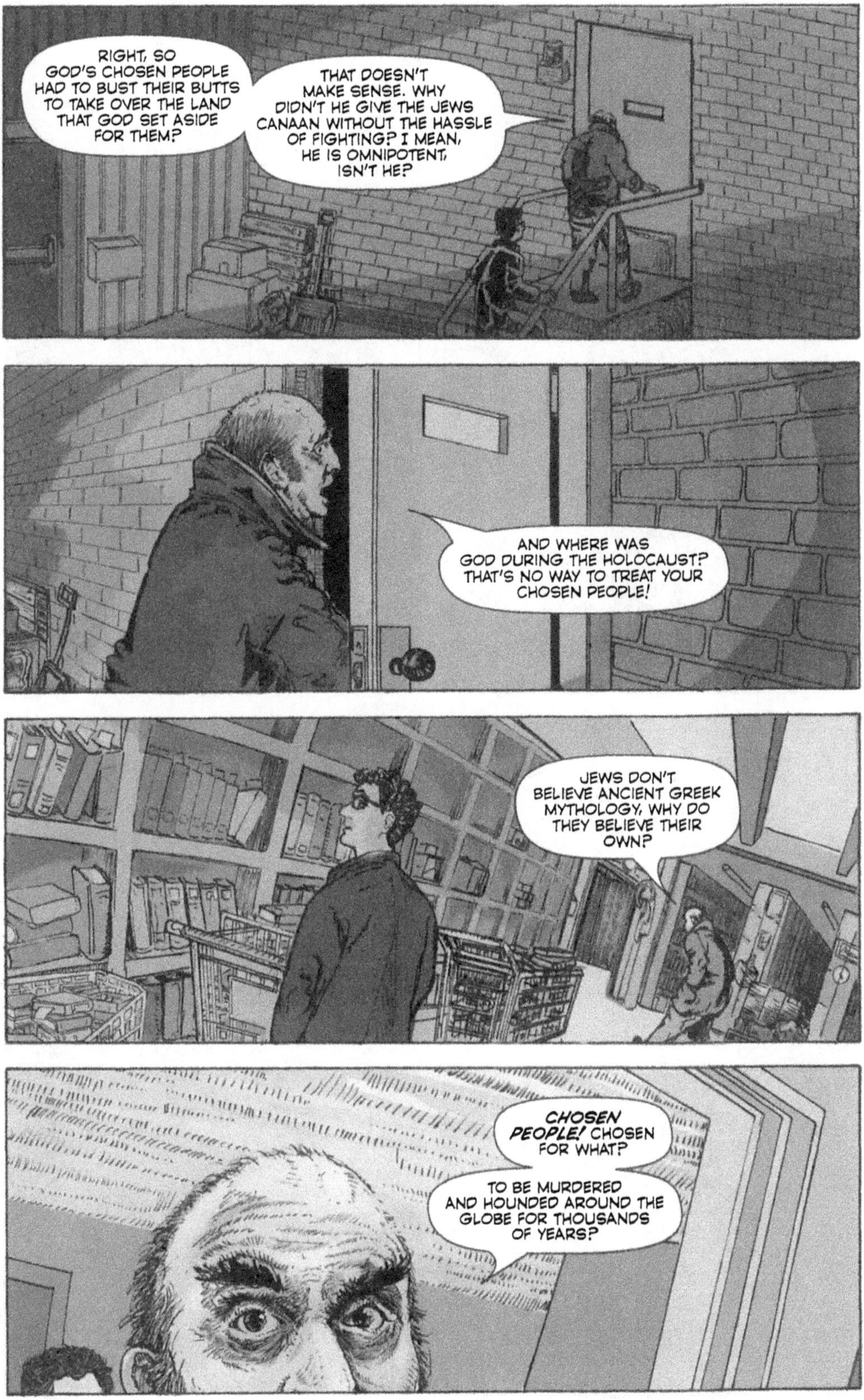
RIGHT, SO GOD'S CHOSEN PEOPLE HAD TO BUST THEIR BUTTS TO TAKE OVER THE LAND THAT GOD SET ASIDE FOR THEM?
THAT DOESN'T MAKE SENSE. WHY DIDN'T HE GIVE THE JEWS CANAAN WITHOUT THE HASSLE OF FIGHTING? I MEAN, HE IS OMNIPOTENT, ISN'T HE?
AND WHERE WAS GOD DURING THE HOLOCAUST? THAT'S NO WAY TO TREAT YOUR CHOSEN PEOPLE!
JEWS DON'T BELIEVE ANCIENT GREEK MYTHOLOGY, WHY DO THEY BELIEVE THEIR OWN?
CHOSEN PEOPLE! CHOSEN FOR WHAT?
TO BE MURDERED AND HOUNDED AROUND THE GLOBE FOR THOUSANDS OF YEARS?

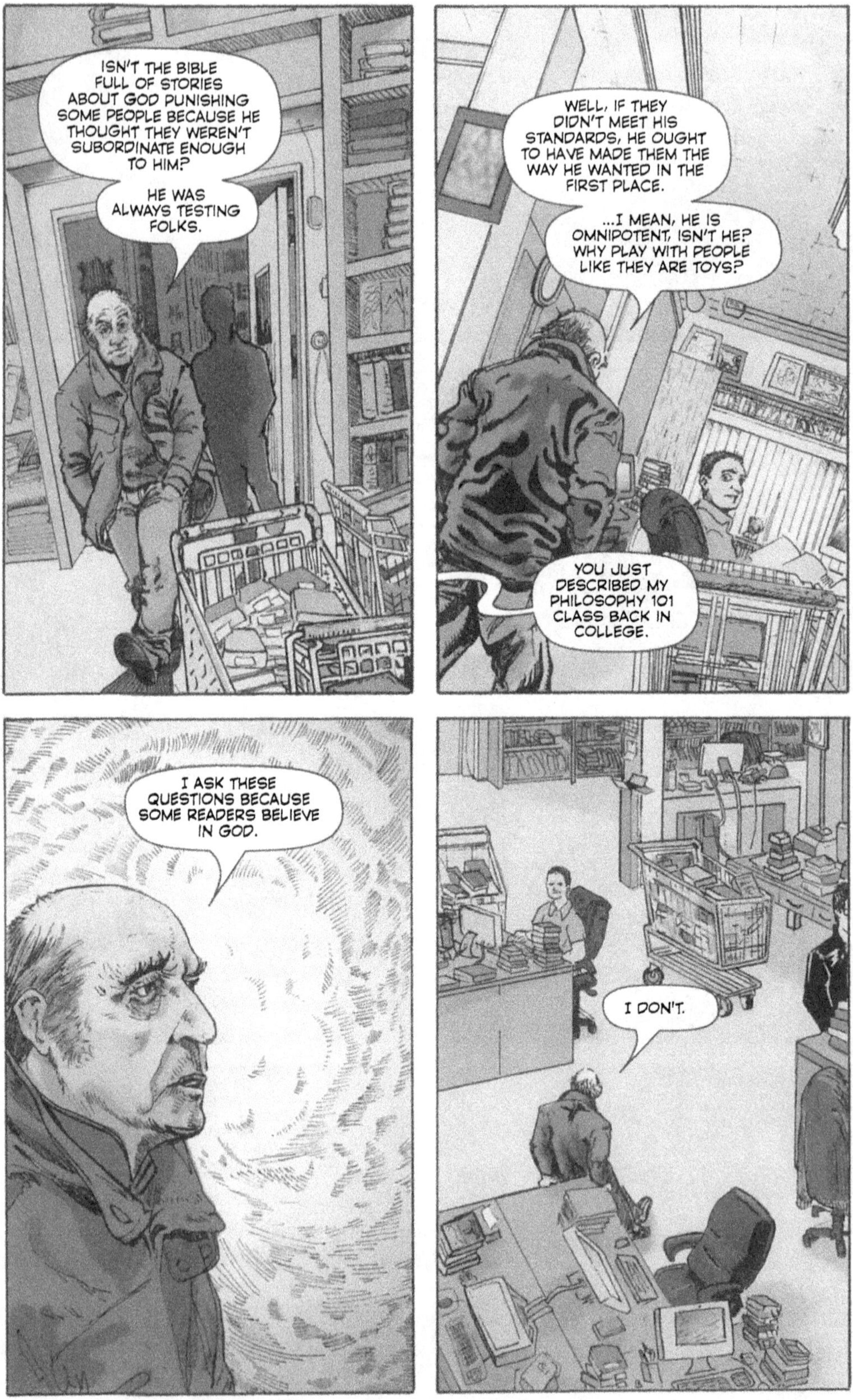
ISN'T THE BIBLE FULL OF STORIES ABOUT GOD PUNISHING SOME PEOPLE BECAUSE HE THOUGHT THEY WEREN'T SUBORDINATE ENOUGH TO HIM?
HE WAS ALWAYS TESTING FOLKS.
WELL, IF THEY DIDN'T MEET HIS STANDARDS, HE OUGHT TO HAVE MADE THEM THE WAY HE WANTED IN THE FIRST PLACE.
...I MEAN, HE IS OMNIPOTENT, ISN'T HE? WHY PLAY WITH PEOPLE LIKE THEY ARE TOYS?
YOU JUST DESCRIBED MY PHILOSOPHY 101 CLASS BACK IN COLLEGE.
I ASK THESE QUESTIONS BECAUSE SOME READERS BELIEVE IN GOD.
I DON'T.

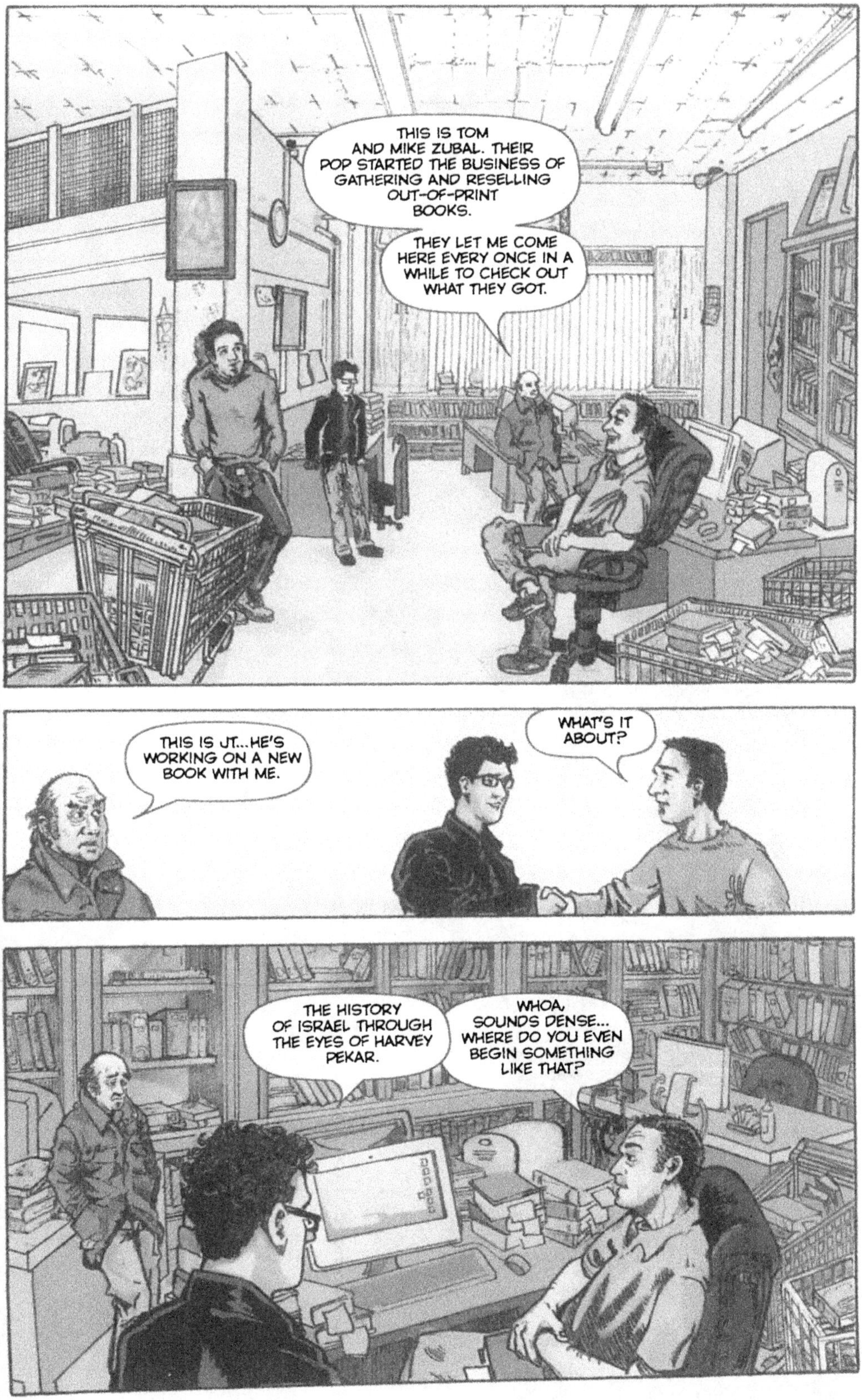
THIS IS TOM AND MIKE ZUBAL. THEIR POP STARTED THE BUSINESS OF GATHERING AND RESELLING OUT-OF-PRINT BOOKS.
THEY LET ME COME HERE EVERY ONCE IN A WHILE TO CHECK OUT WHAT THEY GOT.
THIS IS JT...HE'S WORKING ON A NEW BOOK WITH ME.
WHAT'S IT ABOUT?
THE HISTORY OF ISRAEL THROUGH THE EYES OF HARVEY PEKAR.
WHOA, SOUNDS DENSE... WHERE DO YOU EVEN BEGIN SOMETHING LIKE THAT?

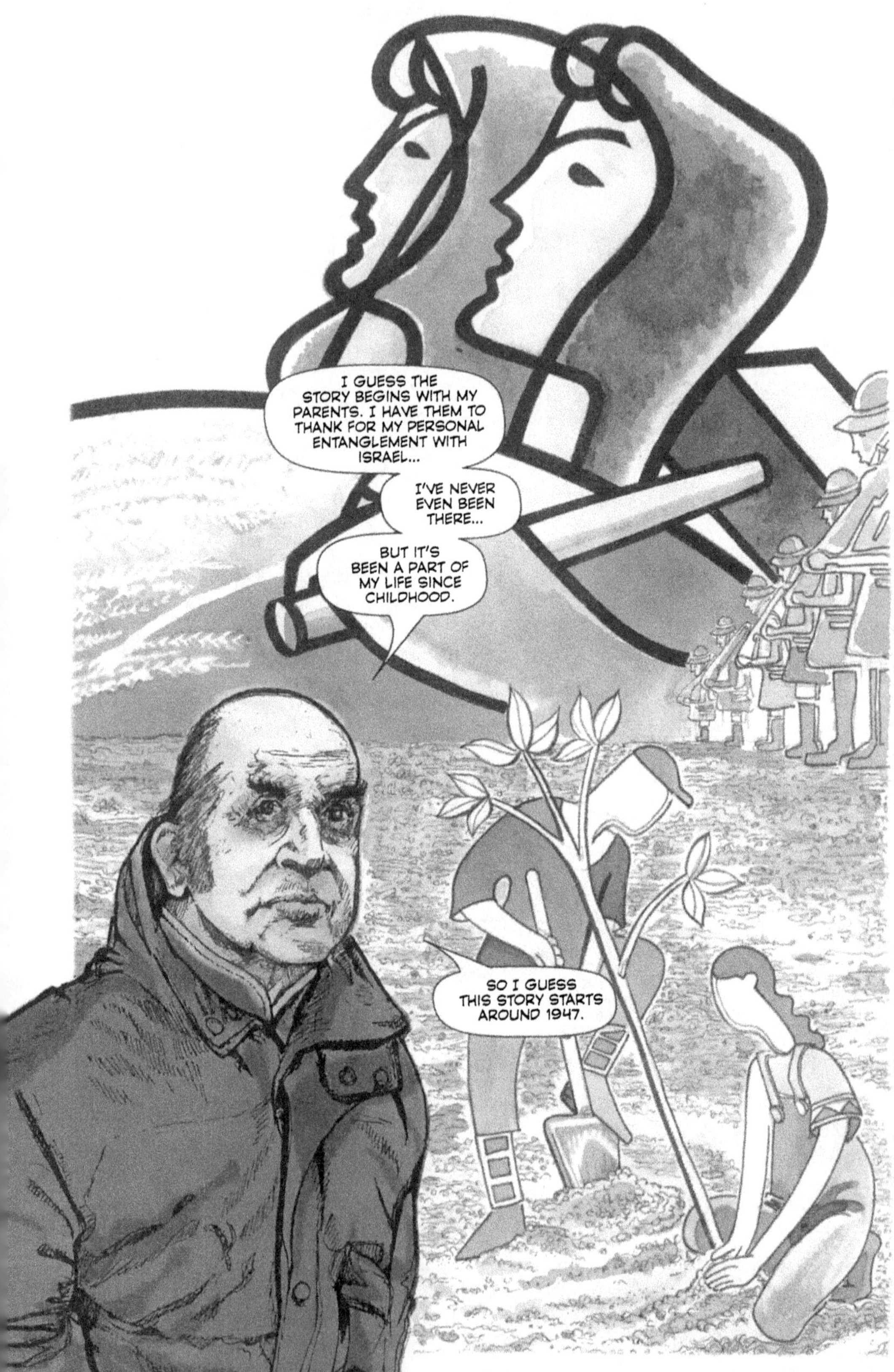
I GUESS THE STORY BEGINS WITH MY PARENTS. I HAVE THEM TO THANK FOR MY PERSONAL ENTANGLEMENT WITH ISRAEL...
I'VE NEVER EVEN BEEN THERE...
BUT IT'S BEEN A PART OF MY LIFE SINCE CHILDHOOD.
SO I GUESS THIS STORY STARTS AROUND 1947.

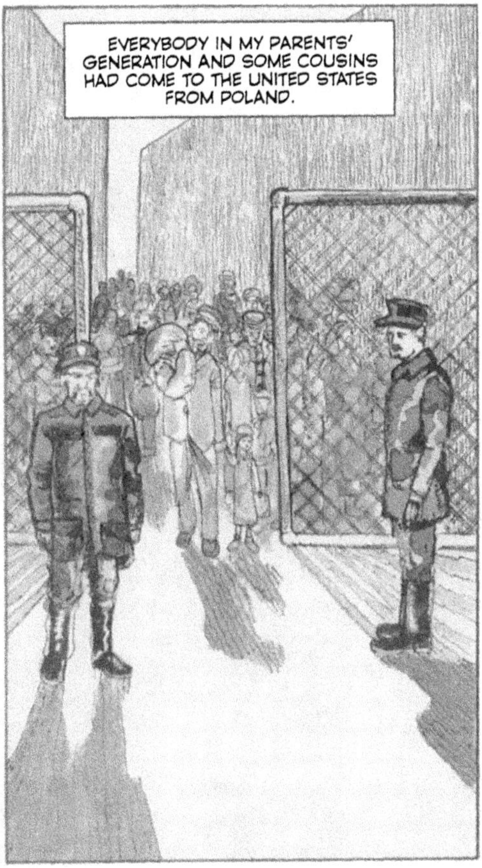
EVERYBODY IN MY PARENTS' GENERATION AND SOME COUSINS HAD COME TO THE UNITED STATES FROM POLAND.

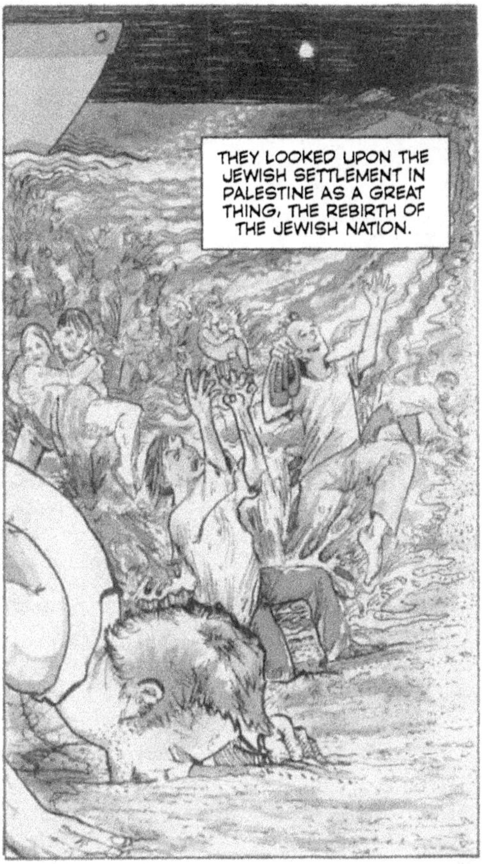
THEY LOOKED UPON THE JEWISH SETTLEMENT IN PALESTINE AS A GREAT THING, THE REBIRTH OF THE JEWISH NATION.

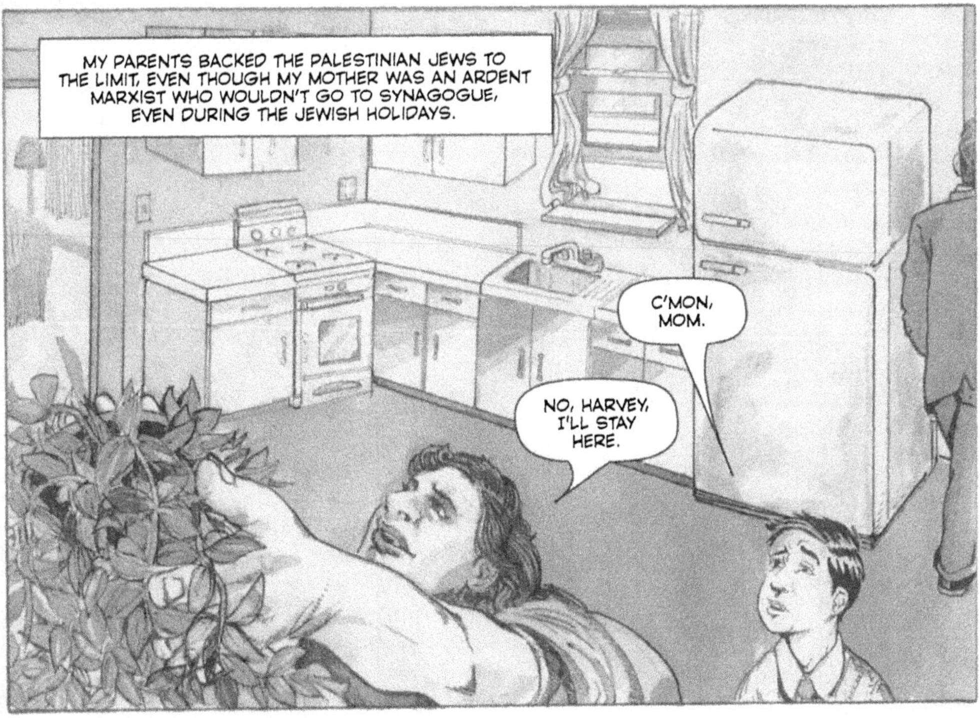
MY PARENTS BACKED THE PALESTINIAN JEWS TO THE LIMIT, EVEN THOUGH MY MOTHER WAS AN ARDENT MARXIST WHO WOULDN'T GO TO SYNAGOGUE, EVEN DURING THE JEWISH HOLIDAYS.
C'MON, MOM.
NO, HARVEY, I'LL STAY HERE.

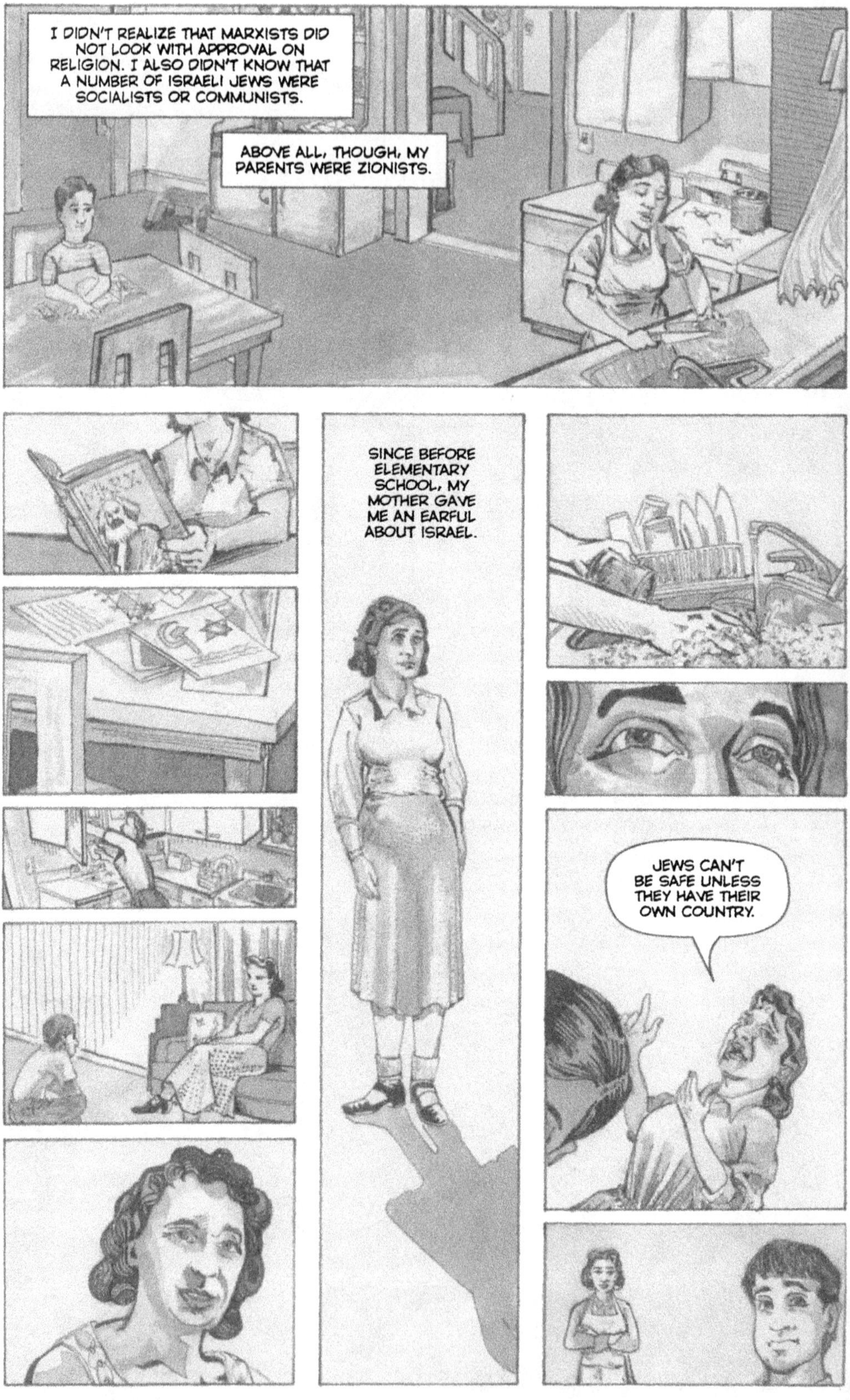
I DIDN'T REALIZE THAT MARXISTS DID NOT LOOK WITH APPROVAL ON RELIGION. I ALSO DIDN'T KNOW THAT A NUMBER OF ISRAELI JEWS WERE SOCIALISTS OR COMMUNISTS.
ABOVE ALL, THOUGH, MY PARENTS WERE ZIONISTS.
SINCE BEFORE ELEMENTARY SCHOOL, MY MOTHER GAVE ME AN EARFUL ABOUT ISRAEL.
JEWS CAN'T BE SAFE UNLESS THEY HAVE THEIR OWN COUNTRY.

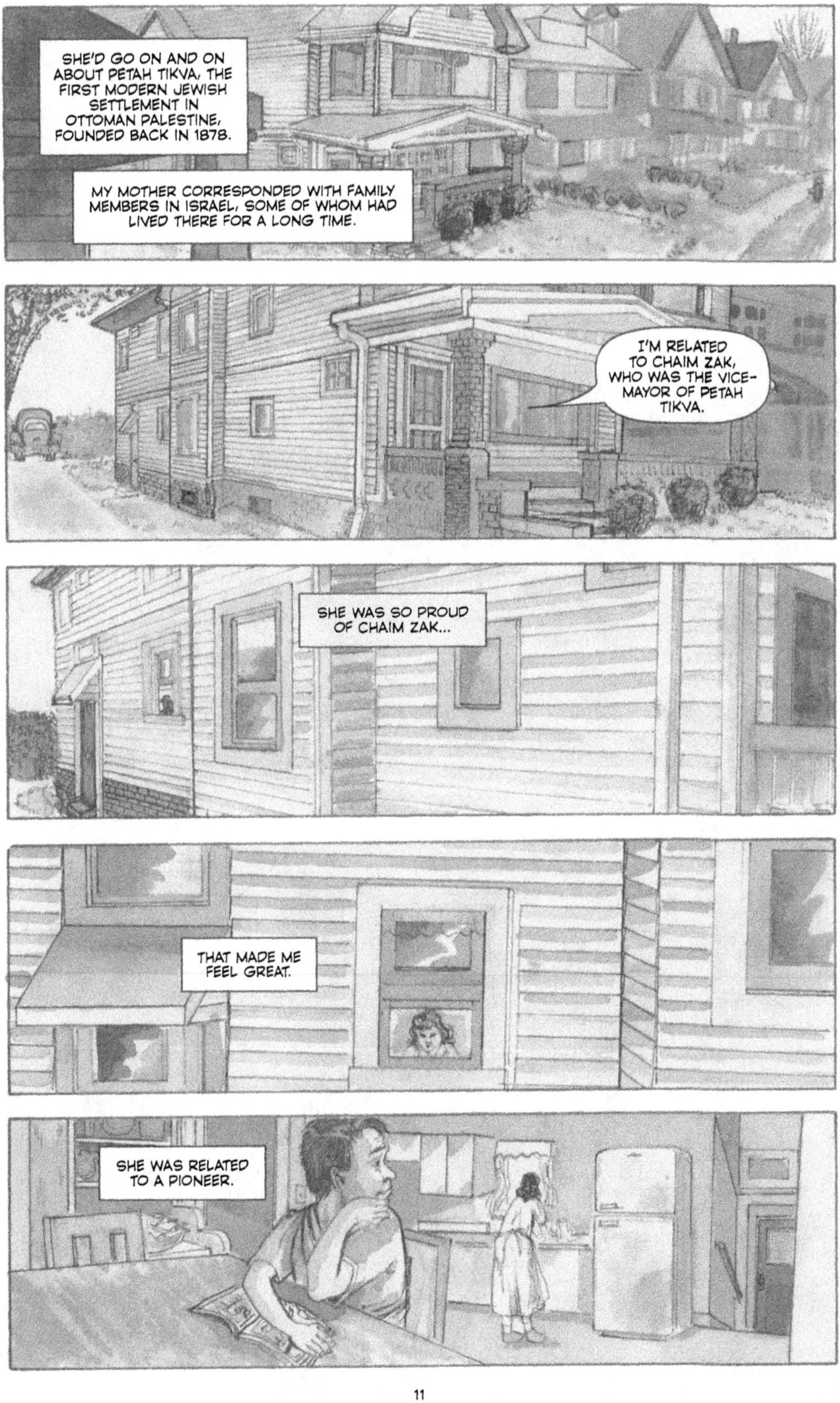
SHE'D GO ON AND ON ABOUT PETAH TIKVA, THE FIRST MODERN JEWISH SETTLEMENT IN OTTOMAN PALESTINE, FOUNDED BACK IN 1878.
MY MOTHER CORRESPONDED WITH FAMILY MEMBERS IN ISRAEL, SOME OF WHOM HAD LIVED THERE FOR A LONG TIME.
I'M RELATED TO CHAIM ZAK, WHO WAS THE VICE-MAYOR OF PETAH TIKVA.
SHE WAS SO PROUD OF CHAIM ZAK...
THAT MADE ME FEEL GREAT.
SHE WAS RELATED TO A PIONEER.

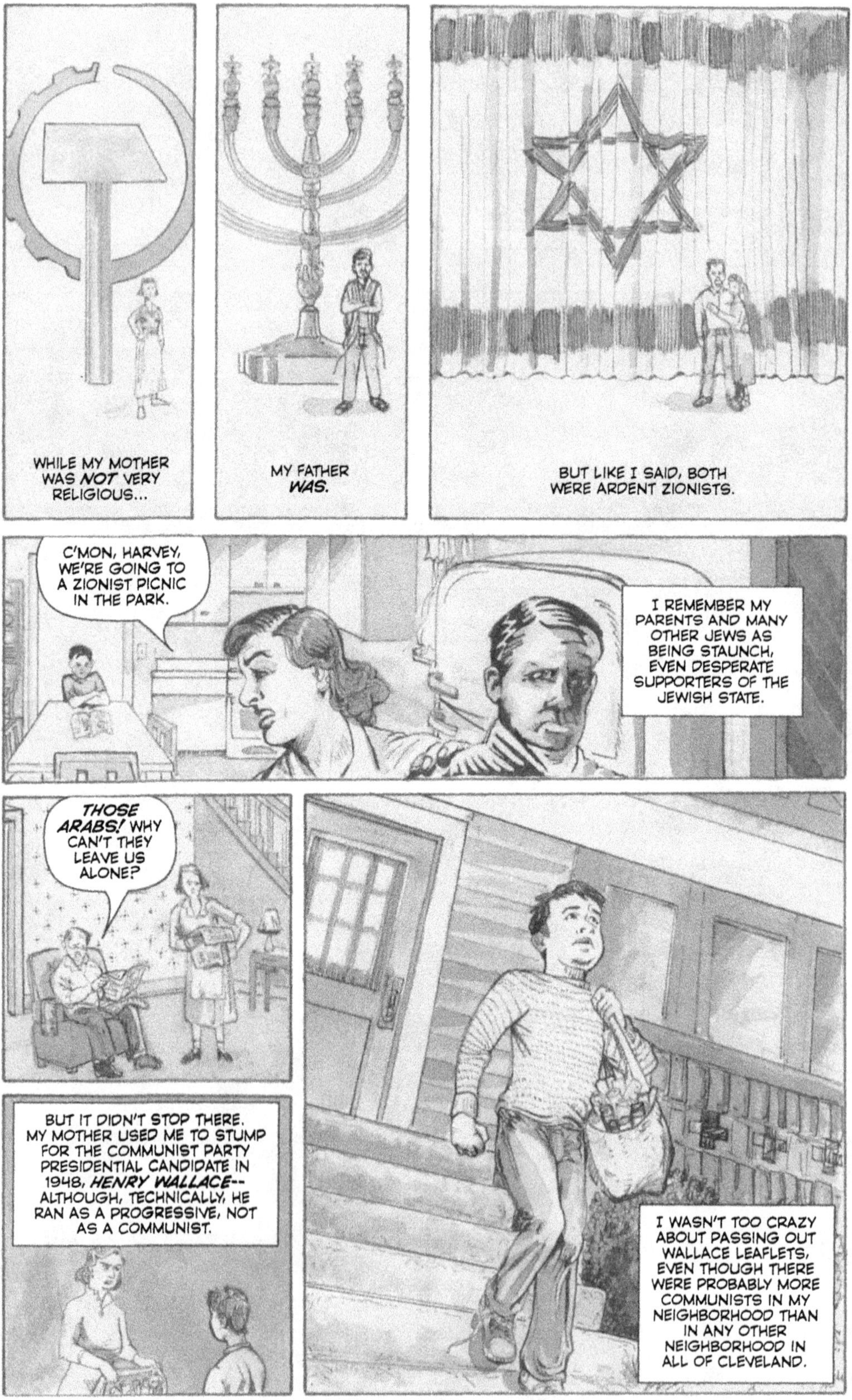
WHILE MY MOTHER WAS *NOT* VERY RELIGIOUS...
MY FATHER *WAS.*
BUT LIKE I SAID, BOTH WERE ARDENT ZIONISTS.
C'MON, HARVEY, WE'RE GOING TO A ZIONIST PICNIC IN THE PARK.
I REMEMBER MY PARENTS AND MANY OTHER JEWS AS BEING STAUNCH, EVEN DESPERATE SUPPORTERS OF THE JEWISH STATE.
THOSE ARABS! WHY CAN'T THEY LEAVE US ALONE?
BUT IT DIDN'T STOP THERE. MY MOTHER USED ME TO STUMP FOR THE COMMUNIST PARTY PRESIDENTIAL CANDIDATE IN 1948, *HENRY WALLACE*-- ALTHOUGH, TECHNICALLY, HE RAN AS A PROGRESSIVE, NOT AS A COMMUNIST.
I WASN'T TOO CRAZY ABOUT PASSING OUT WALLACE LEAFLETS, EVEN THOUGH THERE WERE PROBABLY MORE COMMUNISTS IN MY NEIGHBORHOOD THAN IN ANY OTHER NEIGHBORHOOD IN ALL OF CLEVELAND.

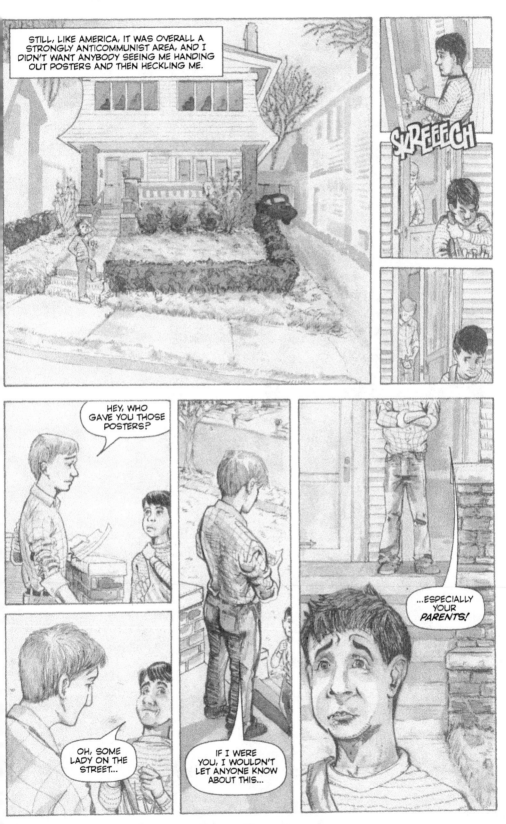

STILL, LIKE AMERICA, IT WAS OVERALL A STRONGLY ANTICOMMUNIST AREA, AND I DIDN'T WANT ANYBODY SEEING ME HANDING OUT POSTERS AND THEN HECKLING ME.

SKREEECH

HEY, WHO GAVE YOU THOSE POSTERS?

OH, SOME LADY ON THE STREET...

IF I WERE YOU, I WOULDN'T LET ANYONE KNOW ABOUT THIS...

...ESPECIALLY YOUR *PARENTS!*

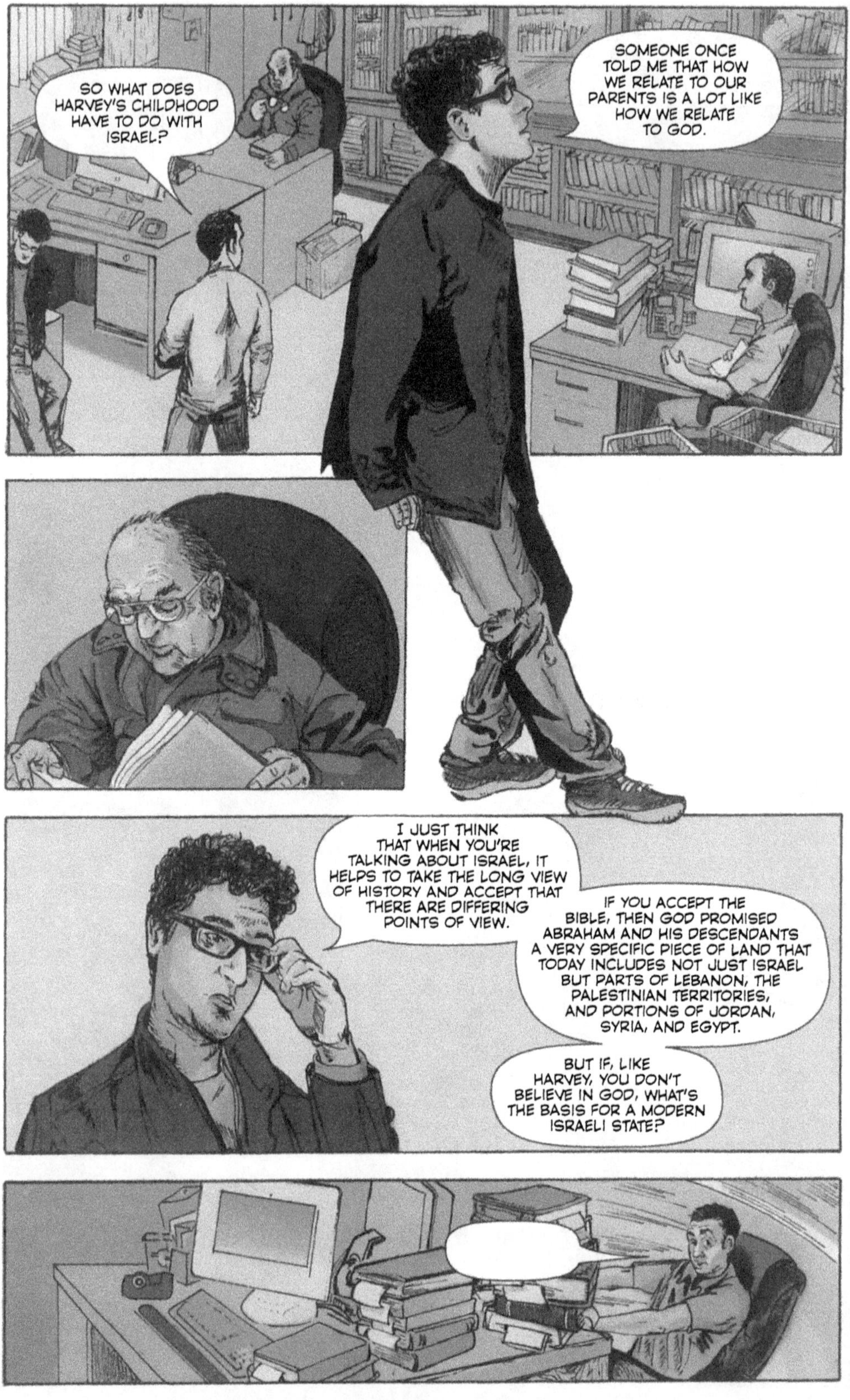
SO WHAT DOES HARVEY'S CHILDHOOD HAVE TO DO WITH ISRAEL?
SOMEONE ONCE TOLD ME THAT HOW WE RELATE TO OUR PARENTS IS A LOT LIKE HOW WE RELATE TO GOD.
I JUST THINK THAT WHEN YOU'RE TALKING ABOUT ISRAEL, IT HELPS TO TAKE THE LONG VIEW OF HISTORY AND ACCEPT THAT THERE ARE DIFFERING POINTS OF VIEW.
IF YOU ACCEPT THE BIBLE, THEN GOD PROMISED ABRAHAM AND HIS DESCENDANTS A VERY SPECIFIC PIECE OF LAND THAT TODAY INCLUDES NOT JUST ISRAEL BUT PARTS OF LEBANON, THE PALESTINIAN TERRITORIES, AND PORTIONS OF JORDAN, SYRIA, AND EGYPT.
BUT IF, LIKE HARVEY, YOU DON'T BELIEVE IN GOD, WHAT'S THE BASIS FOR A MODERN ISRAELI STATE?

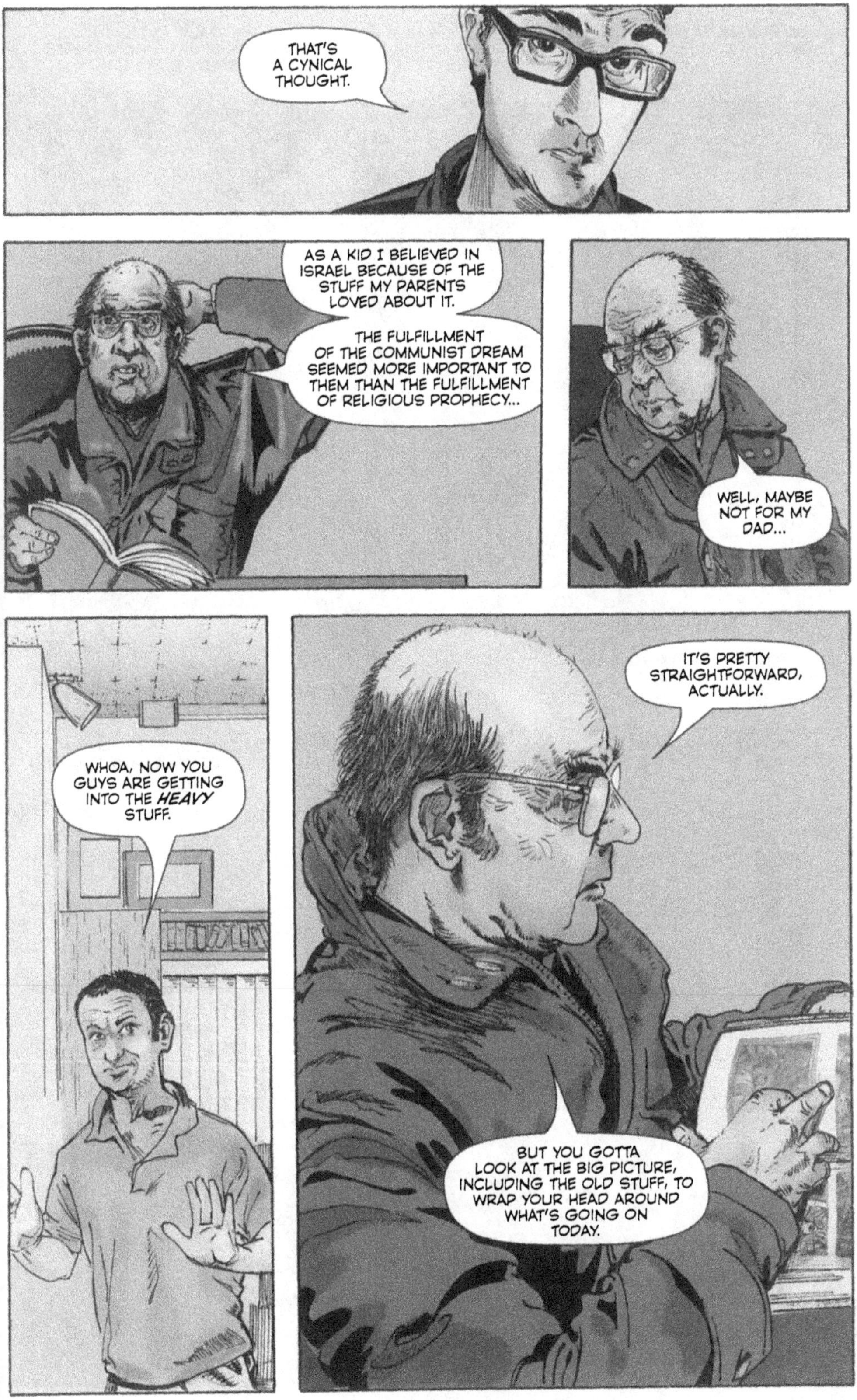
THAT'S A CYNICAL THOUGHT.
AS A KID I BELIEVED IN ISRAEL BECAUSE OF THE STUFF MY PARENTS LOVED ABOUT IT.
THE FULFILLMENT OF THE COMMUNIST DREAM SEEMED MORE IMPORTANT TO THEM THAN THE FULFILLMENT OF RELIGIOUS PROPHECY...
WELL, MAYBE NOT FOR MY DAD...
WHOA, NOW YOU GUYS ARE GETTING INTO THE *HEAVY* STUFF.
IT'S PRETTY STRAIGHTFORWARD, ACTUALLY.
BUT YOU GOTTA LOOK AT THE BIG PICTURE, INCLUDING THE OLD STUFF, TO WRAP YOUR HEAD AROUND WHAT'S GOING ON TODAY.

WE ALL KNOW THE STORY ABOUT ADAM AND EVE, BUT GOD DOESN'T GET REALLY CLOSE TO THE JEWS UNTIL HE MEETS WITH ABRAHAM, A MAN WHO IS FROM UR IN MESOPOTAMIA (THE CHALDEES) AND TRYING TO BETTER THE SITUATION OF HIS FOLLOWERS.

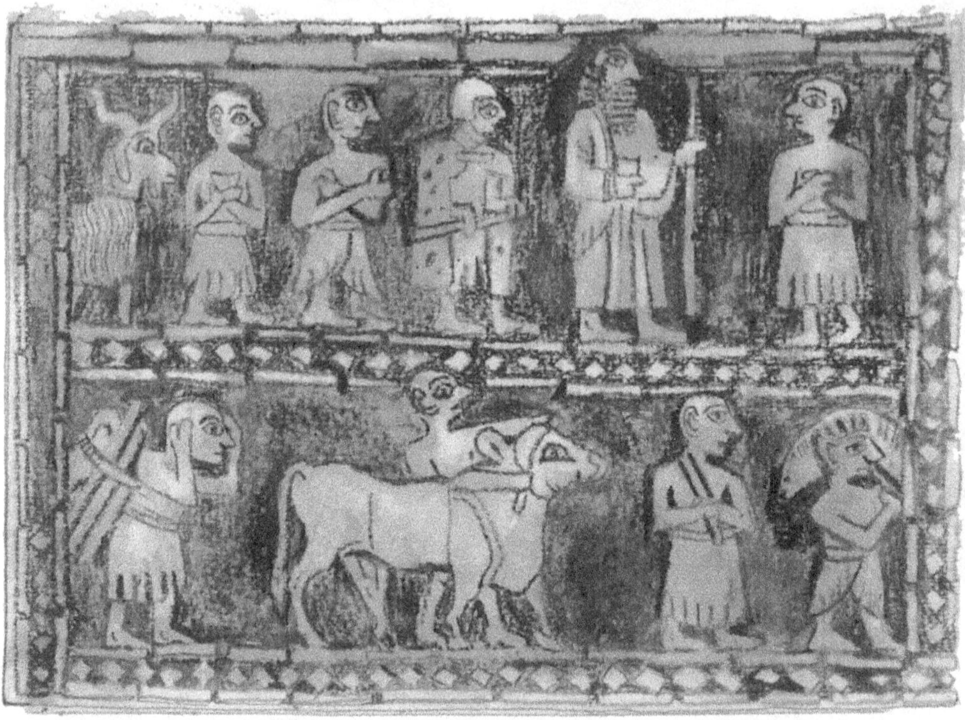

ABRAHAM INITIALLY WORSHIPPED THE STARS, BUT WHEN HE ENCOUNTERED GOD, HE INSTANTLY RECOGNIZED HIM AS KING OF THE UNIVERSE. GOD KNEW THAT ABRAHAM BELIEVED IN HIM AND TOLD HIM:

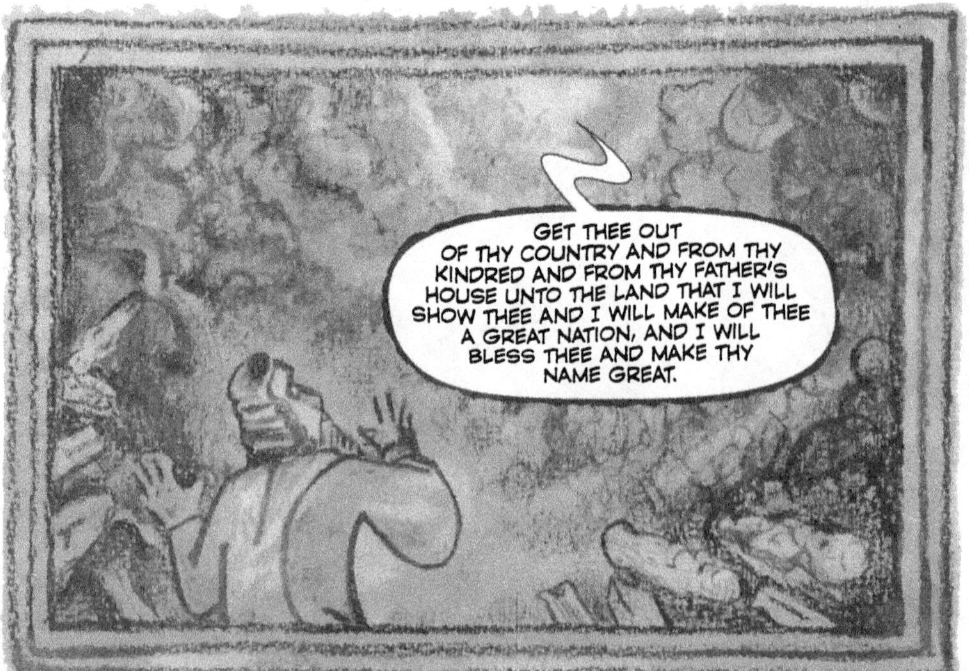
GET THEE OUT OF THY COUNTRY AND FROM THY KINDRED AND FROM THY FATHER'S HOUSE UNTO THE LAND THAT I WILL SHOW THEE AND I WILL MAKE OF THEE A GREAT NATION, AND I WILL BLESS THEE AND MAKE THY NAME GREAT.

ABRAHAM REACHED CANAAN, HIS DESTINATION. HE'D NOT BEEN THERE LONG WHEN THERE WAS FAMINE IN THE LAND, SO HE MOVED ON TO EGYPT, WHERE HE PROSPERED, BUT DREAMED OF RETURNING TO CANAAN.

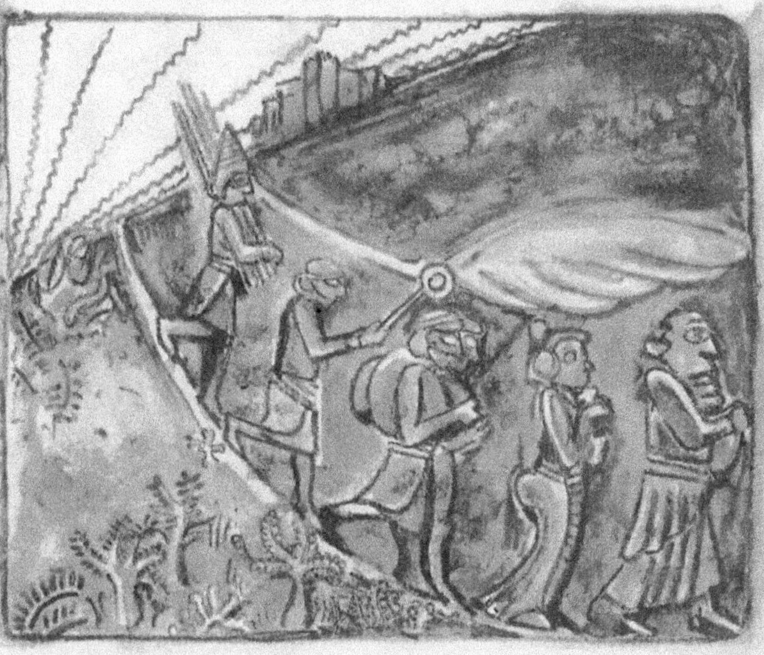

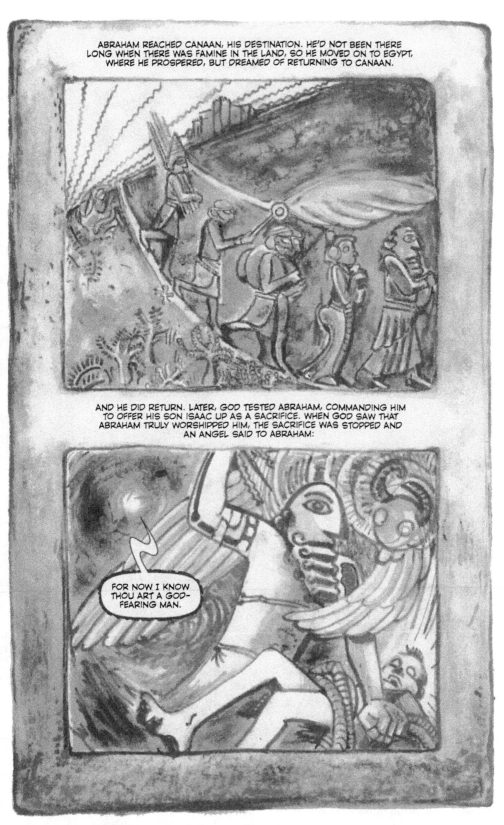

AND HE DID RETURN. LATER, GOD TESTED ABRAHAM, COMMANDING HIM TO OFFER HIS SON ISAAC UP AS A SACRIFICE. WHEN GOD SAW THAT ABRAHAM TRULY WORSHIPPED HIM, THE SACRIFICE WAS STOPPED AND AN ANGEL SAID TO ABRAHAM:

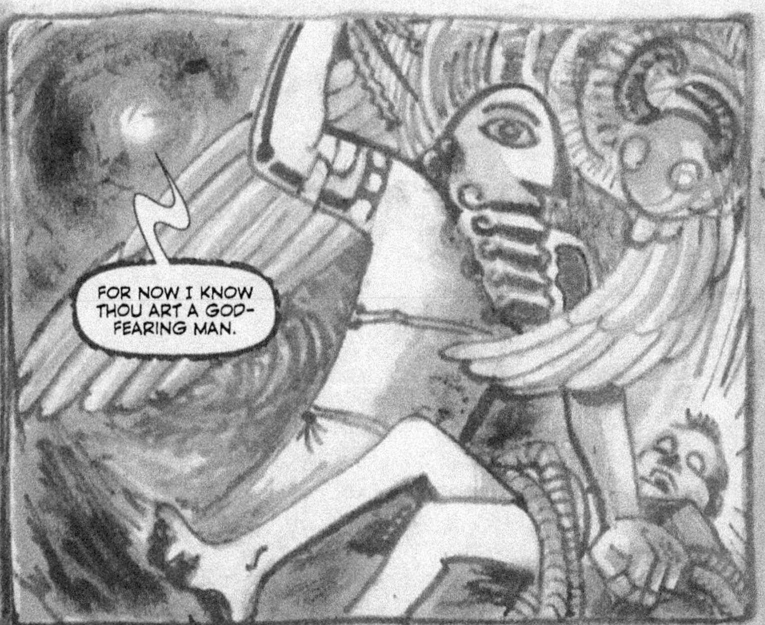
FOR NOW I KNOW THOU ART A GOD-FEARING MAN.

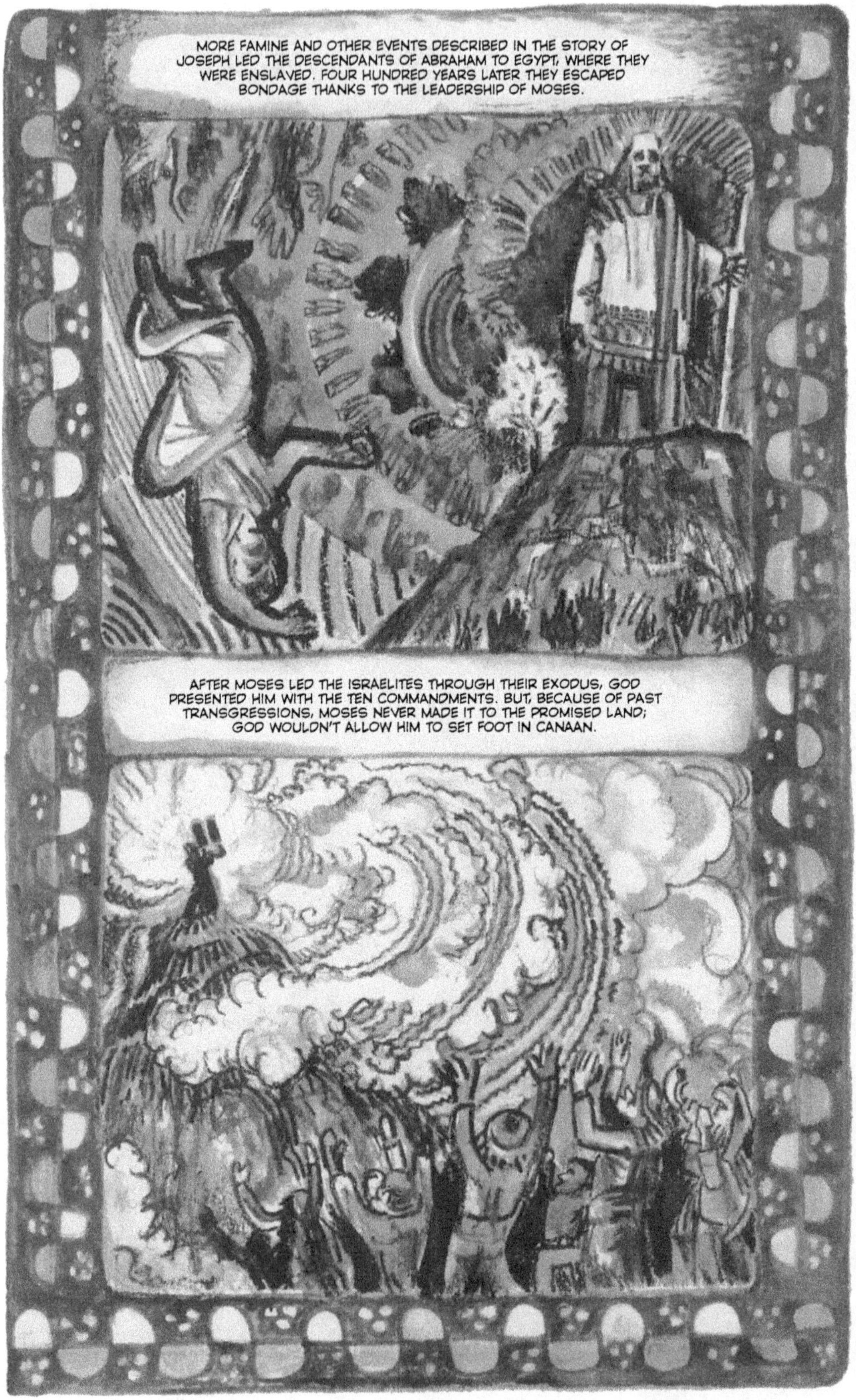
MORE FAMINE AND OTHER EVENTS DESCRIBED IN THE STORY OF JOSEPH LED THE DESCENDANTS OF ABRAHAM TO EGYPT, WHERE THEY WERE ENSLAVED. FOUR HUNDRED YEARS LATER THEY ESCAPED BONDAGE THANKS TO THE LEADERSHIP OF MOSES.
AFTER MOSES LED THE ISRAELITES THROUGH THEIR EXODUS, GOD PRESENTED HIM WITH THE TEN COMMANDMENTS. BUT, BECAUSE OF PAST TRANSGRESSIONS, MOSES NEVER MADE IT TO THE PROMISED LAND; GOD WOULDN'T ALLOW HIM TO SET FOOT IN CANAAN.

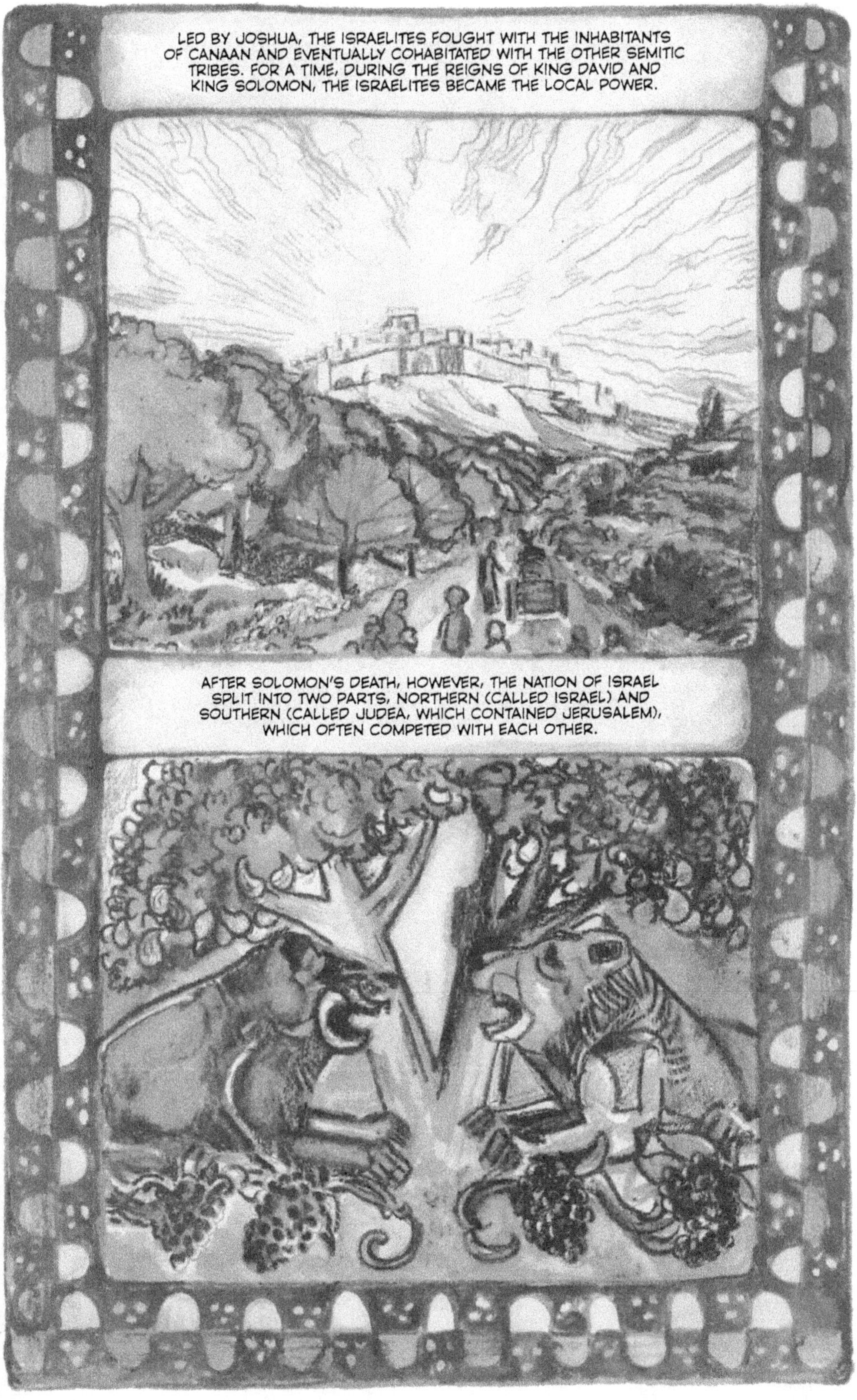
LED BY JOSHUA, THE ISRAELITES FOUGHT WITH THE INHABITANTS OF CANAAN AND EVENTUALLY COHABITATED WITH THE OTHER SEMITIC TRIBES. FOR A TIME, DURING THE REIGNS OF KING DAVID AND KING SOLOMON, THE ISRAELITES BECAME THE LOCAL POWER.
AFTER SOLOMON'S DEATH, HOWEVER, THE NATION OF ISRAEL SPLIT INTO TWO PARTS, NORTHERN (CALLED ISRAEL) AND SOUTHERN (CALLED JUDEA, WHICH CONTAINED JERUSALEM), WHICH OFTEN COMPETED WITH EACH OTHER.

THIS COMPETITION CONTINUED FOR CENTURIES, UNTIL THE ASSYRIANS AND, LATER, THE CHALDEANS, HEADQUARTERED IN BABYLON, DESTROYED THE NORTHERN KINGDOM OF ISRAEL AND THEN THE SOUTHERN KINGDOM OF JUDEA. JERUSALEM WAS CAPTURED AND SOLOMON'S TEMPLE DESTROYED.

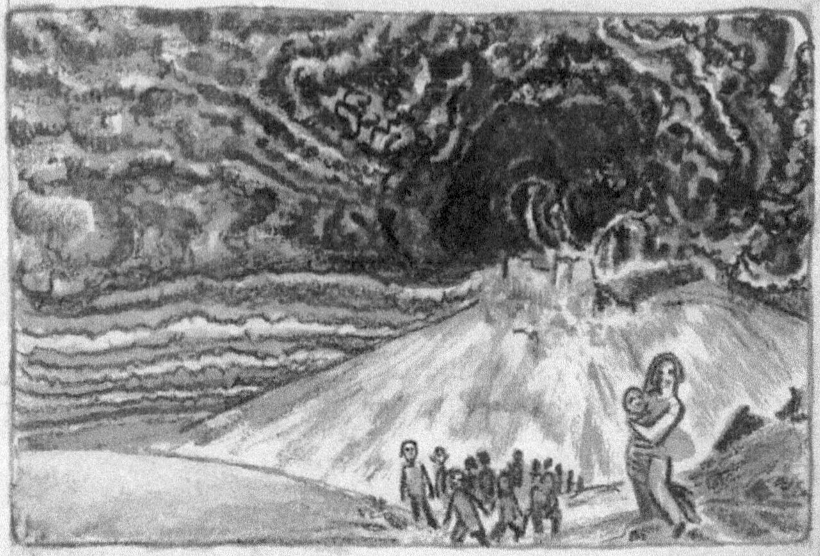

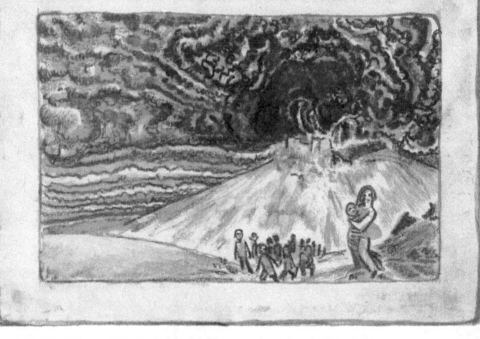

A NUMBER OF PROMINENT JEWS WERE TAKEN FROM THEIR HOMELAND AND EXILED TO BABYLONIA. EVEN THOUGH IT'S KNOWN PEJORATIVELY AS THE BABYLONIAN CAPTIVITY, JEWISH "CAPTIVES" WERE RESPECTED AND ALLOWED, WITH SOME RESTRICTIONS, TO ENTER THE MAINSTREAM OF BABYLONIAN LIFE.

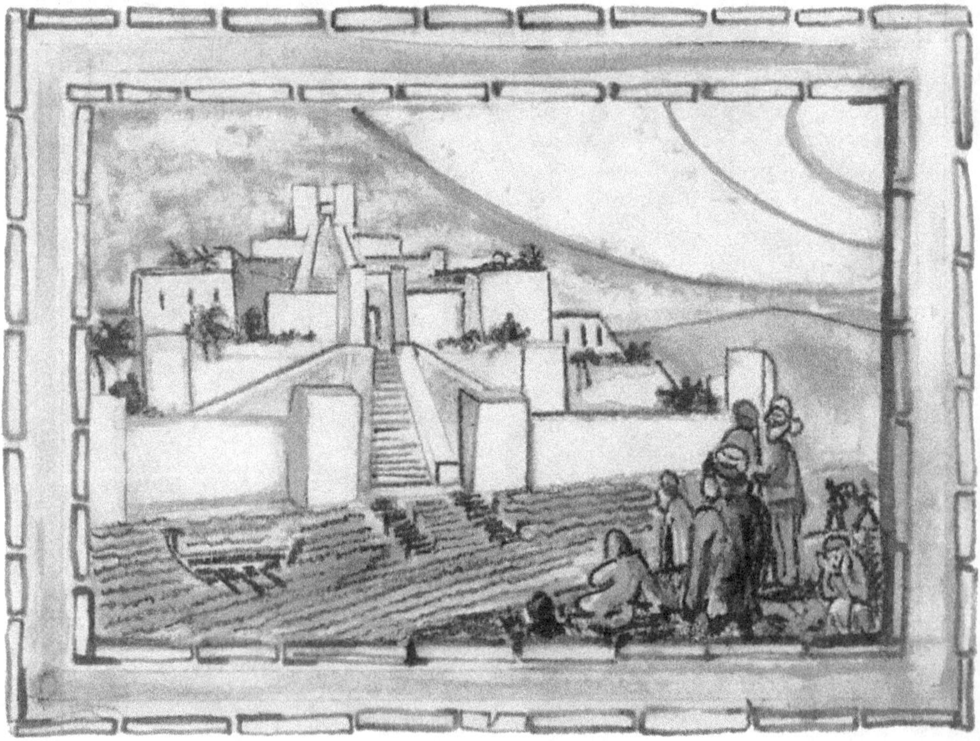

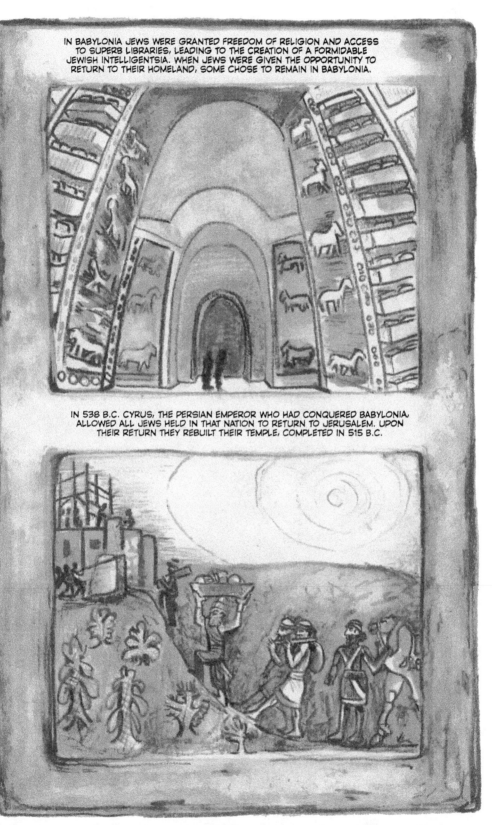

IN BABYLONIA JEWS WERE GRANTED FREEDOM OF RELIGION AND ACCESS TO SUPERB LIBRARIES, LEADING TO THE CREATION OF A FORMIDABLE JEWISH INTELLIGENTSIA. WHEN JEWS WERE GIVEN THE OPPORTUNITY TO RETURN TO THEIR HOMELAND, SOME CHOSE TO REMAIN IN BABYLONIA.

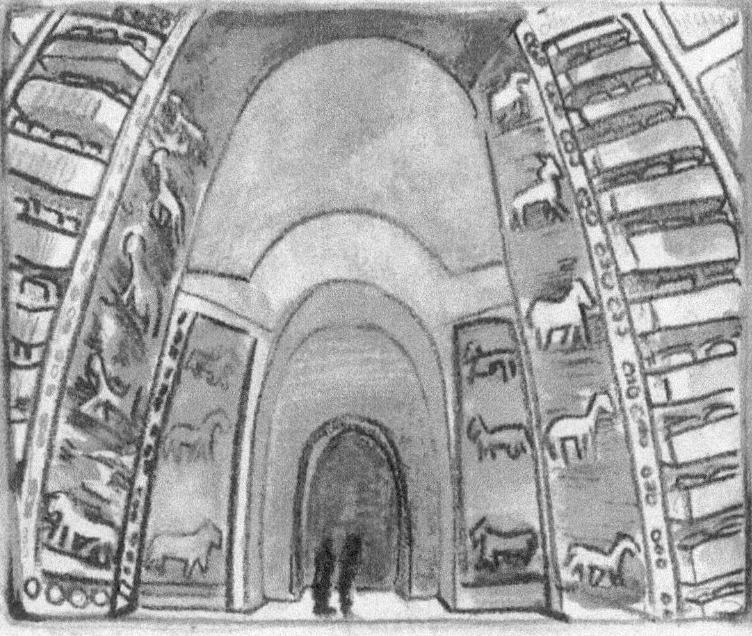

IN 538 B.C. CYRUS, THE PERSIAN EMPEROR WHO HAD CONQUERED BABYLONIA, ALLOWED ALL JEWS HELD IN THAT NATION TO RETURN TO JERUSALEM. UPON THEIR RETURN THEY REBUILT THEIR TEMPLE, COMPLETED IN 515 B.C.

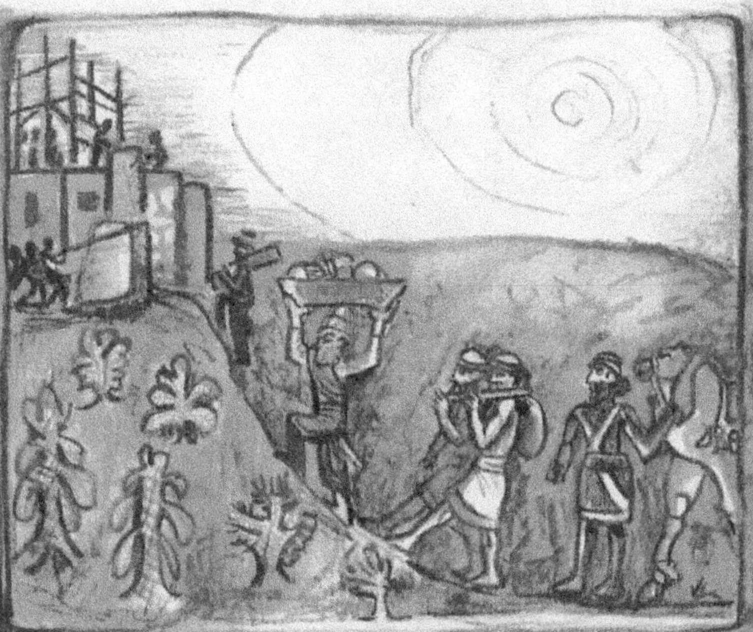

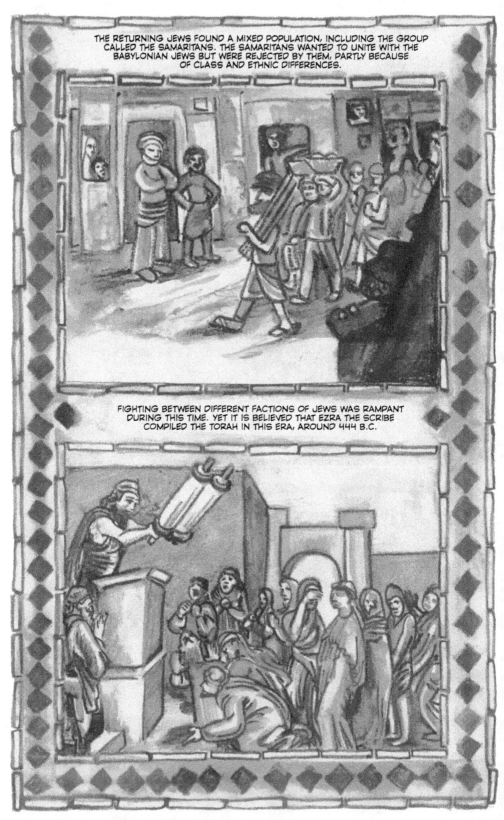

THE RETURNING JEWS FOUND A MIXED POPULATION, INCLUDING THE GROUP CALLED THE SAMARITANS. THE SAMARITANS WANTED TO UNITE WITH THE BABYLONIAN JEWS BUT WERE REJECTED BY THEM, PARTLY BECAUSE OF CLASS AND ETHNIC DIFFERENCES.

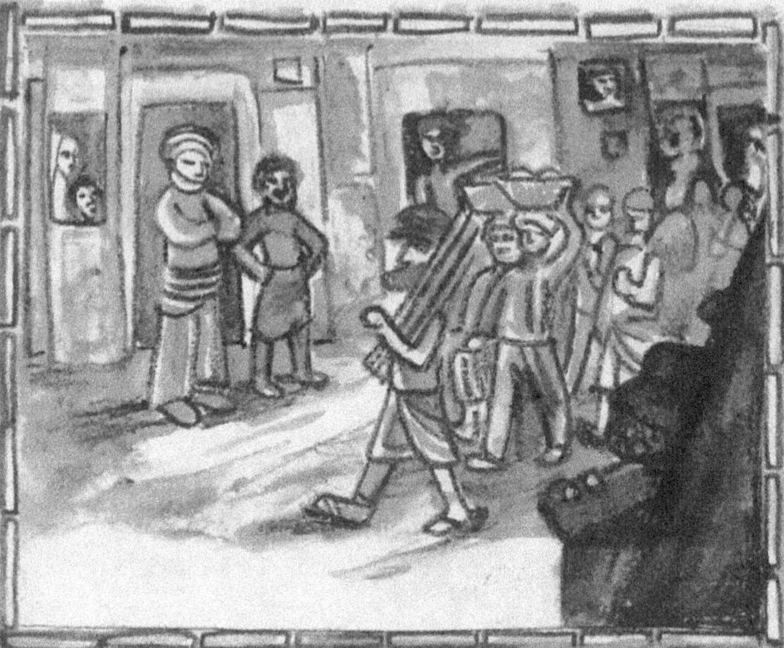

FIGHTING BETWEEN DIFFERENT FACTIONS OF JEWS WAS RAMPANT DURING THIS TIME. YET IT IS BELIEVED THAT EZRA THE SCRIBE COMPILED THE TORAH IN THIS ERA, AROUND 444 B.C.

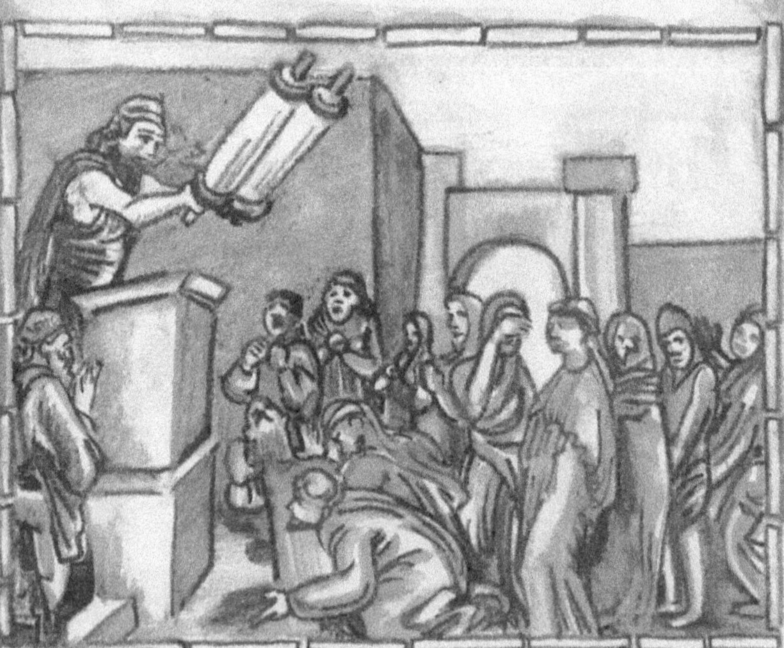

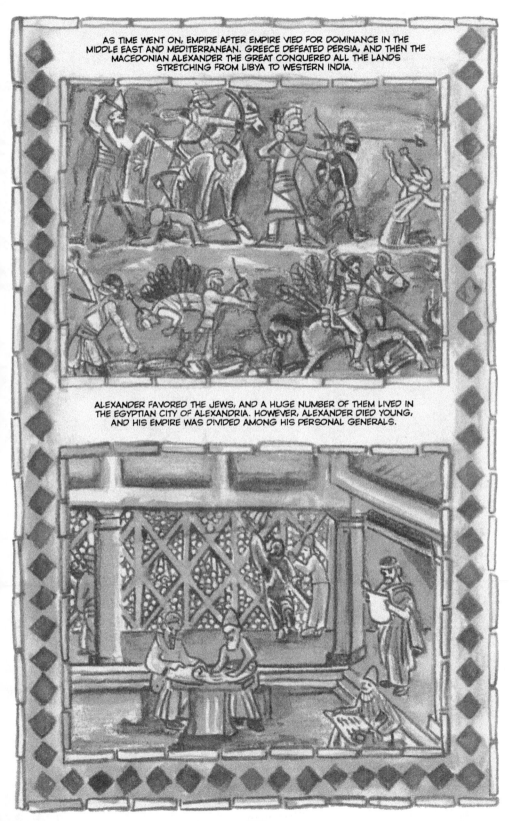

AS TIME WENT ON, EMPIRE AFTER EMPIRE VIED FOR DOMINANCE IN THE MIDDLE EAST AND MEDITERRANEAN. GREECE DEFEATED PERSIA, AND THEN THE MACEDONIAN ALEXANDER THE GREAT CONQUERED ALL THE LANDS STRETCHING FROM LIBYA TO WESTERN INDIA.

ALEXANDER FAVORED THE JEWS, AND A HUGE NUMBER OF THEM LIVED IN THE EGYPTIAN CITY OF ALEXANDRIA. HOWEVER, ALEXANDER DIED YOUNG, AND HIS EMPIRE WAS DIVIDED AMONG HIS PERSONAL GENERALS.

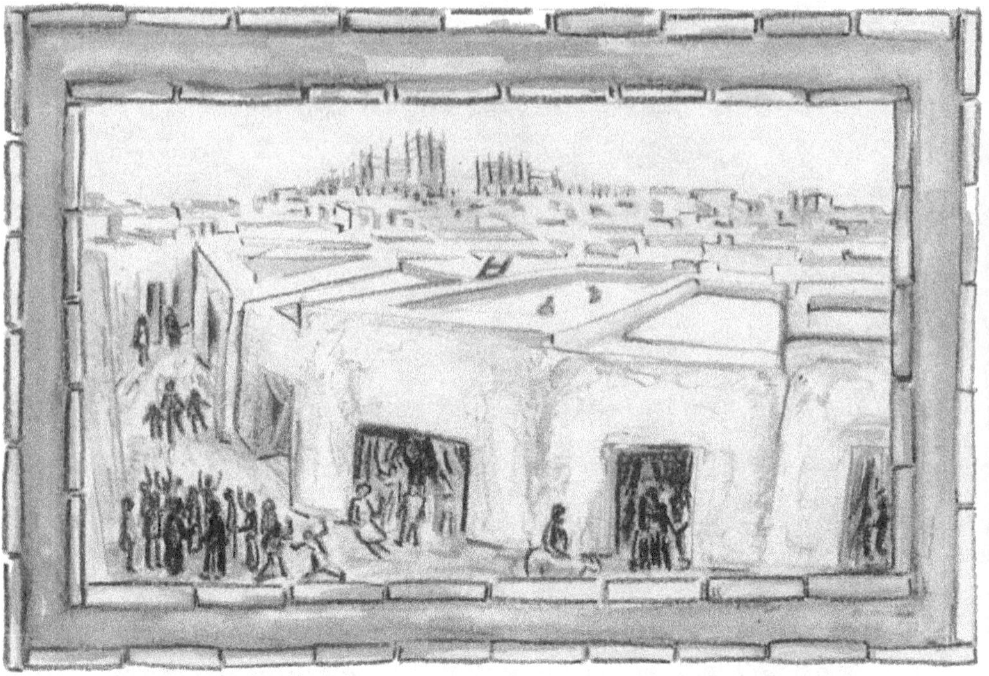

THE JEWS IN ISRAEL WERE RULED BY THE SELEUCID DYNASTY DURING THIS SECOND TEMPLE ERA. THEY CHAFED UNDER FOREIGN RULE AND THERE WERE FIERCE FIGHTS AMONG FACTIONS OF JEWS AS WELL AS WITH OTHER CULTURES.

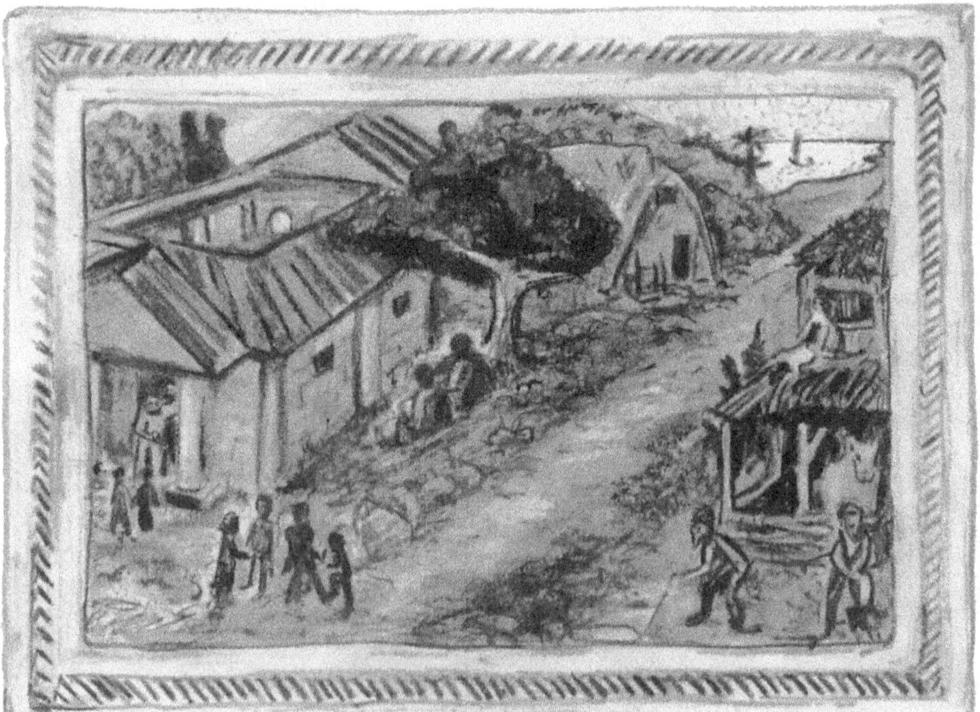

AFTER A BRIEF EXILE IN BABYLONIA, THE JEWISH LEADERS OF THAT ERA BEGAN TO BLEND NATIONALISM WITH THEIR UNIQUE RELIGION, AND THE JEWISH PEOPLE BEGAN TO DISTINGUISH THEMSELVES LIKE NO OTHERS ON EARTH.

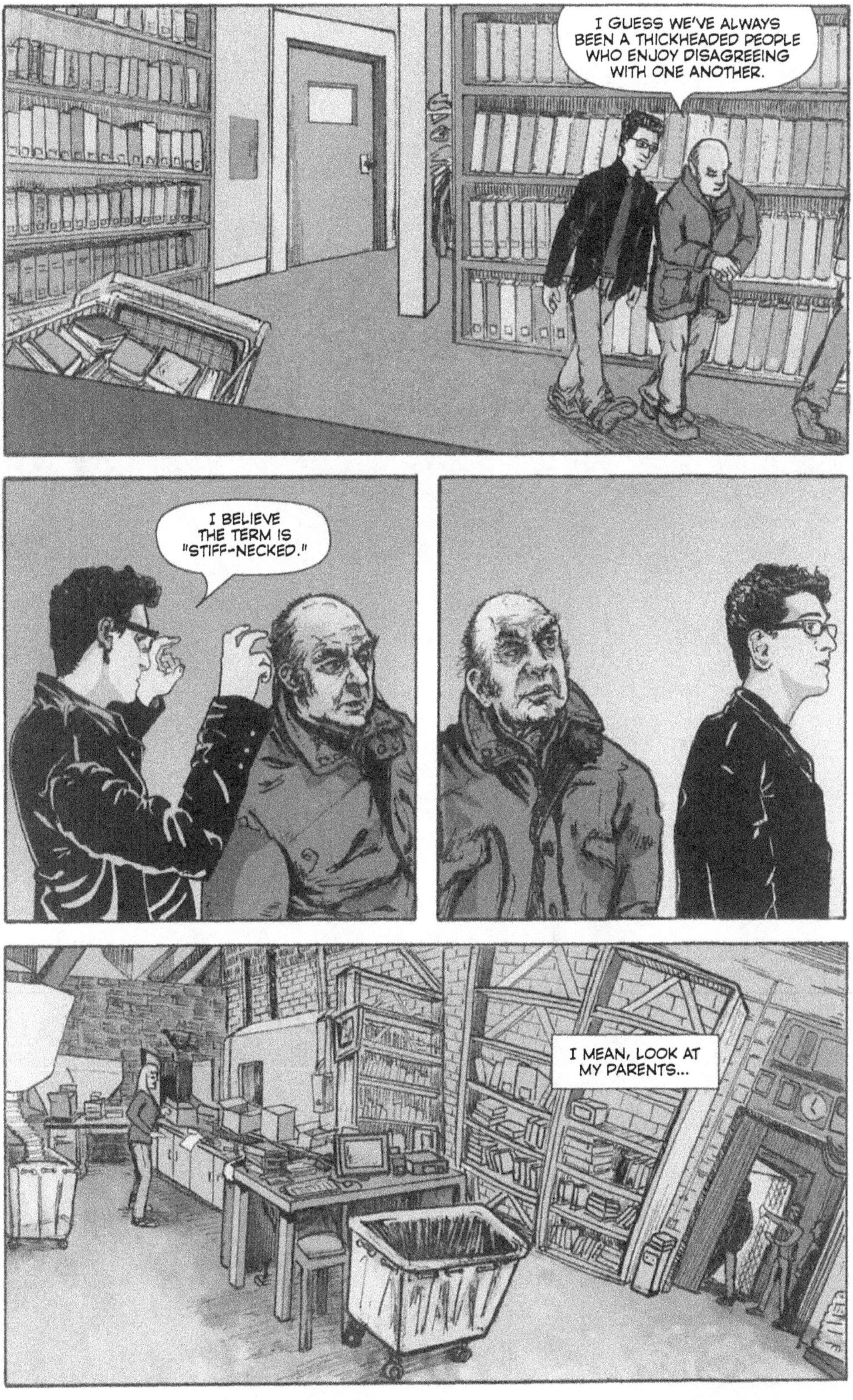
I GUESS WE'VE ALWAYS BEEN A THICKHEADED PEOPLE WHO ENJOY DISAGREEING WITH ONE ANOTHER.
I BELIEVE THE TERM IS "STIFF-NECKED."
I MEAN, LOOK AT MY PARENTS...

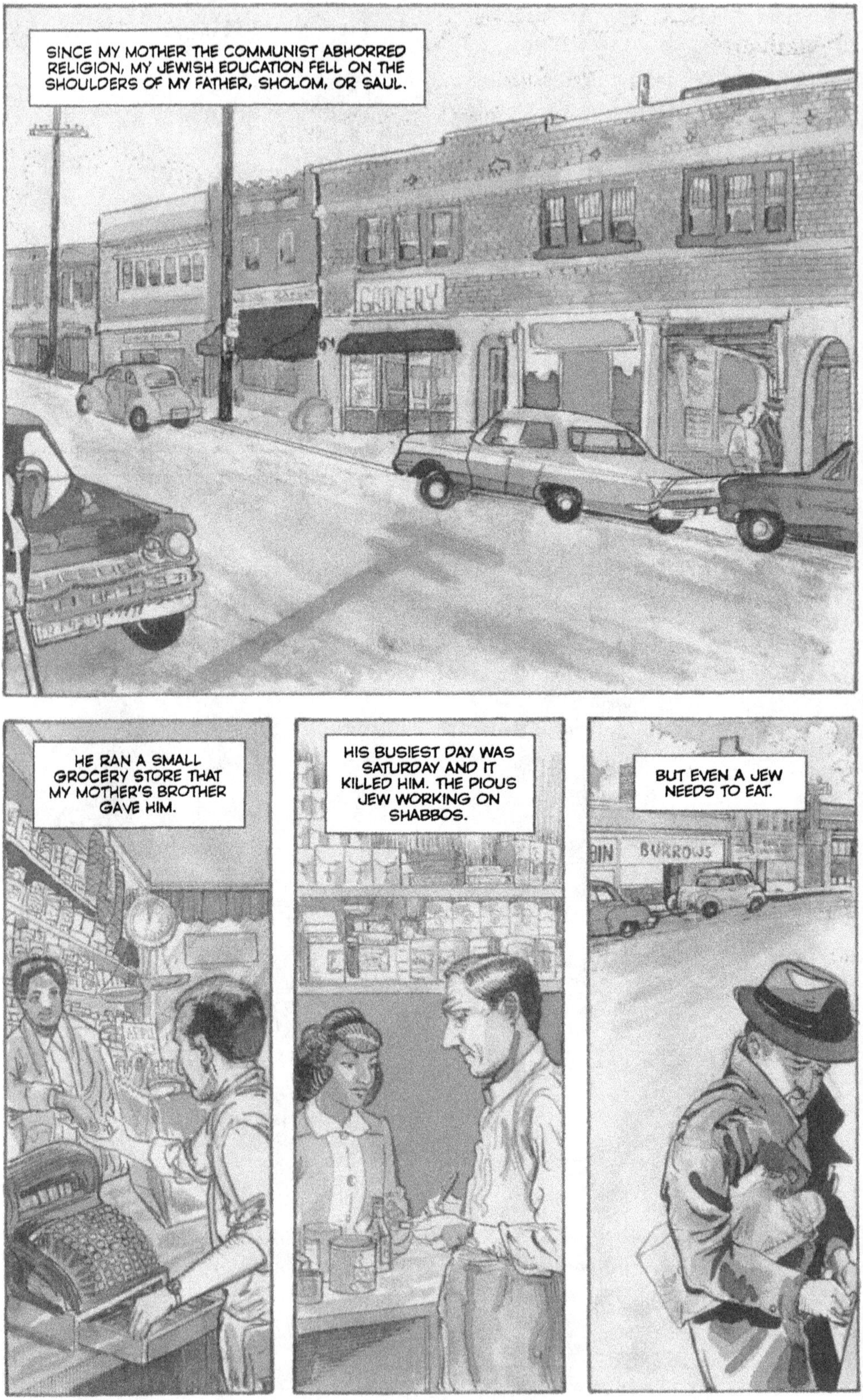
SINCE MY MOTHER THE COMMUNIST ABHORRED RELIGION, MY JEWISH EDUCATION FELL ON THE SHOULDERS OF MY FATHER, SHOLOM, OR SAUL.
GROCERY
HE RAN A SMALL GROCERY STORE THAT MY MOTHER'S BROTHER GAVE HIM.
HIS BUSIEST DAY WAS SATURDAY AND IT KILLED HIM. THE PIOUS JEW WORKING ON SHABBOS.
BUT EVEN A JEW NEEDS TO EAT.
BURROWS

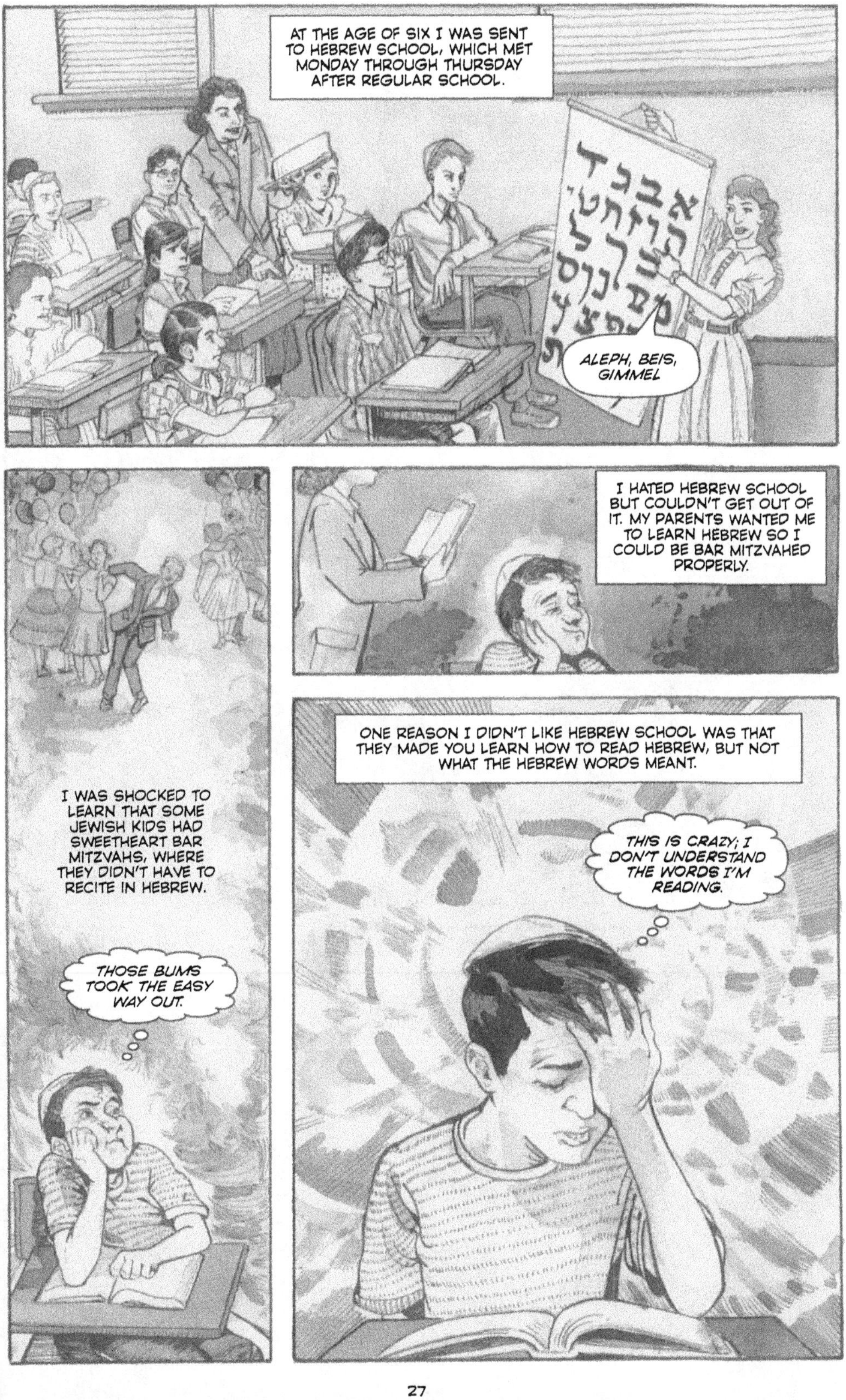
AT THE AGE OF SIX I WAS SENT TO HEBREW SCHOOL, WHICH MET MONDAY THROUGH THURSDAY AFTER REGULAR SCHOOL.
ALEPH, BEIS, GIMMEL
I HATED HEBREW SCHOOL BUT COULDN'T GET OUT OF IT. MY PARENTS WANTED ME TO LEARN HEBREW SO I COULD BE BAR MITZVAHED PROPERLY.
I WAS SHOCKED TO LEARN THAT SOME JEWISH KIDS HAD SWEETHEART BAR MITZVAHS, WHERE THEY DIDN'T HAVE TO RECITE IN HEBREW.
THOSE BUMS TOOK THE EASY WAY OUT.
ONE REASON I DIDN'T LIKE HEBREW SCHOOL WAS THAT THEY MADE YOU LEARN HOW TO READ HEBREW, BUT NOT WHAT THE HEBREW WORDS MEANT.
THIS IS CRAZY; I DON'T UNDERSTAND THE WORDS I'M READING.

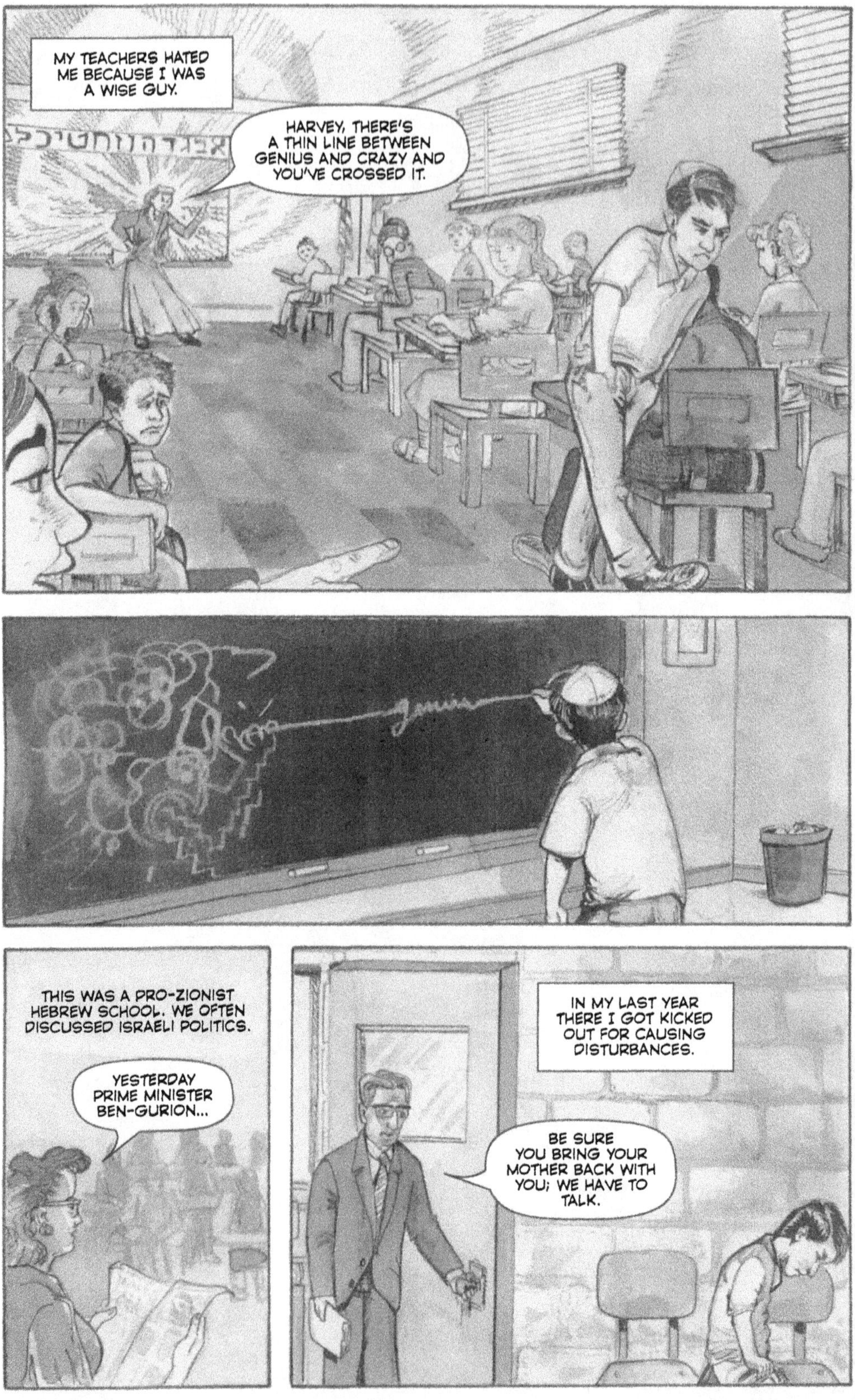
MY TEACHERS HATED ME BECAUSE I WAS A WISE GUY.
HARVEY, THERE'S A THIN LINE BETWEEN GENIUS AND CRAZY AND YOU'VE CROSSED IT.
THIS WAS A PRO-ZIONIST HEBREW SCHOOL. WE OFTEN DISCUSSED ISRAELI POLITICS.
YESTERDAY PRIME MINISTER BEN-GURION...
IN MY LAST YEAR THERE I GOT KICKED OUT FOR CAUSING DISTURBANCES.
BE SURE YOU BRING YOUR MOTHER BACK WITH YOU; WE HAVE TO TALK.

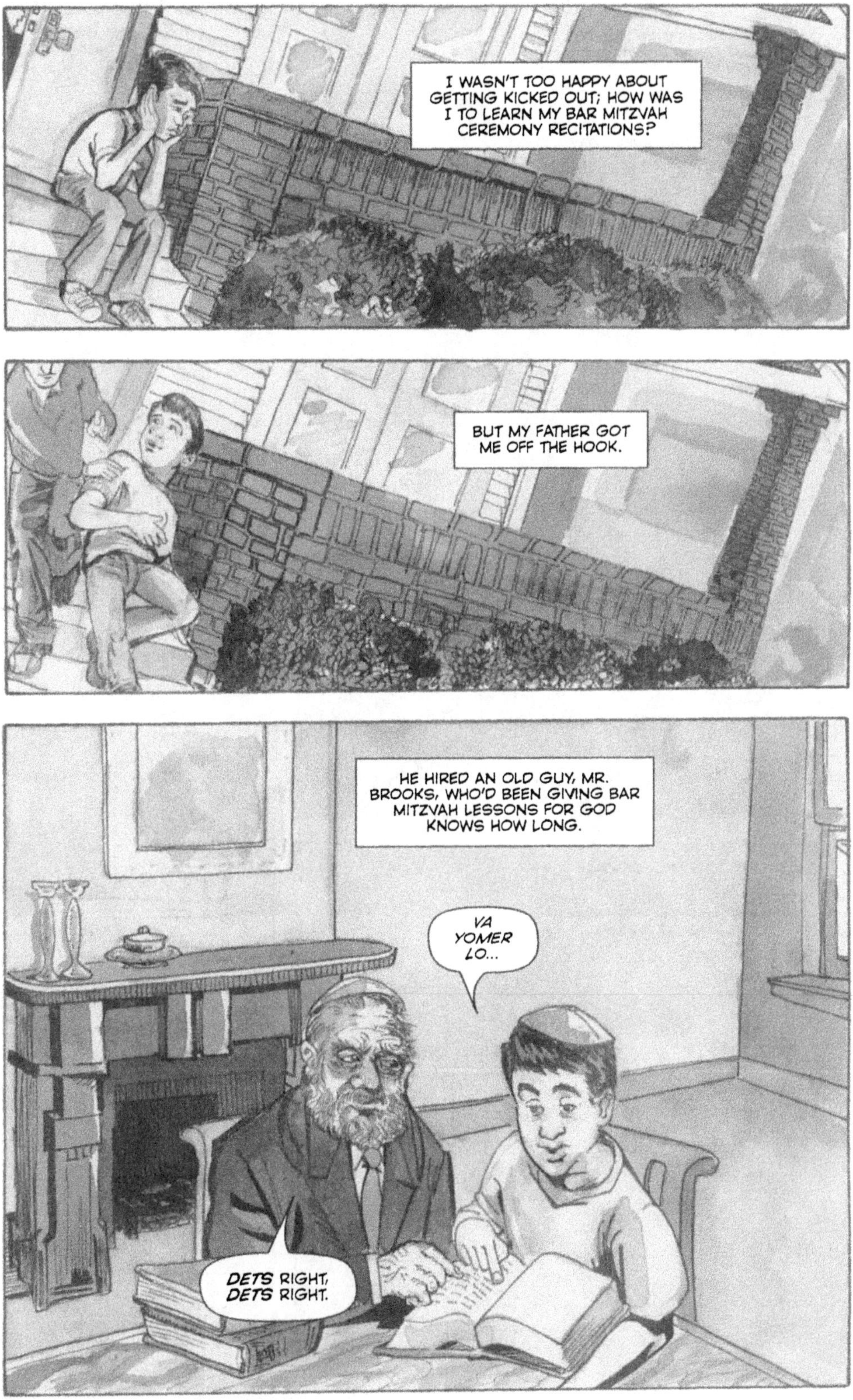
I WASN'T TOO HAPPY ABOUT GETTING KICKED OUT; HOW WAS I TO LEARN MY BAR MITZVAH CEREMONY RECITATIONS?
BUT MY FATHER GOT ME OFF THE HOOK.
HE HIRED AN OLD GUY, MR. BROOKS, WHO'D BEEN GIVING BAR MITZVAH LESSONS FOR GOD KNOWS HOW LONG.
VA YOMER LO...
DETS RIGHT, DETS RIGHT.

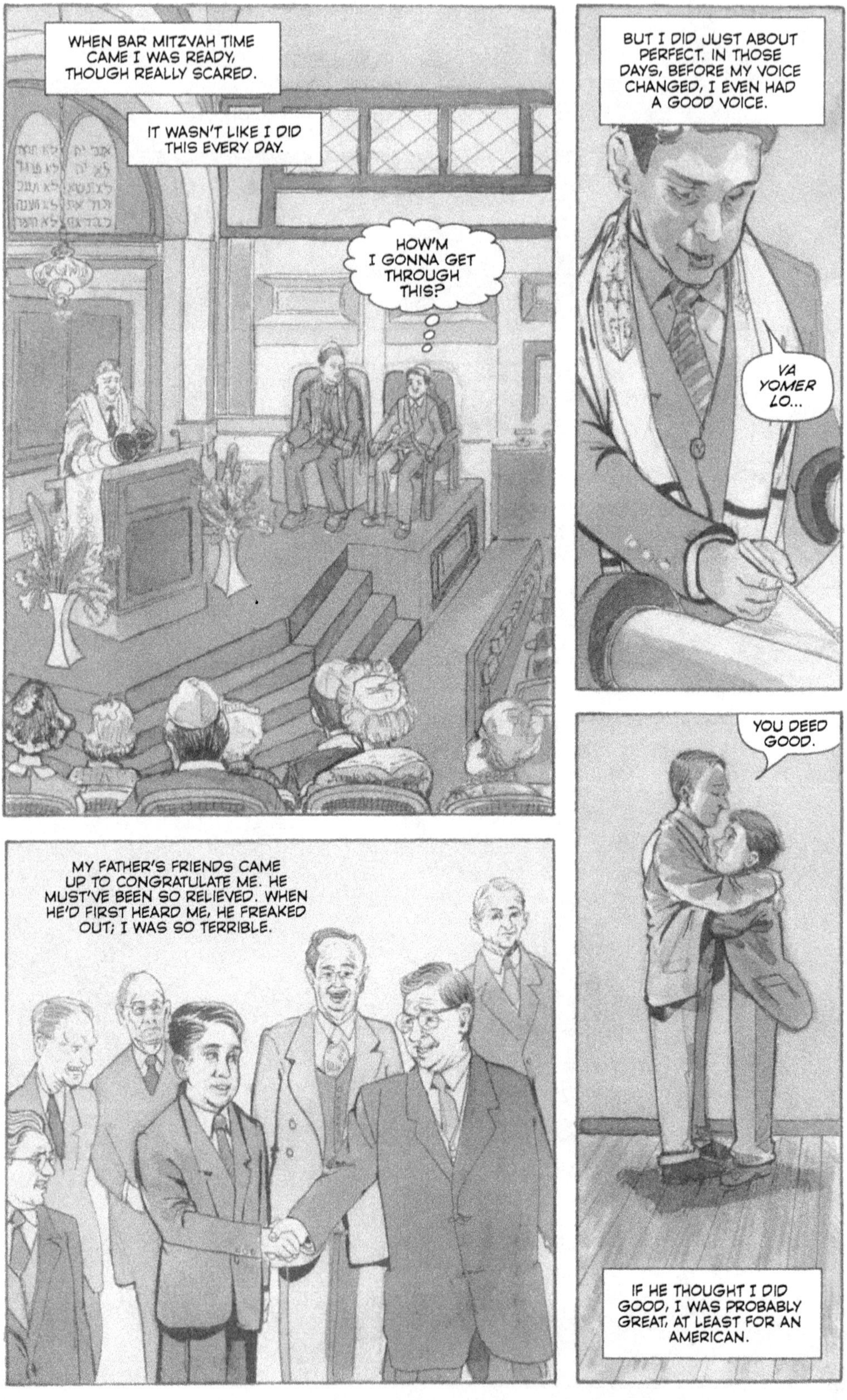
WHEN BAR MITZVAH TIME CAME I WAS READY, THOUGH REALLY SCARED.
IT WASN'T LIKE I DID THIS EVERY DAY.
HOW'M I GONNA GET THROUGH THIS?
BUT I DID JUST ABOUT PERFECT. IN THOSE DAYS, BEFORE MY VOICE CHANGED, I EVEN HAD A GOOD VOICE.
VA YOMER LO...
MY FATHER'S FRIENDS CAME UP TO CONGRATULATE ME. HE MUST'VE BEEN SO RELIEVED. WHEN HE'D FIRST HEARD ME, HE FREAKED OUT; I WAS SO TERRIBLE.
YOU DEED GOOD.
IF HE THOUGHT I DID GOOD, I WAS PROBABLY GREAT, AT LEAST FOR AN AMERICAN.

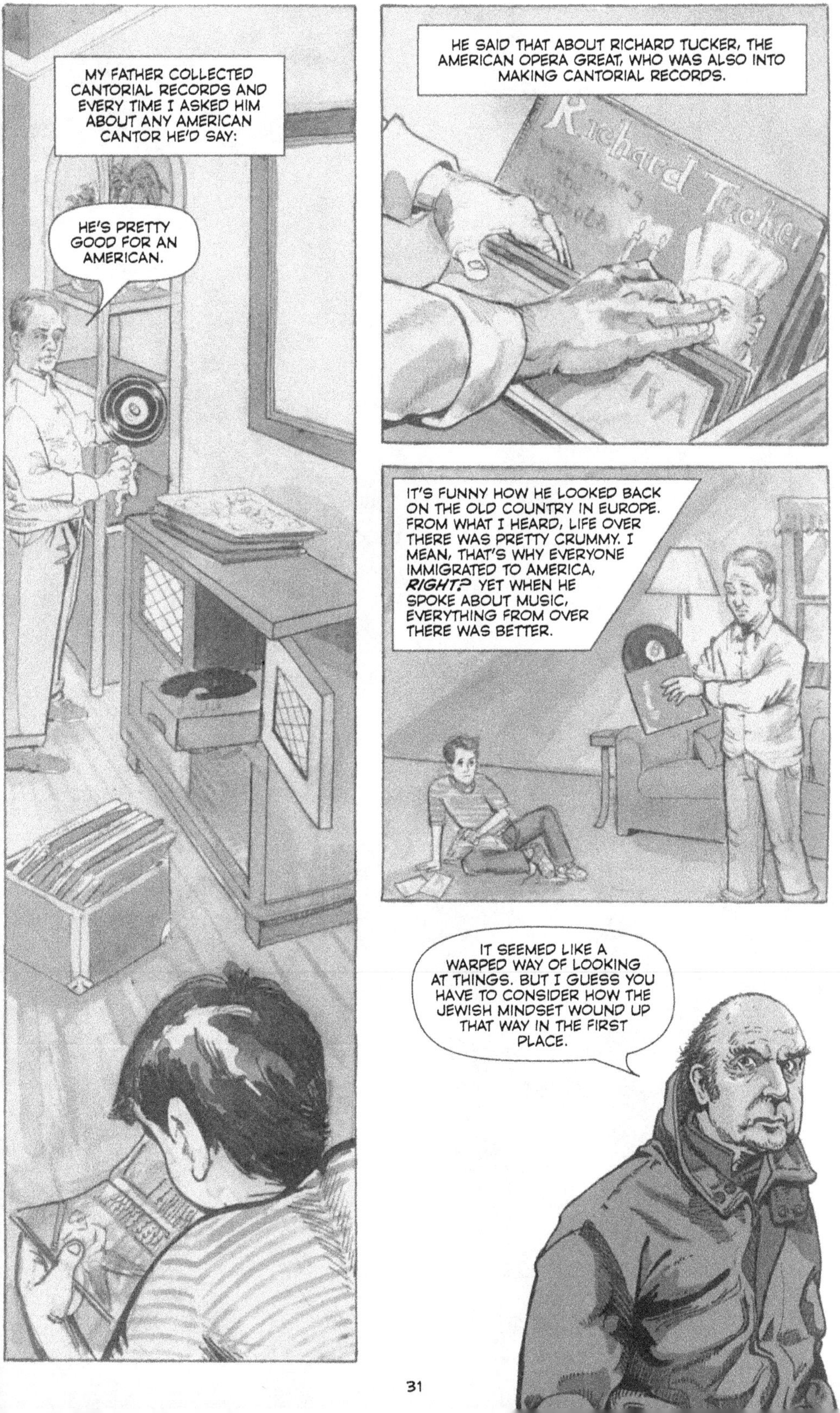
MY FATHER COLLECTED CANTORIAL RECORDS AND EVERY TIME I ASKED HIM ABOUT ANY AMERICAN CANTOR HE'D SAY:
HE'S PRETTY GOOD FOR AN AMERICAN.
HE SAID THAT ABOUT RICHARD TUCKER, THE AMERICAN OPERA GREAT, WHO WAS ALSO INTO MAKING CANTORIAL RECORDS.
Richard Tucker
IT'S FUNNY HOW HE LOOKED BACK ON THE OLD COUNTRY IN EUROPE. FROM WHAT I HEARD, LIFE OVER THERE WAS PRETTY CRUMMY. I MEAN, THAT'S WHY EVERYONE IMMIGRATED TO AMERICA, *RIGHT?* YET WHEN HE SPOKE ABOUT MUSIC, EVERYTHING FROM OVER THERE WAS BETTER.
IT SEEMED LIKE A WARPED WAY OF LOOKING AT THINGS. BUT I GUESS YOU HAVE TO CONSIDER HOW THE JEWISH MINDSET WOUND UP THAT WAY IN THE FIRST PLACE.

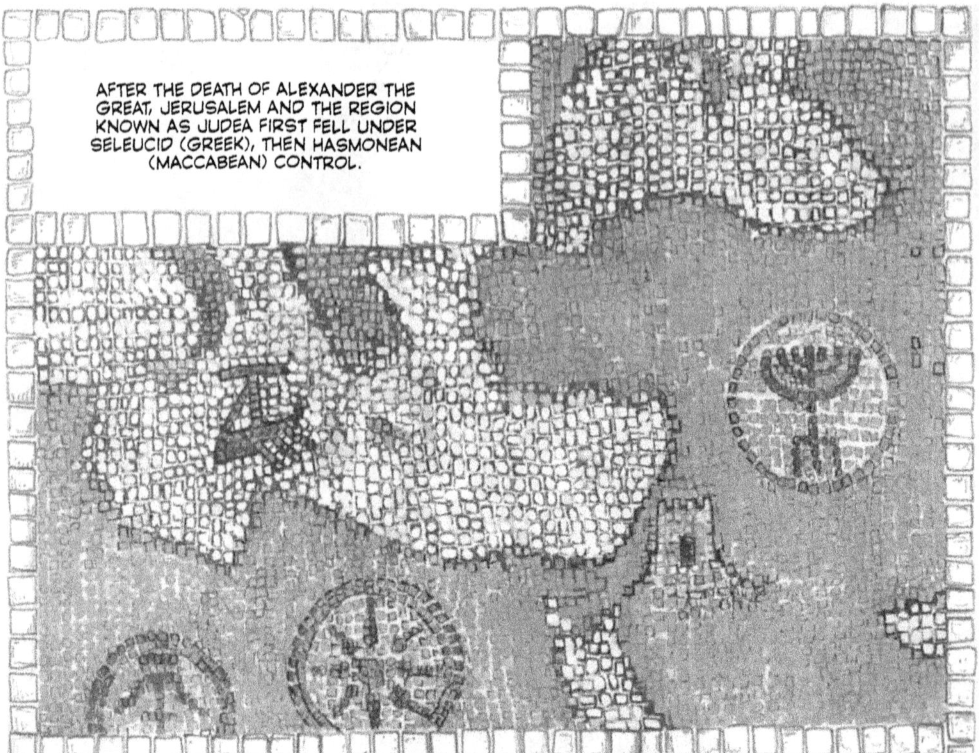
AFTER THE DEATH OF ALEXANDER THE GREAT, JERUSALEM AND THE REGION KNOWN AS JUDEA FIRST FELL UNDER SELEUCID (GREEK), THEN HASMONEAN (MACCABEAN) CONTROL.

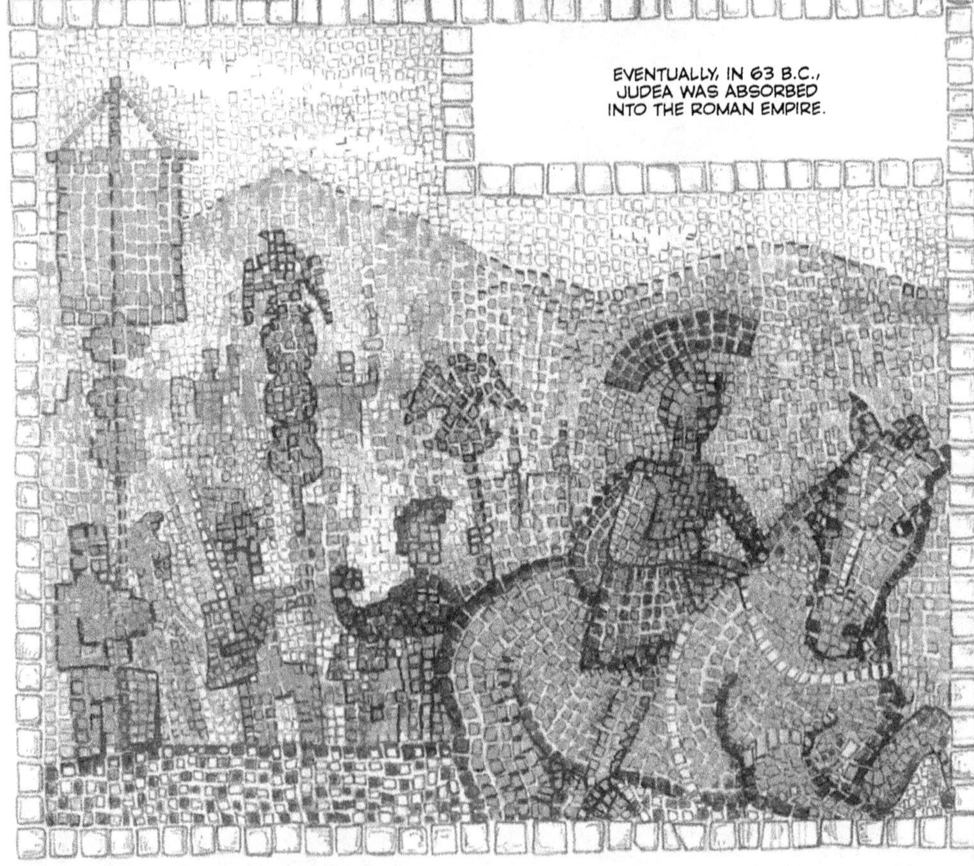
EVENTUALLY, IN 63 B.C., JUDEA WAS ABSORBED INTO THE ROMAN EMPIRE.

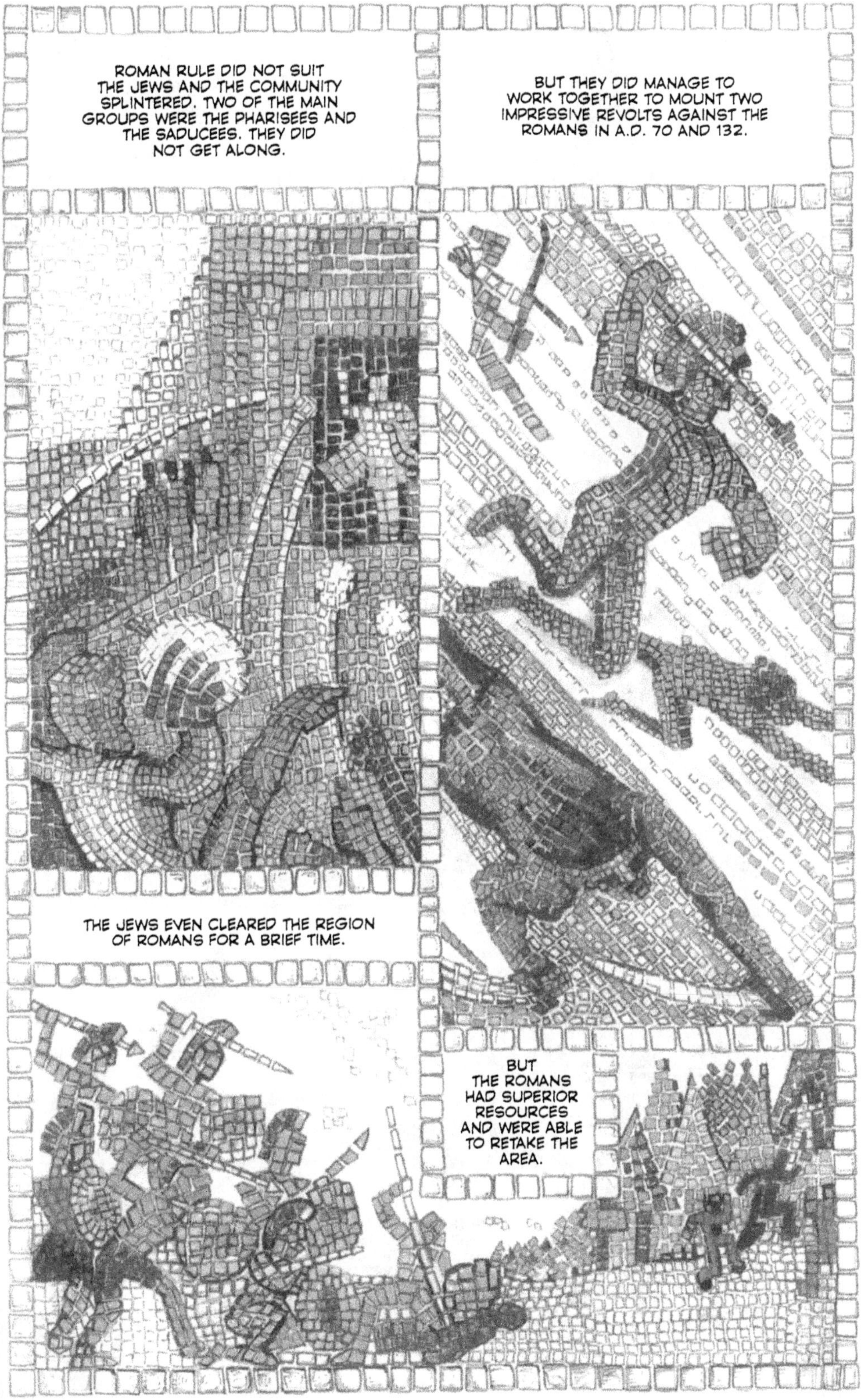
ROMAN RULE DID NOT SUIT THE JEWS AND THE COMMUNITY SPLINTERED. TWO OF THE MAIN GROUPS WERE THE PHARISEES AND THE SADUCEES. THEY DID NOT GET ALONG.
BUT THEY DID MANAGE TO WORK TOGETHER TO MOUNT TWO IMPRESSIVE REVOLTS AGAINST THE ROMANS IN A.D. 70 AND 132.
THE JEWS EVEN CLEARED THE REGION OF ROMANS FOR A BRIEF TIME.
BUT THE ROMANS HAD SUPERIOR RESOURCES AND WERE ABLE TO RETAKE THE AREA.

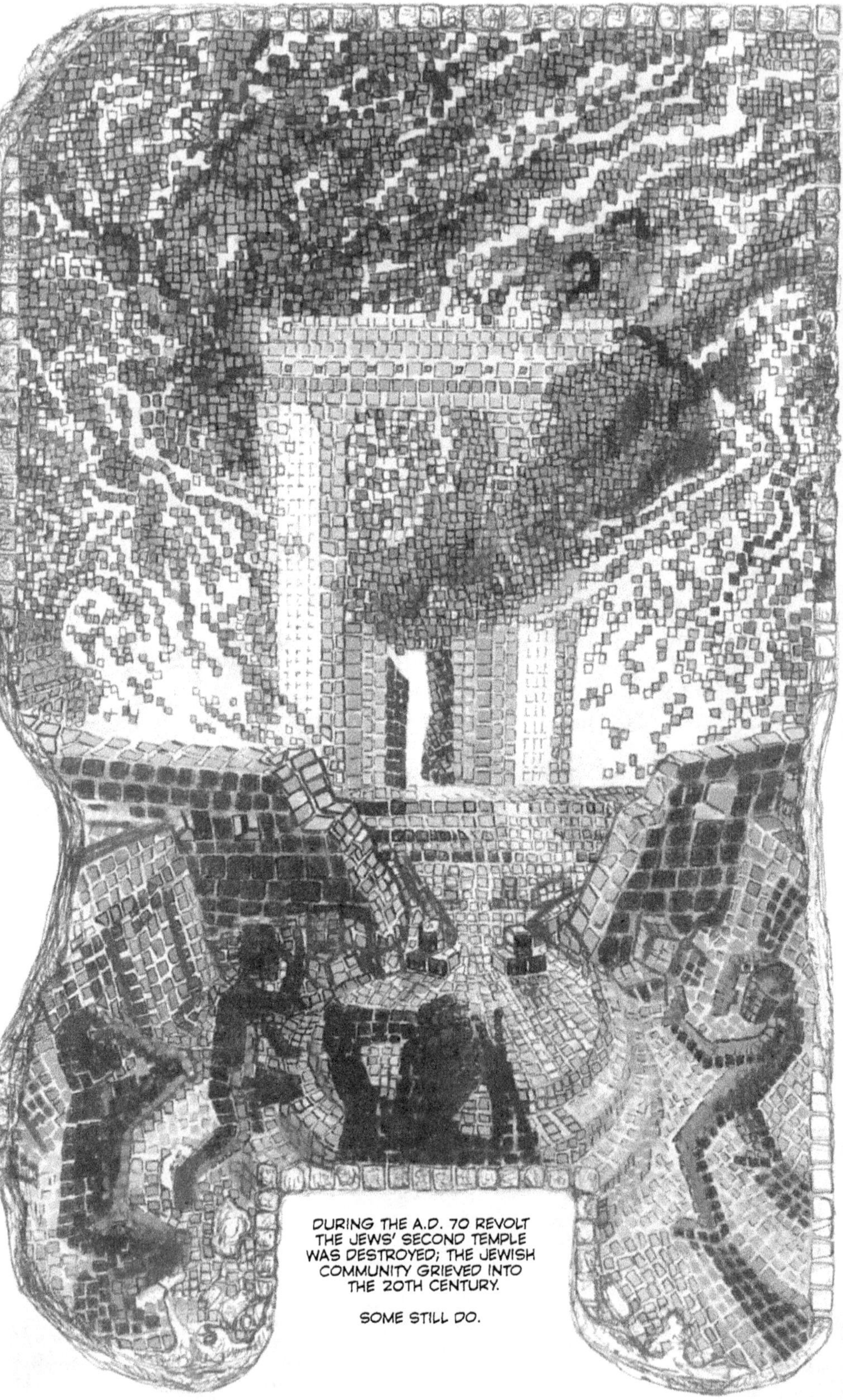
DURING THE A.D. 70 REVOLT THE JEWS' SECOND TEMPLE WAS DESTROYED; THE JEWISH COMMUNITY GRIEVED INTO THE 20TH CENTURY.
SOME STILL DO.

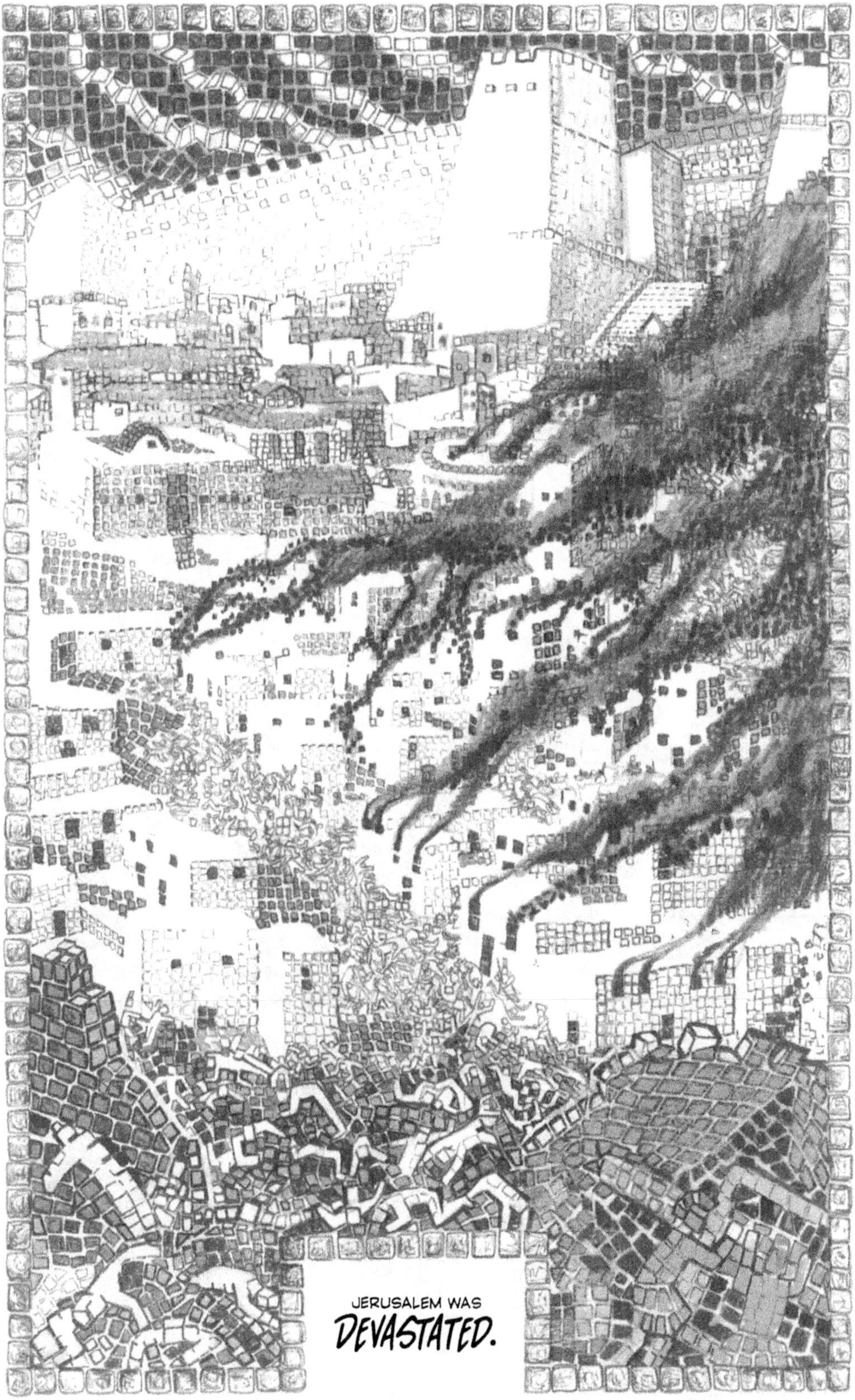
JERUSALEM WAS
DEVASTATED.

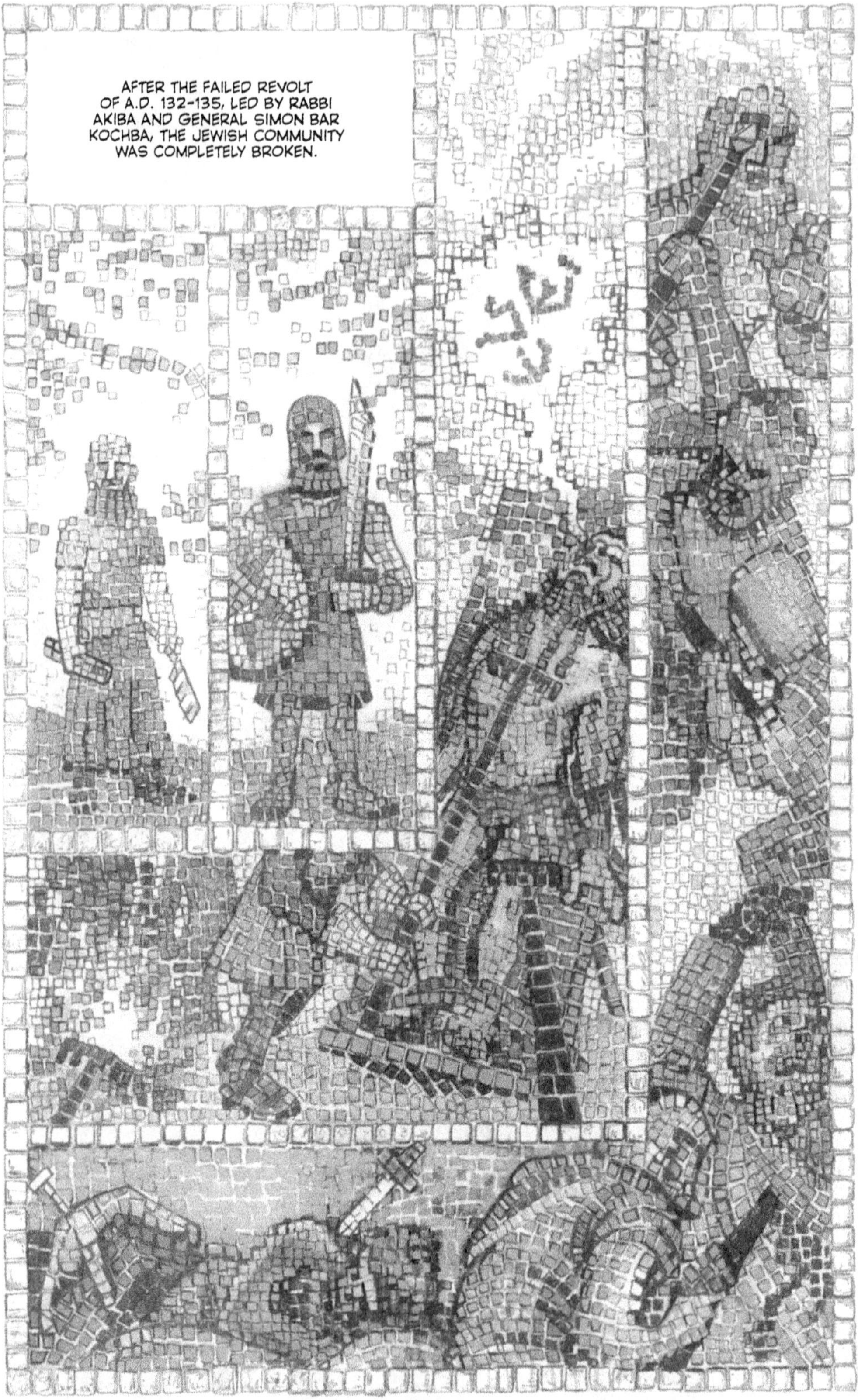
AFTER THE FAILED REVOLT OF A.D. 132-135, LED BY RABBI AKIBA AND GENERAL SIMON BAR KOCHBA, THE JEWISH COMMUNITY WAS COMPLETELY BROKEN.

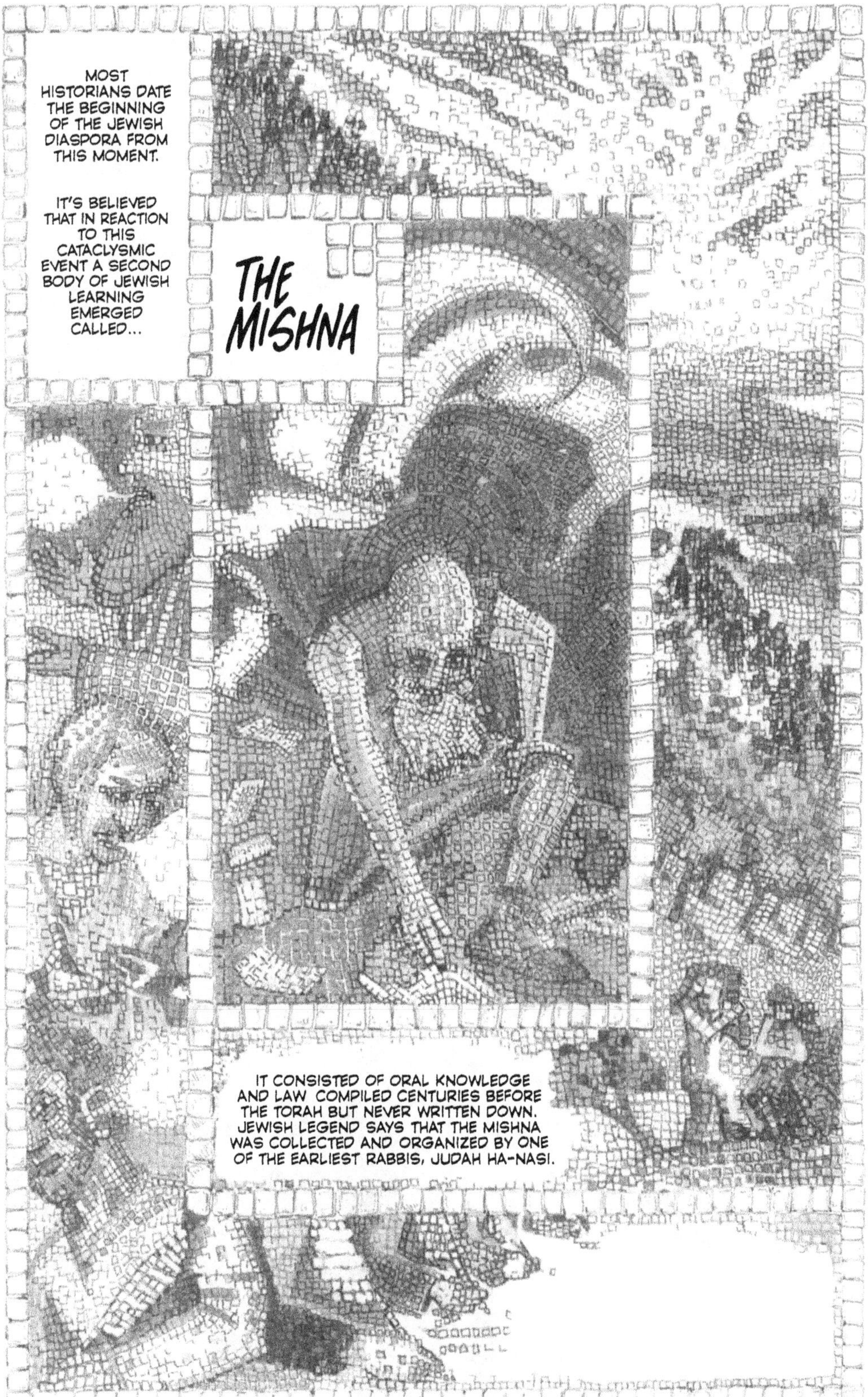
MOST HISTORIANS DATE THE BEGINNING OF THE JEWISH DIASPORA FROM THIS MOMENT.
IT'S BELIEVED THAT IN REACTION TO THIS CATACLYSMIC EVENT A SECOND BODY OF JEWISH LEARNING EMERGED CALLED...
THE MISHNA
IT CONSISTED OF ORAL KNOWLEDGE AND LAW COMPILED CENTURIES BEFORE THE TORAH BUT NEVER WRITTEN DOWN. JEWISH LEGEND SAYS THAT THE MISHNA WAS COLLECTED AND ORGANIZED BY ONE OF THE EARLIEST RABBIS, JUDAH HA-NASI.

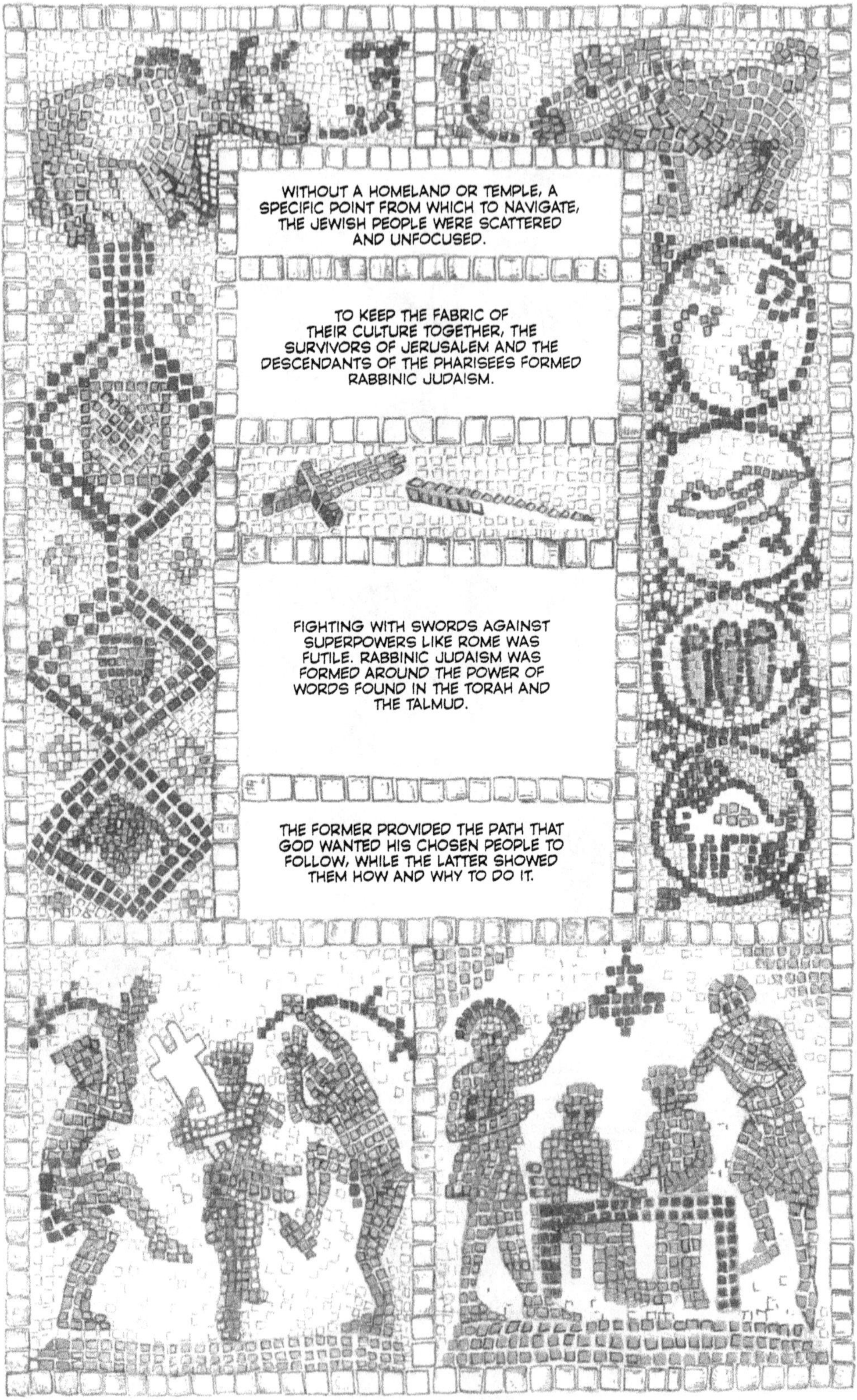
WITHOUT A HOMELAND OR TEMPLE, A SPECIFIC POINT FROM WHICH TO NAVIGATE, THE JEWISH PEOPLE WERE SCATTERED AND UNFOCUSED.
TO KEEP THE FABRIC OF THEIR CULTURE TOGETHER, THE SURVIVORS OF JERUSALEM AND THE DESCENDANTS OF THE PHARISEES FORMED RABBINIC JUDAISM.
FIGHTING WITH SWORDS AGAINST SUPERPOWERS LIKE ROME WAS FUTILE. RABBINIC JUDAISM WAS FORMED AROUND THE POWER OF WORDS FOUND IN THE TORAH AND THE TALMUD.
THE FORMER PROVIDED THE PATH THAT GOD WANTED HIS CHOSEN PEOPLE TO FOLLOW, WHILE THE LATTER SHOWED THEM HOW AND WHY TO DO IT.

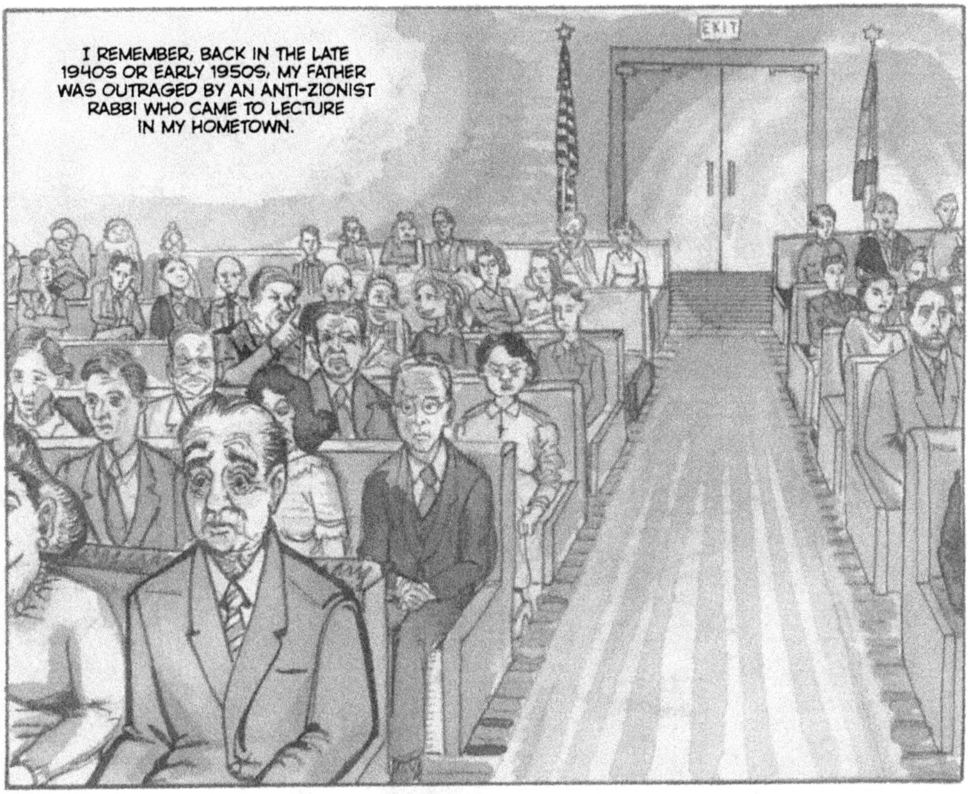
I REMEMBER, BACK IN THE LATE 1940S OR EARLY 1950S, MY FATHER WAS OUTRAGED BY AN ANTI-ZIONIST RABBI WHO CAME TO LECTURE IN MY HOMETOWN.
EXIT

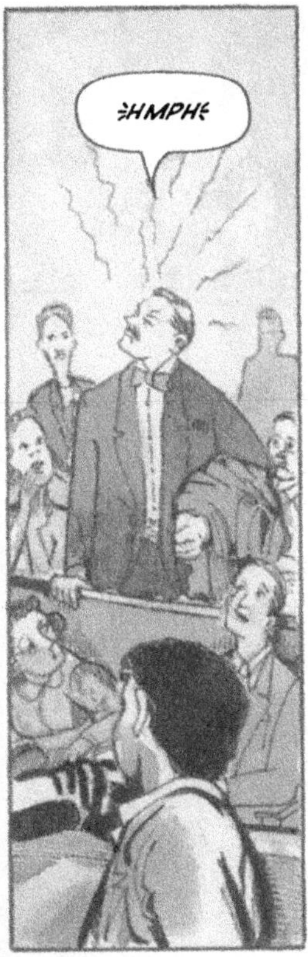
HMPH

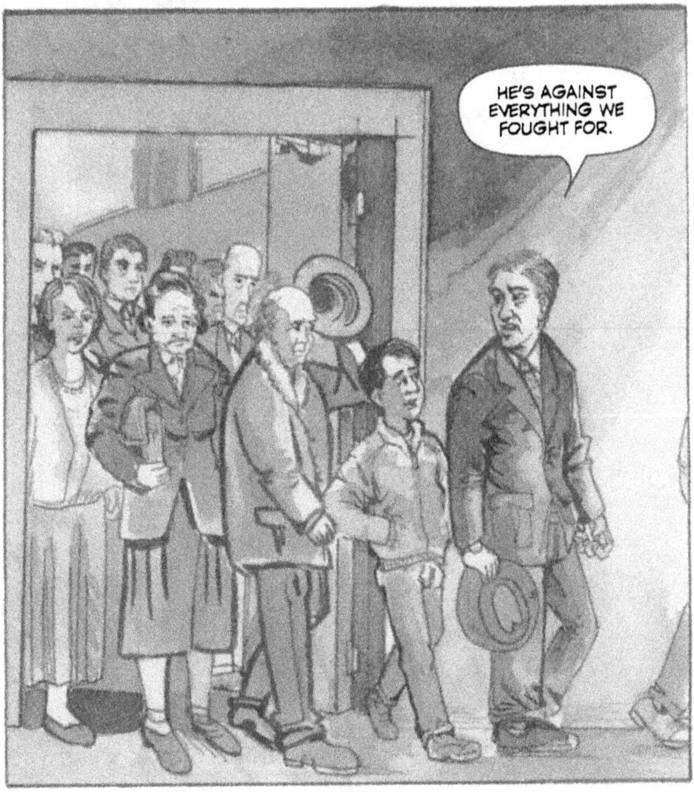
HE'S AGAINST EVERYTHING WE FOUGHT FOR.

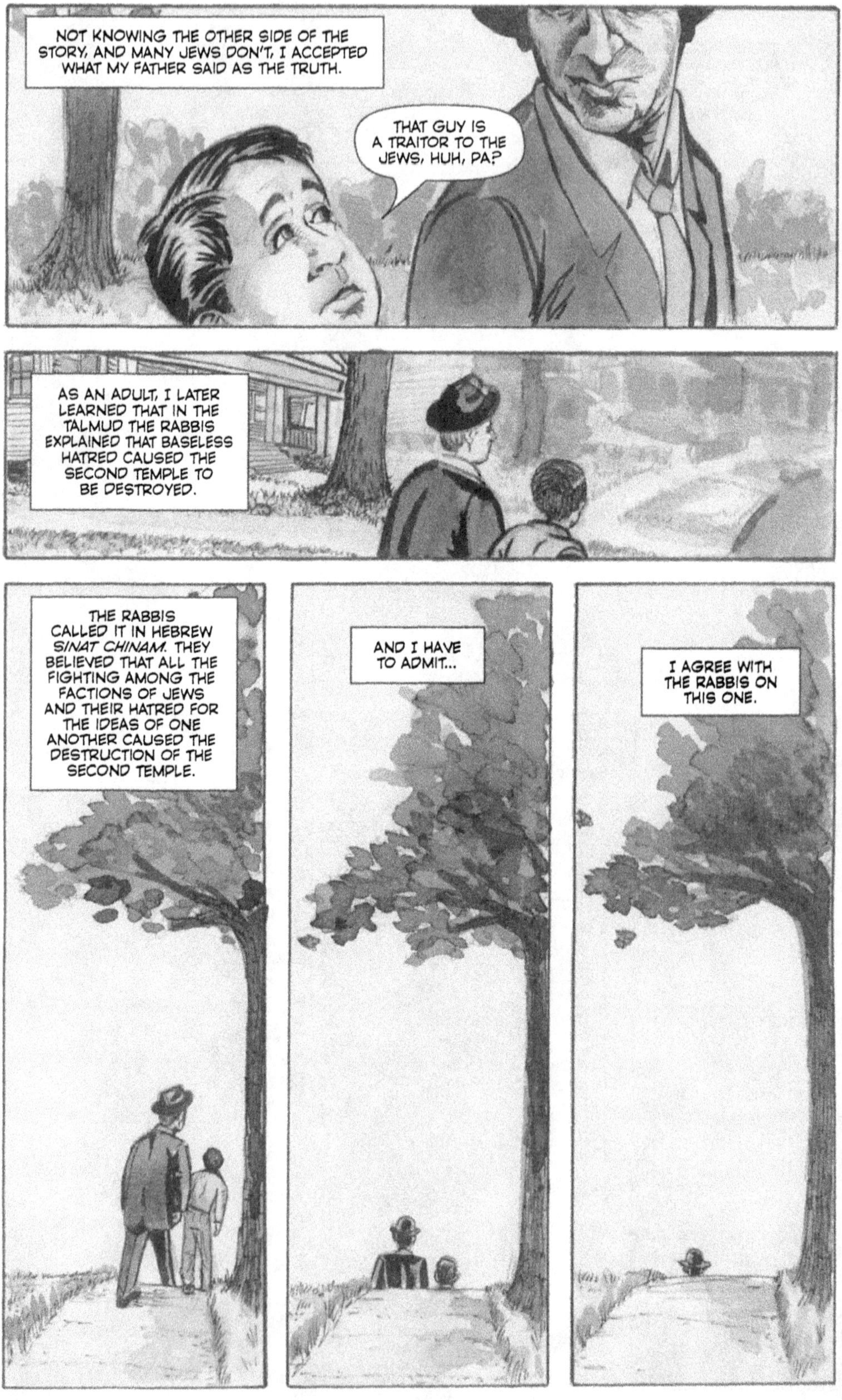
NOT KNOWING THE OTHER SIDE OF THE STORY, AND MANY JEWS DON'T, I ACCEPTED WHAT MY FATHER SAID AS THE TRUTH.
THAT GUY IS A TRAITOR TO THE JEWS, HUH, PA?
AS AN ADULT, I LATER LEARNED THAT IN THE TALMUD THE RABBIS EXPLAINED THAT BASELESS HATRED CAUSED THE SECOND TEMPLE TO BE DESTROYED.
THE RABBIS CALLED IT IN HEBREW *SINAT CHINAM*. THEY BELIEVED THAT ALL THE FIGHTING AMONG THE FACTIONS OF JEWS AND THEIR HATRED FOR THE IDEAS OF ONE ANOTHER CAUSED THE DESTRUCTION OF THE SECOND TEMPLE.
AND I HAVE TO ADMIT...
I AGREE WITH THE RABBIS ON THIS ONE.

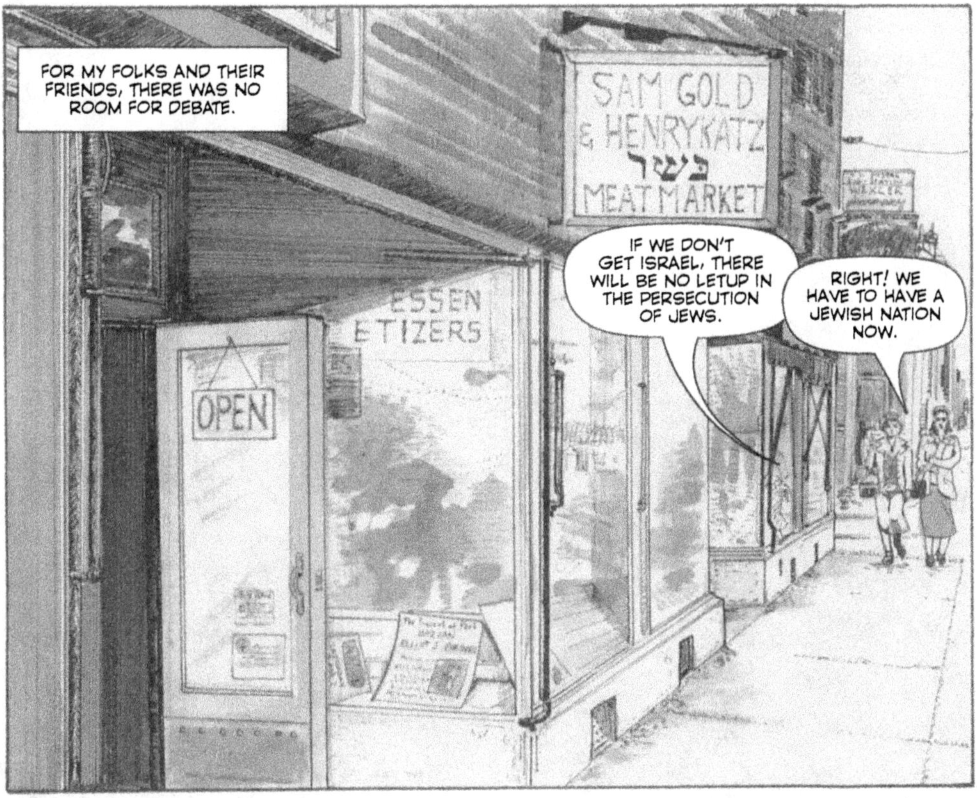
FOR MY FOLKS AND THEIR FRIENDS, THERE WAS NO ROOM FOR DEBATE.
SAM GOLD
& HENRY KATZ
בשר
MEAT MARKET
OPEN
IF WE DON'T GET ISRAEL, THERE WILL BE NO LETUP IN THE PERSECUTION OF JEWS.
RIGHT! WE HAVE TO HAVE A JEWISH NATION NOW.

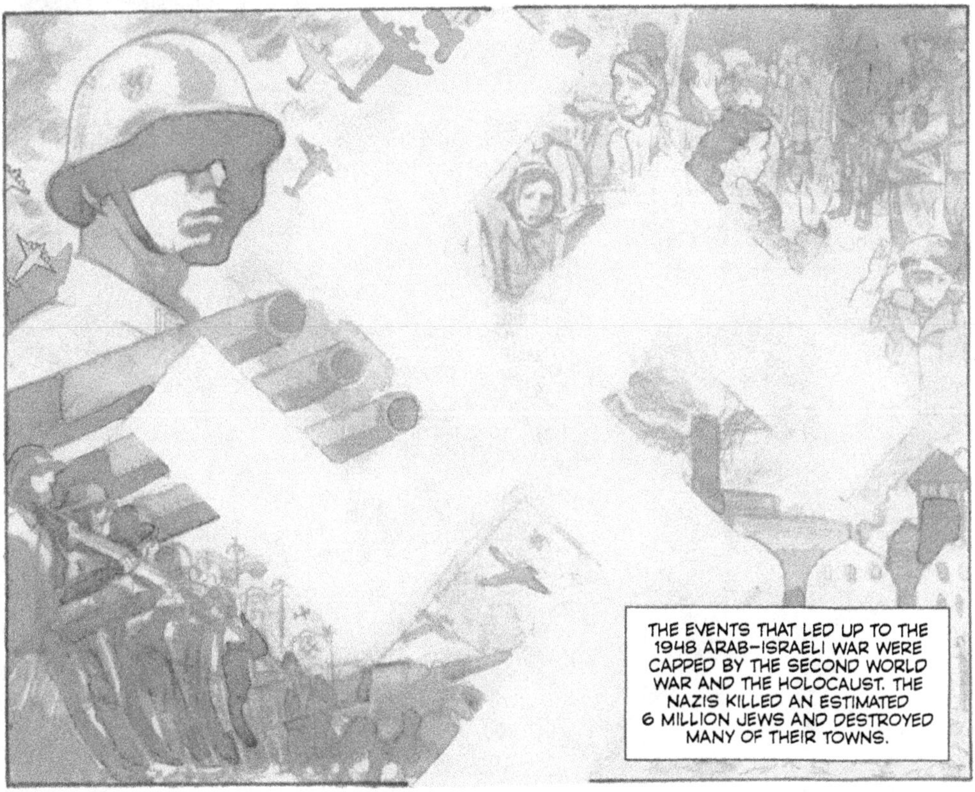
THE EVENTS THAT LED UP TO THE 1948 ARAB-ISRAELI WAR WERE CAPPED BY THE SECOND WORLD WAR AND THE HOLOCAUST. THE NAZIS KILLED AN ESTIMATED 6 MILLION JEWS AND DESTROYED MANY OF THEIR TOWNS.

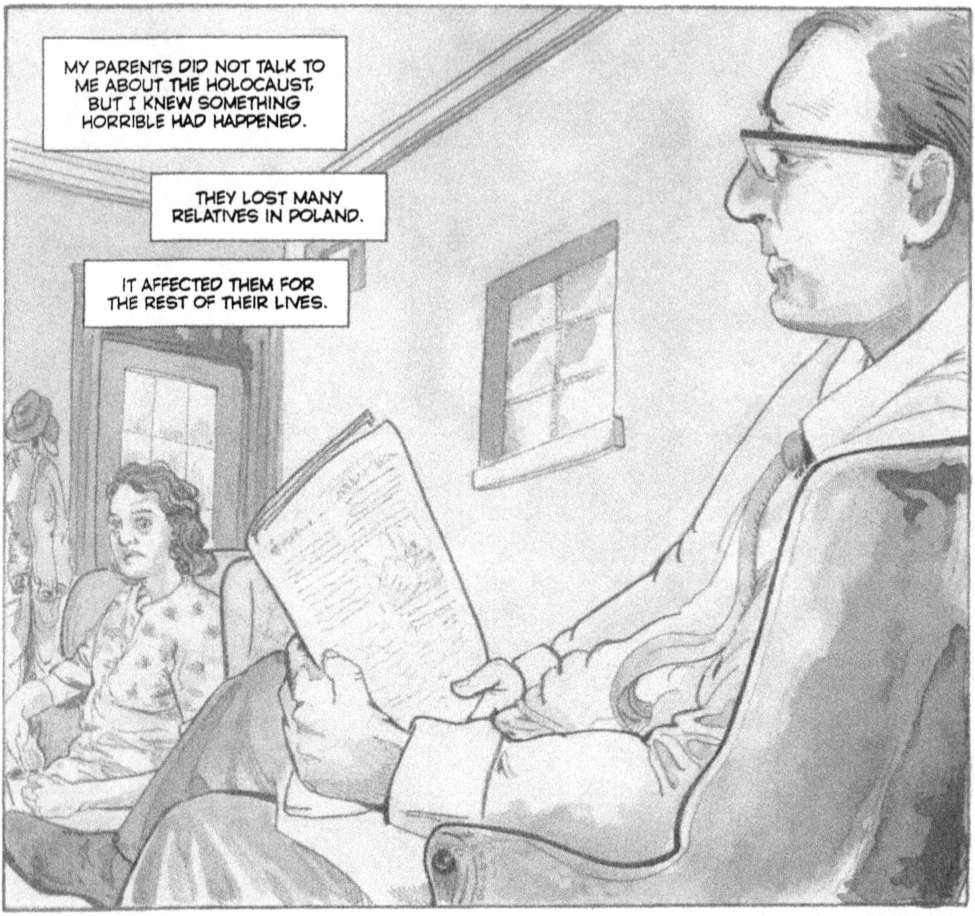
MY PARENTS DID NOT TALK TO ME ABOUT THE HOLOCAUST, BUT I KNEW SOMETHING HORRIBLE HAD HAPPENED.
THEY LOST MANY RELATIVES IN POLAND.
IT AFFECTED THEM FOR THE REST OF THEIR LIVES.

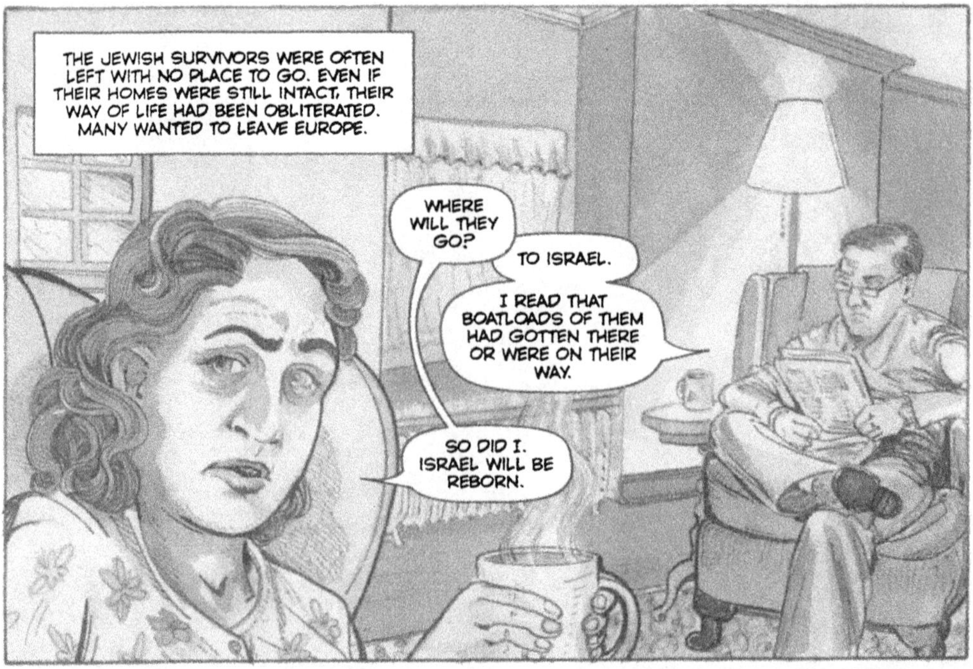
THE JEWISH SURVIVORS WERE OFTEN LEFT WITH NO PLACE TO GO. EVEN IF THEIR HOMES WERE STILL INTACT, THEIR WAY OF LIFE HAD BEEN OBLITERATED. MANY WANTED TO LEAVE EUROPE.
WHERE WILL THEY GO?
TO ISRAEL.
I READ THAT BOATLOADS OF THEM HAD GOTTEN THERE OR WERE ON THEIR WAY.
SO DID I. ISRAEL WILL BE REBORN.

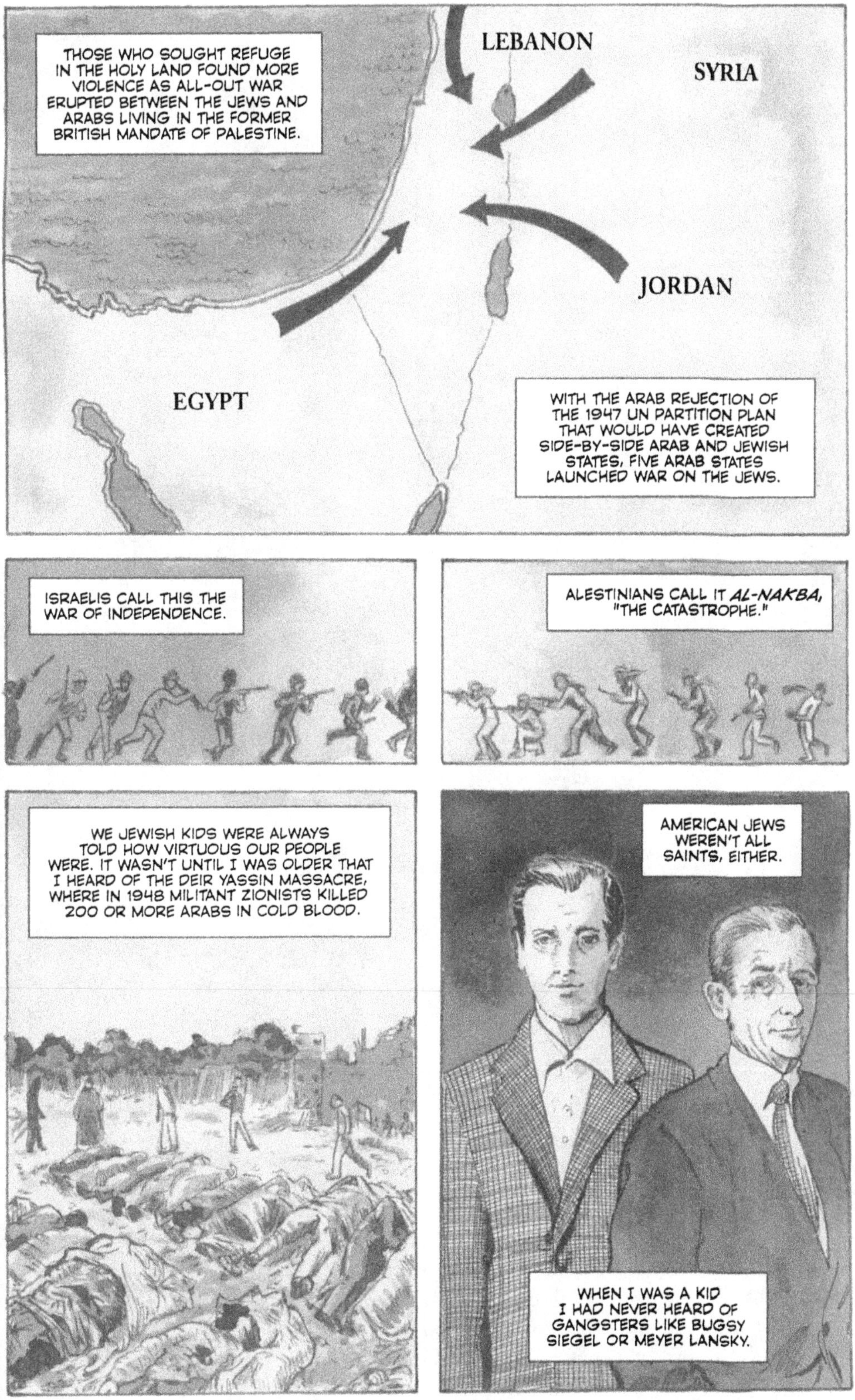
THOSE WHO SOUGHT REFUGE IN THE HOLY LAND FOUND MORE VIOLENCE AS ALL-OUT WAR ERUPTED BETWEEN THE JEWS AND ARABS LIVING IN THE FORMER BRITISH MANDATE OF PALESTINE.
LEBANON
SYRIA
JORDAN
EGYPT
WITH THE ARAB REJECTION OF THE 1947 UN PARTITION PLAN THAT WOULD HAVE CREATED SIDE-BY-SIDE ARAB AND JEWISH STATES, FIVE ARAB STATES LAUNCHED WAR ON THE JEWS.
ISRAELIS CALL THIS THE WAR OF INDEPENDENCE.
ALESTINIANS CALL IT *AL-NAKBA,* "THE CATASTROPHE."
WE JEWISH KIDS WERE ALWAYS TOLD HOW VIRTUOUS OUR PEOPLE WERE. IT WASN'T UNTIL I WAS OLDER THAT I HEARD OF THE DEIR YASSIN MASSACRE, WHERE IN 1948 MILITANT ZIONISTS KILLED 200 OR MORE ARABS IN COLD BLOOD.
AMERICAN JEWS WEREN'T ALL SAINTS, EITHER.
WHEN I WAS A KID I HAD NEVER HEARD OF GANGSTERS LIKE BUGSY SIEGEL OR MEYER LANSKY.

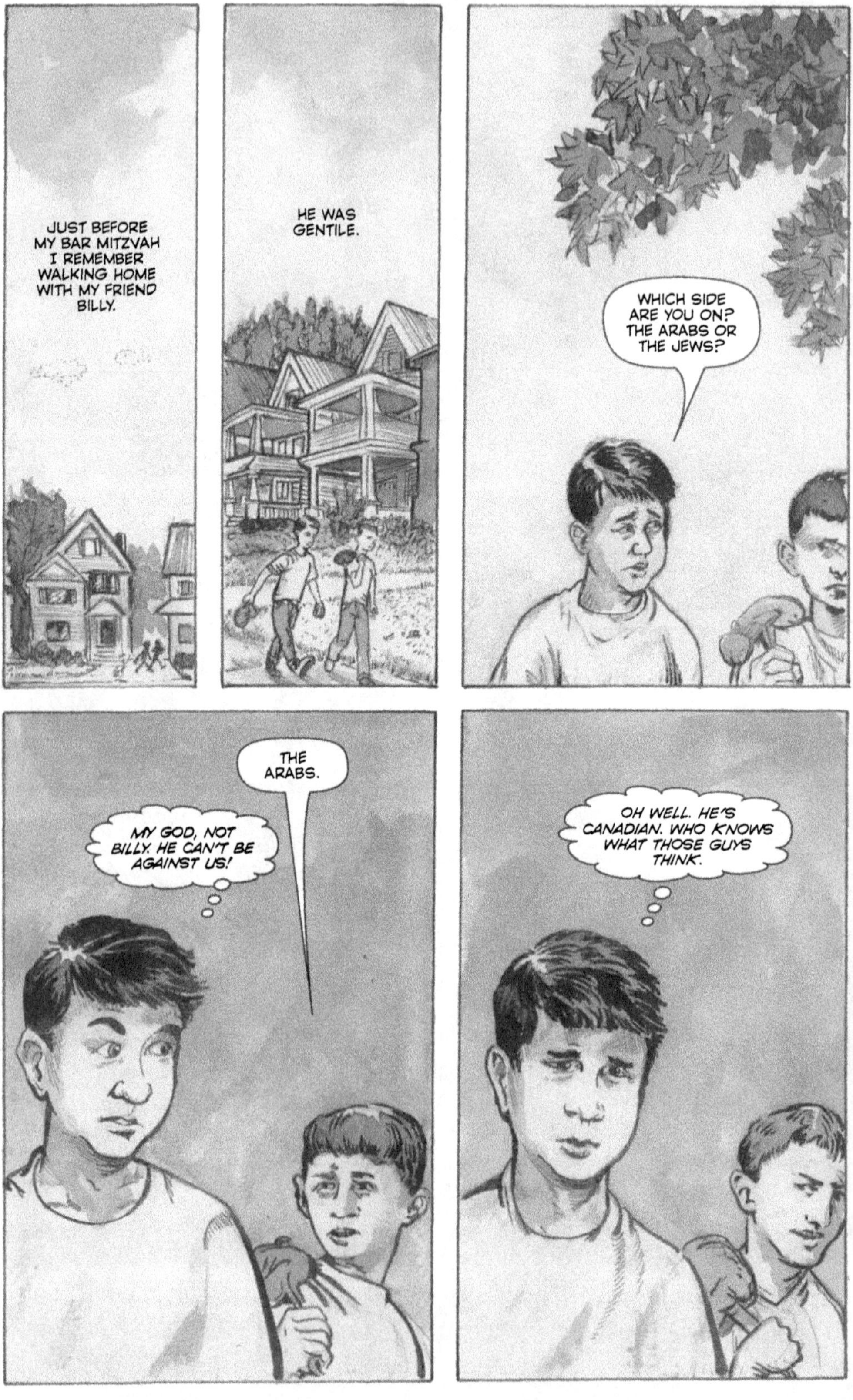
JUST BEFORE MY BAR MITZVAH I REMEMBER WALKING HOME WITH MY FRIEND BILLY.
HE WAS GENTILE.
WHICH SIDE ARE YOU ON? THE ARABS OR THE JEWS?
THE ARABS.
MY GOD, NOT BILLY. HE CAN'T BE AGAINST US!
OH WELL. HE'S CANADIAN. WHO KNOWS WHAT THOSE GUYS THINK.

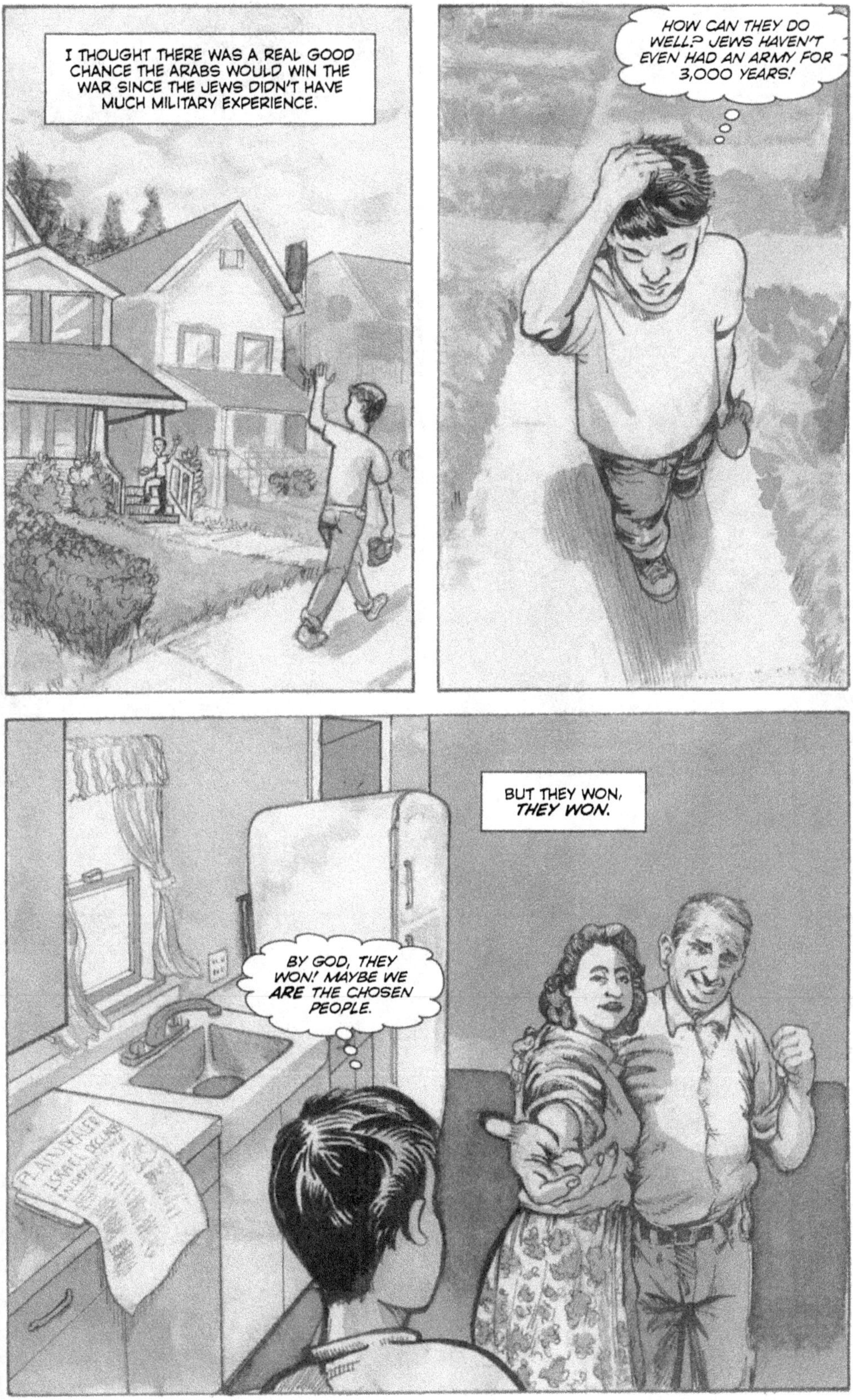
I THOUGHT THERE WAS A REAL GOOD CHANCE THE ARABS WOULD WIN THE WAR SINCE THE JEWS DIDN'T HAVE MUCH MILITARY EXPERIENCE.
HOW CAN THEY DO WELL? JEWS HAVEN'T EVEN HAD AN ARMY FOR 3,000 YEARS!
BUT THEY WON, THEY WON.
BY GOD, THEY WON! MAYBE WE ARE THE CHOSEN PEOPLE.

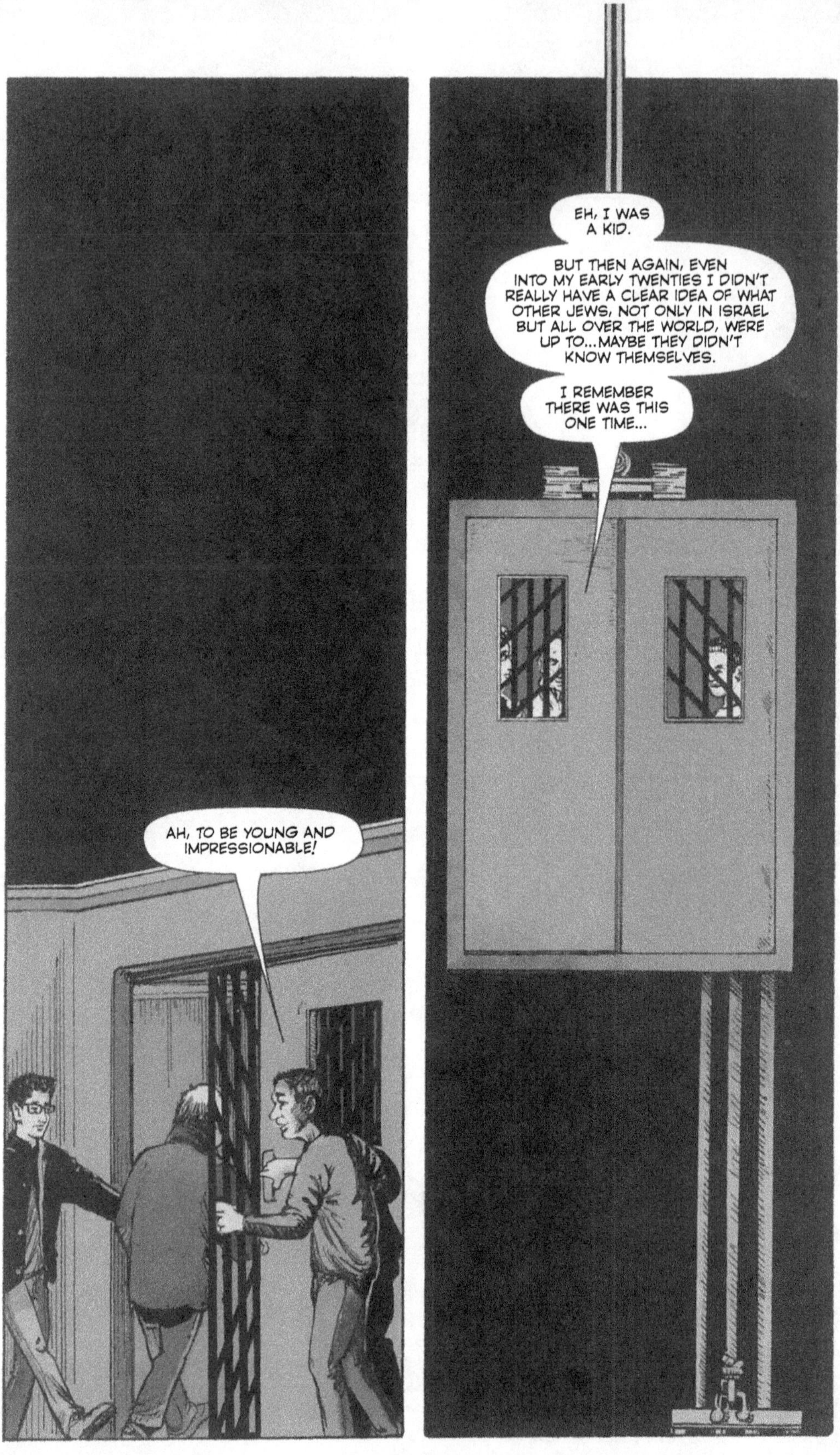
AH, TO BE YOUNG AND IMPRESSIONABLE!
EH, I WAS A KID.
BUT THEN AGAIN, EVEN INTO MY EARLY TWENTIES I DIDN'T REALLY HAVE A CLEAR IDEA OF WHAT OTHER JEWS, NOT ONLY IN ISRAEL BUT ALL OVER THE WORLD, WERE UP TO...MAYBE THEY DIDN'T KNOW THEMSELVES.
I REMEMBER THERE WAS THIS ONE TIME...

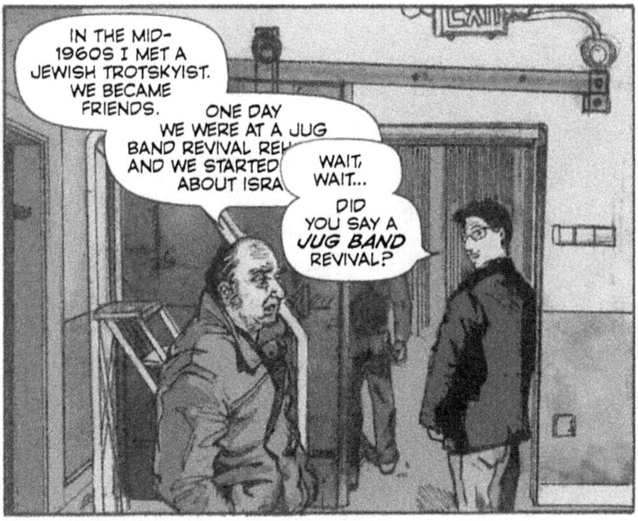
IN THE MID-1960S I MET A JEWISH TROTSKYIST. WE BECAME FRIENDS.
ONE DAY WE WERE AT A JUG BAND REVIVAL REH AND WE STARTED ABOUT ISRA
WAIT, WAIT...
DID YOU SAY A JUG BAND REVIVAL?

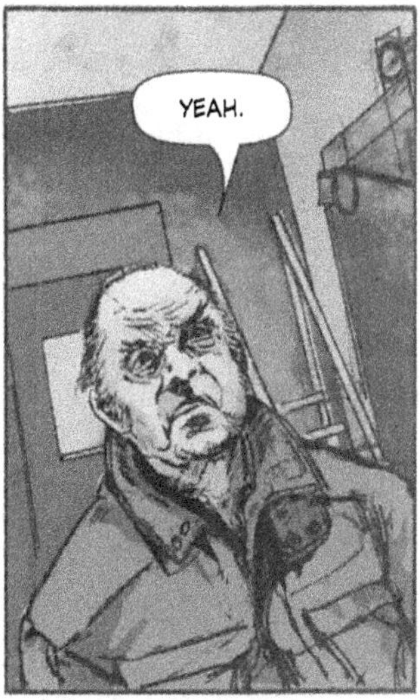
YEAH.

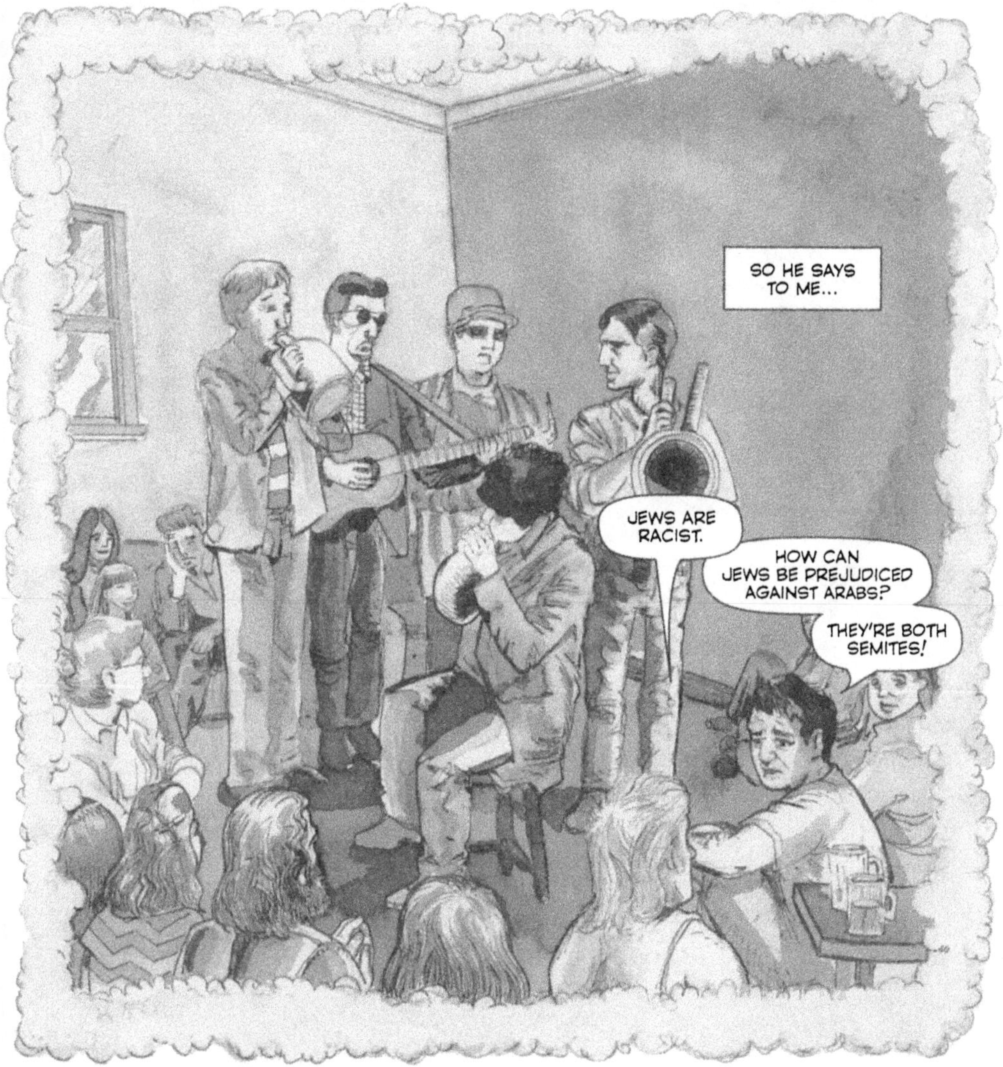
SO HE SAYS TO ME...
JEWS ARE RACIST.
HOW CAN JEWS BE PREJUDICED AGAINST ARABS?
THEY'RE BOTH SEMITES!

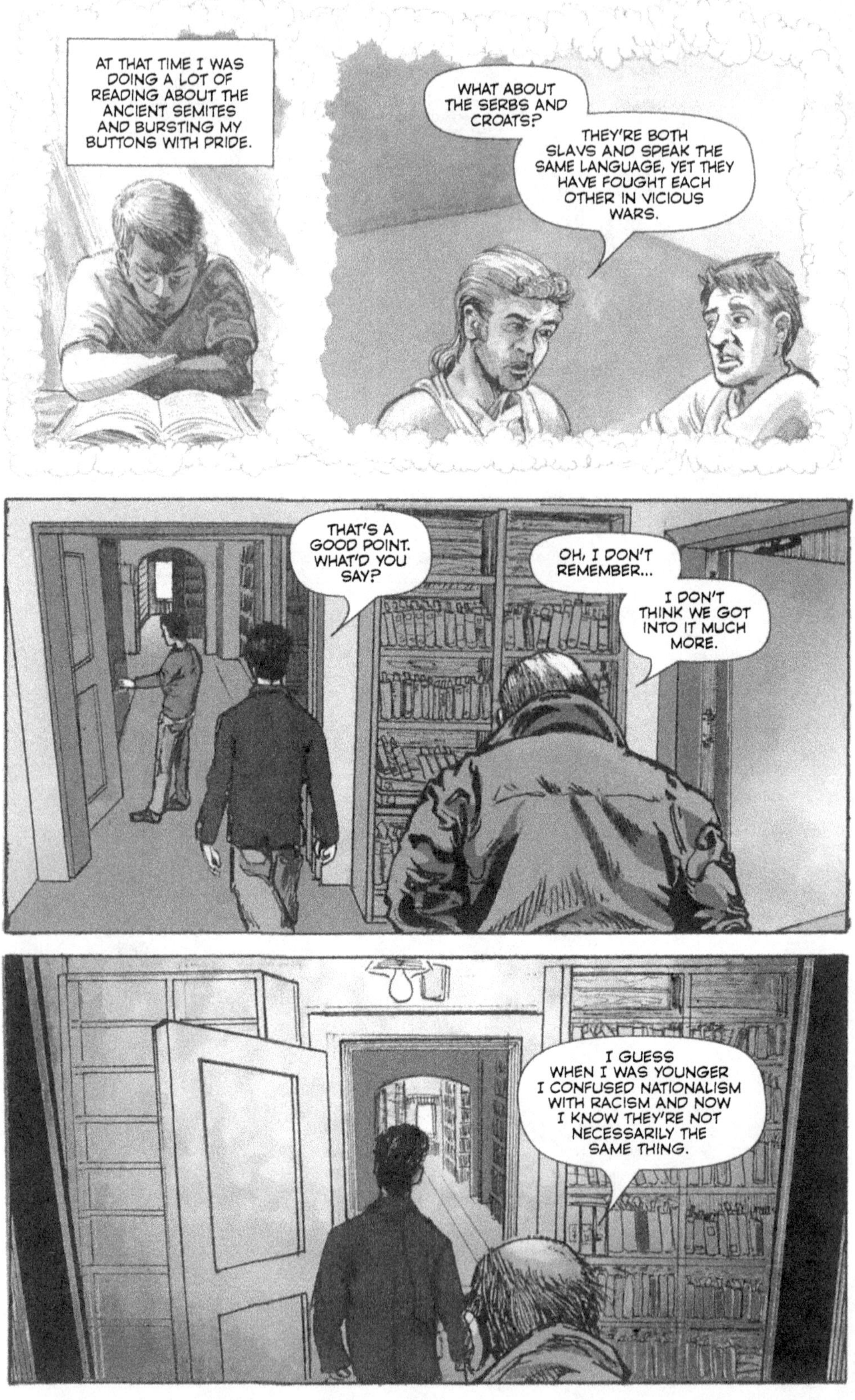
AT THAT TIME I WAS DOING A LOT OF READING ABOUT THE ANCIENT SEMITES AND BURSTING MY BUTTONS WITH PRIDE.
WHAT ABOUT THE SERBS AND CROATS?
THEY'RE BOTH SLAVS AND SPEAK THE SAME LANGUAGE, YET THEY HAVE FOUGHT EACH OTHER IN VICIOUS WARS.
THAT'S A GOOD POINT. WHAT'D YOU SAY?
OH, I DON'T REMEMBER...
I DON'T THINK WE GOT INTO IT MUCH MORE.
I GUESS WHEN I WAS YOUNGER I CONFUSED NATIONALISM WITH RACISM AND NOW I KNOW THEY'RE NOT NECESSARILY THE SAME THING.

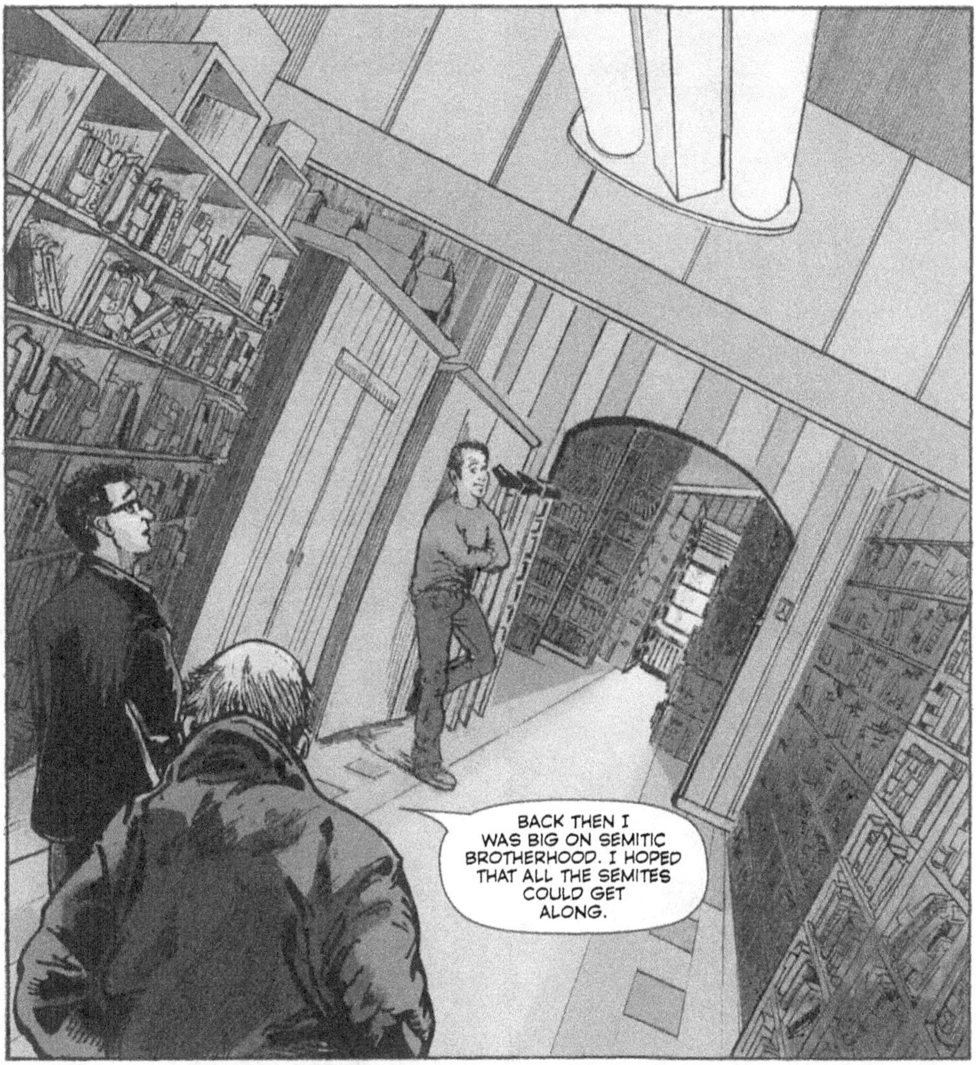
BACK THEN I WAS BIG ON SEMITIC BROTHERHOOD. I HOPED THAT ALL THE SEMITES COULD GET ALONG.

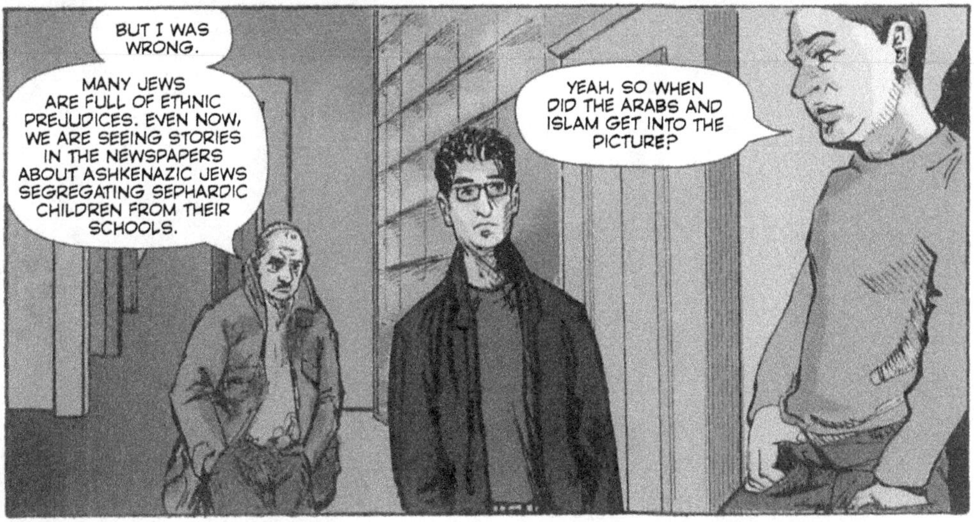
BUT I WAS WRONG.
MANY JEWS ARE FULL OF ETHNIC PREJUDICES. EVEN NOW, WE ARE SEEING STORIES IN THE NEWSPAPERS ABOUT ASHKENAZIC JEWS SEGREGATING SEPHARDIC CHILDREN FROM THEIR SCHOOLS.
YEAH, SO WHEN DID THE ARABS AND ISLAM GET INTO THE PICTURE?

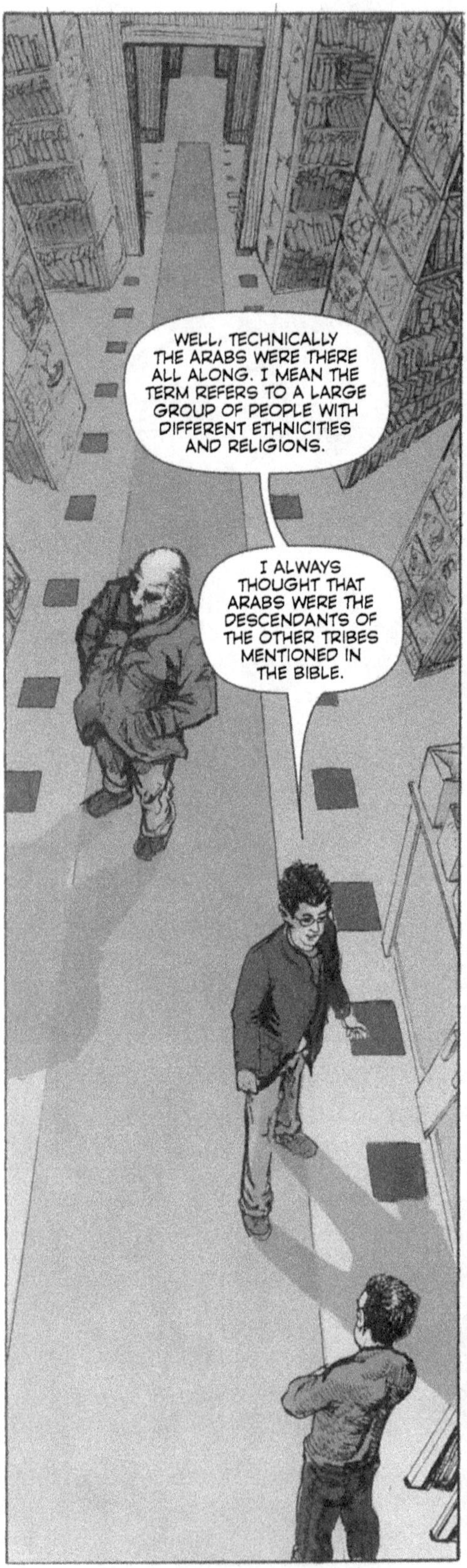
WELL, TECHNICALLY THE ARABS WERE THERE ALL ALONG. I MEAN THE TERM REFERS TO A LARGE GROUP OF PEOPLE WITH DIFFERENT ETHNICITIES AND RELIGIONS.
I ALWAYS THOUGHT THAT ARABS WERE THE DESCENDANTS OF THE OTHER TRIBES MENTIONED IN THE BIBLE.

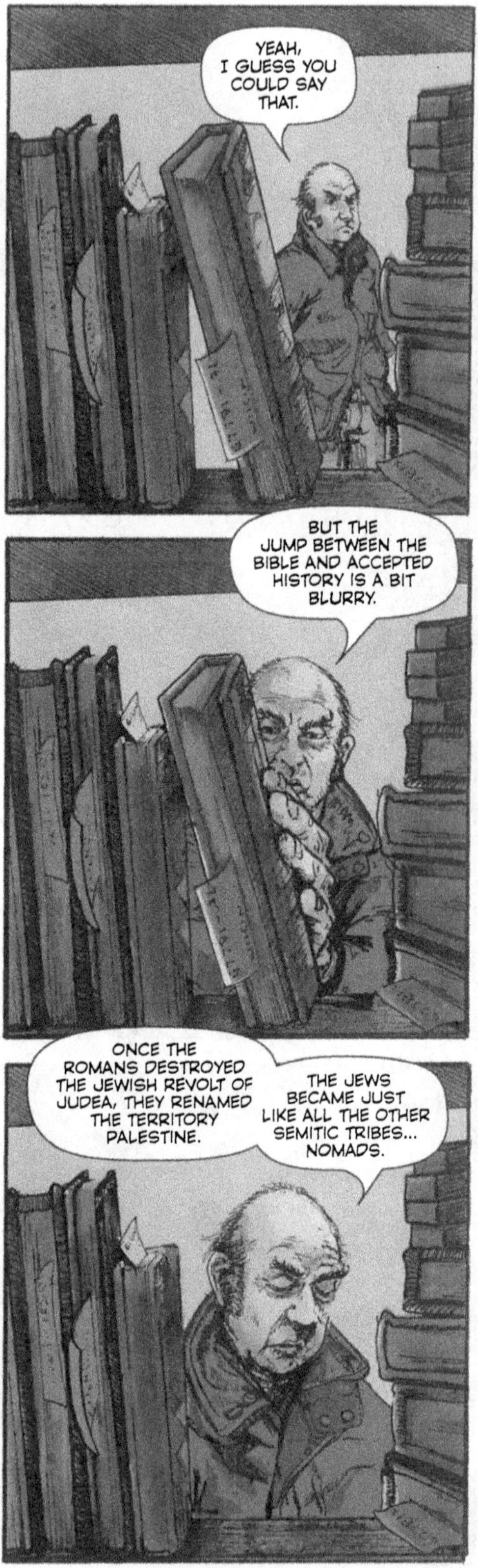
YEAH, I GUESS YOU COULD SAY THAT.
BUT THE JUMP BETWEEN THE BIBLE AND ACCEPTED HISTORY IS A BIT BLURRY.
ONCE THE ROMANS DESTROYED THE JEWISH REVOLT OF JUDEA, THEY RENAMED THE TERRITORY PALESTINE.
THE JEWS BECAME JUST LIKE ALL THE OTHER SEMITIC TRIBES... NOMADS.

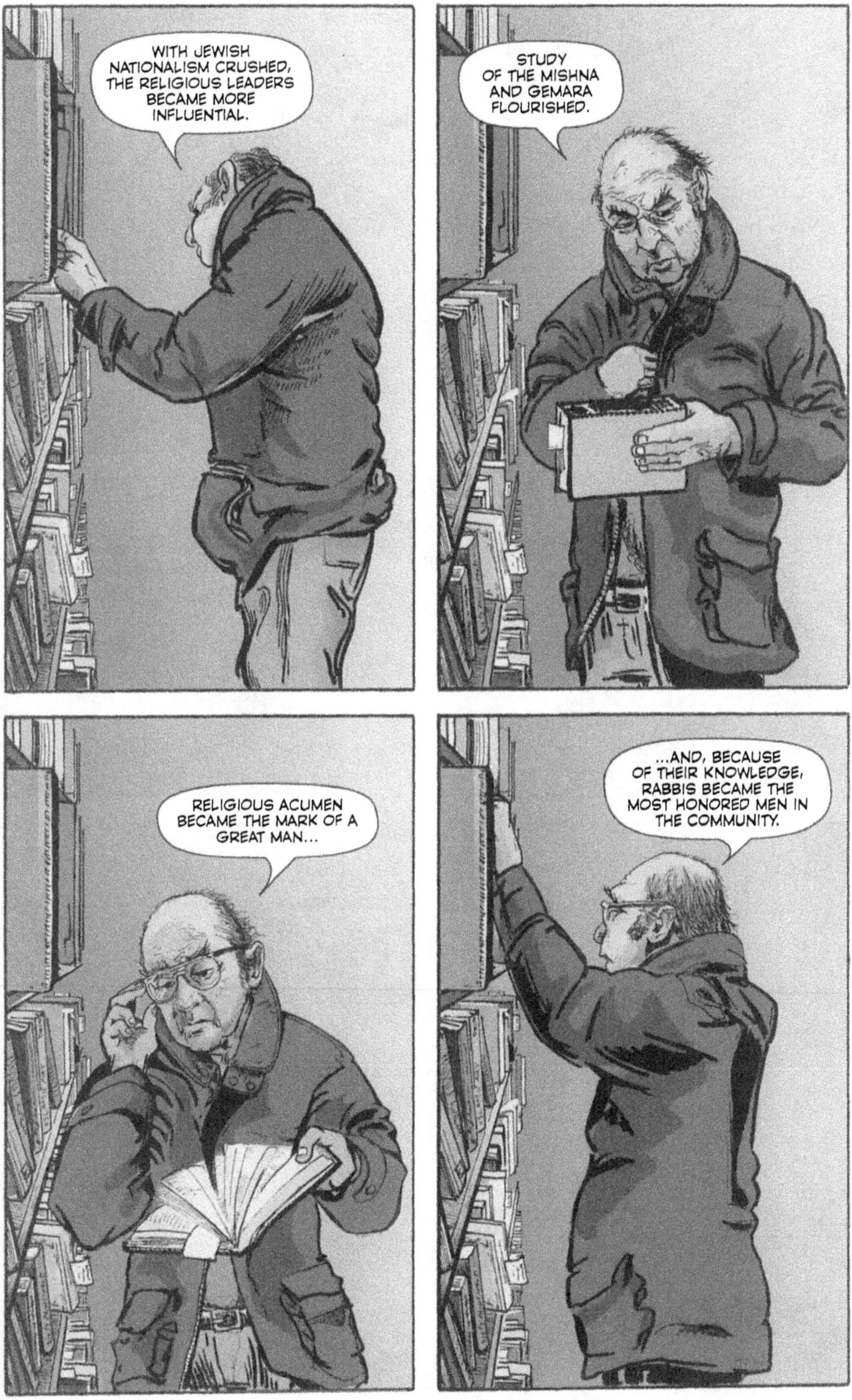
WITH JEWISH NATIONALISM CRUSHED, THE RELIGIOUS LEADERS BECAME MORE INFLUENTIAL.
STUDY OF THE MISHNA AND GEMARA FLOURISHED.
RELIGIOUS ACUMEN BECAME THE MARK OF A GREAT MAN...
...AND, BECAUSE OF THEIR KNOWLEDGE, RABBIS BECAME THE MOST HONORED MEN IN THE COMMUNITY.

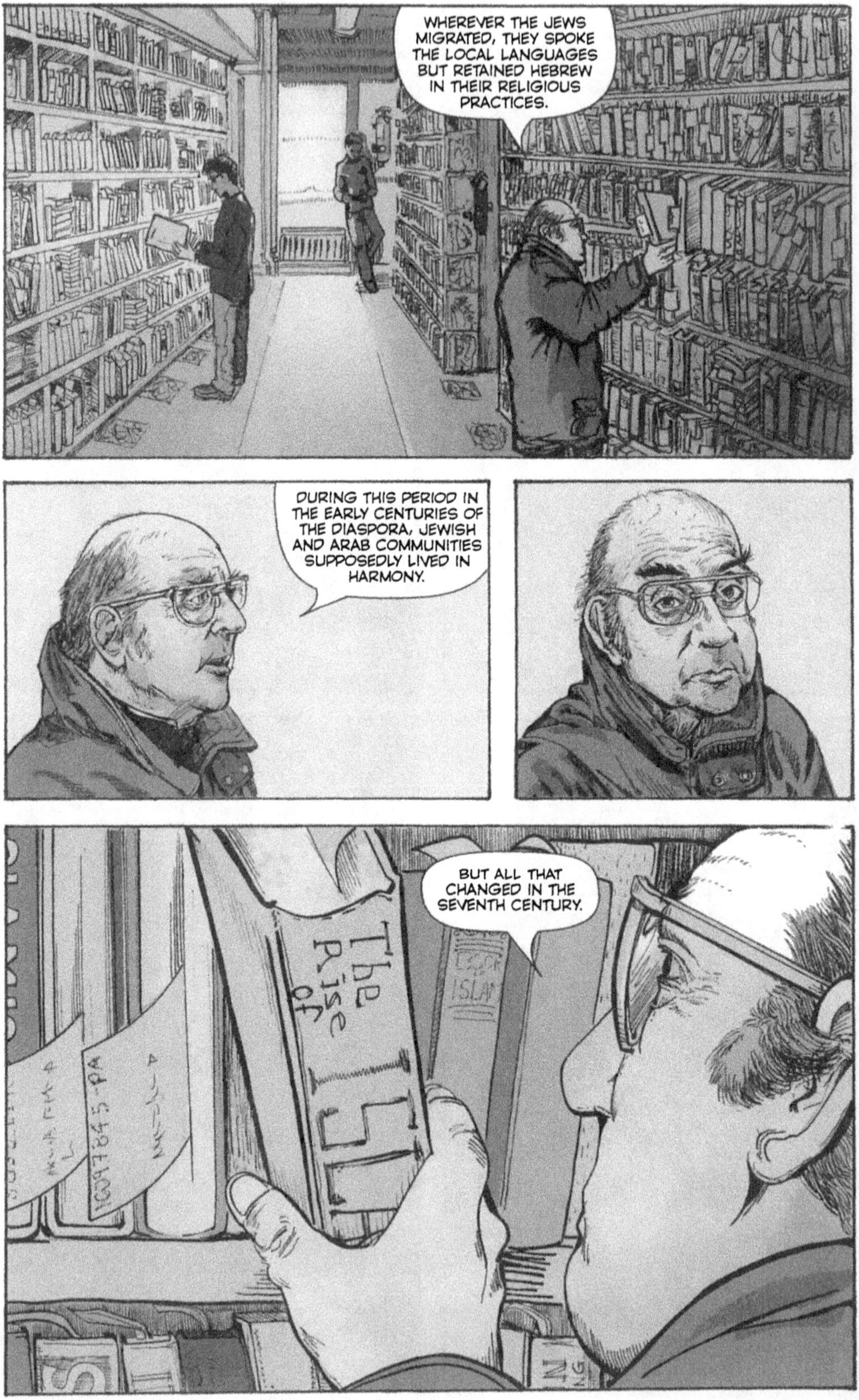
WHEREVER THE JEWS MIGRATED, THEY SPOKE THE LOCAL LANGUAGES BUT RETAINED HEBREW IN THEIR RELIGIOUS PRACTICES.
DURING THIS PERIOD IN THE EARLY CENTURIES OF THE DIASPORA, JEWISH AND ARAB COMMUNITIES SUPPOSEDLY LIVED IN HARMONY.
BUT ALL THAT CHANGED IN THE SEVENTH CENTURY.

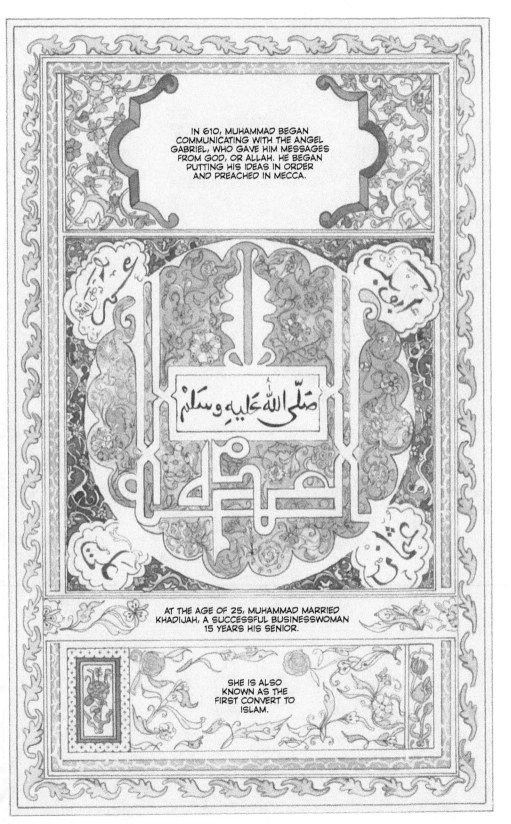

IN 610, MUHAMMAD BEGAN
COMMUNICATING WITH THE ANGEL
GABRIEL, WHO GAVE HIM MESSAGES
FROM GOD, OR ALLAH. HE BEGAN
PUTTING HIS IDEAS IN ORDER
AND PREACHED IN MECCA.

AT THE AGE OF 25, MUHAMMAD MARRIED
KHADIJAH, A SUCCESSFUL BUSINESSWOMAN
15 YEARS HIS SENIOR.

SHE IS ALSO
KNOWN AS THE
FIRST CONVERT TO
ISLAM.

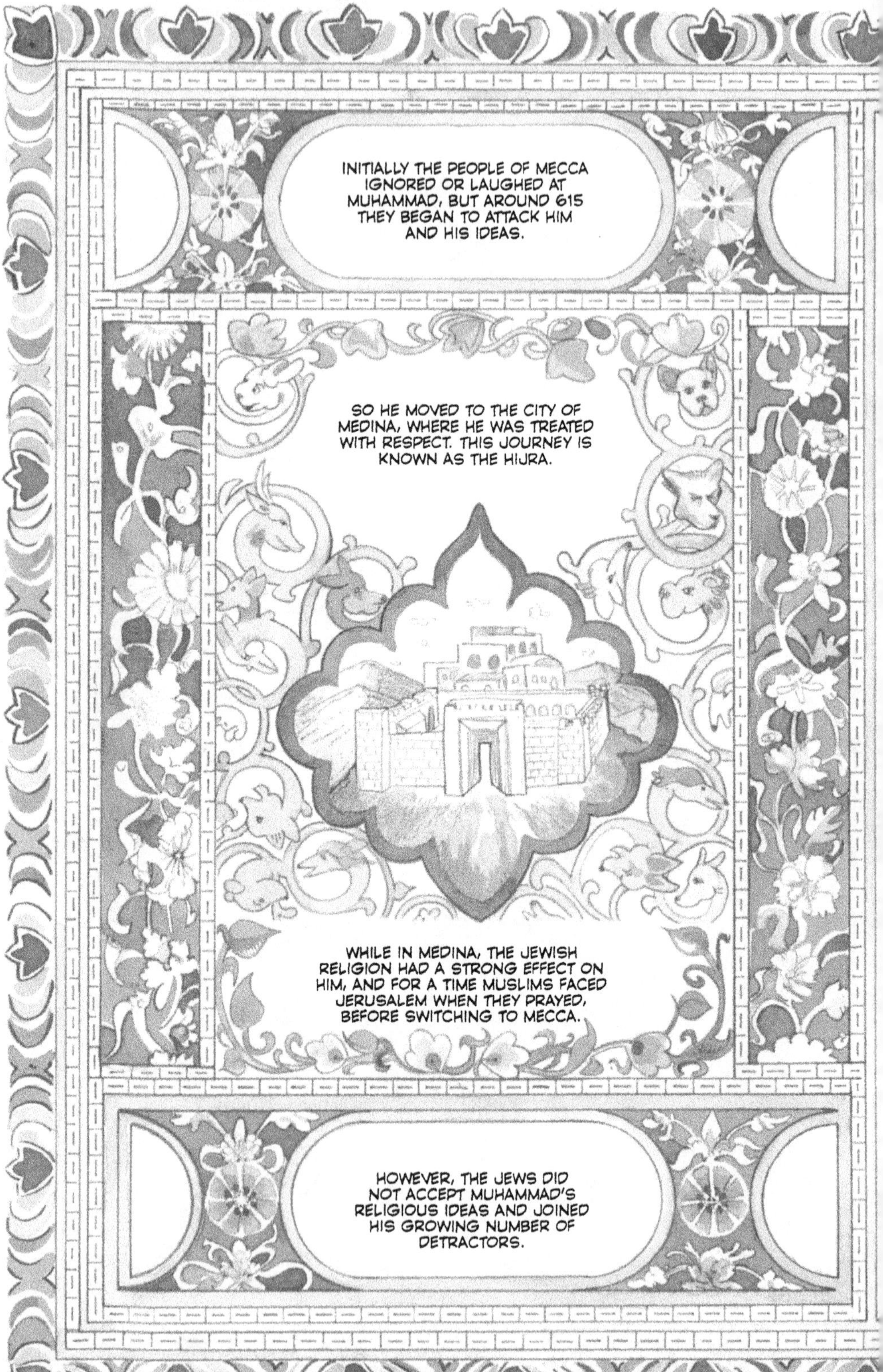
INITIALLY THE PEOPLE OF MECCA IGNORED OR LAUGHED AT MUHAMMAD, BUT AROUND 615 THEY BEGAN TO ATTACK HIM AND HIS IDEAS.
SO HE MOVED TO THE CITY OF MEDINA, WHERE HE WAS TREATED WITH RESPECT. THIS JOURNEY IS KNOWN AS THE HIJRA.
WHILE IN MEDINA, THE JEWISH RELIGION HAD A STRONG EFFECT ON HIM, AND FOR A TIME MUSLIMS FACED JERUSALEM WHEN THEY PRAYED, BEFORE SWITCHING TO MECCA.
HOWEVER, THE JEWS DID NOT ACCEPT MUHAMMAD'S RELIGIOUS IDEAS AND JOINED HIS GROWING NUMBER OF DETRACTORS.

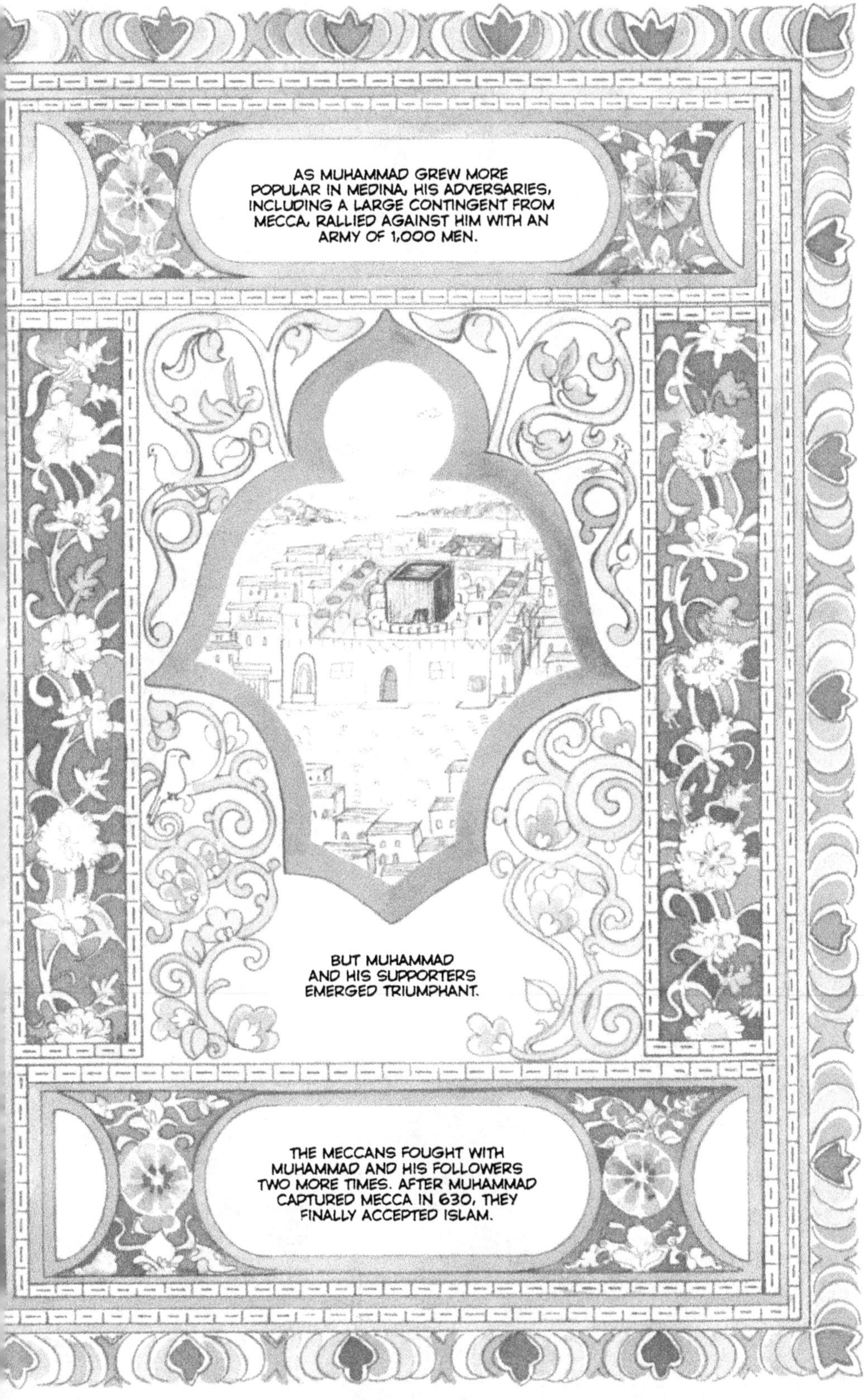
AS MUHAMMAD GREW MORE POPULAR IN MEDINA, HIS ADVERSARIES, INCLUDING A LARGE CONTINGENT FROM MECCA, RALLIED AGAINST HIM WITH AN ARMY OF 1,000 MEN.
BUT MUHAMMAD AND HIS SUPPORTERS EMERGED TRIUMPHANT.
THE MECCANS FOUGHT WITH MUHAMMAD AND HIS FOLLOWERS TWO MORE TIMES. AFTER MUHAMMAD CAPTURED MECCA IN 630, THEY FINALLY ACCEPTED ISLAM.

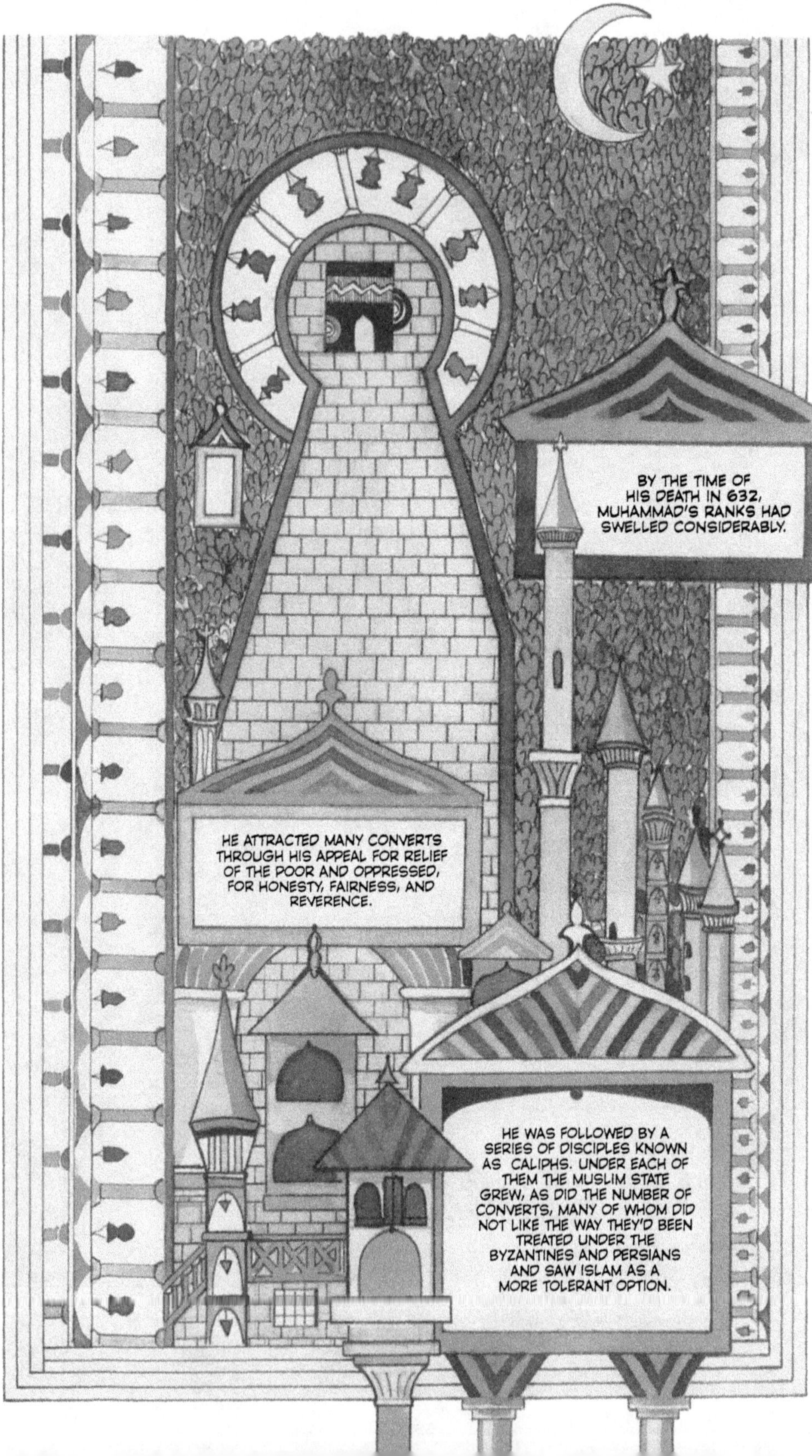
BY THE TIME OF HIS DEATH IN 632, MUHAMMAD'S RANKS HAD SWELLED CONSIDERABLY.
HE ATTRACTED MANY CONVERTS THROUGH HIS APPEAL FOR RELIEF OF THE POOR AND OPPRESSED, FOR HONESTY, FAIRNESS, AND REVERENCE.
HE WAS FOLLOWED BY A SERIES OF DISCIPLES KNOWN AS CALIPHS. UNDER EACH OF THEM THE MUSLIM STATE GREW, AS DID THE NUMBER OF CONVERTS, MANY OF WHOM DID NOT LIKE THE WAY THEY'D BEEN TREATED UNDER THE BYZANTINES AND PERSIANS AND SAW ISLAM AS A MORE TOLERANT OPTION.

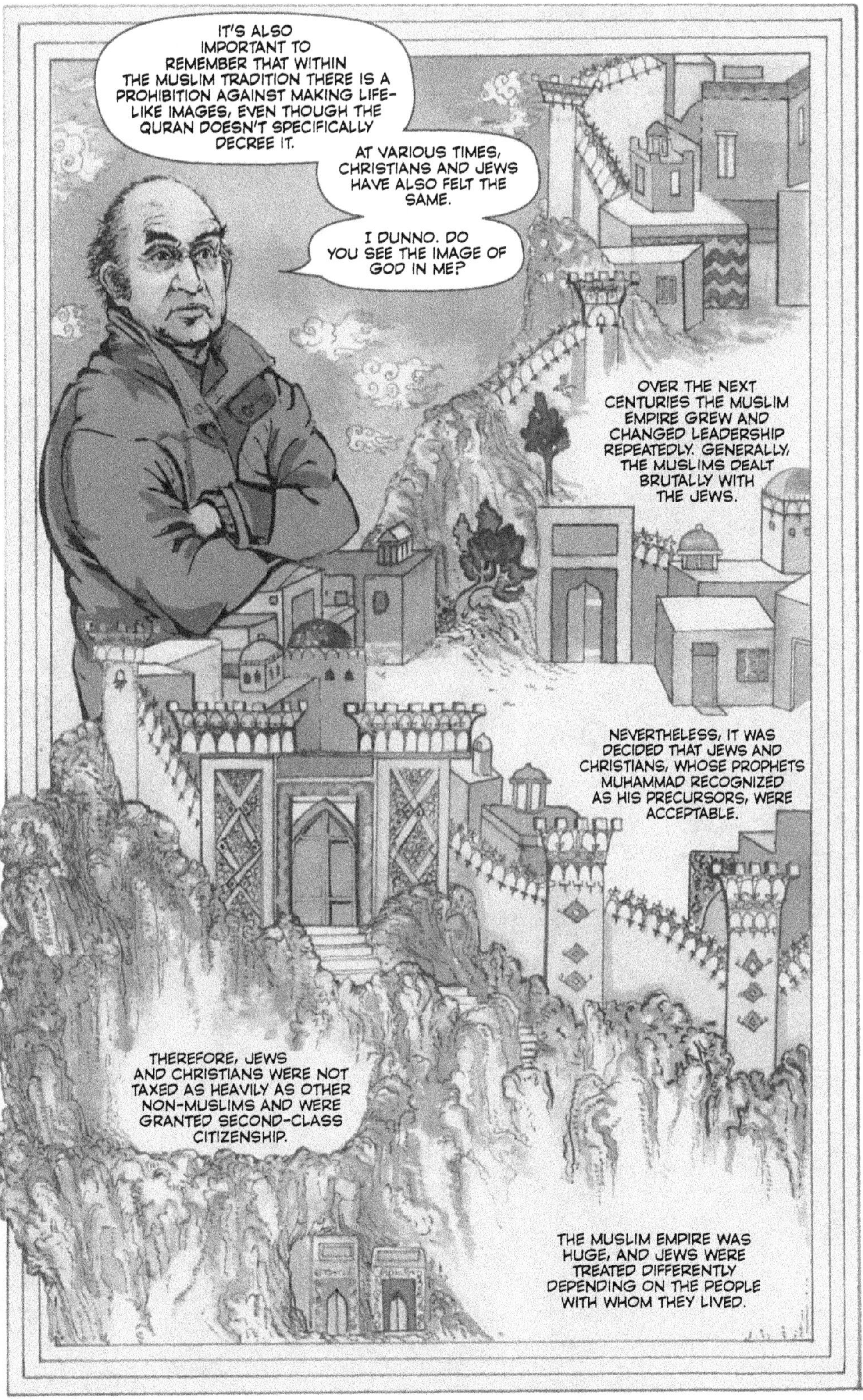
IT'S ALSO IMPORTANT TO REMEMBER THAT WITHIN THE MUSLIM TRADITION THERE IS A PROHIBITION AGAINST MAKING LIFE-LIKE IMAGES, EVEN THOUGH THE QURAN DOESN'T SPECIFICALLY DECREE IT.
AT VARIOUS TIMES, CHRISTIANS AND JEWS HAVE ALSO FELT THE SAME.
I DUNNO. DO YOU SEE THE IMAGE OF GOD IN ME?
OVER THE NEXT CENTURIES THE MUSLIM EMPIRE GREW AND CHANGED LEADERSHIP REPEATEDLY. GENERALLY, THE MUSLIMS DEALT BRUTALLY WITH THE JEWS.
NEVERTHELESS, IT WAS DECIDED THAT JEWS AND CHRISTIANS, WHOSE PROPHETS MUHAMMAD RECOGNIZED AS HIS PRECURSORS, WERE ACCEPTABLE.
THEREFORE, JEWS AND CHRISTIANS WERE NOT TAXED AS HEAVILY AS OTHER NON-MUSLIMS AND WERE GRANTED SECOND-CLASS CITIZENSHIP.
THE MUSLIM EMPIRE WAS HUGE, AND JEWS WERE TREATED DIFFERENTLY DEPENDING ON THE PEOPLE WITH WHOM THEY LIVED.

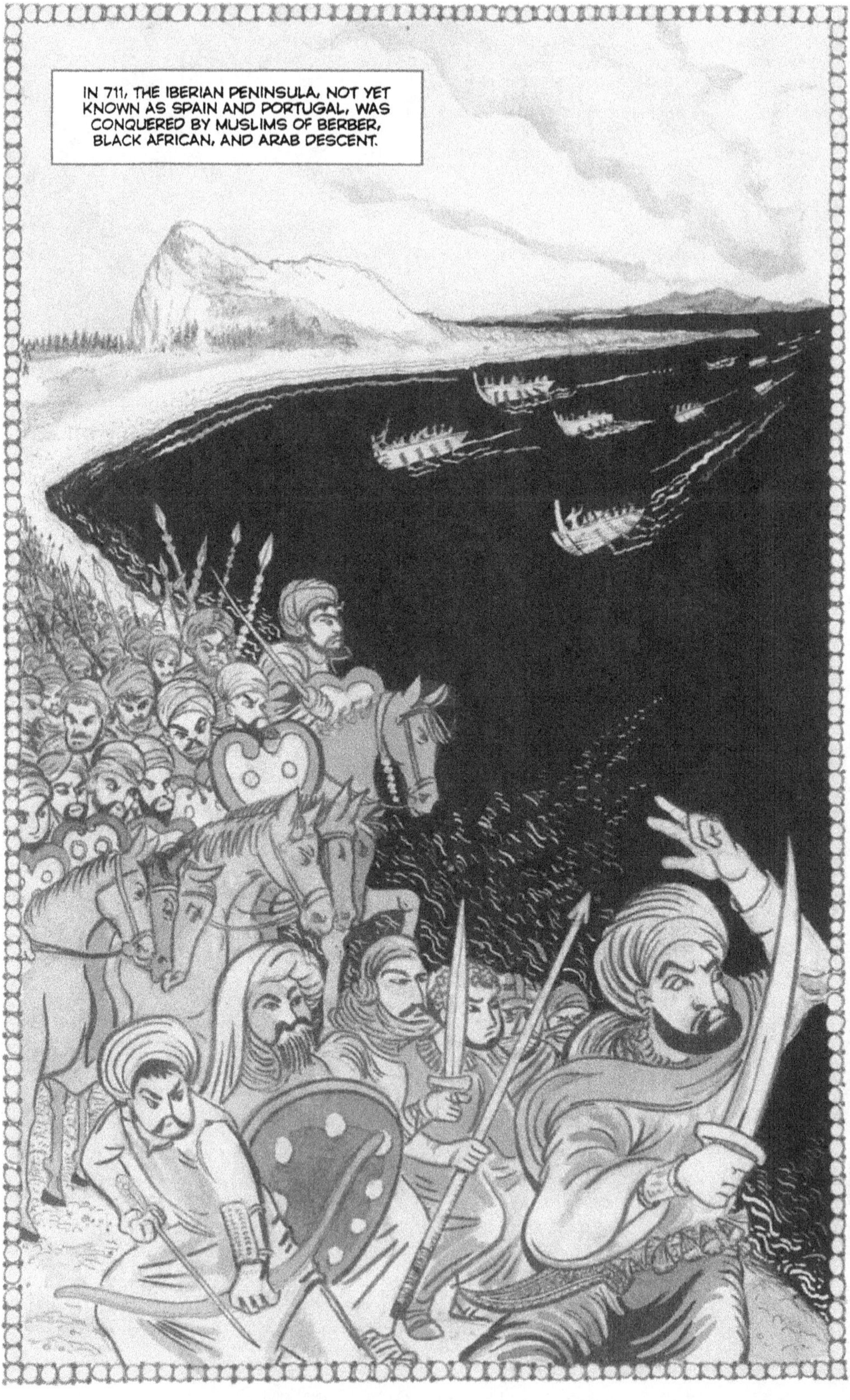
IN 711, THE IBERIAN PENINSULA, NOT YET KNOWN AS SPAIN AND PORTUGAL, WAS CONQUERED BY MUSLIMS OF BERBER, BLACK AFRICAN, AND ARAB DESCENT.

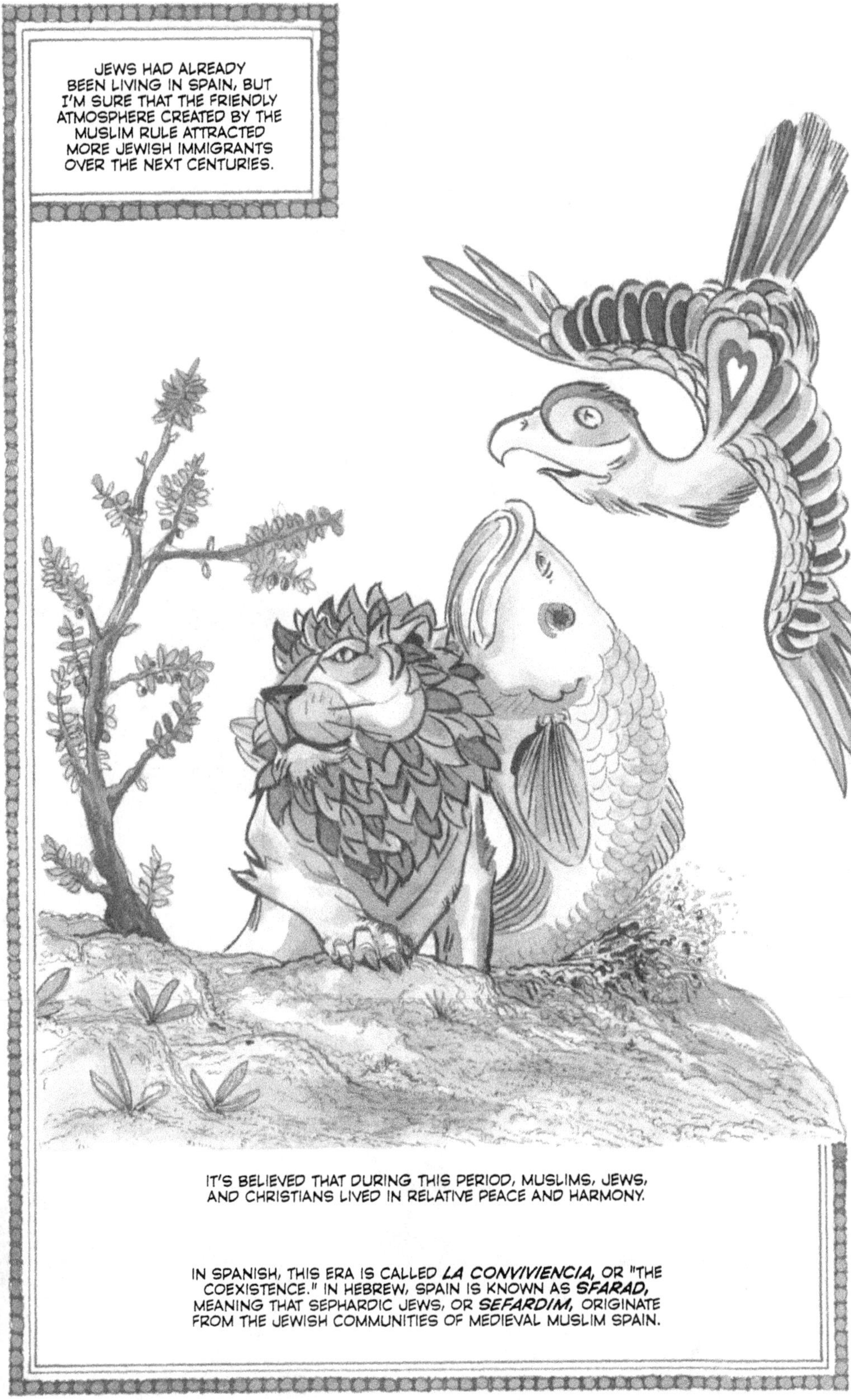
JEWS HAD ALREADY BEEN LIVING IN SPAIN, BUT I'M SURE THAT THE FRIENDLY ATMOSPHERE CREATED BY THE MUSLIM RULE ATTRACTED MORE JEWISH IMMIGRANTS OVER THE NEXT CENTURIES.
IT'S BELIEVED THAT DURING THIS PERIOD, MUSLIMS, JEWS, AND CHRISTIANS LIVED IN RELATIVE PEACE AND HARMONY.
IN SPANISH, THIS ERA IS CALLED ***LA CONVIVIENCIA,*** OR "THE COEXISTENCE." IN HEBREW, SPAIN IS KNOWN AS ***SFARAD,*** MEANING THAT SEPHARDIC JEWS, OR ***SEFARDIM,*** ORIGINATE FROM THE JEWISH COMMUNITIES OF MEDIEVAL MUSLIM SPAIN.

JEWS LIVING IN THIS GOLDEN AGE WERE PRETTY MUCH LEFT ALONE.

A NUMBER OF GREAT JEWISH SCIENTISTS AND PHILOSOPHERS FLOURISHED DURING THIS TIME, INCLUDING MAIMONIDES. SOMETIMES CALLED THE RAMBAM, MAIMONIDES WAS A RELIGIOUS SCHOLAR, PHILOSOPHER, AND PHYSICIAN.

BORN IN CORDOBA, HE LEFT THE CITY AFTER FANATICAL BERBERS FROM NORTH AFRICA CAPTURED IT IN 1148. HE THEN MOVED TO EGYPT AND WAS A COURT PHYSICIAN TO THE LEGENDARY SALADIN.

רמב״ם

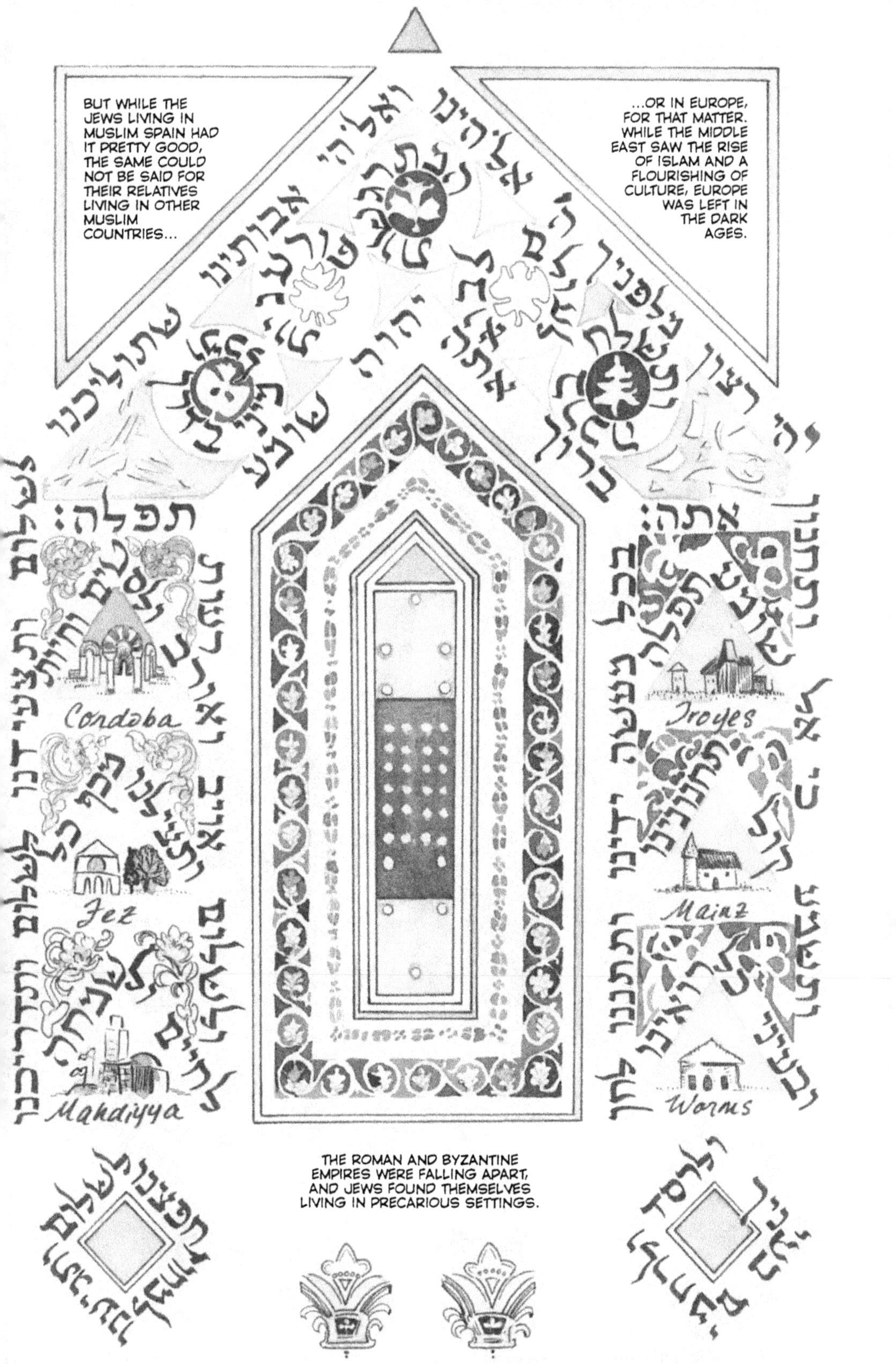
BUT WHILE THE JEWS LIVING IN MUSLIM SPAIN HAD IT PRETTY GOOD, THE SAME COULD NOT BE SAID FOR THEIR RELATIVES LIVING IN OTHER MUSLIM COUNTRIES...
...OR IN EUROPE, FOR THAT MATTER. WHILE THE MIDDLE EAST SAW THE RISE OF ISLAM AND A FLOURISHING OF CULTURE, EUROPE WAS LEFT IN THE DARK AGES.
Cordoba
Fez
Mahdiyya
Troyes
Mainz
Worms
THE ROMAN AND BYZANTINE EMPIRES WERE FALLING APART, AND JEWS FOUND THEMSELVES LIVING IN PRECARIOUS SETTINGS.

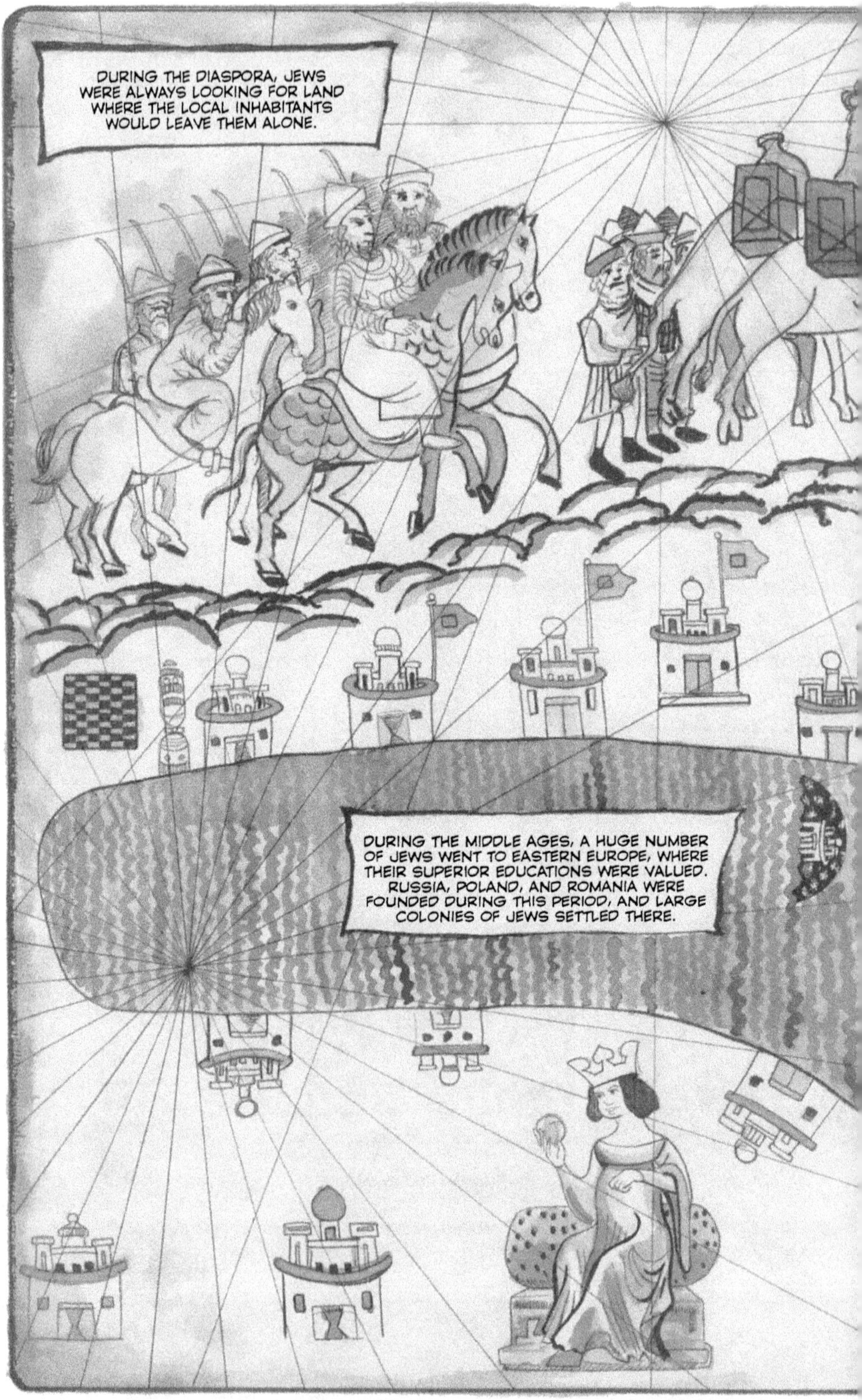
DURING THE DIASPORA, JEWS WERE ALWAYS LOOKING FOR LAND WHERE THE LOCAL INHABITANTS WOULD LEAVE THEM ALONE.
DURING THE MIDDLE AGES, A HUGE NUMBER OF JEWS WENT TO EASTERN EUROPE, WHERE THEIR SUPERIOR EDUCATIONS WERE VALUED. RUSSIA, POLAND, AND ROMANIA WERE FOUNDED DURING THIS PERIOD, AND LARGE COLONIES OF JEWS SETTLED THERE.

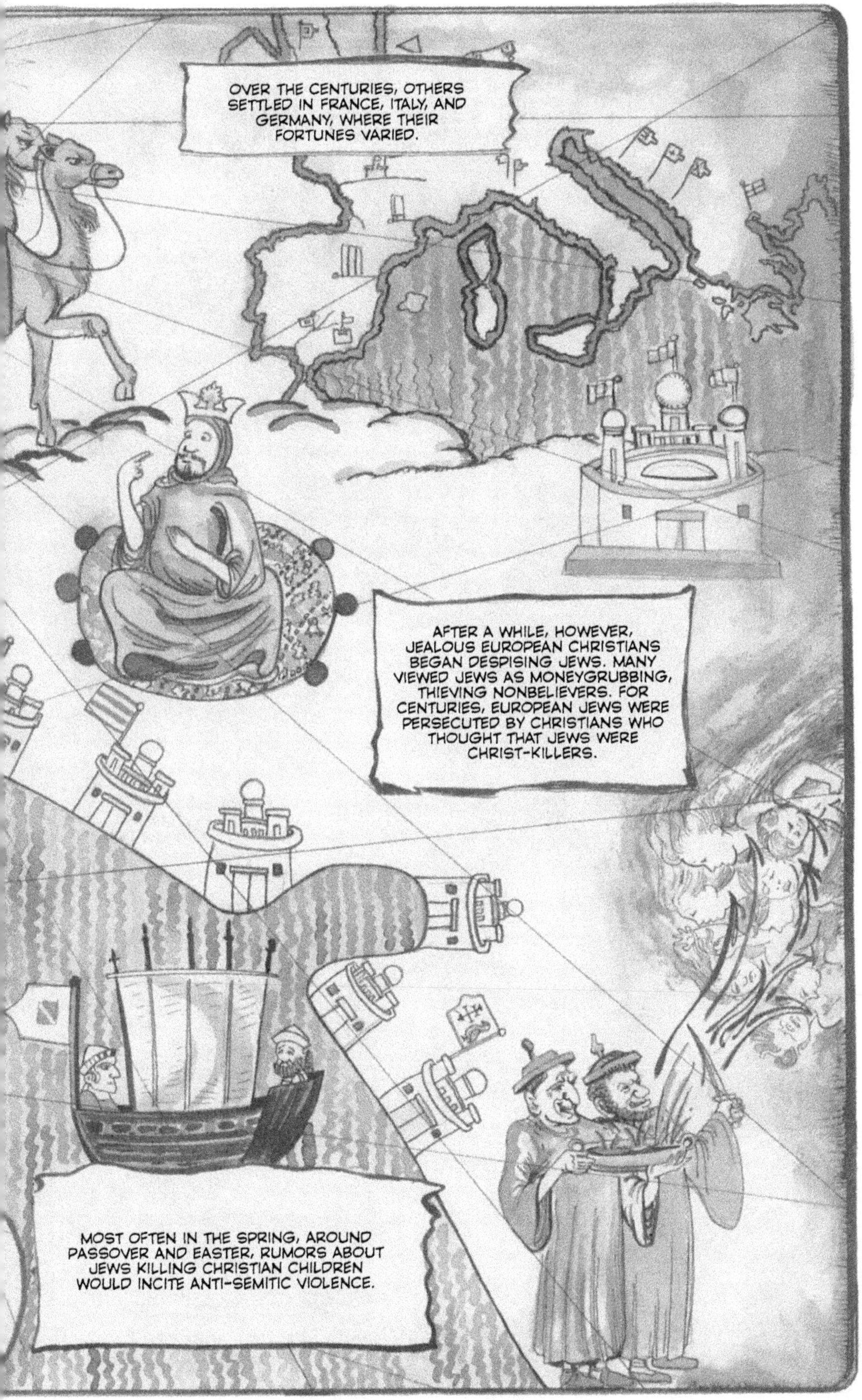
OVER THE CENTURIES, OTHERS SETTLED IN FRANCE, ITALY, AND GERMANY, WHERE THEIR FORTUNES VARIED.
AFTER A WHILE, HOWEVER, JEALOUS EUROPEAN CHRISTIANS BEGAN DESPISING JEWS. MANY VIEWED JEWS AS MONEYGRUBBING, THIEVING NONBELIEVERS. FOR CENTURIES, EUROPEAN JEWS WERE PERSECUTED BY CHRISTIANS WHO THOUGHT THAT JEWS WERE CHRIST-KILLERS.
MOST OFTEN IN THE SPRING, AROUND PASSOVER AND EASTER, RUMORS ABOUT JEWS KILLING CHRISTIAN CHILDREN WOULD INCITE ANTI-SEMITIC VIOLENCE.

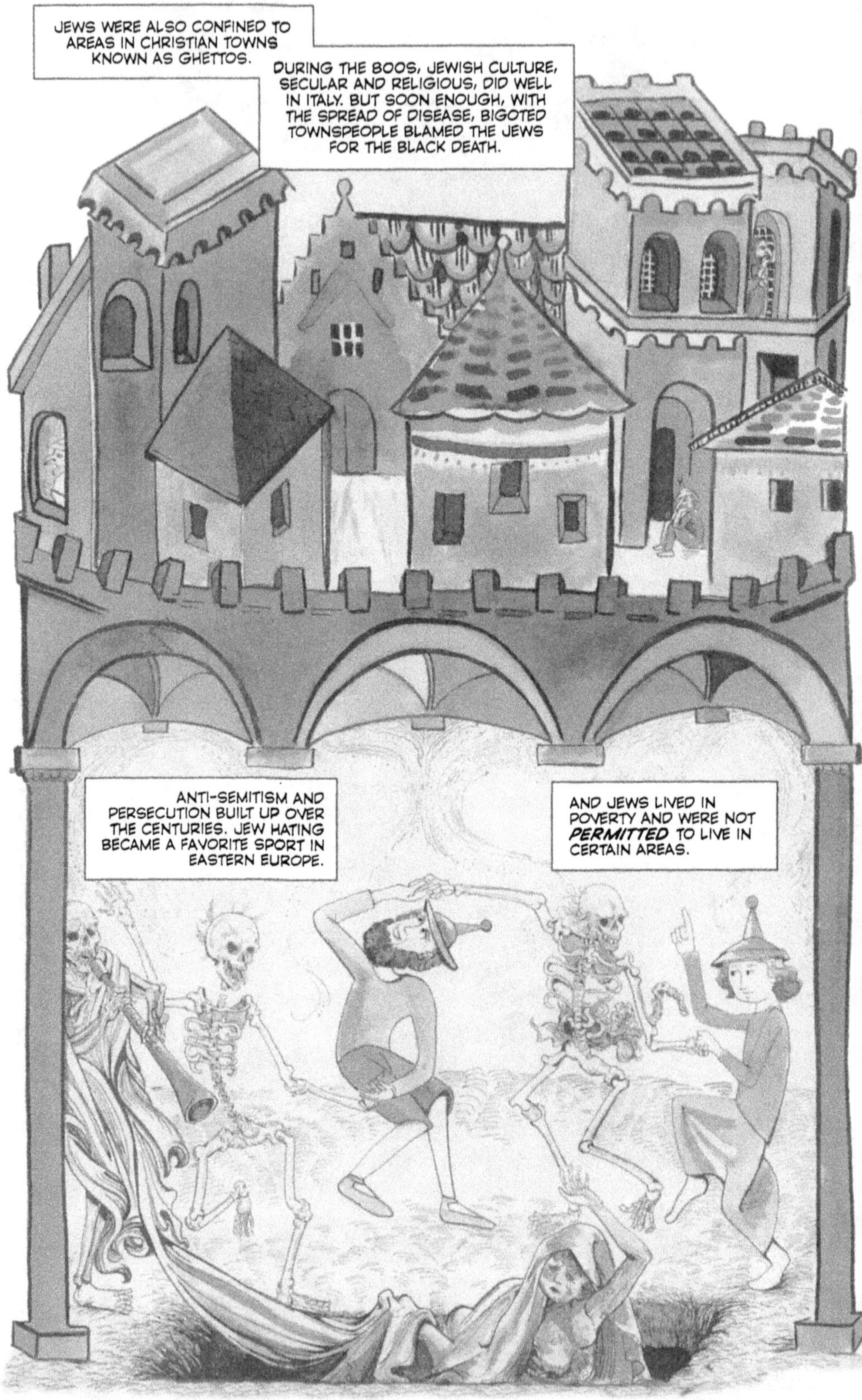
JEWS WERE ALSO CONFINED TO AREAS IN CHRISTIAN TOWNS KNOWN AS GHETTOS.
DURING THE 800S, JEWISH CULTURE, SECULAR AND RELIGIOUS, DID WELL IN ITALY. BUT SOON ENOUGH, WITH THE SPREAD OF DISEASE, BIGOTED TOWNSPEOPLE BLAMED THE JEWS FOR THE BLACK DEATH.
ANTI-SEMITISM AND PERSECUTION BUILT UP OVER THE CENTURIES. JEW HATING BECAME A FAVORITE SPORT IN EASTERN EUROPE.
AND JEWS LIVED IN POVERTY AND WERE NOT PERMITTED TO LIVE IN CERTAIN AREAS.

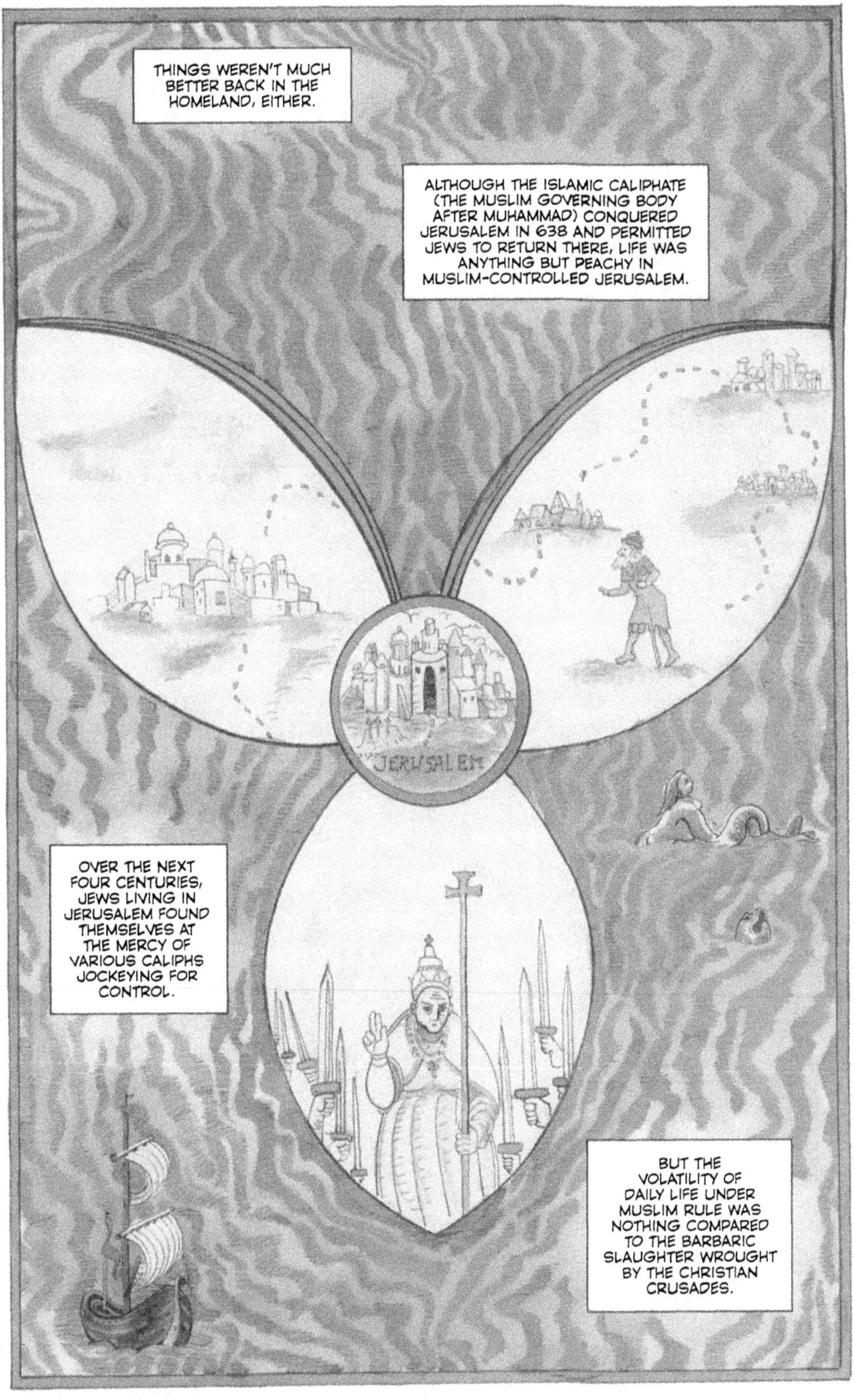
THINGS WEREN'T MUCH BETTER BACK IN THE HOMELAND, EITHER.
ALTHOUGH THE ISLAMIC CALIPHATE (THE MUSLIM GOVERNING BODY AFTER MUHAMMAD) CONQUERED JERUSALEM IN 638 AND PERMITTED JEWS TO RETURN THERE, LIFE WAS ANYTHING BUT PEACHY IN MUSLIM-CONTROLLED JERUSALEM.
JERUSALEM
OVER THE NEXT FOUR CENTURIES, JEWS LIVING IN JERUSALEM FOUND THEMSELVES AT THE MERCY OF VARIOUS CALIPHS JOCKEYING FOR CONTROL.
BUT THE VOLATILITY OF DAILY LIFE UNDER MUSLIM RULE WAS NOTHING COMPARED TO THE BARBARIC SLAUGHTER WROUGHT BY THE CHRISTIAN CRUSADES.

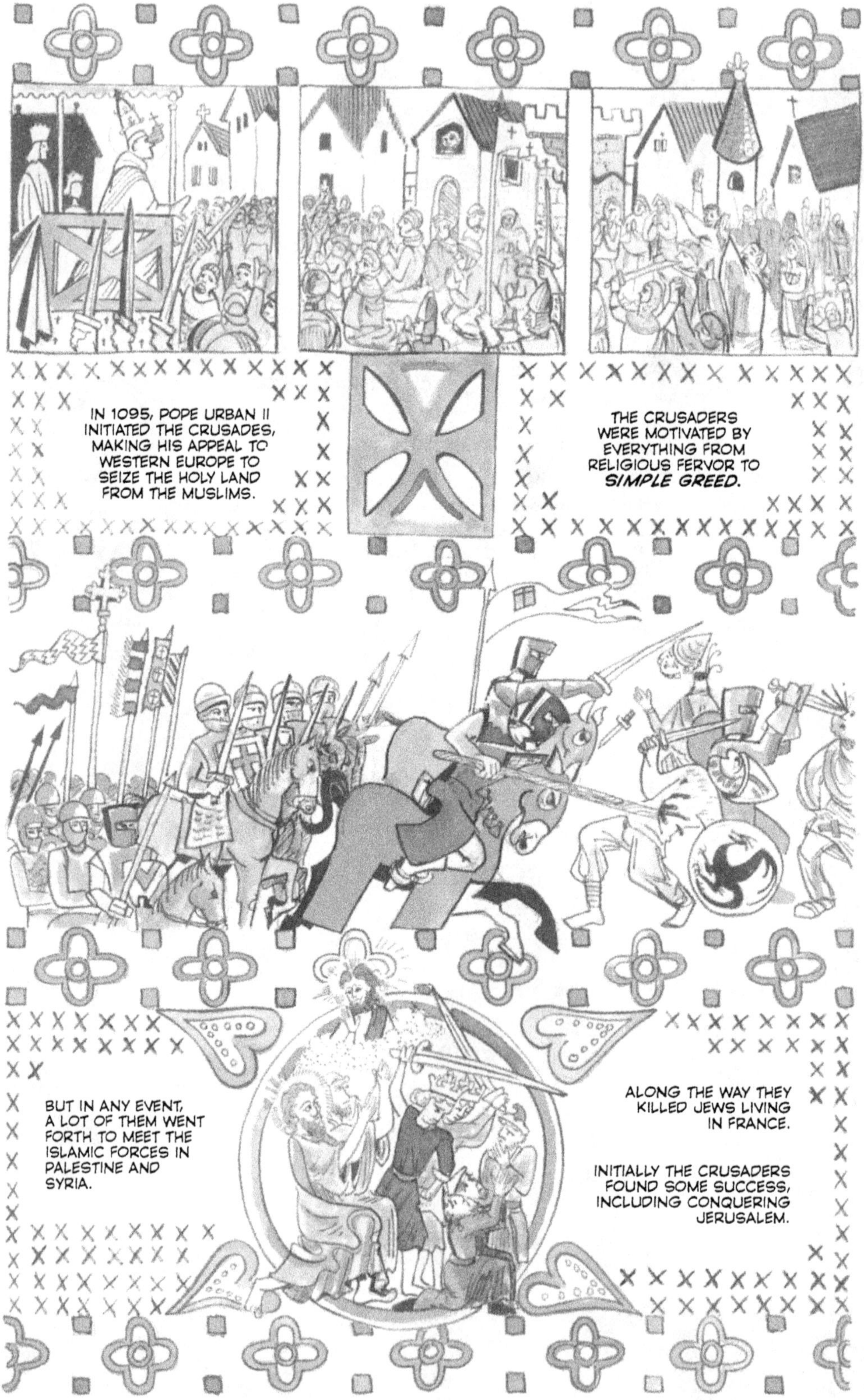
IN 1095, POPE URBAN II INITIATED THE CRUSADES, MAKING HIS APPEAL TO WESTERN EUROPE TO SEIZE THE HOLY LAND FROM THE MUSLIMS.
THE CRUSADERS WERE MOTIVATED BY EVERYTHING FROM RELIGIOUS FERVOR TO ***SIMPLE GREED.***
BUT IN ANY EVENT, A LOT OF THEM WENT FORTH TO MEET THE ISLAMIC FORCES IN PALESTINE AND SYRIA.
ALONG THE WAY THEY KILLED JEWS LIVING IN FRANCE.
INITIALLY THE CRUSADERS FOUND SOME SUCCESS, INCLUDING CONQUERING JERUSALEM.

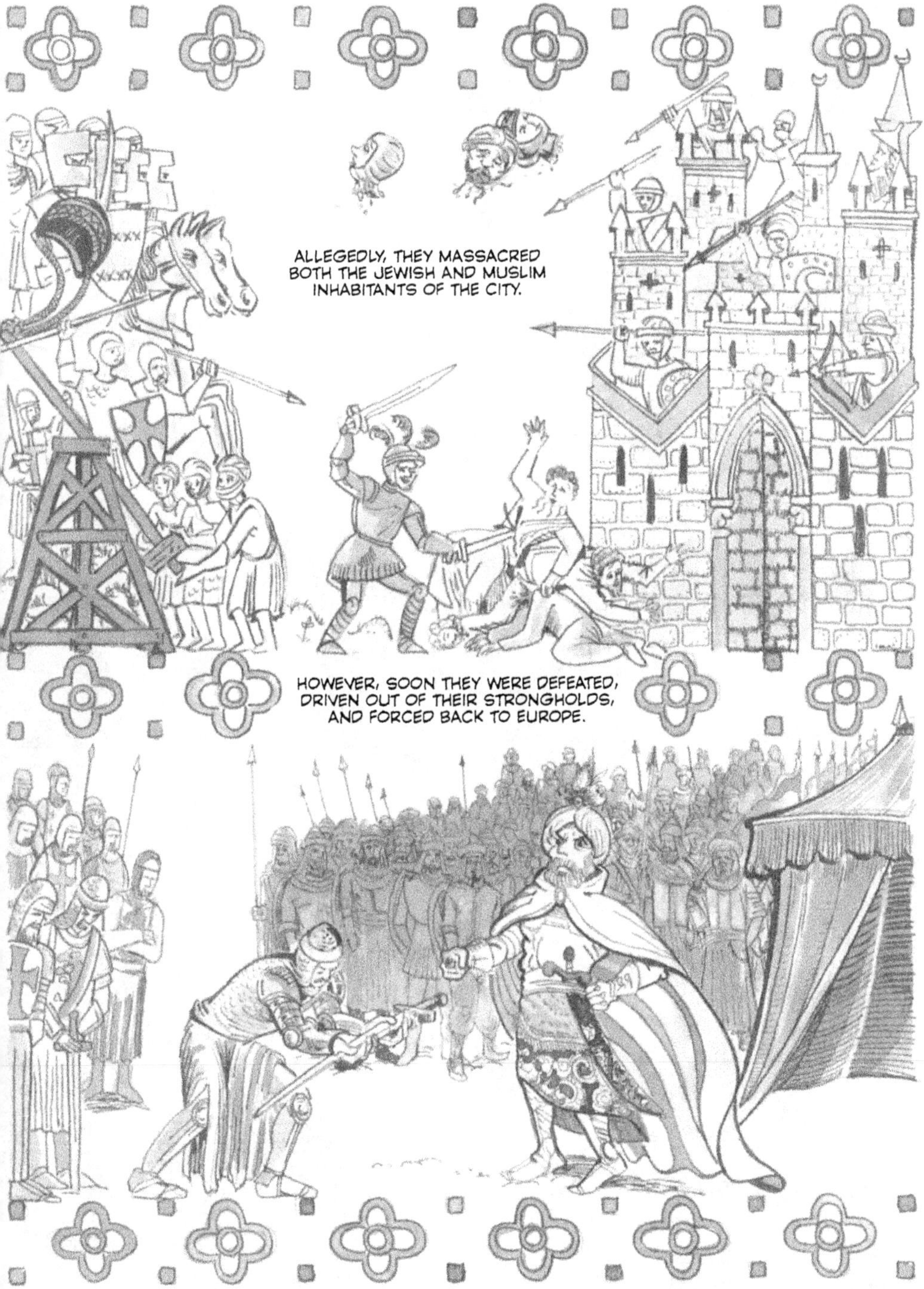
ALLEGEDLY, THEY MASSACRED BOTH THE JEWISH AND MUSLIM INHABITANTS OF THE CITY.
HOWEVER, SOON THEY WERE DEFEATED, DRIVEN OUT OF THEIR STRONGHOLDS, AND FORCED BACK TO EUROPE.

COINCIDENTALLY, ONE OF THE HEROES TO EMERGE FROM THESE EARLY CRUSADES WAS SALADIN, THE KURDISH LEADER OF A DYNASTY BASED IN EGYPT. HE WAS A TOP-NOTCH MILITARY LEADER AND TOOK BACK JERUSALEM FROM THE CRUSADERS.

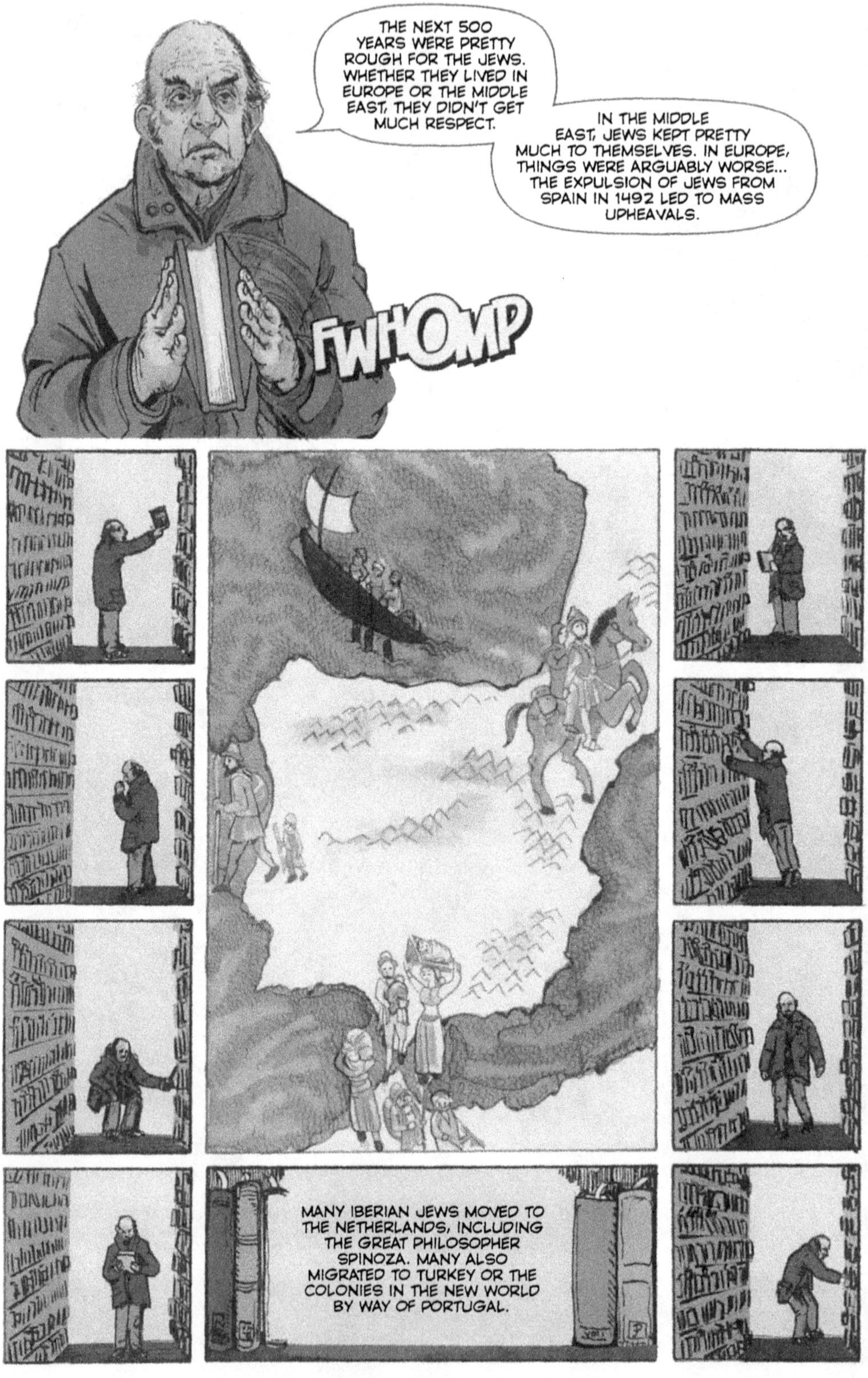
THE NEXT 500 YEARS WERE PRETTY ROUGH FOR THE JEWS. WHETHER THEY LIVED IN EUROPE OR THE MIDDLE EAST, THEY DIDN'T GET MUCH RESPECT.
IN THE MIDDLE EAST, JEWS KEPT PRETTY MUCH TO THEMSELVES. IN EUROPE, THINGS WERE ARGUABLY WORSE... THE EXPULSION OF JEWS FROM SPAIN IN 1492 LED TO MASS UPHEAVALS.
FWHOMP
MANY IBERIAN JEWS MOVED TO THE NETHERLANDS, INCLUDING THE GREAT PHILOSOPHER SPINOZA. MANY ALSO MIGRATED TO TURKEY OR THE COLONIES IN THE NEW WORLD BY WAY OF PORTUGAL.

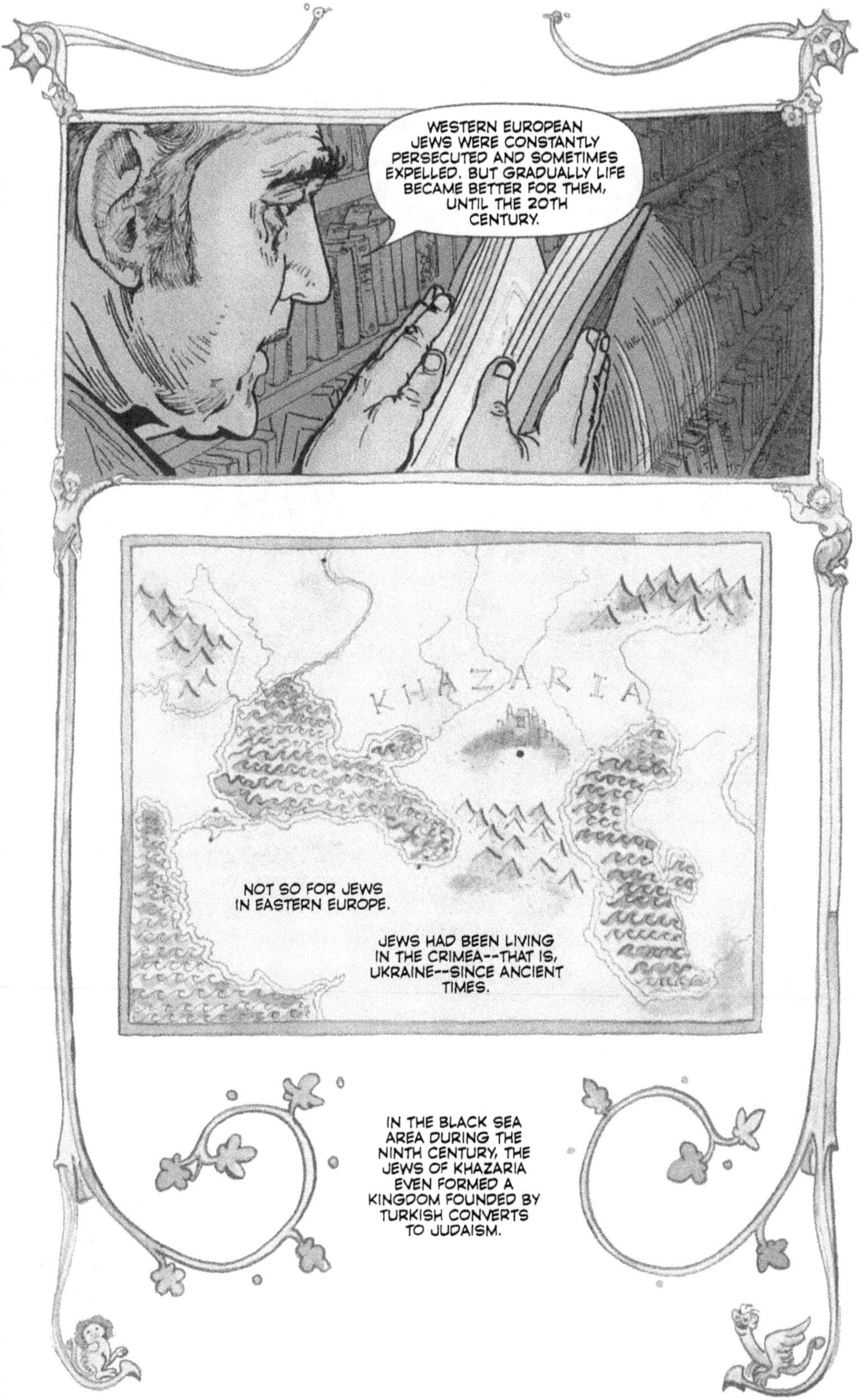
WESTERN EUROPEAN JEWS WERE CONSTANTLY PERSECUTED AND SOMETIMES EXPELLED. BUT GRADUALLY LIFE BECAME BETTER FOR THEM, UNTIL THE 20TH CENTURY.
KHAZARIA
NOT SO FOR JEWS IN EASTERN EUROPE.
JEWS HAD BEEN LIVING IN THE CRIMEA--THAT IS, UKRAINE--SINCE ANCIENT TIMES.
IN THE BLACK SEA AREA DURING THE NINTH CENTURY, THE JEWS OF KHAZARIA EVEN FORMED A KINGDOM FOUNDED BY TURKISH CONVERTS TO JUDAISM.

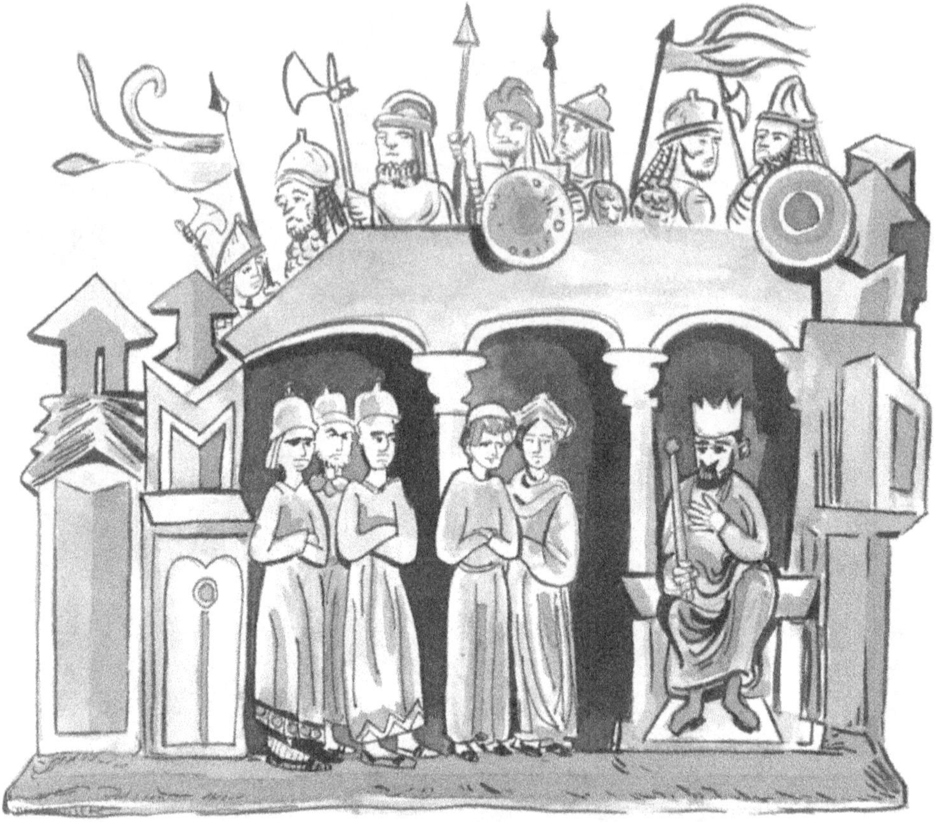

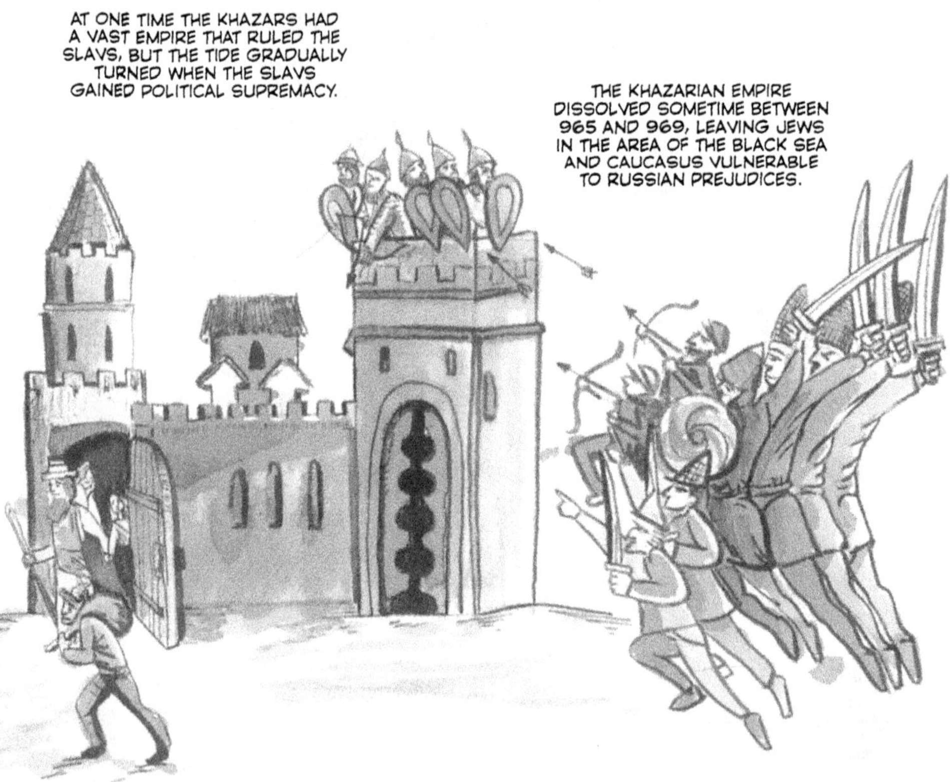
AT ONE TIME THE KHAZARS HAD A VAST EMPIRE THAT RULED THE SLAVS, BUT THE TIDE GRADUALLY TURNED WHEN THE SLAVS GAINED POLITICAL SUPREMACY.
THE KHAZARIAN EMPIRE DISSOLVED SOMETIME BETWEEN 965 AND 969, LEAVING JEWS IN THE AREA OF THE BLACK SEA AND CAUCASUS VULNERABLE TO RUSSIAN PREJUDICES.

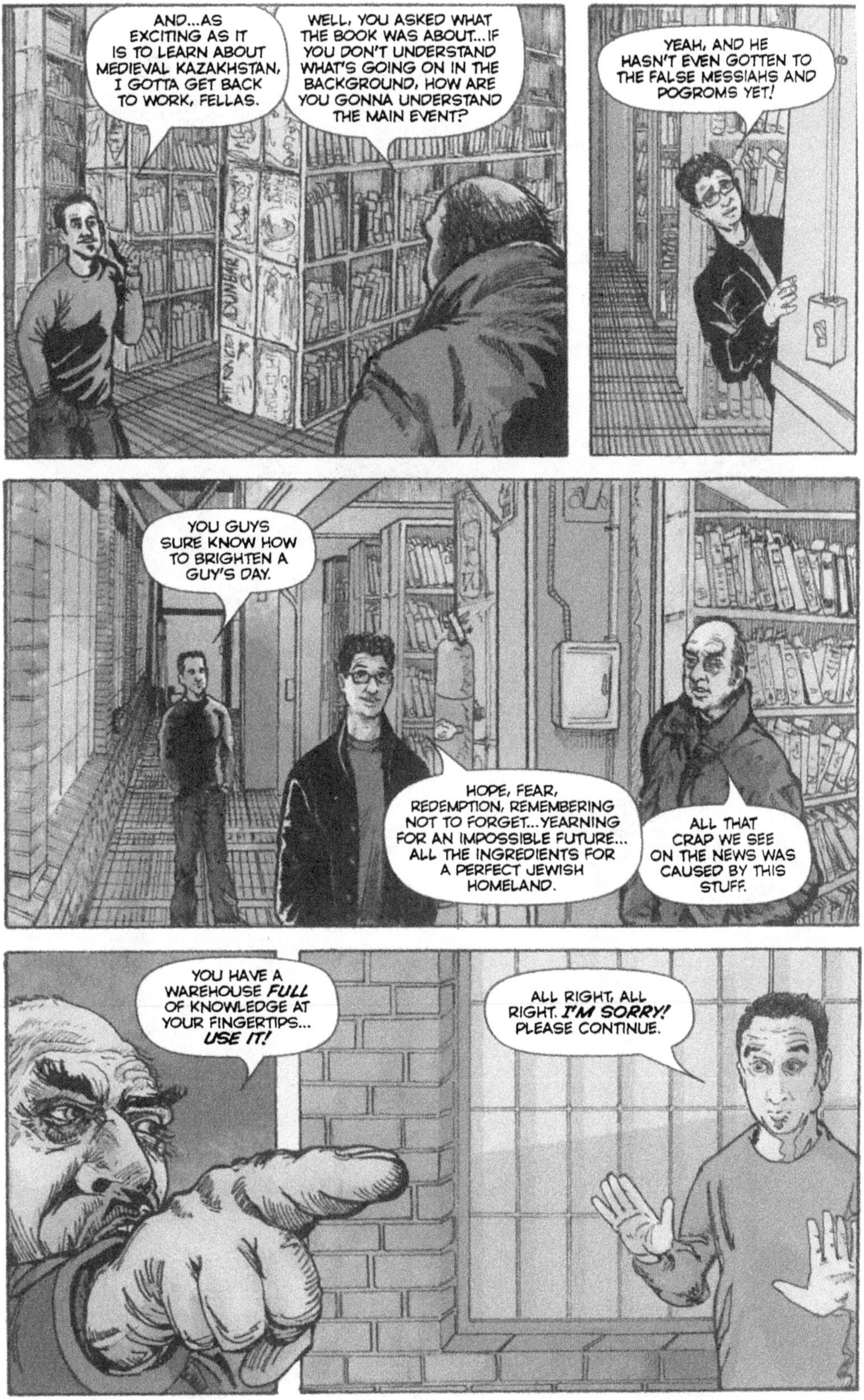
AND...AS EXCITING AS IT IS TO LEARN ABOUT MEDIEVAL KAZAKHSTAN, I GOTTA GET BACK TO WORK, FELLAS.
WELL, YOU ASKED WHAT THE BOOK WAS ABOUT...IF YOU DON'T UNDERSTAND WHAT'S GOING ON IN THE BACKGROUND, HOW ARE YOU GONNA UNDERSTAND THE MAIN EVENT?
YEAH, AND HE HASN'T EVEN GOTTEN TO THE FALSE MESSIAHS AND POGROMS YET!
YOU GUYS SURE KNOW HOW TO BRIGHTEN A GUY'S DAY.
HOPE, FEAR, REDEMPTION, REMEMBERING NOT TO FORGET...YEARNING FOR AN IMPOSSIBLE FUTURE... ALL THE INGREDIENTS FOR A PERFECT JEWISH HOMELAND.
ALL THAT CRAP WE SEE ON THE NEWS WAS CAUSED BY THIS STUFF.
YOU HAVE A WAREHOUSE ***FULL*** OF KNOWLEDGE AT YOUR FINGERTIPS... ***USE IT!***
ALL RIGHT, ALL RIGHT. ***I'M SORRY!*** PLEASE CONTINUE.

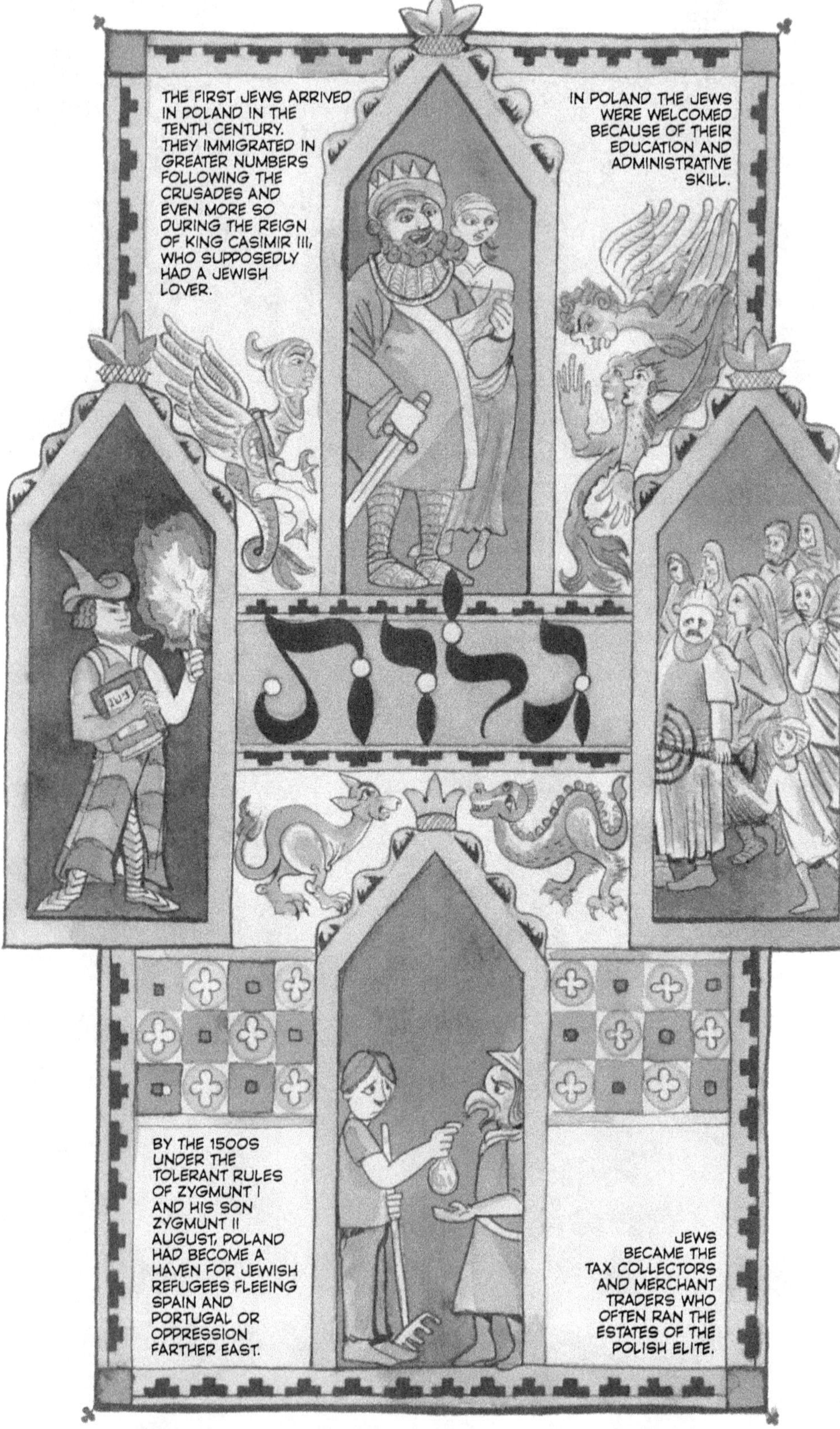
THE FIRST JEWS ARRIVED IN POLAND IN THE TENTH CENTURY. THEY IMMIGRATED IN GREATER NUMBERS FOLLOWING THE CRUSADES AND EVEN MORE SO DURING THE REIGN OF KING CASIMIR III, WHO SUPPOSEDLY HAD A JEWISH LOVER.
IN POLAND THE JEWS WERE WELCOMED BECAUSE OF THEIR EDUCATION AND ADMINISTRATIVE SKILL.
גלות
BY THE 1500S UNDER THE TOLERANT RULES OF ZYGMUNT I AND HIS SON ZYGMUNT II AUGUST, POLAND HAD BECOME A HAVEN FOR JEWISH REFUGEES FLEEING SPAIN AND PORTUGAL OR OPPRESSION FARTHER EAST.
JEWS BECAME THE TAX COLLECTORS AND MERCHANT TRADERS WHO OFTEN RAN THE ESTATES OF THE POLISH ELITE.

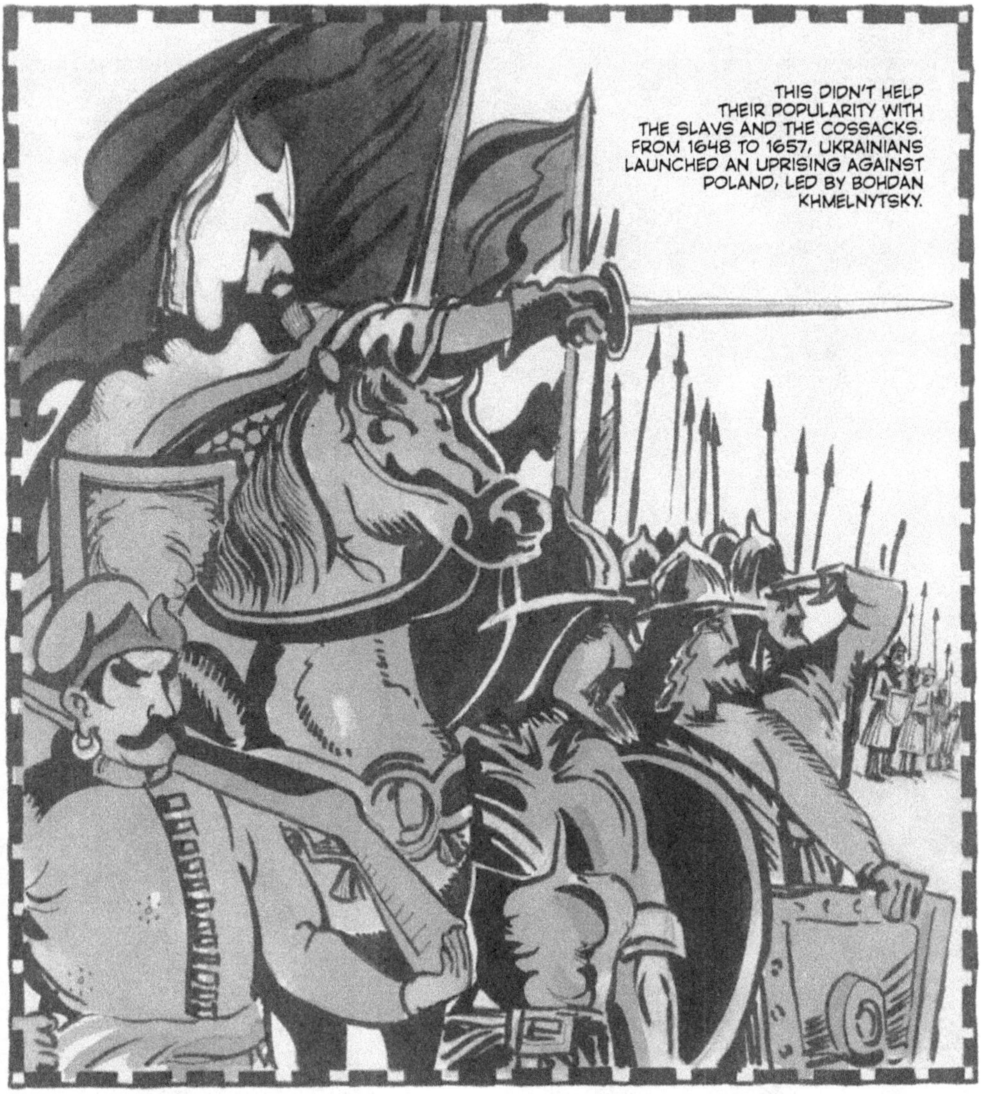
THIS DIDN'T HELP THEIR POPULARITY WITH THE SLAVS AND THE COSSACKS. FROM 1648 TO 1657, UKRAINIANS LAUNCHED AN UPRISING AGAINST POLAND, LED BY BOHDAN KHMELNYTSKY.

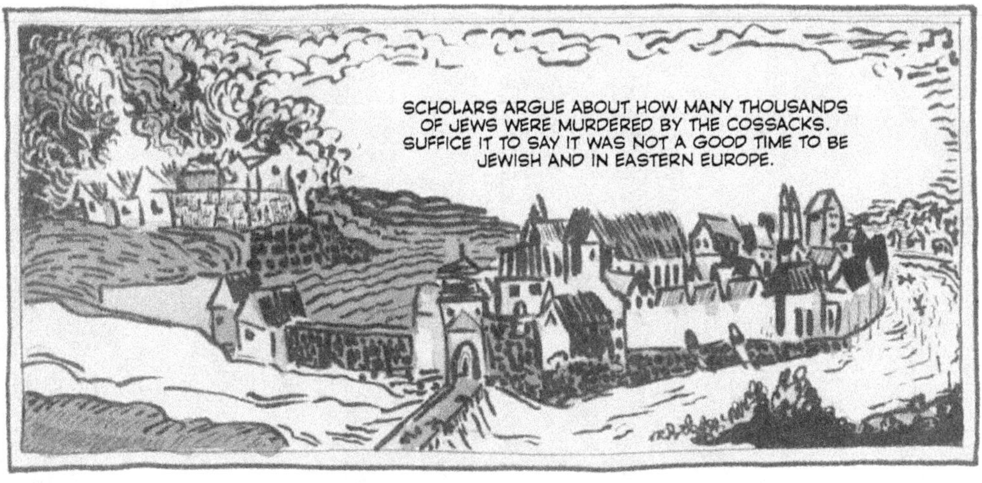
SCHOLARS ARGUE ABOUT HOW MANY THOUSANDS OF JEWS WERE MURDERED BY THE COSSACKS. SUFFICE IT TO SAY IT WAS NOT A GOOD TIME TO BE JEWISH AND IN EASTERN EUROPE.

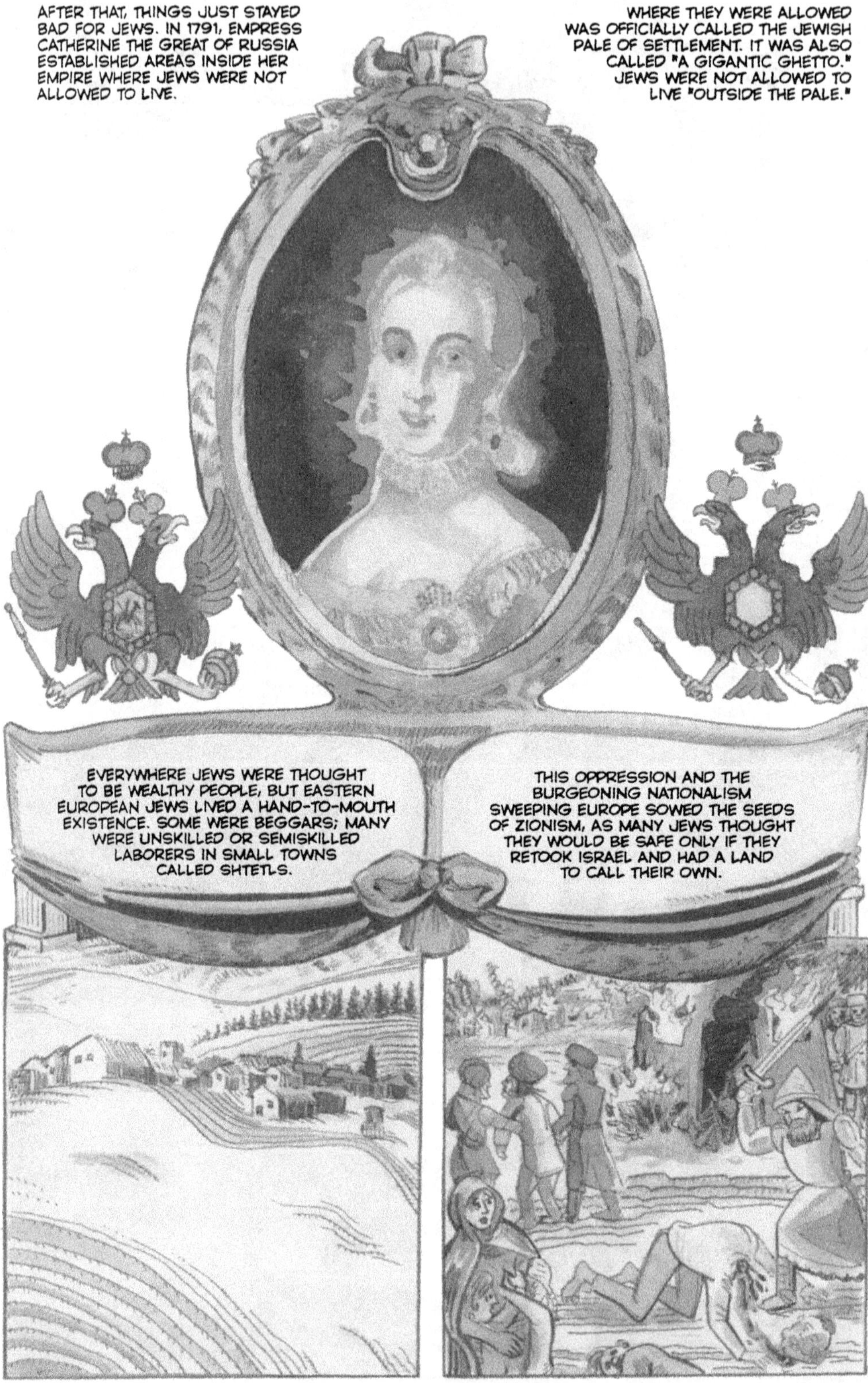
AFTER THAT, THINGS JUST STAYED BAD FOR JEWS. IN 1791, EMPRESS CATHERINE THE GREAT OF RUSSIA ESTABLISHED AREAS INSIDE HER EMPIRE WHERE JEWS WERE NOT ALLOWED TO LIVE.
WHERE THEY WERE ALLOWED WAS OFFICIALLY CALLED THE JEWISH PALE OF SETTLEMENT. IT WAS ALSO CALLED "A GIGANTIC GHETTO." JEWS WERE NOT ALLOWED TO LIVE "OUTSIDE THE PALE."
EVERYWHERE JEWS WERE THOUGHT TO BE WEALTHY PEOPLE, BUT EASTERN EUROPEAN JEWS LIVED A HAND-TO-MOUTH EXISTENCE. SOME WERE BEGGARS; MANY WERE UNSKILLED OR SEMISKILLED LABORERS IN SMALL TOWNS CALLED SHTETLS.
THIS OPPRESSION AND THE BURGEONING NATIONALISM SWEEPING EUROPE SOWED THE SEEDS OF ZIONISM, AS MANY JEWS THOUGHT THEY WOULD BE SAFE ONLY IF THEY RETOOK ISRAEL AND HAD A LAND TO CALL THEIR OWN.

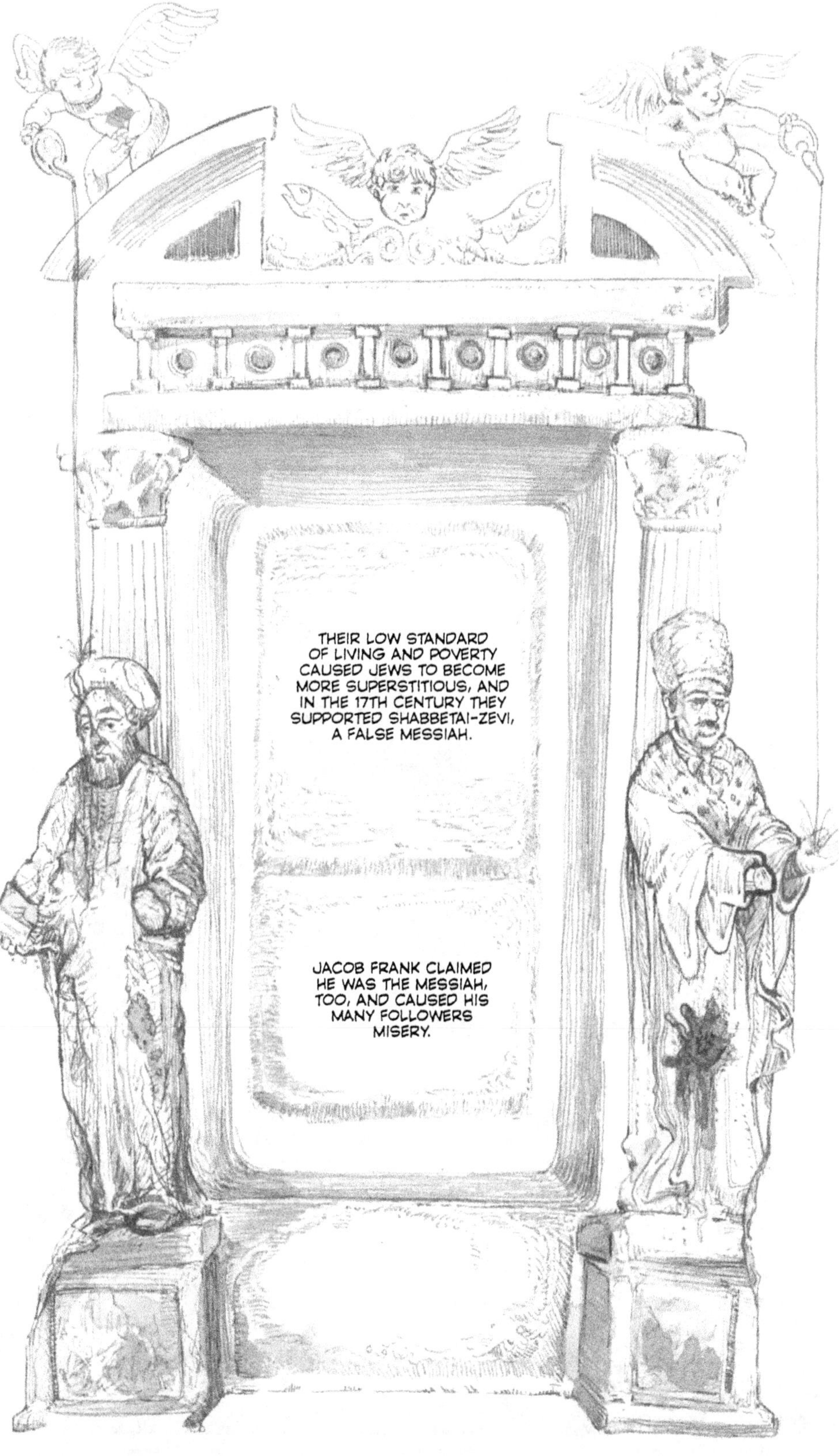
THEIR LOW STANDARD OF LIVING AND POVERTY CAUSED JEWS TO BECOME MORE SUPERSTITIOUS, AND IN THE 17TH CENTURY THEY SUPPORTED SHABBETAI-ZEVI, A FALSE MESSIAH.
JACOB FRANK CLAIMED HE WAS THE MESSIAH, TOO, AND CAUSED HIS MANY FOLLOWERS MISERY.

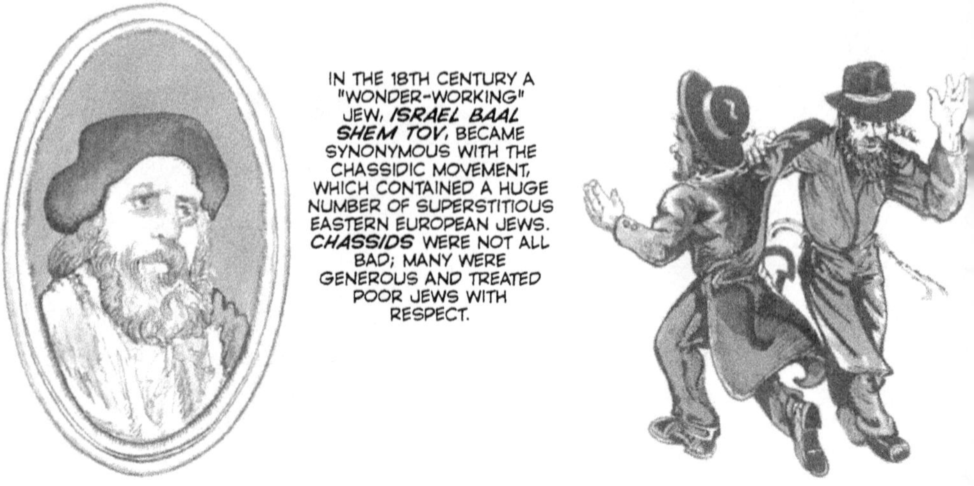
IN THE 18TH CENTURY A "WONDER-WORKING" JEW, *ISRAEL BAAL SHEM TOV*, BECAME SYNONYMOUS WITH THE CHASSIDIC MOVEMENT, WHICH CONTAINED A HUGE NUMBER OF SUPERSTITIOUS EASTERN EUROPEAN JEWS. *CHASSIDS* WERE NOT ALL BAD; MANY WERE GENEROUS AND TREATED POOR JEWS WITH RESPECT.

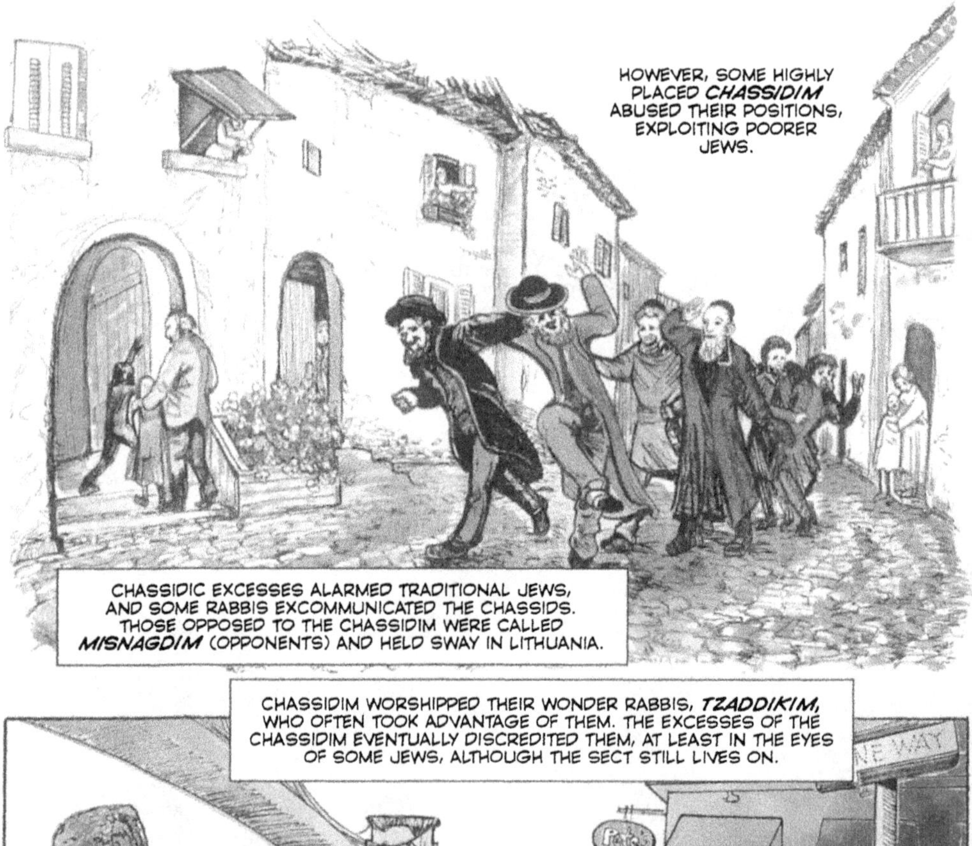
HOWEVER, SOME HIGHLY PLACED *CHASSIDIM* ABUSED THEIR POSITIONS, EXPLOITING POORER JEWS.
CHASSIDIC EXCESSES ALARMED TRADITIONAL JEWS, AND SOME RABBIS EXCOMMUNICATED THE CHASSIDS. THOSE OPPOSED TO THE CHASSIDIM WERE CALLED *MISNAGDIM* (OPPONENTS) AND HELD SWAY IN LITHUANIA.

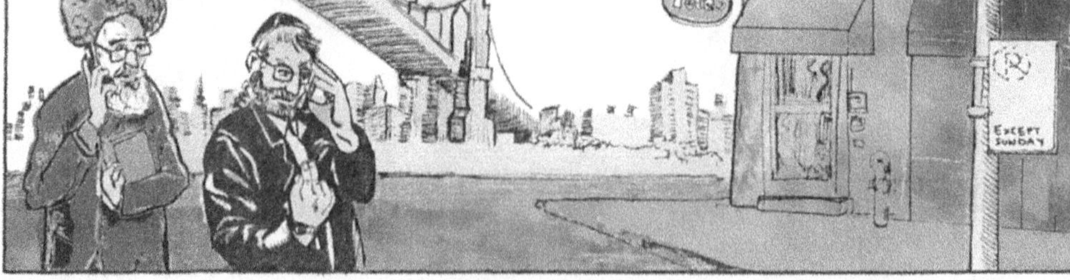
CHASSIDIM WORSHIPPED THEIR WONDER RABBIS, *TZADDIKIM*, WHO OFTEN TOOK ADVANTAGE OF THEM. THE EXCESSES OF THE CHASSIDIM EVENTUALLY DISCREDITED THEM, AT LEAST IN THE EYES OF SOME JEWS, ALTHOUGH THE SECT STILL LIVES ON.
EXCEPT SUNDAY

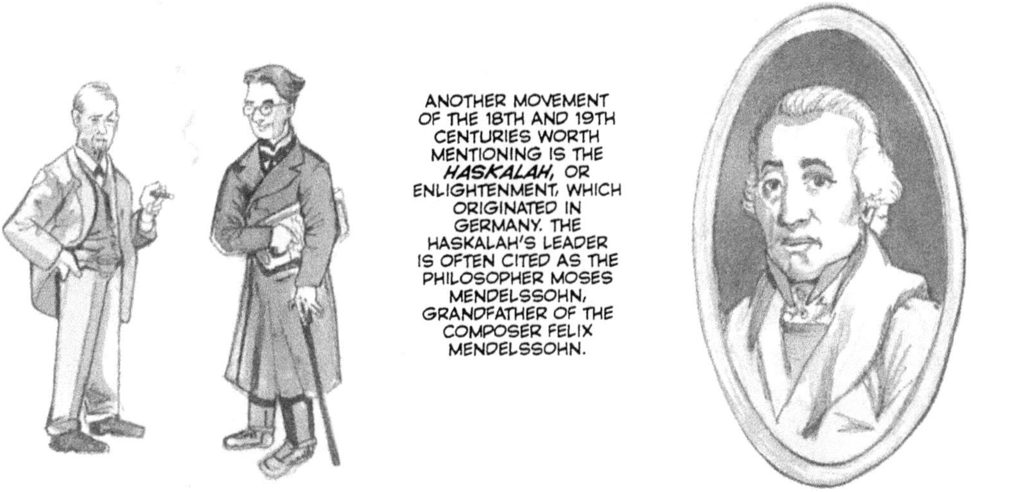
ANOTHER MOVEMENT OF THE 18TH AND 19TH CENTURIES WORTH MENTIONING IS THE *HASKALAH,* OR ENLIGHTENMENT, WHICH ORIGINATED IN GERMANY. THE HASKALAH'S LEADER IS OFTEN CITED AS THE PHILOSOPHER MOSES MENDELSSOHN, GRANDFATHER OF THE COMPOSER FELIX MENDELSSOHN.

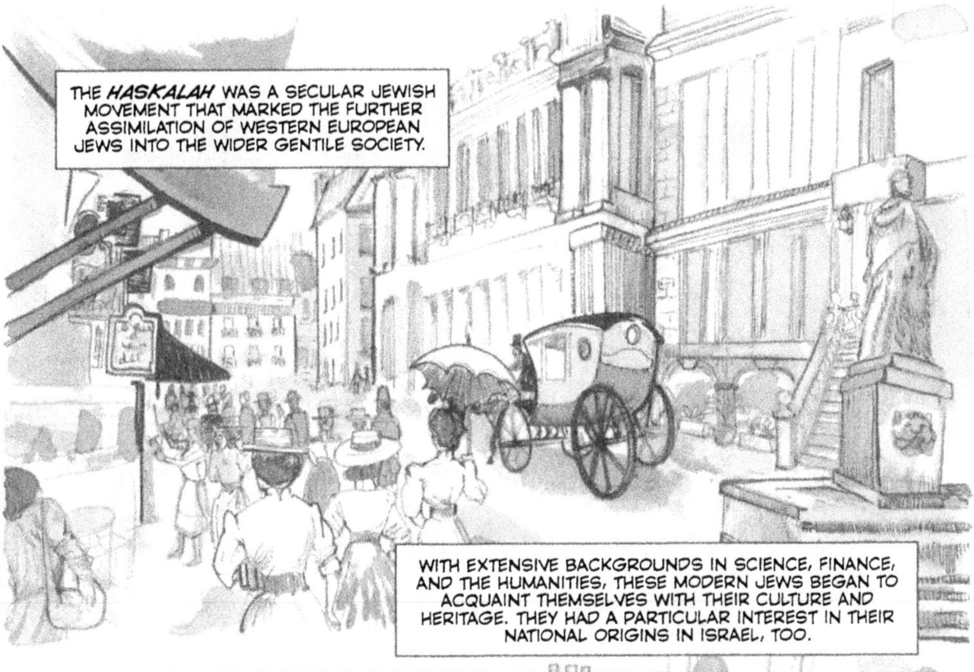
THE *HASKALAH* WAS A SECULAR JEWISH MOVEMENT THAT MARKED THE FURTHER ASSIMILATION OF WESTERN EUROPEAN JEWS INTO THE WIDER GENTILE SOCIETY.
WITH EXTENSIVE BACKGROUNDS IN SCIENCE, FINANCE, AND THE HUMANITIES, THESE MODERN JEWS BEGAN TO ACQUAINT THEMSELVES WITH THEIR CULTURE AND HERITAGE. THEY HAD A PARTICULAR INTEREST IN THEIR NATIONAL ORIGINS IN ISRAEL, TOO.

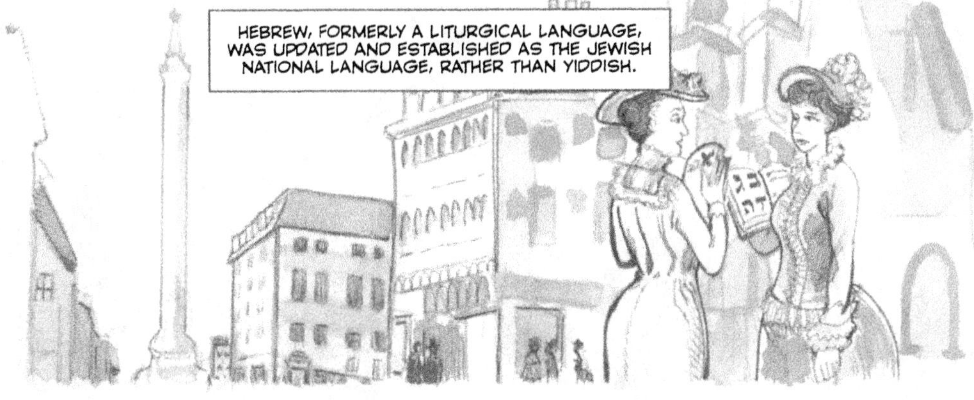
HEBREW, FORMERLY A LITURGICAL LANGUAGE, WAS UPDATED AND ESTABLISHED AS THE JEWISH NATIONAL LANGUAGE, RATHER THAN YIDDISH.

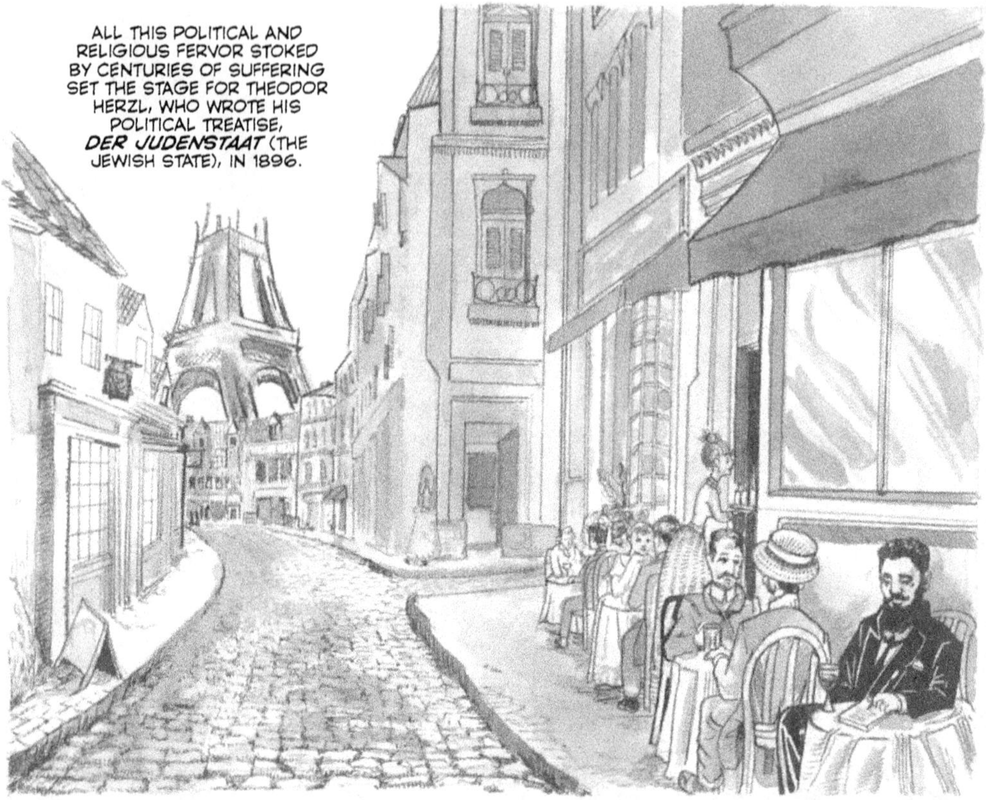
ALL THIS POLITICAL AND RELIGIOUS FERVOR STOKED BY CENTURIES OF SUFFERING SET THE STAGE FOR THEODOR HERZL, WHO WROTE HIS POLITICAL TREATISE, ***DER JUDENSTAAT*** (THE JEWISH STATE), IN 1896.

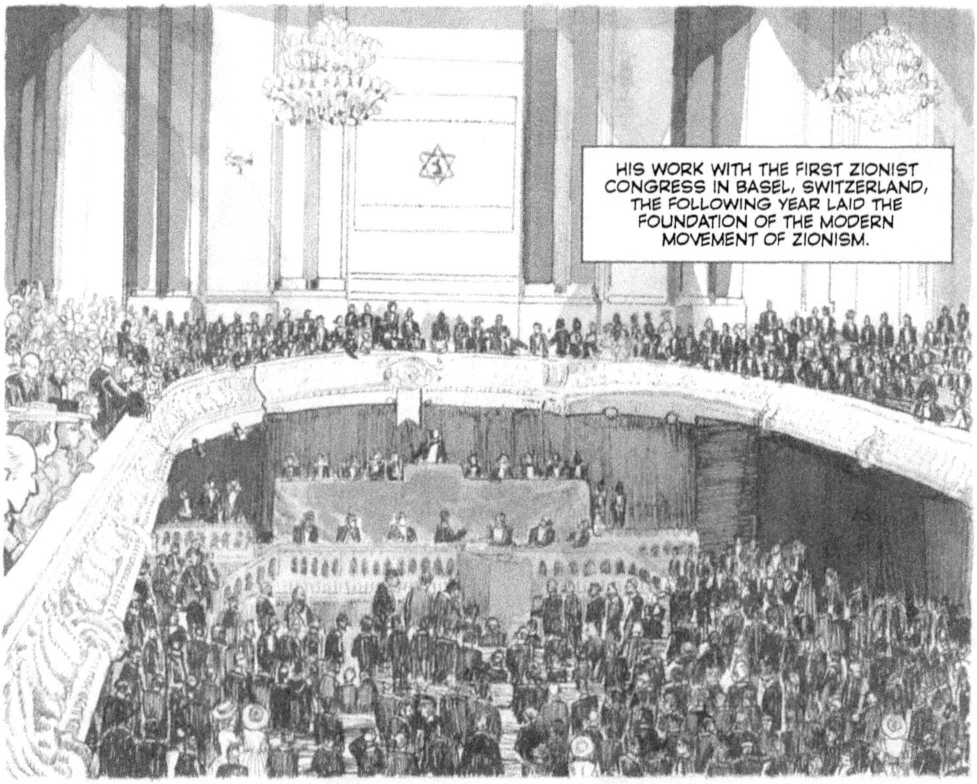
HIS WORK WITH THE FIRST ZIONIST CONGRESS IN BASEL, SWITZERLAND, THE FOLLOWING YEAR LAID THE FOUNDATION OF THE MODERN MOVEMENT OF ZIONISM.

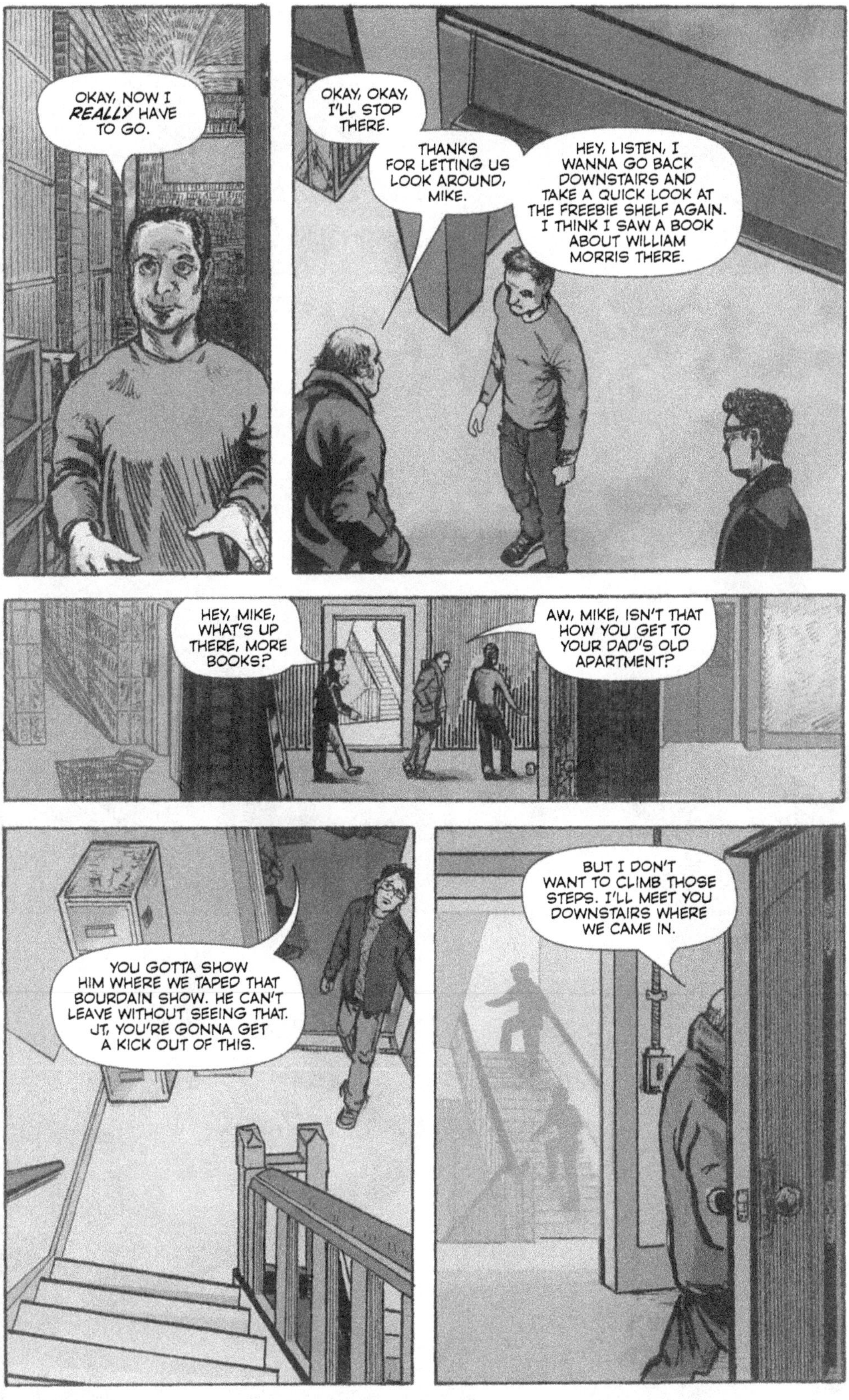
OKAY, NOW I *REALLY* HAVE TO GO.
OKAY, OKAY, I'LL STOP THERE.
THANKS FOR LETTING US LOOK AROUND, MIKE.
HEY, LISTEN, I WANNA GO BACK DOWNSTAIRS AND TAKE A QUICK LOOK AT THE FREEBIE SHELF AGAIN. I THINK I SAW A BOOK ABOUT WILLIAM MORRIS THERE.
HEY, MIKE, WHAT'S UP THERE, MORE BOOKS?
AW, MIKE, ISN'T THAT HOW YOU GET TO YOUR DAD'S OLD APARTMENT?
YOU GOTTA SHOW HIM WHERE WE TAPED THAT BOURDAIN SHOW. HE CAN'T LEAVE WITHOUT SEEING THAT. JT, YOU'RE GONNA GET A KICK OUT OF THIS.
BUT I DON'T WANT TO CLIMB THOSE STEPS. I'LL MEET YOU DOWNSTAIRS WHERE WE CAME IN.

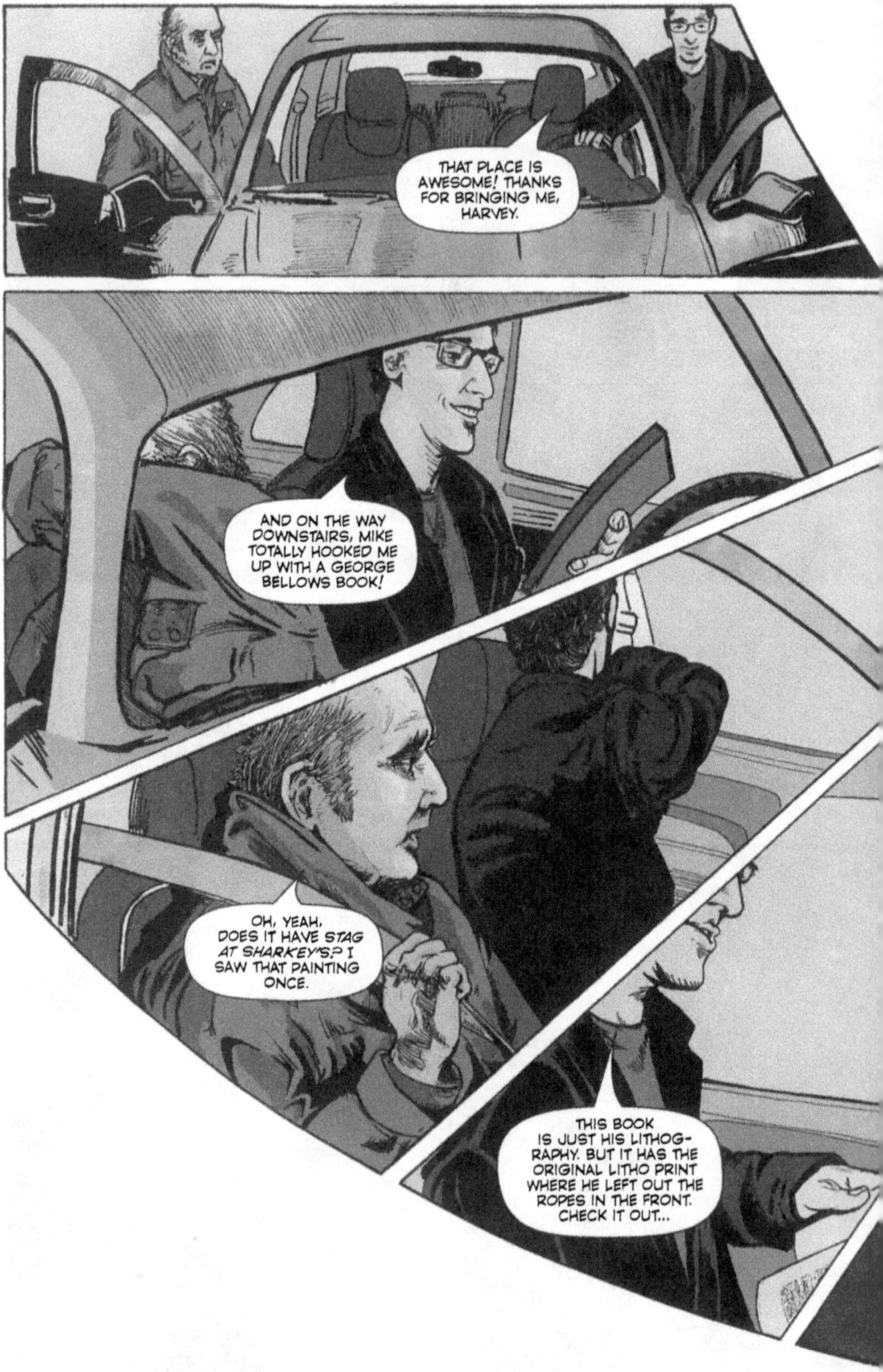
THAT PLACE IS AWESOME! THANKS FOR BRINGING ME, HARVEY.
AND ON THE WAY DOWNSTAIRS, MIKE TOTALLY HOOKED ME UP WITH A GEORGE BELLOWS BOOK!
OH, YEAH, DOES IT HAVE *STAG AT SHARKEY'S*? I SAW THAT PAINTING ONCE.
THIS BOOK IS JUST HIS LITHOG-RAPHY. BUT IT HAS THE ORIGINAL LITHO PRINT WHERE HE LEFT OUT THE ROPES IN THE FRONT. CHECK IT OUT...

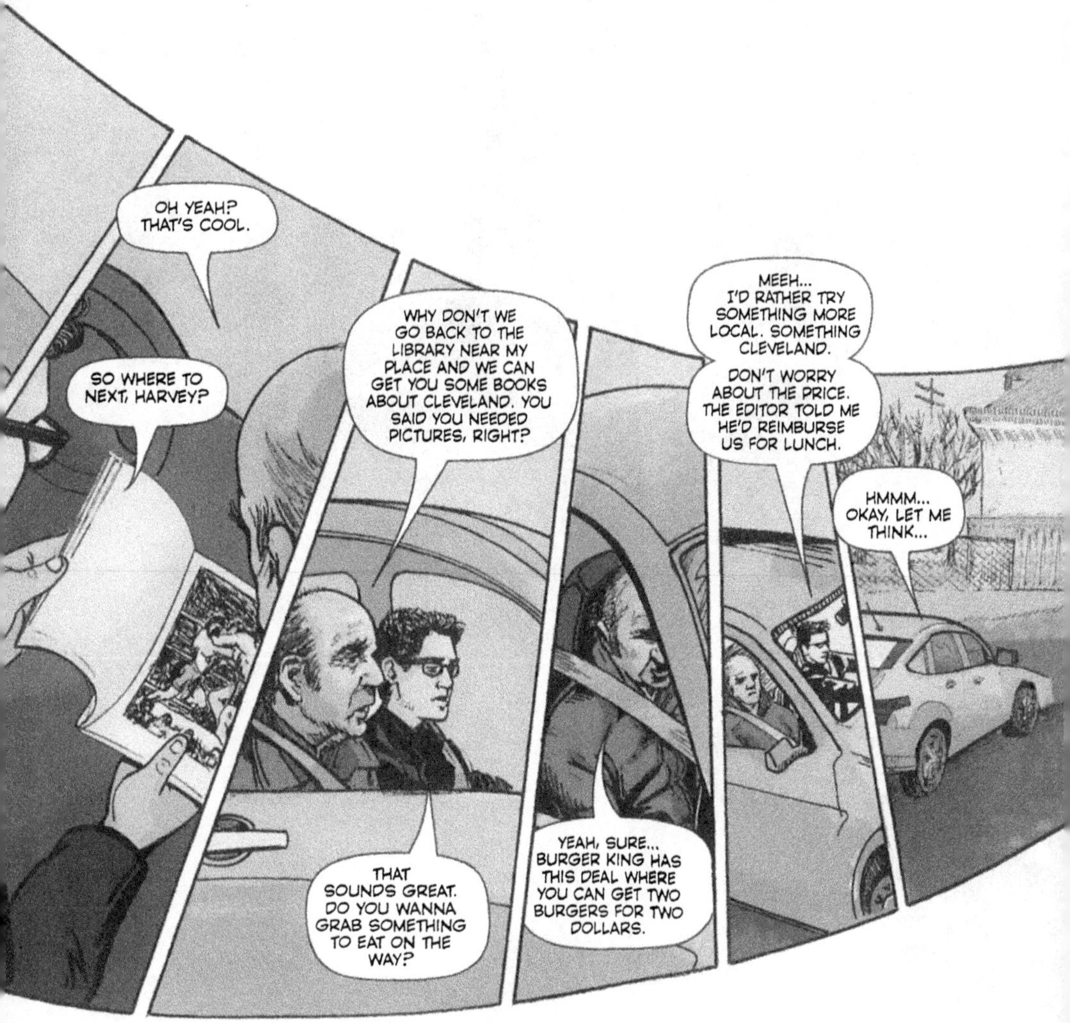
OH YEAH? THAT'S COOL.
SO WHERE TO NEXT, HARVEY?
WHY DON'T WE GO BACK TO THE LIBRARY NEAR MY PLACE AND WE CAN GET YOU SOME BOOKS ABOUT CLEVELAND. YOU SAID YOU NEEDED PICTURES, RIGHT?
THAT SOUNDS GREAT. DO YOU WANNA GRAB SOMETHING TO EAT ON THE WAY?
YEAH, SURE... BURGER KING HAS THIS DEAL WHERE YOU CAN GET TWO BURGERS FOR TWO DOLLARS.
MEEH... I'D RATHER TRY SOMETHING MORE LOCAL. SOMETHING CLEVELAND.
DON'T WORRY ABOUT THE PRICE. THE EDITOR TOLD ME HE'D REIMBURSE US FOR LUNCH.
HMMM... OKAY, LET ME THINK...

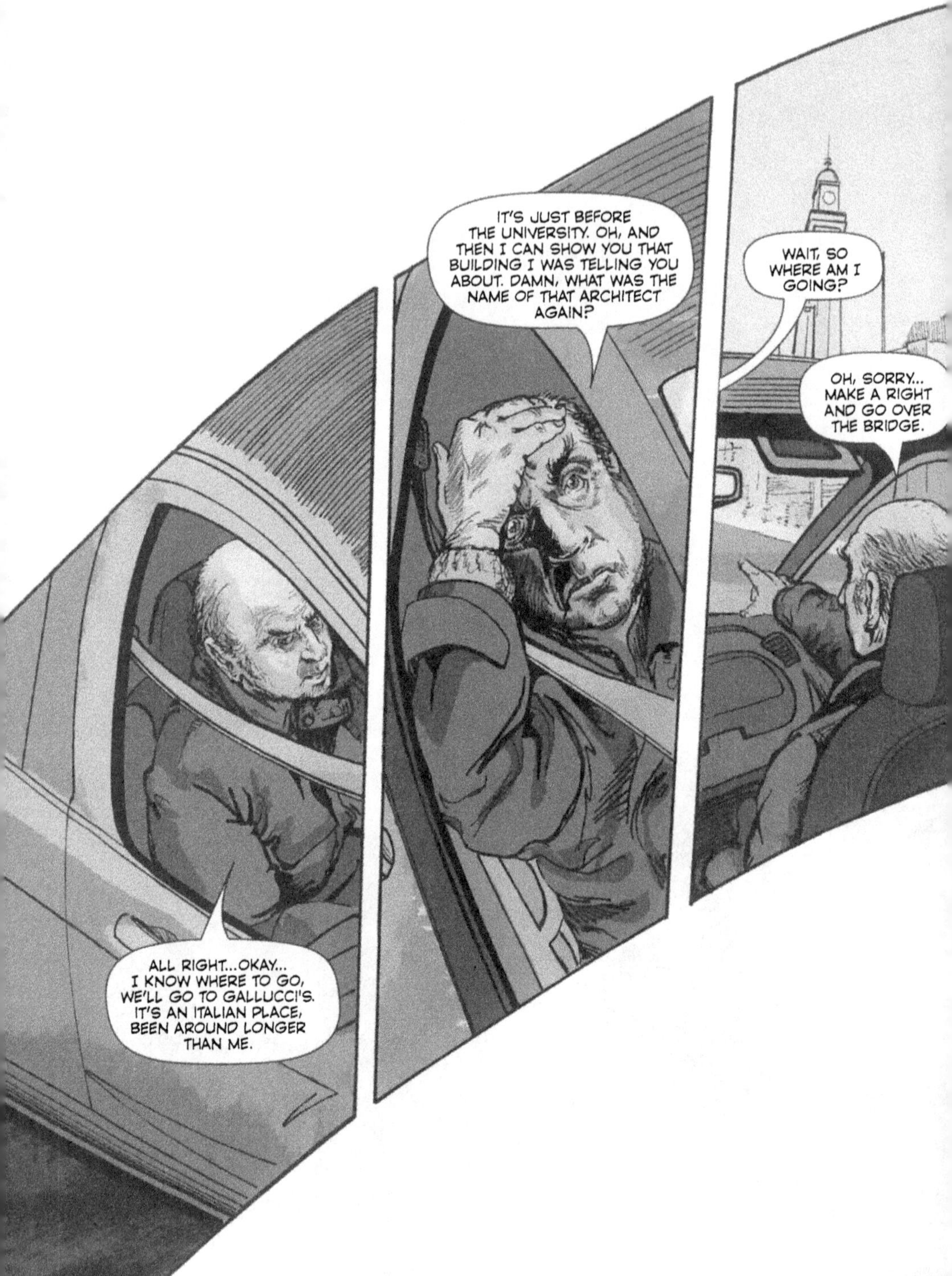
ALL RIGHT...OKAY... I KNOW WHERE TO GO, WE'LL GO TO GALLUCCI'S. IT'S AN ITALIAN PLACE, BEEN AROUND LONGER THAN ME.
IT'S JUST BEFORE THE UNIVERSITY. OH, AND THEN I CAN SHOW YOU THAT BUILDING I WAS TELLING YOU ABOUT. DAMN, WHAT WAS THE NAME OF THAT ARCHITECT AGAIN?
WAIT, SO WHERE AM I GOING?
OH, SORRY... MAKE A RIGHT AND GO OVER THE BRIDGE.

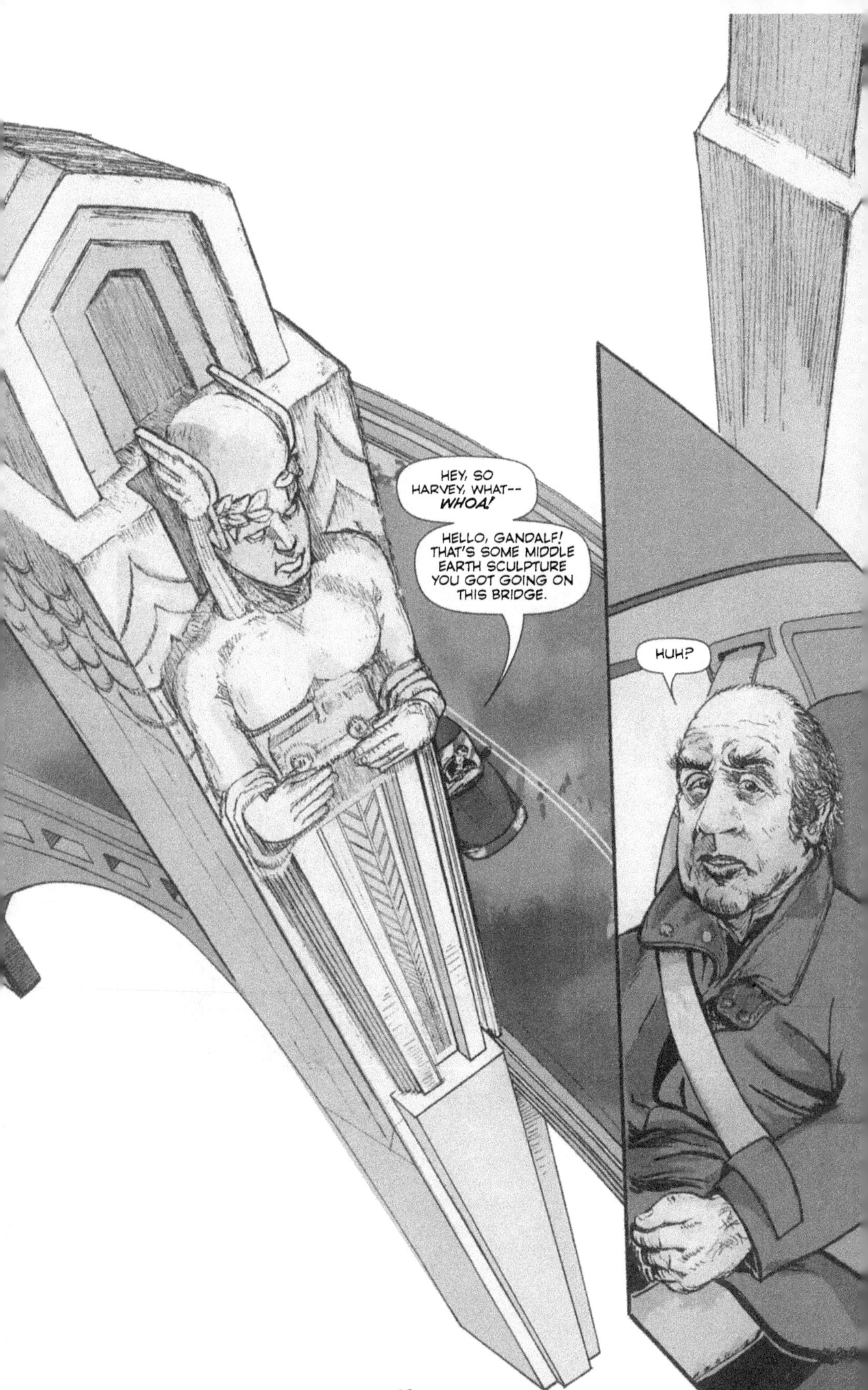

HEY, SO HARVEY, WHAT-- *WHOA!*
HELLO, GANDALF! THAT'S SOME MIDDLE EARTH SCULPTURE YOU GOT GOING ON THIS BRIDGE.
HUH?

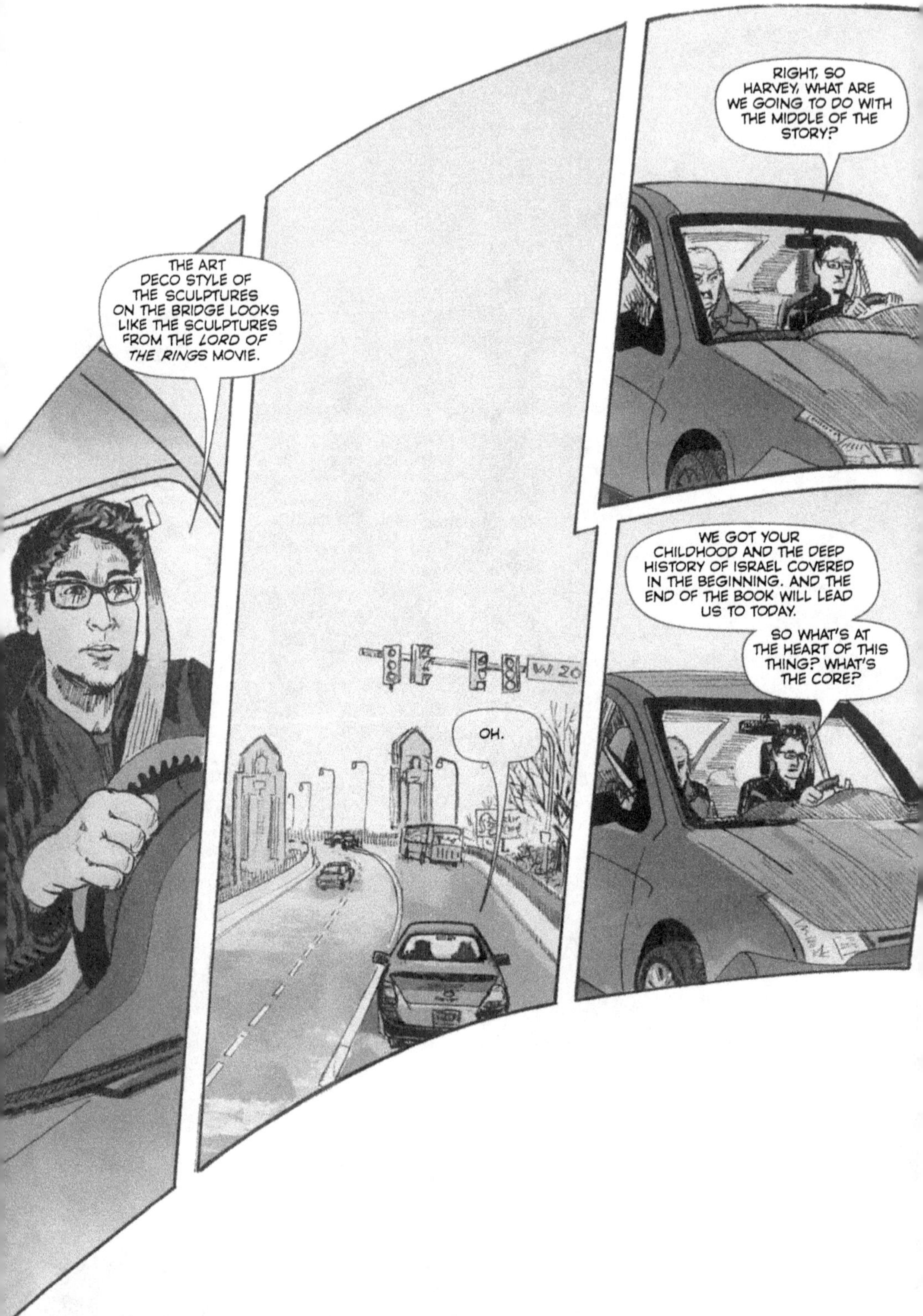
THE ART DECO STYLE OF THE SCULPTURES ON THE BRIDGE LOOKS LIKE THE SCULPTURES FROM THE *LORD OF THE RINGS* MOVIE.
OH.
RIGHT, SO HARVEY, WHAT ARE WE GOING TO DO WITH THE MIDDLE OF THE STORY?
WE GOT YOUR CHILDHOOD AND THE DEEP HISTORY OF ISRAEL COVERED IN THE BEGINNING. AND THE END OF THE BOOK WILL LEAD US TO TODAY.
SO WHAT'S AT THE HEART OF THIS THING? WHAT'S THE CORE?

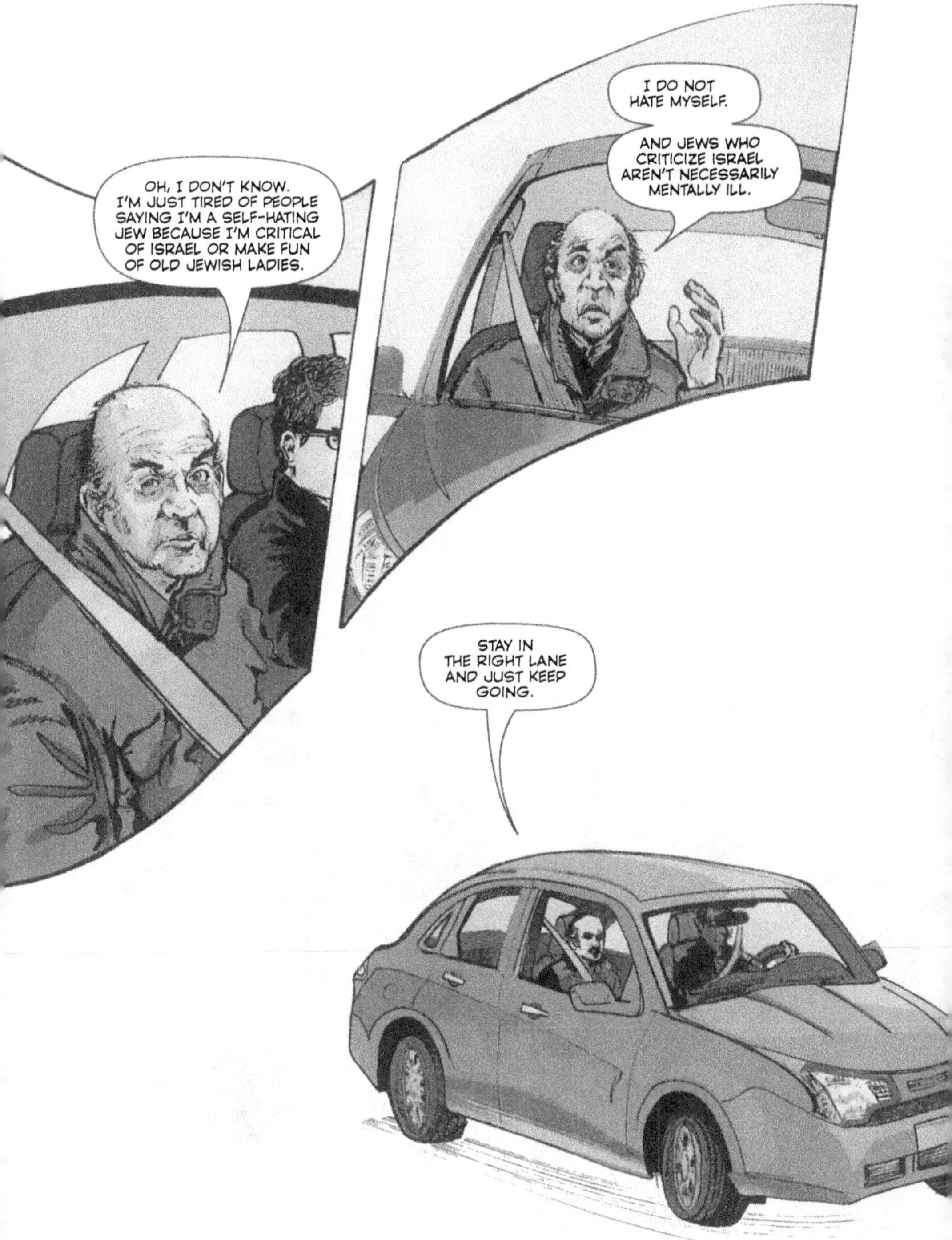
OH, I DON'T KNOW. I'M JUST TIRED OF PEOPLE SAYING I'M A SELF-HATING JEW BECAUSE I'M CRITICAL OF ISRAEL OR MAKE FUN OF OLD JEWISH LADIES.
I DO NOT HATE MYSELF.
AND JEWS WHO CRITICIZE ISRAEL AREN'T NECESSARILY MENTALLY ILL.
STAY IN THE RIGHT LANE AND JUST KEEP GOING.

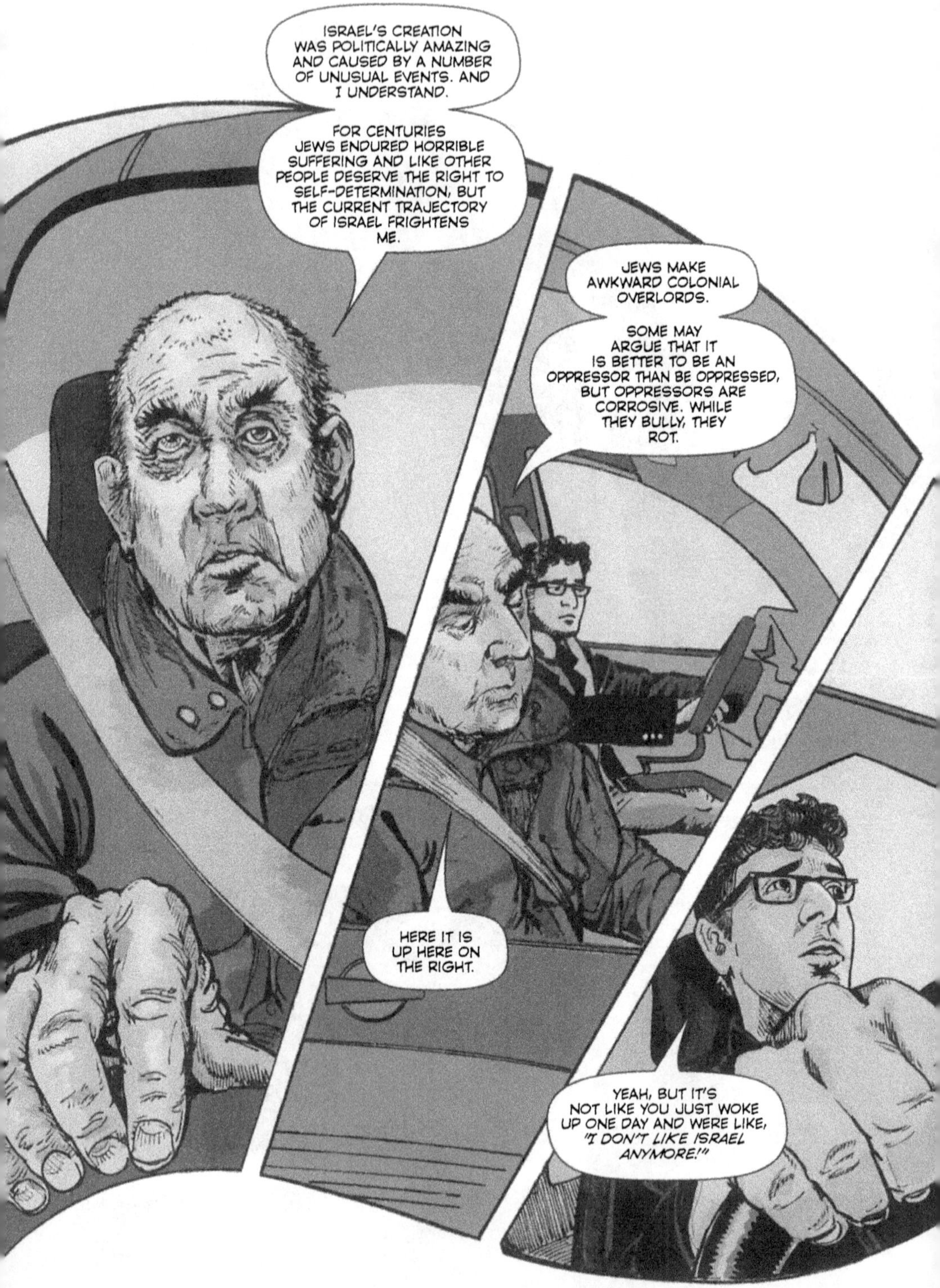
ISRAEL'S CREATION WAS POLITICALLY AMAZING AND CAUSED BY A NUMBER OF UNUSUAL EVENTS. AND I UNDERSTAND.
FOR CENTURIES JEWS ENDURED HORRIBLE SUFFERING AND LIKE OTHER PEOPLE DESERVE THE RIGHT TO SELF-DETERMINATION, BUT THE CURRENT TRAJECTORY OF ISRAEL FRIGHTENS ME.
JEWS MAKE AWKWARD COLONIAL OVERLORDS.
SOME MAY ARGUE THAT IT IS BETTER TO BE AN OPPRESSOR THAN BE OPPRESSED, BUT OPPRESSORS ARE CORROSIVE. WHILE THEY BULLY, THEY ROT.
HERE IT IS UP HERE ON THE RIGHT.
YEAH, BUT IT'S NOT LIKE YOU JUST WOKE UP ONE DAY AND WERE LIKE, *"I DON'T LIKE ISRAEL ANYMORE!"*

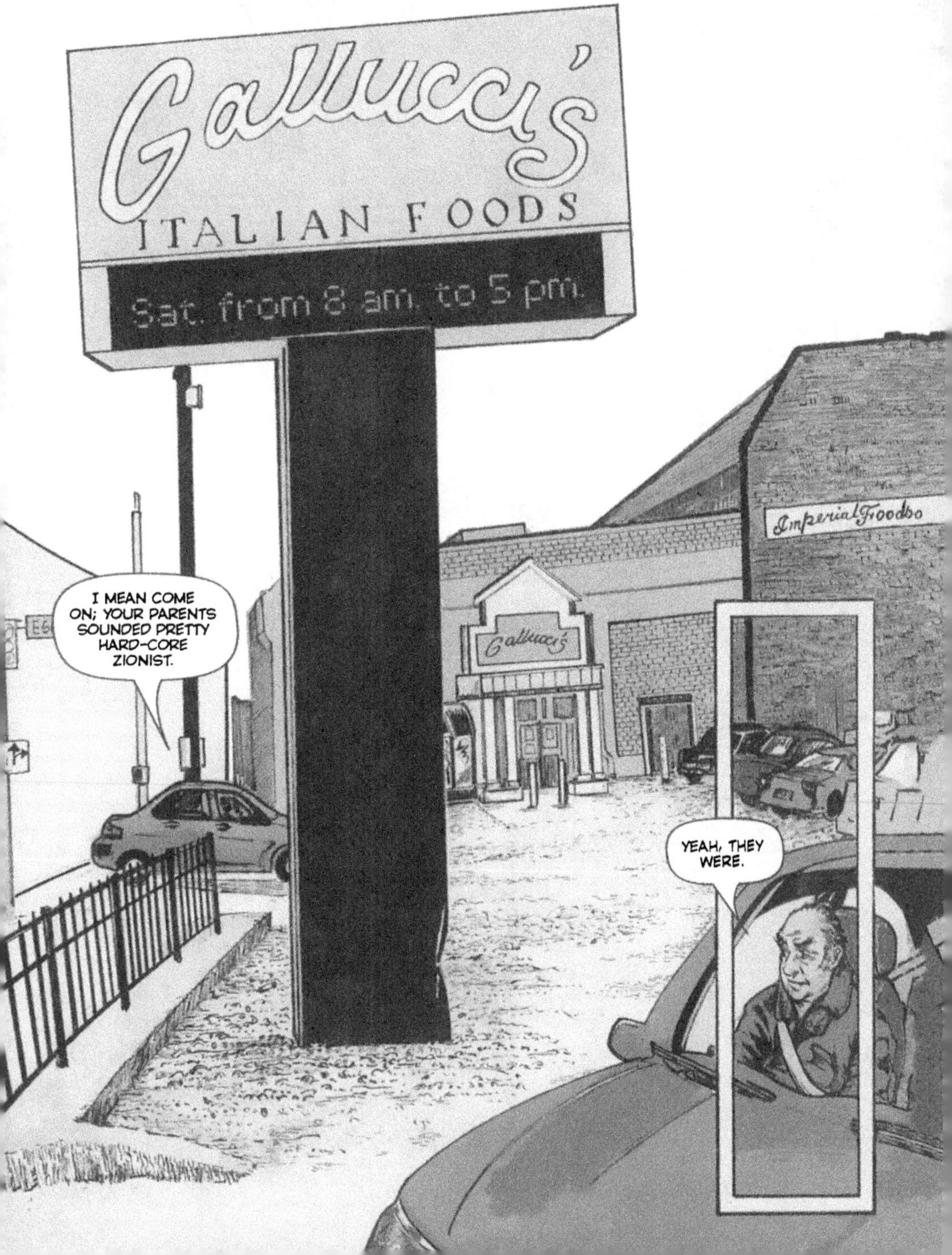
Gallucci's
ITALIAN FOODS
Sat. from 8 am. to 5 pm.
Gallucci's
I MEAN COME ON; YOUR PARENTS SOUNDED PRETTY HARD-CORE ZIONIST.
YEAH, THEY WERE.

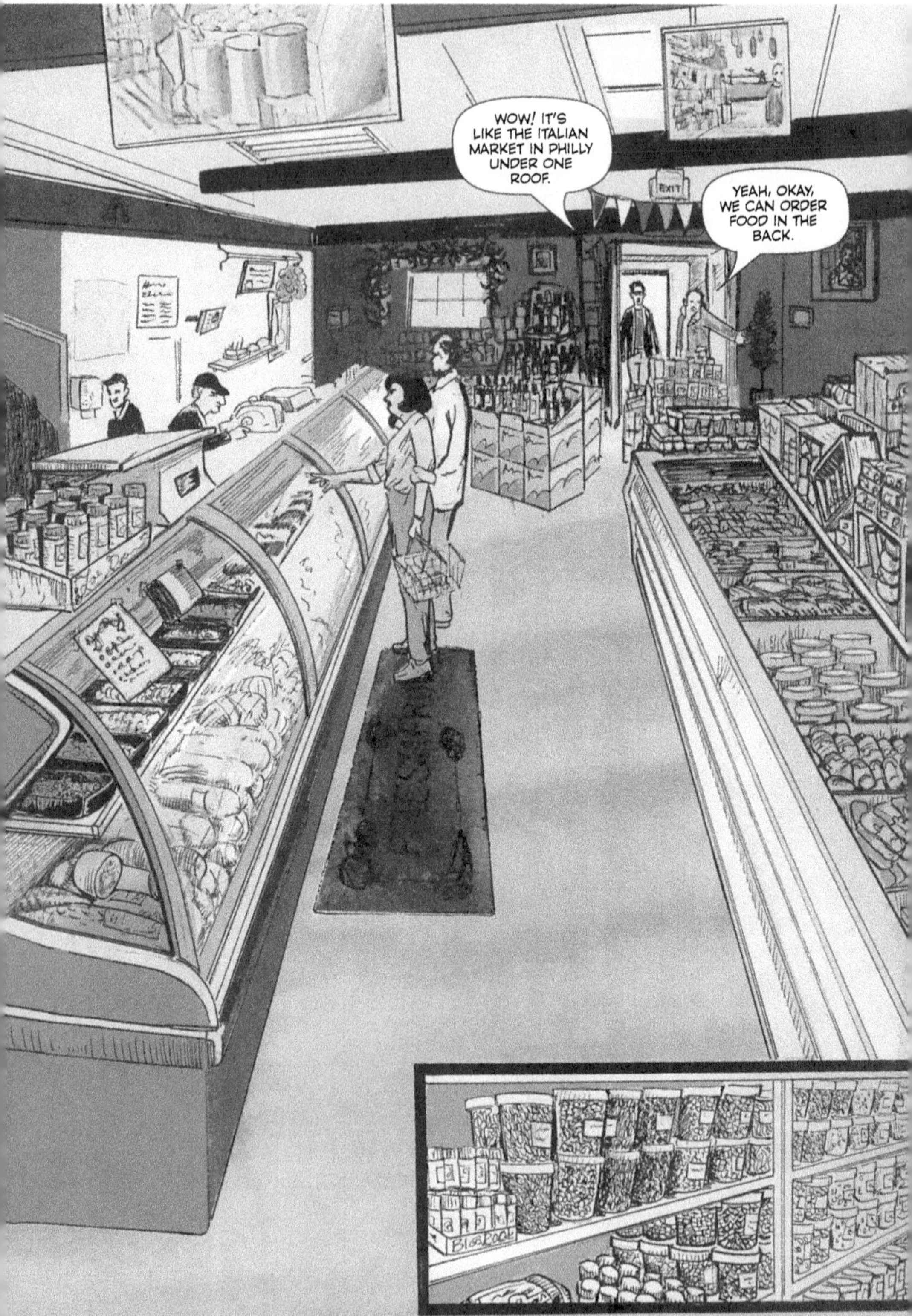
WOW! IT'S LIKE THE ITALIAN MARKET IN PHILLY UNDER ONE ROOF.
YEAH, OKAY, WE CAN ORDER FOOD IN THE BACK.
EXIT

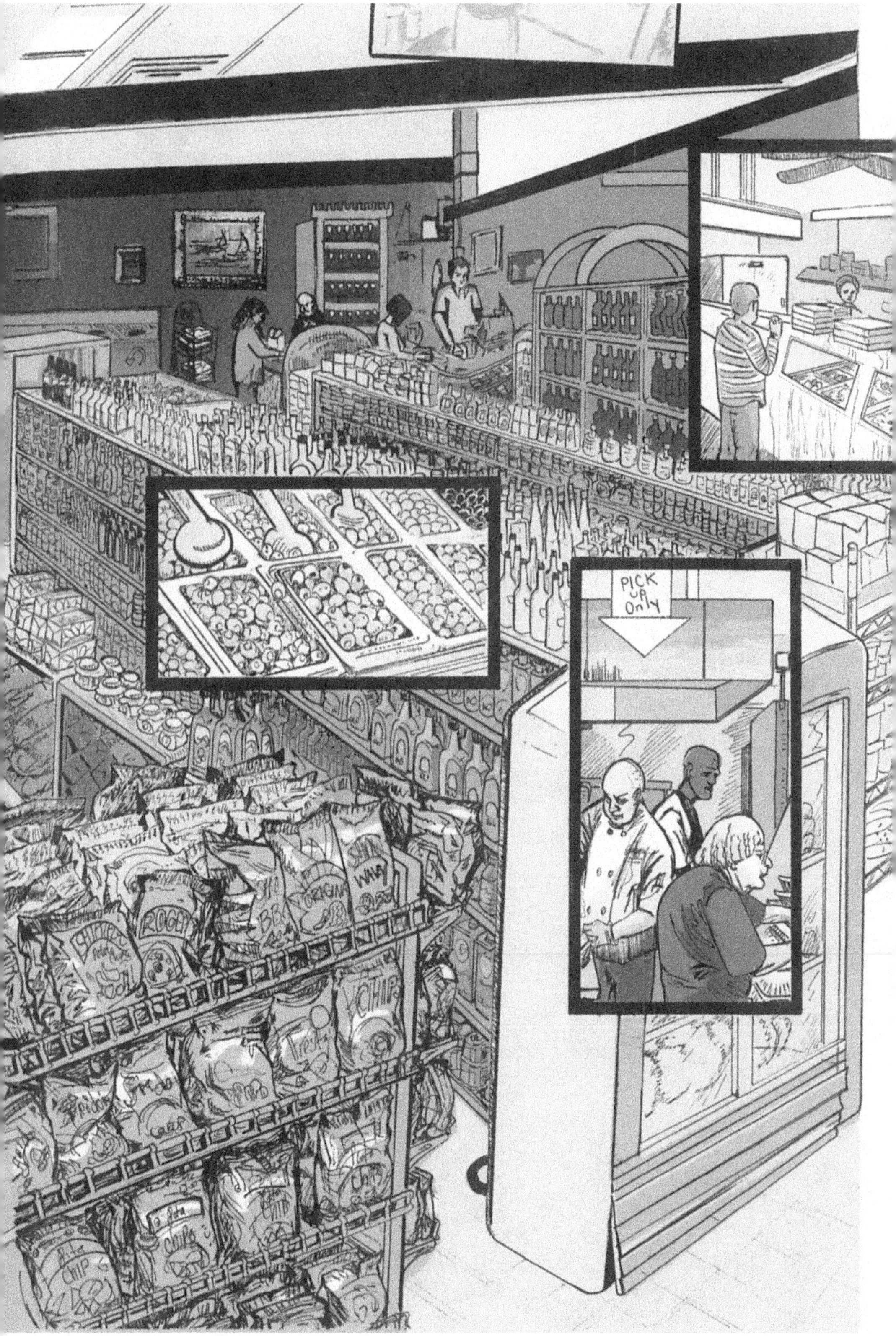
PICK
up
Only

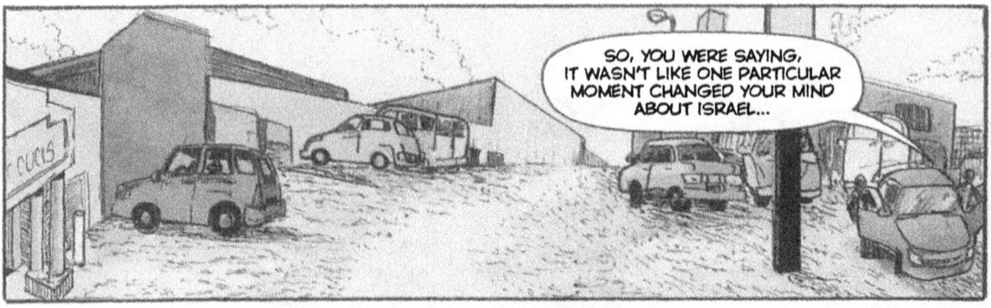
SO, YOU WERE SAYING, IT WASN'T LIKE ONE PARTICULAR MOMENT CHANGED YOUR MIND ABOUT ISRAEL...

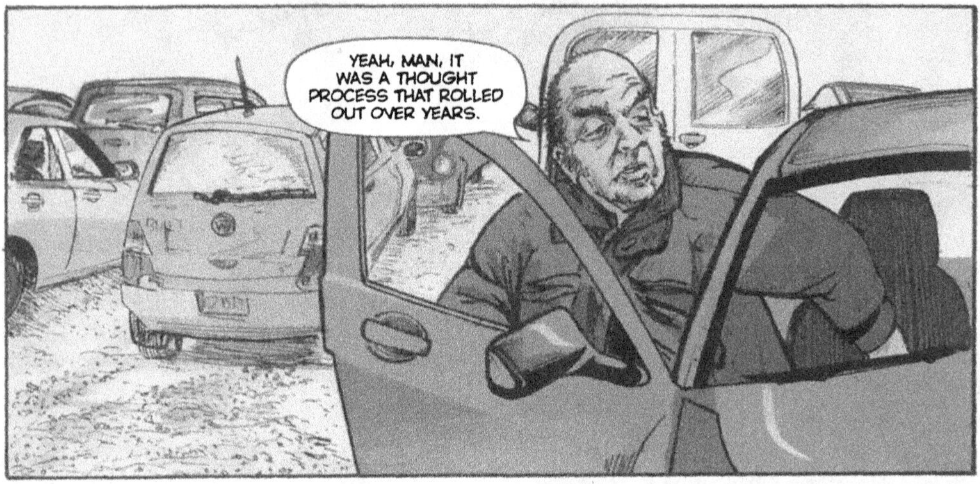
YEAH, MAN, IT WAS A THOUGHT PROCESS THAT ROLLED OUT OVER YEARS.

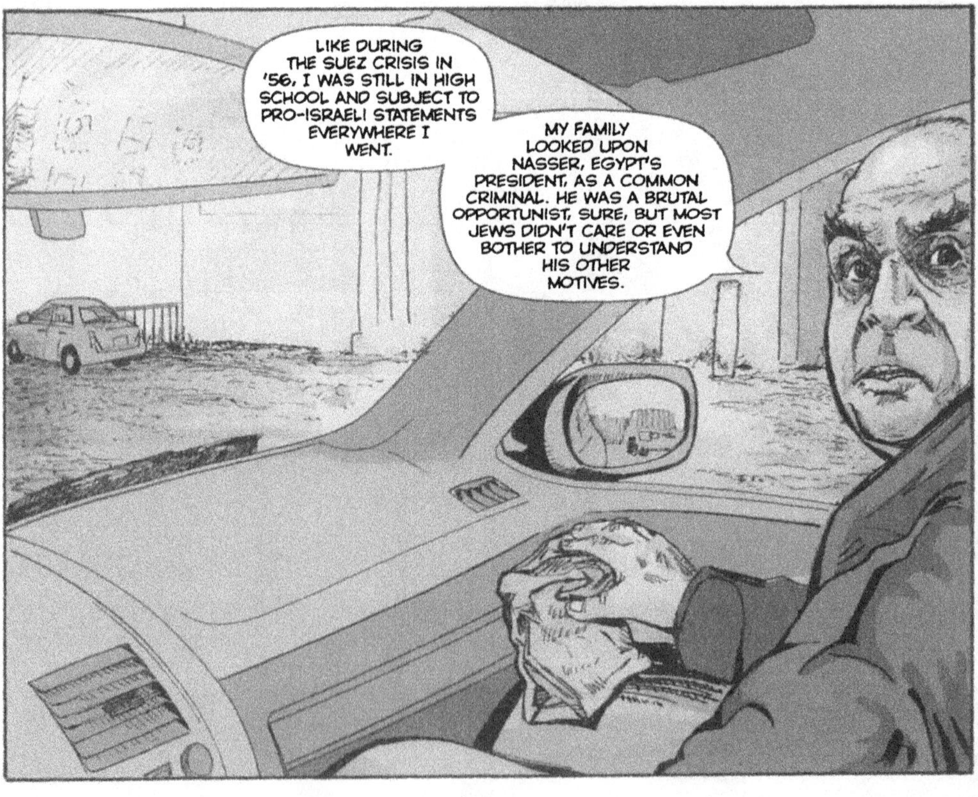
LIKE DURING THE SUEZ CRISIS IN '56, I WAS STILL IN HIGH SCHOOL AND SUBJECT TO PRO-ISRAELI STATEMENTS EVERYWHERE I WENT.
MY FAMILY LOOKED UPON NASSER, EGYPT'S PRESIDENT, AS A COMMON CRIMINAL. HE WAS A BRUTAL OPPORTUNIST, SURE, BUT MOST JEWS DIDN'T CARE OR EVEN BOTHER TO UNDERSTAND HIS OTHER MOTIVES.

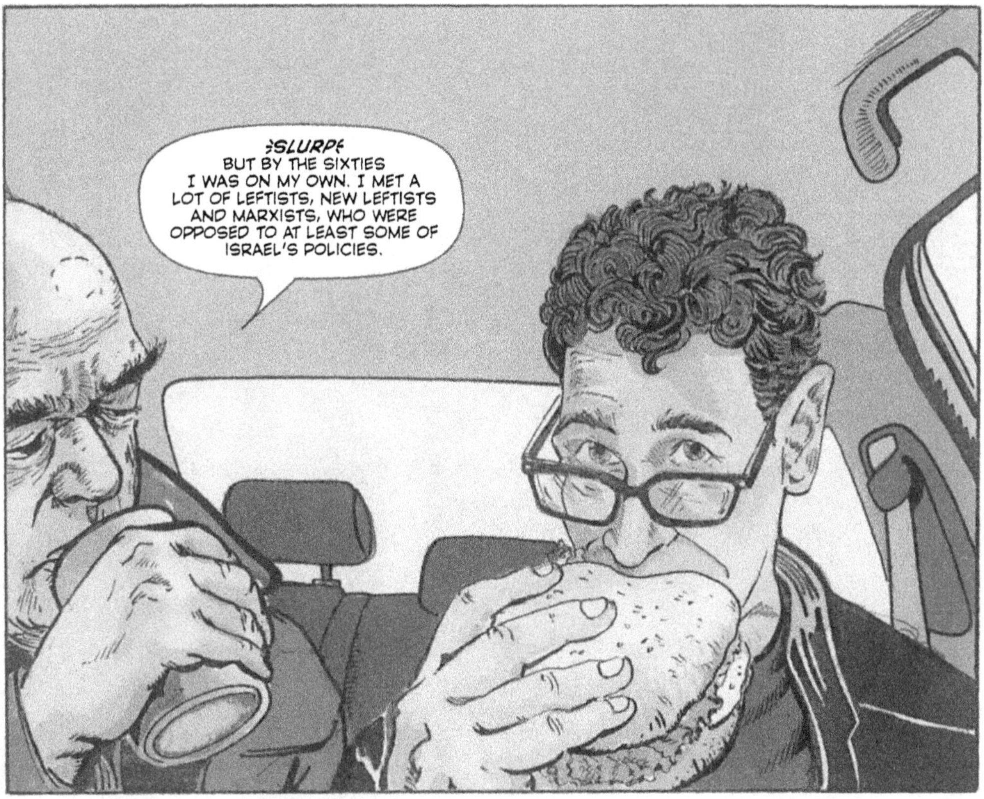
SLURP
BUT BY THE SIXTIES I WAS ON MY OWN. I MET A LOT OF LEFTISTS, NEW LEFTISTS AND MARXISTS, WHO WERE OPPOSED TO AT LEAST SOME OF ISRAEL'S POLICIES.

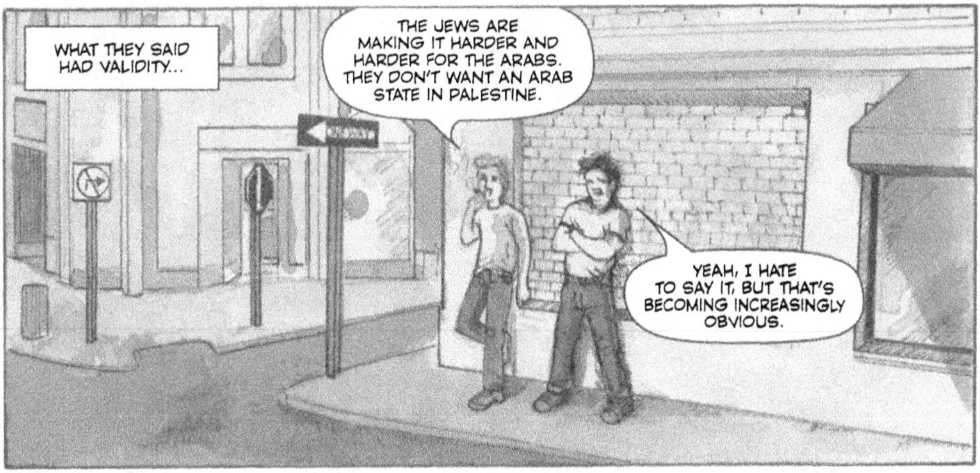
WHAT THEY SAID HAD VALIDITY...
THE JEWS ARE MAKING IT HARDER AND HARDER FOR THE ARABS. THEY DON'T WANT AN ARAB STATE IN PALESTINE.
YEAH, I HATE TO SAY IT, BUT THAT'S BECOMING INCREASINGLY OBVIOUS.

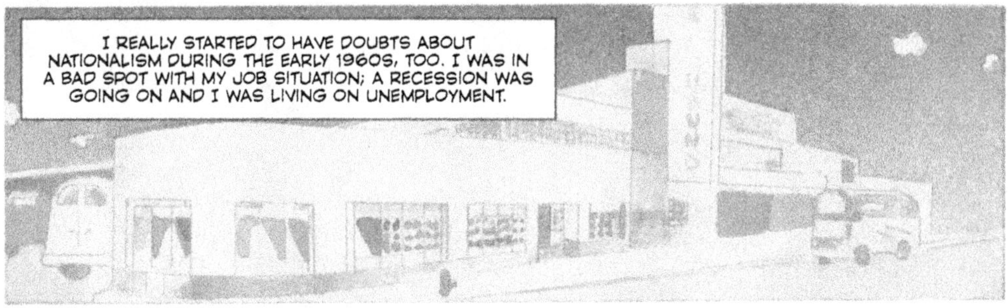
I REALLY STARTED TO HAVE DOUBTS ABOUT NATIONALISM DURING THE EARLY 1960S, TOO. I WAS IN A BAD SPOT WITH MY JOB SITUATION; A RECESSION WAS GOING ON AND I WAS LIVING ON UNEMPLOYMENT.

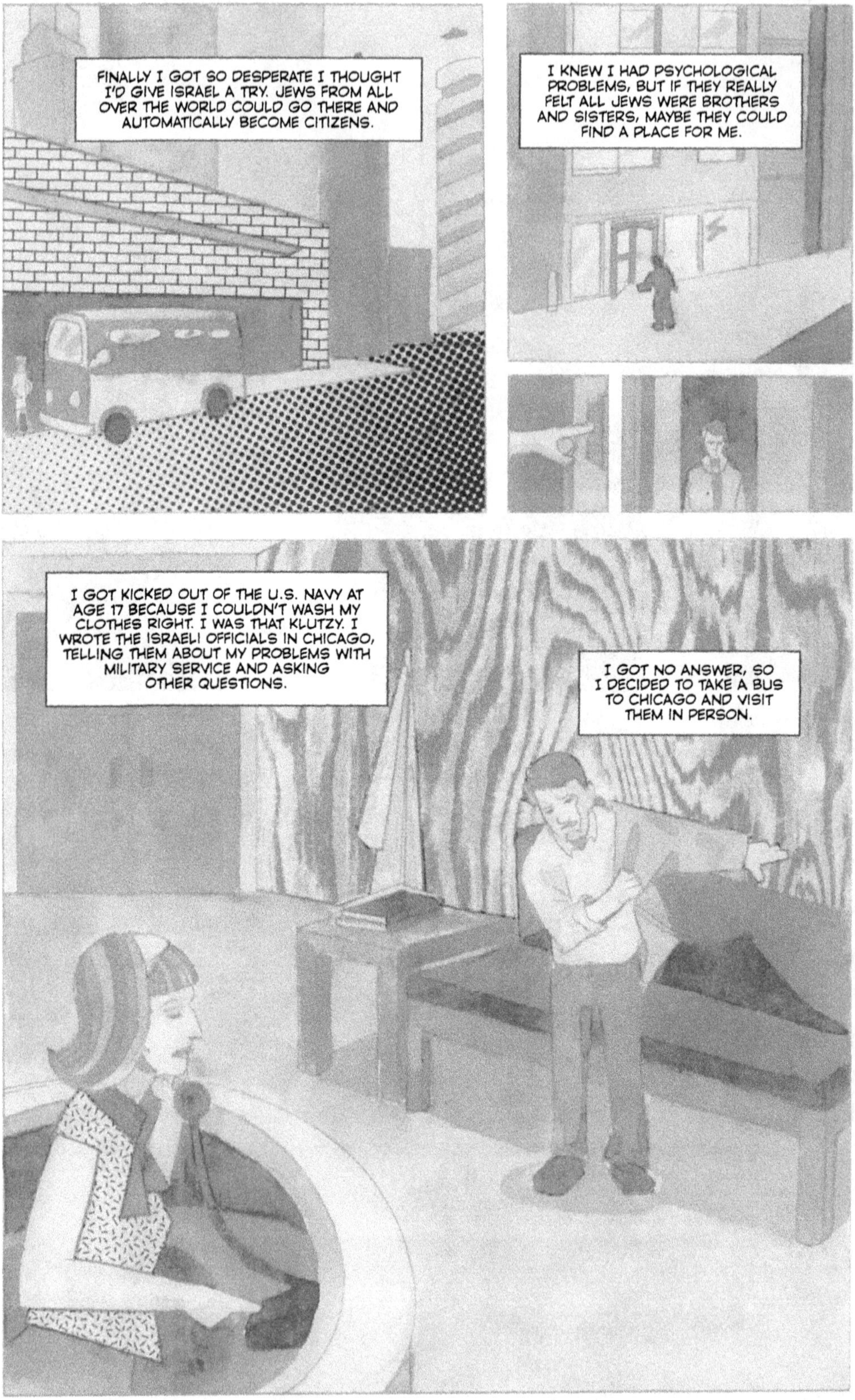
FINALLY I GOT SO DESPERATE I THOUGHT I'D GIVE ISRAEL A TRY. JEWS FROM ALL OVER THE WORLD COULD GO THERE AND AUTOMATICALLY BECOME CITIZENS.
I KNEW I HAD PSYCHOLOGICAL PROBLEMS, BUT IF THEY REALLY FELT ALL JEWS WERE BROTHERS AND SISTERS, MAYBE THEY COULD FIND A PLACE FOR ME.
I GOT KICKED OUT OF THE U.S. NAVY AT AGE 17 BECAUSE I COULDN'T WASH MY CLOTHES RIGHT. I WAS THAT KLUTZY. I WROTE THE ISRAELI OFFICIALS IN CHICAGO, TELLING THEM ABOUT MY PROBLEMS WITH MILITARY SERVICE AND ASKING OTHER QUESTIONS.
I GOT NO ANSWER, SO I DECIDED TO TAKE A BUS TO CHICAGO AND VISIT THEM IN PERSON.

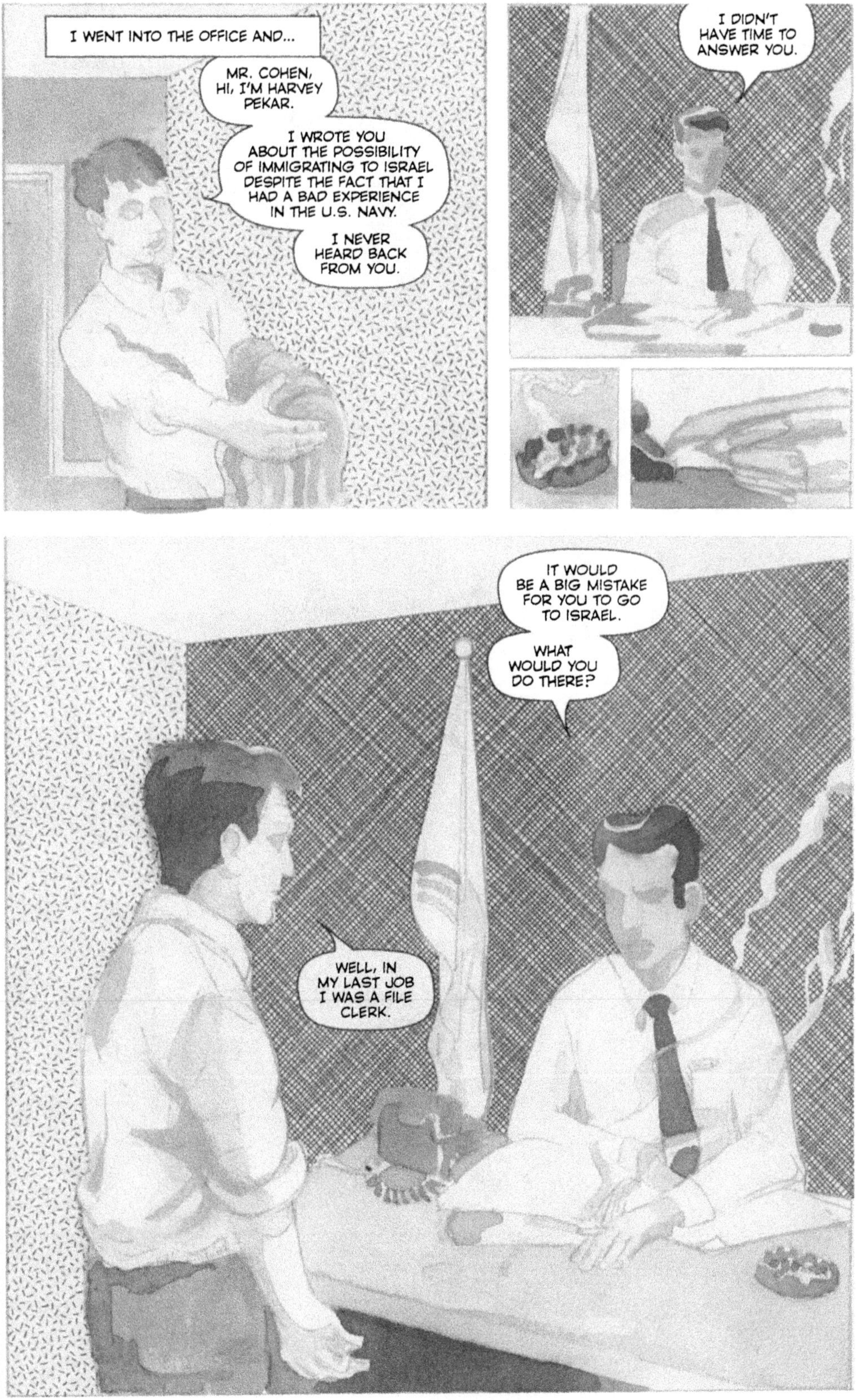
I WENT INTO THE OFFICE AND...
MR. COHEN, HI, I'M HARVEY PEKAR.
I WROTE YOU ABOUT THE POSSIBILITY OF IMMIGRATING TO ISRAEL DESPITE THE FACT THAT I HAD A BAD EXPERIENCE IN THE U.S. NAVY.
I NEVER HEARD BACK FROM YOU.
I DIDN'T HAVE TIME TO ANSWER YOU.
IT WOULD BE A BIG MISTAKE FOR YOU TO GO TO ISRAEL.
WHAT WOULD YOU DO THERE?
WELL, IN MY LAST JOB I WAS A FILE CLERK.

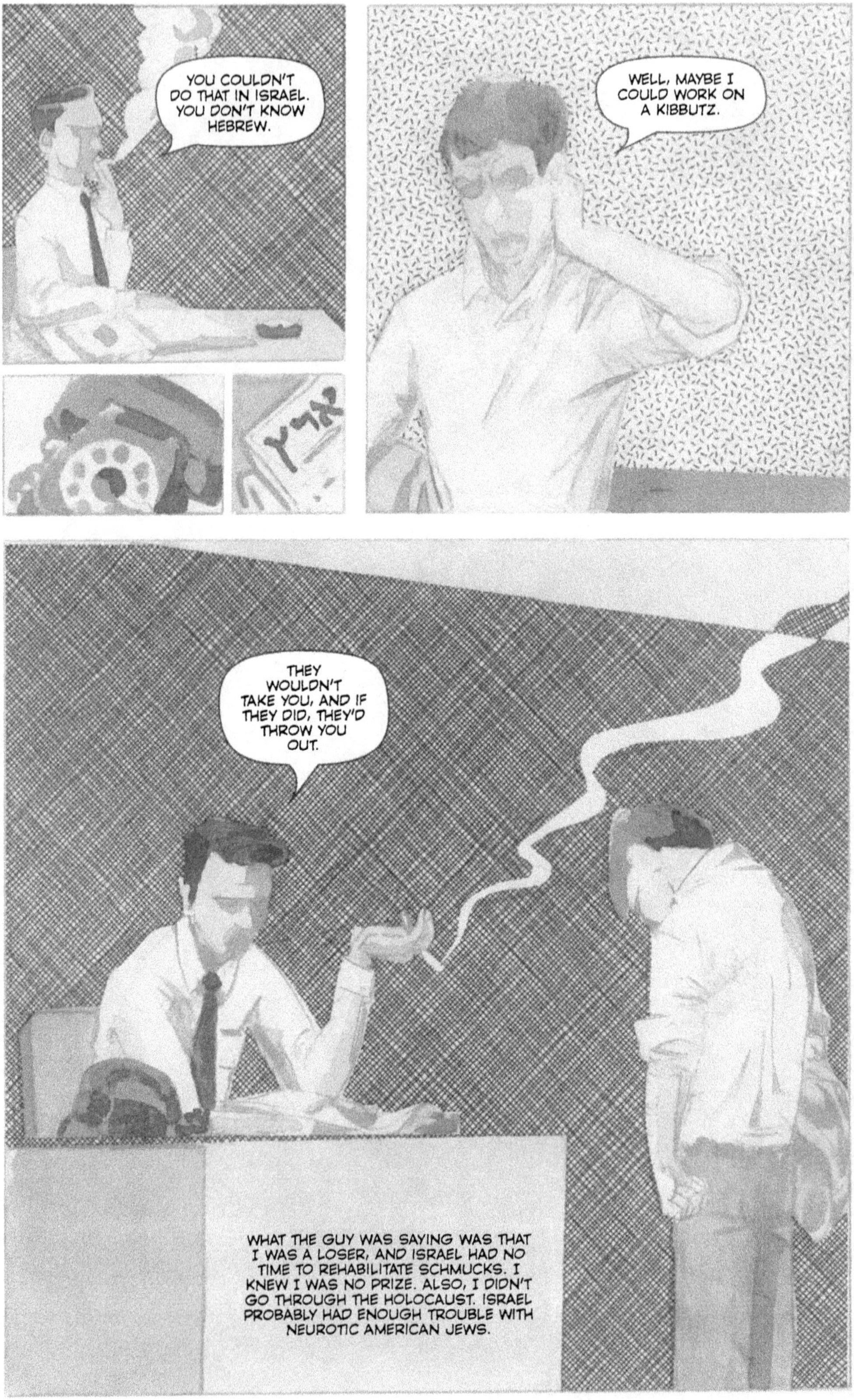
YOU COULDN'T DO THAT IN ISRAEL. YOU DON'T KNOW HEBREW.
WELL, MAYBE I COULD WORK ON A KIBBUTZ.
THEY WOULDN'T TAKE YOU, AND IF THEY DID, THEY'D THROW YOU OUT.
WHAT THE GUY WAS SAYING WAS THAT I WAS A LOSER, AND ISRAEL HAD NO TIME TO REHABILITATE SCHMUCKS. I KNEW I WAS NO PRIZE. ALSO, I DIDN'T GO THROUGH THE HOLOCAUST. ISRAEL PROBABLY HAD ENOUGH TROUBLE WITH NEUROTIC AMERICAN JEWS.

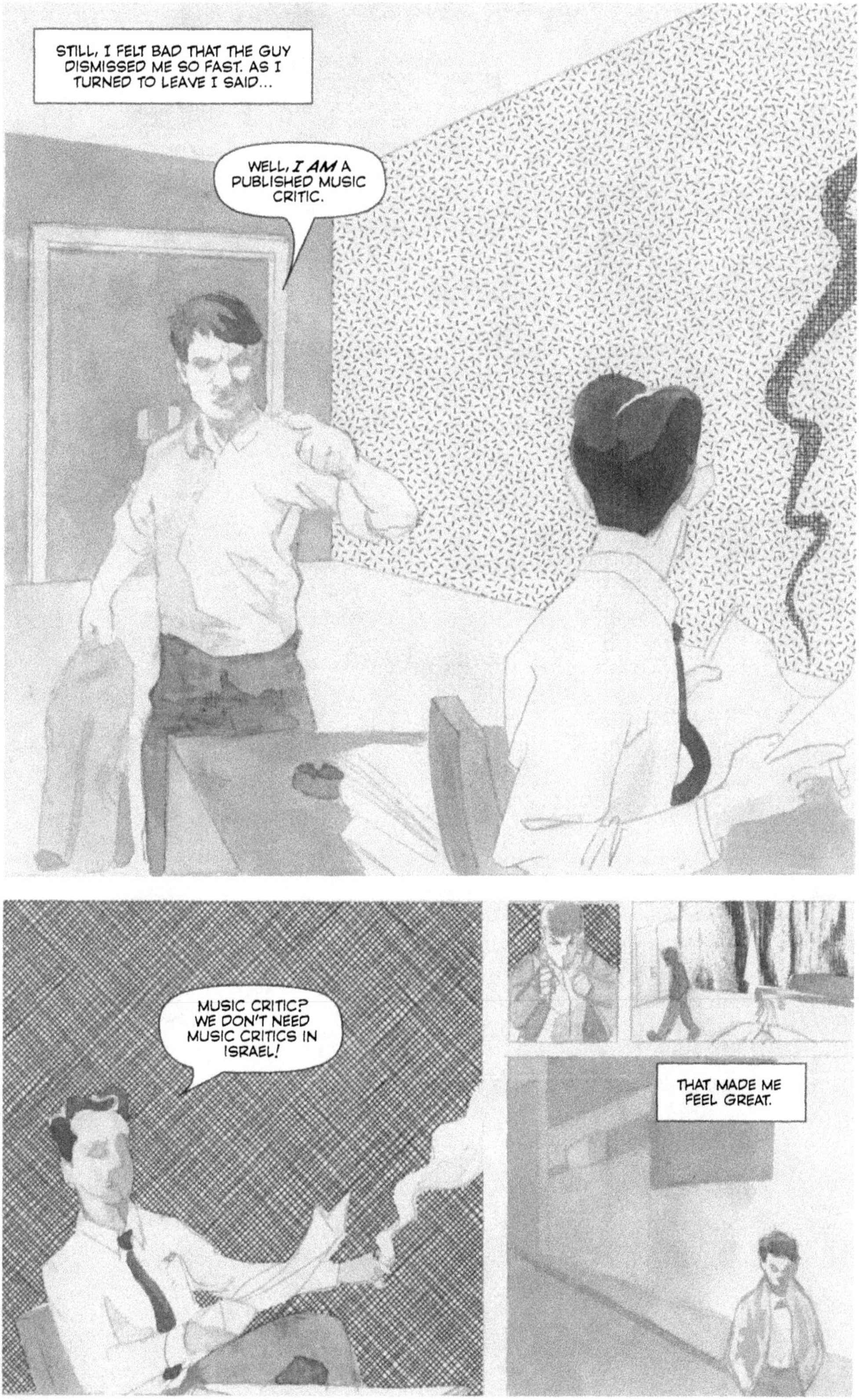
STILL, I FELT BAD THAT THE GUY DISMISSED ME SO FAST. AS I TURNED TO LEAVE I SAID...
WELL, *I AM* A PUBLISHED MUSIC CRITIC.
MUSIC CRITIC? WE DON'T NEED MUSIC CRITICS IN ISRAEL!
THAT MADE ME FEEL GREAT.

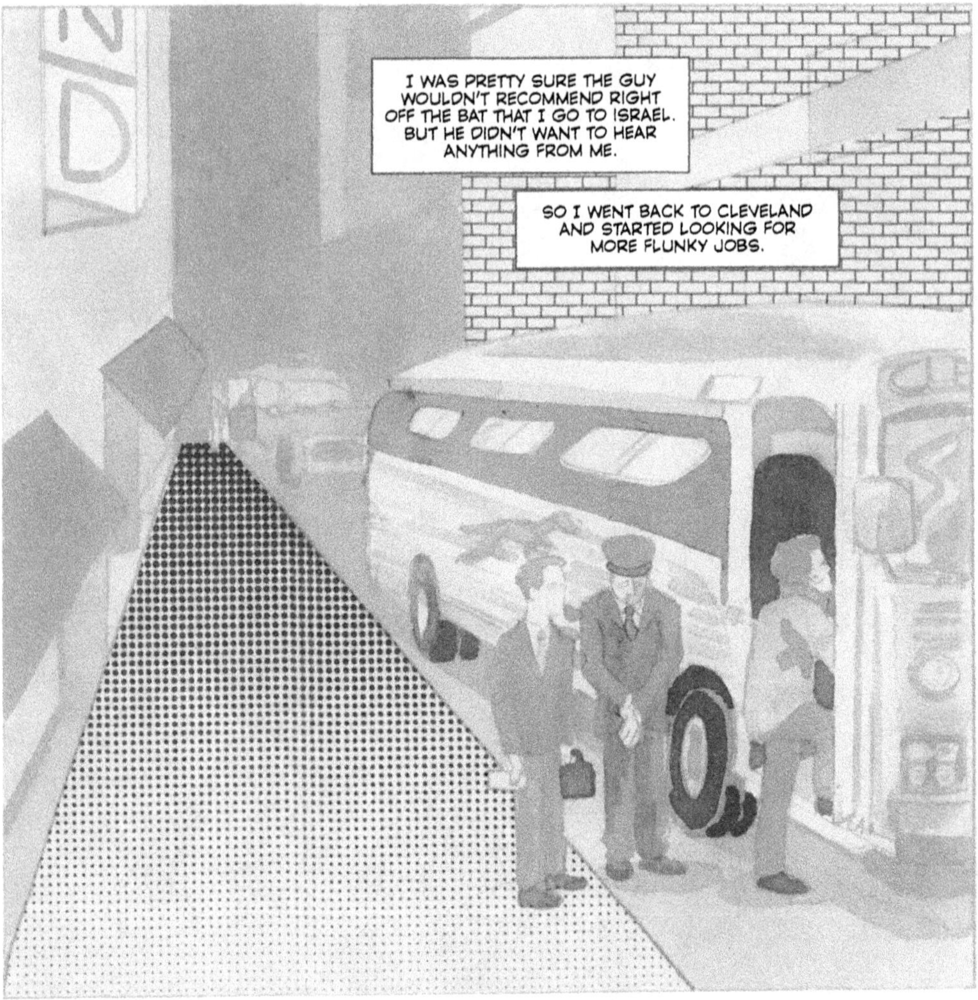
I WAS PRETTY SURE THE GUY WOULDN'T RECOMMEND RIGHT OFF THE BAT THAT I GO TO ISRAEL. BUT HE DIDN'T WANT TO HEAR ANYTHING FROM ME.
SO I WENT BACK TO CLEVELAND AND STARTED LOOKING FOR MORE FLUNKY JOBS.

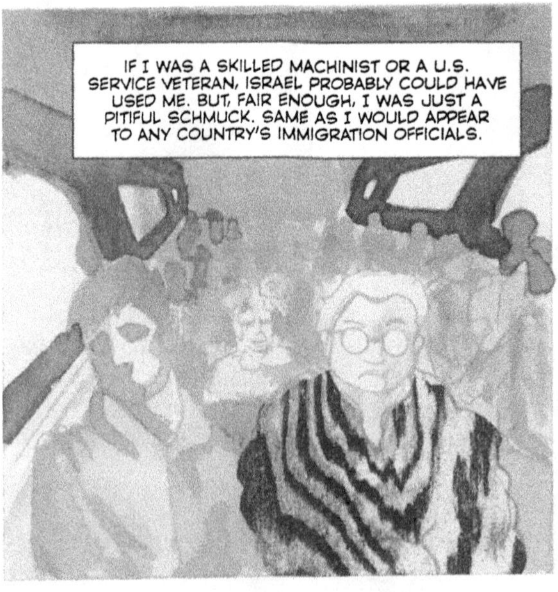
IF I WAS A SKILLED MACHINIST OR A U.S. SERVICE VETERAN, ISRAEL PROBABLY COULD HAVE USED ME. BUT, FAIR ENOUGH, I WAS JUST A PITIFUL SCHMUCK. SAME AS I WOULD APPEAR TO ANY COUNTRY'S IMMIGRATION OFFICIALS.

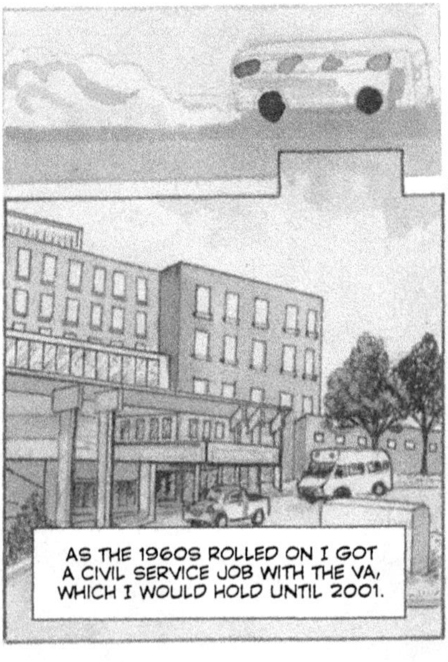
AS THE 1960S ROLLED ON I GOT A CIVIL SERVICE JOB WITH THE VA, WHICH I WOULD HOLD UNTIL 2001.

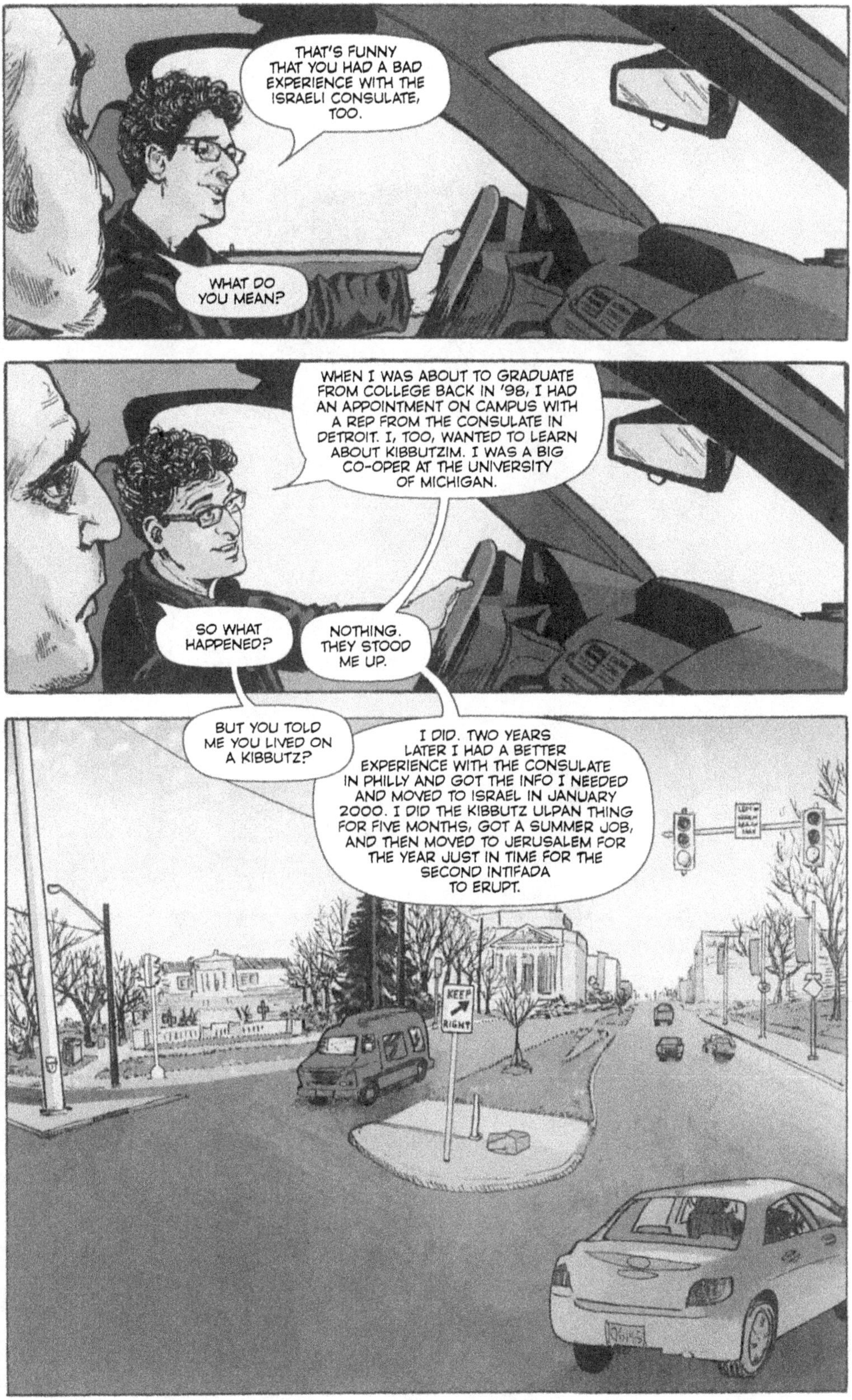
THAT'S FUNNY THAT YOU HAD A BAD EXPERIENCE WITH THE ISRAELI CONSULATE, TOO.
WHAT DO YOU MEAN?
WHEN I WAS ABOUT TO GRADUATE FROM COLLEGE BACK IN '98, I HAD AN APPOINTMENT ON CAMPUS WITH A REP FROM THE CONSULATE IN DETROIT. I, TOO, WANTED TO LEARN ABOUT KIBBUTZIM. I WAS A BIG CO-OPER AT THE UNIVERSITY OF MICHIGAN.
SO WHAT HAPPENED?
NOTHING. THEY STOOD ME UP.
BUT YOU TOLD ME YOU LIVED ON A KIBBUTZ?
I DID. TWO YEARS LATER I HAD A BETTER EXPERIENCE WITH THE CONSULATE IN PHILLY AND GOT THE INFO I NEEDED AND MOVED TO ISRAEL IN JANUARY 2000. I DID THE KIBBUTZ ULPAN THING FOR FIVE MONTHS, GOT A SUMMER JOB, AND THEN MOVED TO JERUSALEM FOR THE YEAR JUST IN TIME FOR THE SECOND INTIFADA TO ERUPT.
KEEP RIGHT

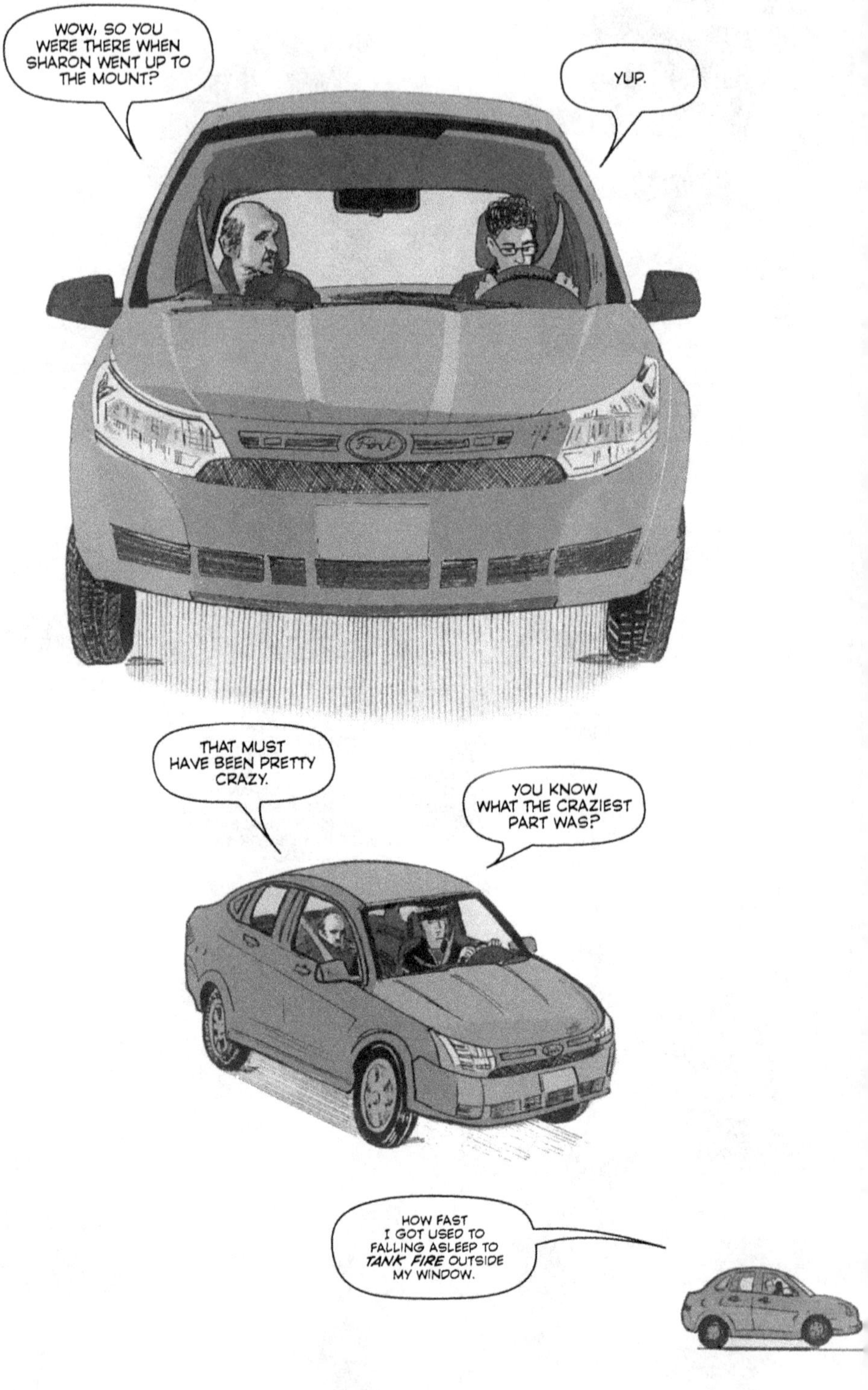
WOW, SO YOU WERE THERE WHEN SHARON WENT UP TO THE MOUNT?
YUP.
THAT MUST HAVE BEEN PRETTY CRAZY.
YOU KNOW WHAT THE CRAZIEST PART WAS?
HOW FAST I GOT USED TO FALLING ASLEEP TO *TANK FIRE* OUTSIDE MY WINDOW.

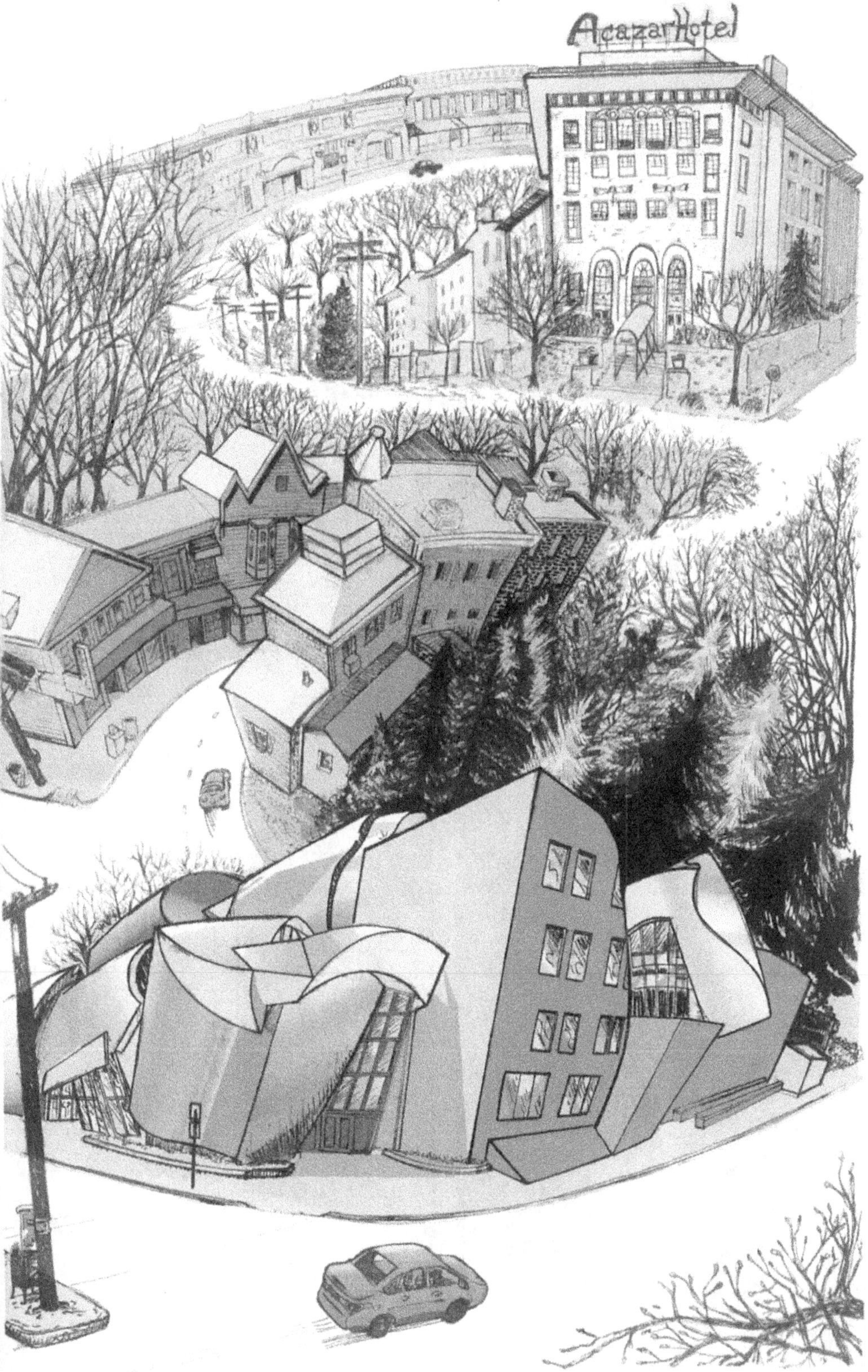
AcazarHotel

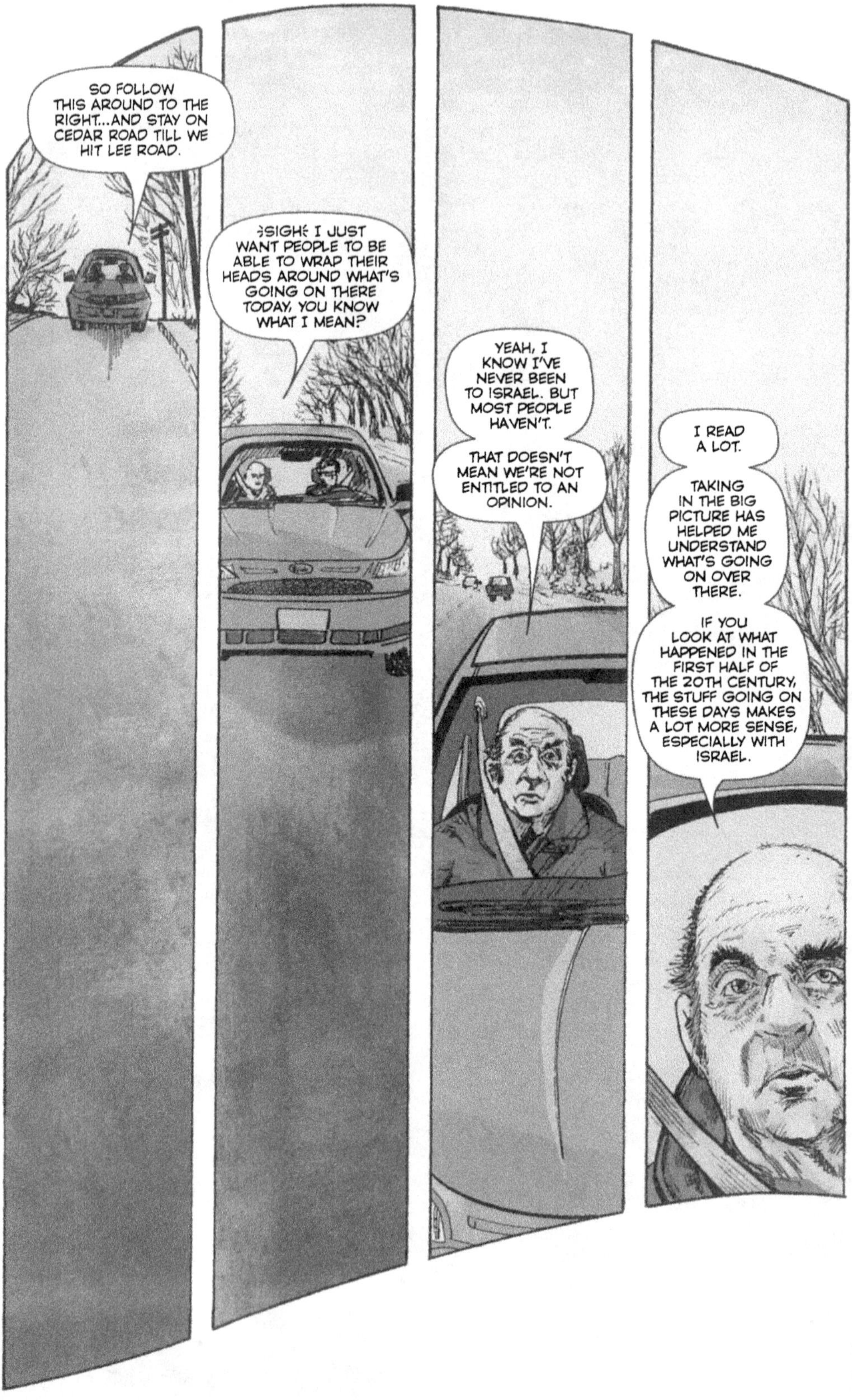
SO FOLLOW THIS AROUND TO THE RIGHT...AND STAY ON CEDAR ROAD TILL WE HIT LEE ROAD.
⸗SIGH⸗ I JUST WANT PEOPLE TO BE ABLE TO WRAP THEIR HEADS AROUND WHAT'S GOING ON THERE TODAY, YOU KNOW WHAT I MEAN?
YEAH, I KNOW I'VE NEVER BEEN TO ISRAEL. BUT MOST PEOPLE HAVEN'T.
THAT DOESN'T MEAN WE'RE NOT ENTITLED TO AN OPINION.
I READ A LOT.
TAKING IN THE BIG PICTURE HAS HELPED ME UNDERSTAND WHAT'S GOING ON OVER THERE.
IF YOU LOOK AT WHAT HAPPENED IN THE FIRST HALF OF THE 20TH CENTURY, THE STUFF GOING ON THESE DAYS MAKES A LOT MORE SENSE, ESPECIALLY WITH ISRAEL.

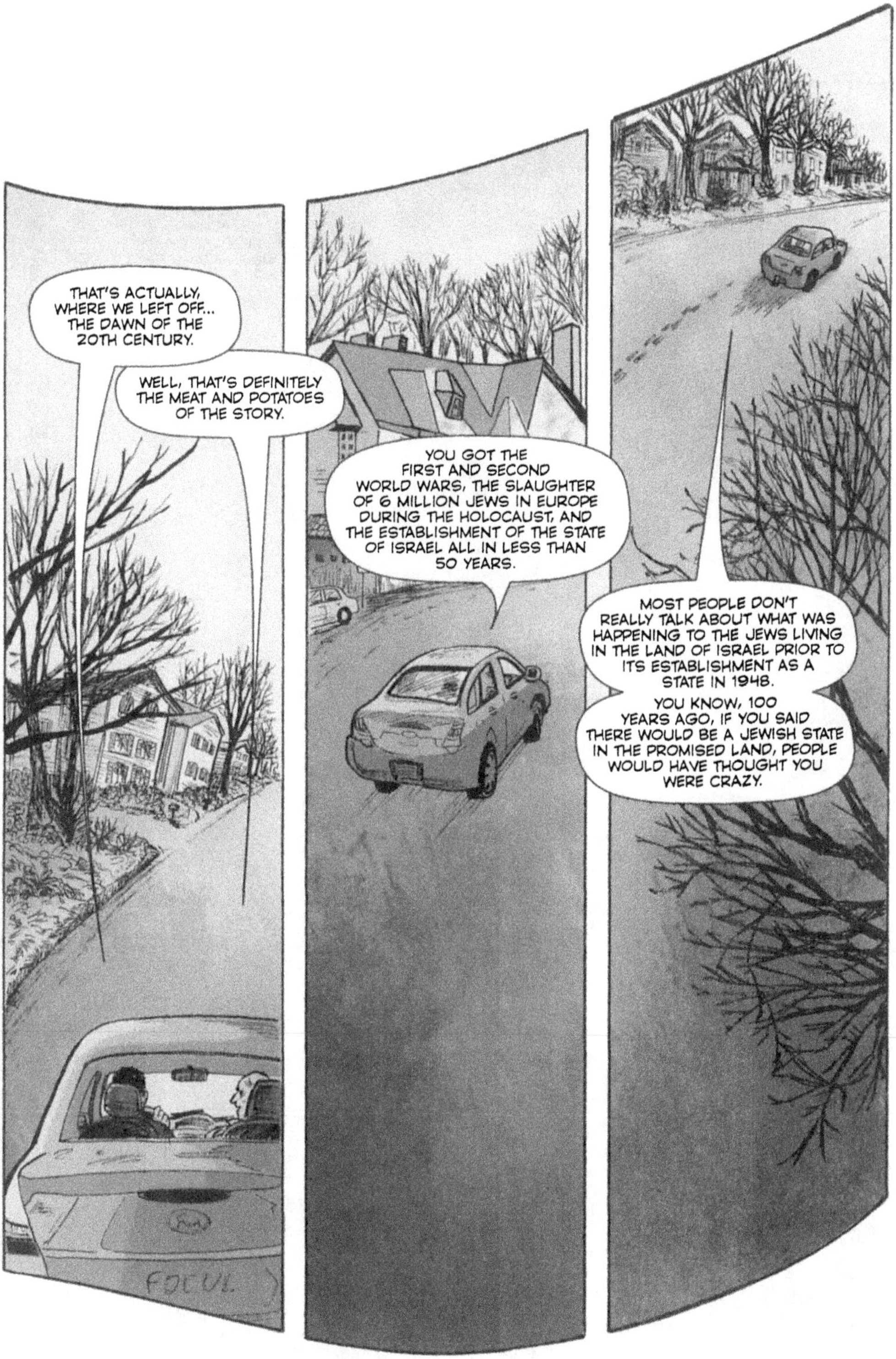
THAT'S ACTUALLY, WHERE WE LEFT OFF... THE DAWN OF THE 20TH CENTURY.
WELL, THAT'S DEFINITELY THE MEAT AND POTATOES OF THE STORY.
FOCUS
YOU GOT THE FIRST AND SECOND WORLD WARS, THE SLAUGHTER OF 6 MILLION JEWS IN EUROPE DURING THE HOLOCAUST, AND THE ESTABLISHMENT OF THE STATE OF ISRAEL ALL IN LESS THAN 50 YEARS.
MOST PEOPLE DON'T REALLY TALK ABOUT WHAT WAS HAPPENING TO THE JEWS LIVING IN THE LAND OF ISRAEL PRIOR TO ITS ESTABLISHMENT AS A STATE IN 1948.
YOU KNOW, 100 YEARS AGO, IF YOU SAID THERE WOULD BE A JEWISH STATE IN THE PROMISED LAND, PEOPLE WOULD HAVE THOUGHT YOU WERE CRAZY.

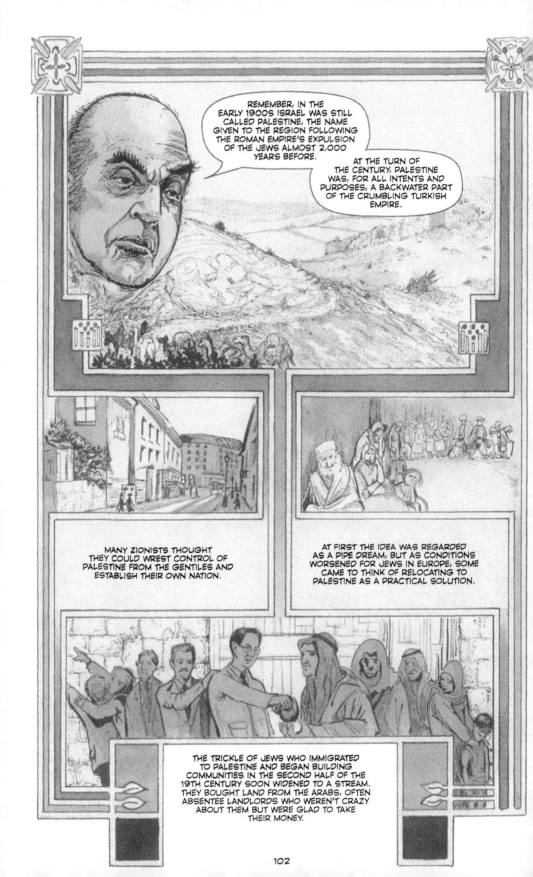

REMEMBER, IN THE EARLY 1900s ISRAEL WAS STILL CALLED PALESTINE, THE NAME GIVEN TO THE REGION FOLLOWING THE ROMAN EMPIRE'S EXPULSION OF THE JEWS ALMOST 2,000 YEARS BEFORE.

AT THE TURN OF THE CENTURY, PALESTINE WAS, FOR ALL INTENTS AND PURPOSES, A BACKWATER PART OF THE CRUMBLING TURKISH EMPIRE.

MANY ZIONISTS THOUGHT THEY COULD WREST CONTROL OF PALESTINE FROM THE GENTILES AND ESTABLISH THEIR OWN NATION.

AT FIRST THE IDEA WAS REGARDED AS A PIPE DREAM, BUT AS CONDITIONS WORSENED FOR JEWS IN EUROPE, SOME CAME TO THINK OF RELOCATING TO PALESTINE AS A PRACTICAL SOLUTION.

THE TRICKLE OF JEWS WHO IMMIGRATED TO PALESTINE AND BEGAN BUILDING COMMUNITIES IN THE SECOND HALF OF THE 19TH CENTURY SOON WIDENED TO A STREAM. THEY BOUGHT LAND FROM THE ARABS, OFTEN ABSENTEE LANDLORDS WHO WEREN'T CRAZY ABOUT THEM BUT WERE GLAD TO TAKE THEIR MONEY.

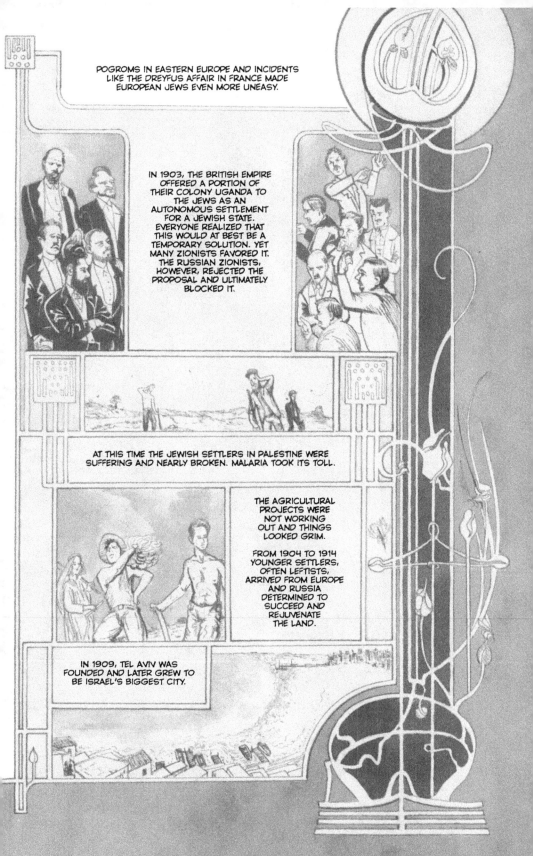

POGROMS IN EASTERN EUROPE AND INCIDENTS LIKE THE DREYFUS AFFAIR IN FRANCE MADE EUROPEAN JEWS EVEN MORE UNEASY.

IN 1903, THE BRITISH EMPIRE OFFERED A PORTION OF THEIR COLONY UGANDA TO THE JEWS AS AN AUTONOMOUS SETTLEMENT FOR A JEWISH STATE. EVERYONE REALIZED THAT THIS WOULD AT BEST BE A TEMPORARY SOLUTION. YET MANY ZIONISTS FAVORED IT. THE RUSSIAN ZIONISTS, HOWEVER, REJECTED THE PROPOSAL AND ULTIMATELY BLOCKED IT.

AT THIS TIME THE JEWISH SETTLERS IN PALESTINE WERE SUFFERING AND NEARLY BROKEN. MALARIA TOOK ITS TOLL.

THE AGRICULTURAL PROJECTS WERE NOT WORKING OUT AND THINGS LOOKED GRIM.

FROM 1904 TO 1914 YOUNGER SETTLERS, OFTEN LEFTISTS, ARRIVED FROM EUROPE AND RUSSIA DETERMINED TO SUCCEED AND REJUVENATE THE LAND.

IN 1909, TEL AVIV WAS FOUNDED AND LATER GREW TO BE ISRAEL'S BIGGEST CITY.

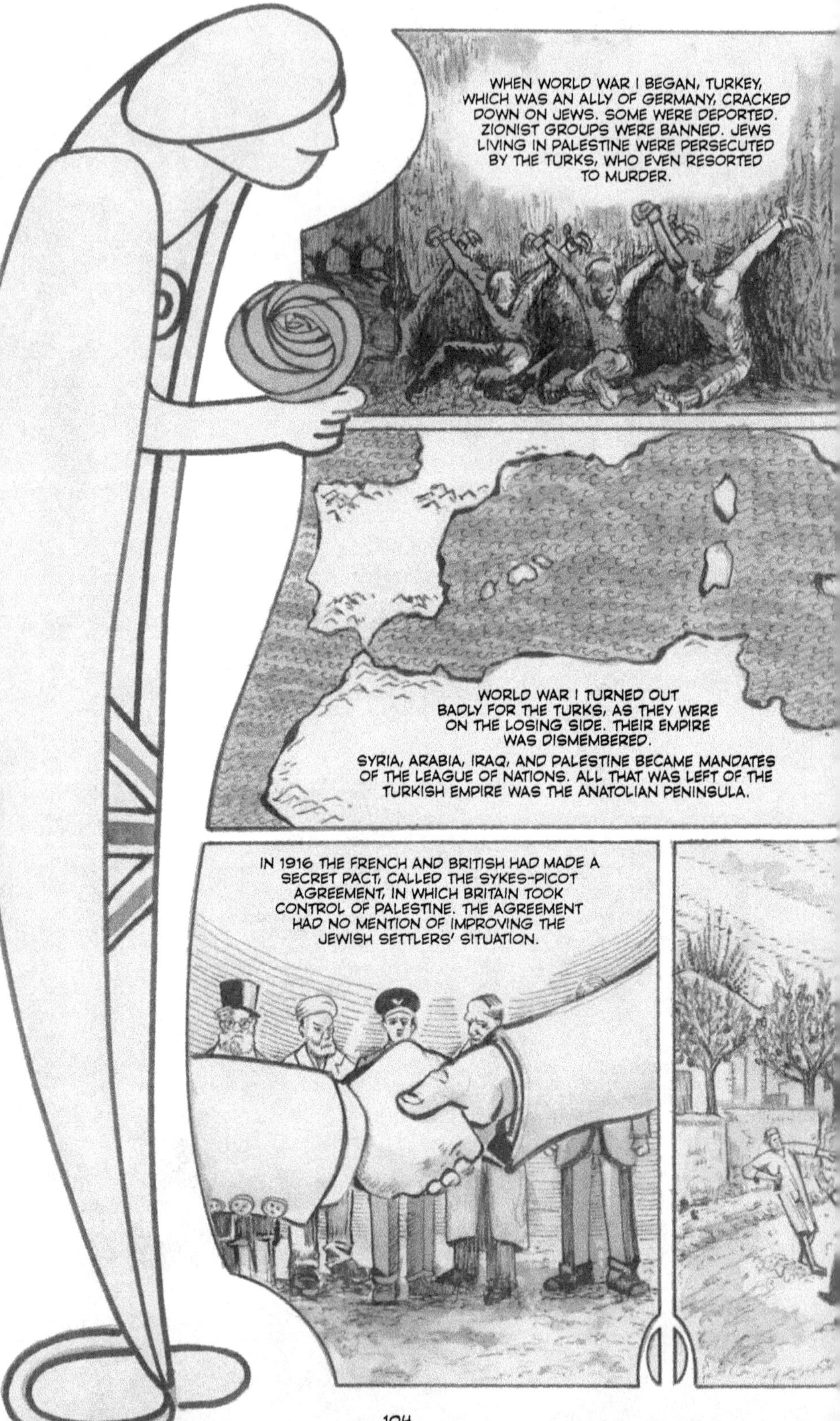
WHEN WORLD WAR I BEGAN, TURKEY, WHICH WAS AN ALLY OF GERMANY, CRACKED DOWN ON JEWS. SOME WERE DEPORTED. ZIONIST GROUPS WERE BANNED. JEWS LIVING IN PALESTINE WERE PERSECUTED BY THE TURKS, WHO EVEN RESORTED TO MURDER.
WORLD WAR I TURNED OUT BADLY FOR THE TURKS, AS THEY WERE ON THE LOSING SIDE. THEIR EMPIRE WAS DISMEMBERED.
SYRIA, ARABIA, IRAQ, AND PALESTINE BECAME MANDATES OF THE LEAGUE OF NATIONS. ALL THAT WAS LEFT OF THE TURKISH EMPIRE WAS THE ANATOLIAN PENINSULA.
IN 1916 THE FRENCH AND BRITISH HAD MADE A SECRET PACT, CALLED THE SYKES-PICOT AGREEMENT, IN WHICH BRITAIN TOOK CONTROL OF PALESTINE. THE AGREEMENT HAD NO MENTION OF IMPROVING THE JEWISH SETTLERS' SITUATION.

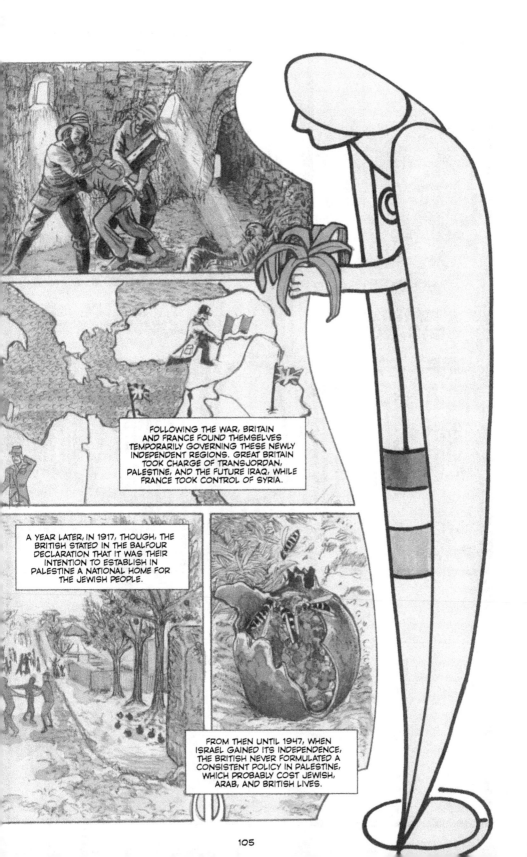

FOLLOWING THE WAR, BRITAIN AND FRANCE FOUND THEMSELVES TEMPORARILY GOVERNING THESE NEWLY INDEPENDENT REGIONS. GREAT BRITAIN TOOK CHARGE OF TRANSJORDAN, PALESTINE, AND THE FUTURE IRAQ, WHILE FRANCE TOOK CONTROL OF SYRIA.

A YEAR LATER, IN 1917, THOUGH, THE BRITISH STATED IN THE BALFOUR DECLARATION THAT IT WAS THEIR INTENTION TO ESTABLISH IN PALESTINE A NATIONAL HOME FOR THE JEWISH PEOPLE.

FROM THEN UNTIL 1947, WHEN ISRAEL GAINED ITS INDEPENDENCE, THE BRITISH NEVER FORMULATED A CONSISTENT POLICY IN PALESTINE, WHICH PROBABLY COST JEWISH, ARAB, AND BRITISH LIVES.

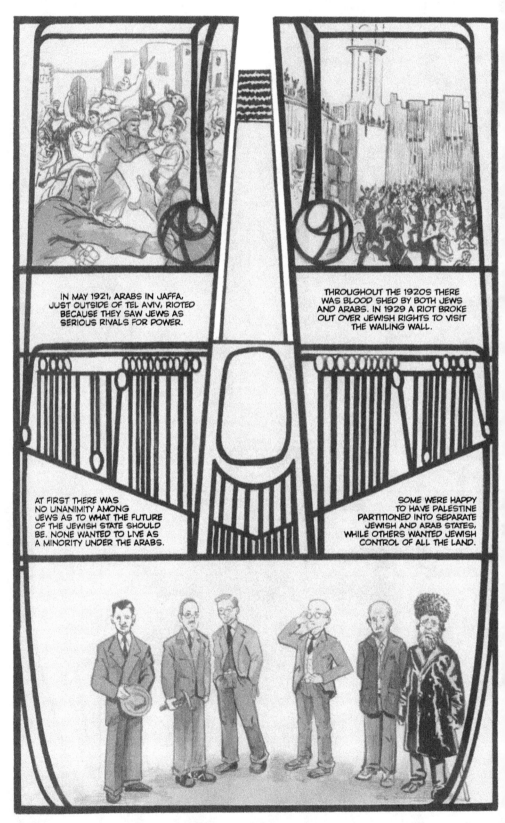

IN MAY 1921, ARABS IN JAFFA, JUST OUTSIDE OF TEL AVIV, RIOTED BECAUSE THEY SAW JEWS AS SERIOUS RIVALS FOR POWER.

THROUGHOUT THE 1920S THERE WAS BLOOD SHED BY BOTH JEWS AND ARABS. IN 1929 A RIOT BROKE OUT OVER JEWISH RIGHTS TO VISIT THE WAILING WALL.

AT FIRST THERE WAS NO UNANIMITY AMONG JEWS AS TO WHAT THE FUTURE OF THE JEWISH STATE SHOULD BE. NONE WANTED TO LIVE AS A MINORITY UNDER THE ARABS.

SOME WERE HAPPY TO HAVE PALESTINE PARTITIONED INTO SEPARATE JEWISH AND ARAB STATES, WHILE OTHERS WANTED JEWISH CONTROL OF ALL THE LAND.

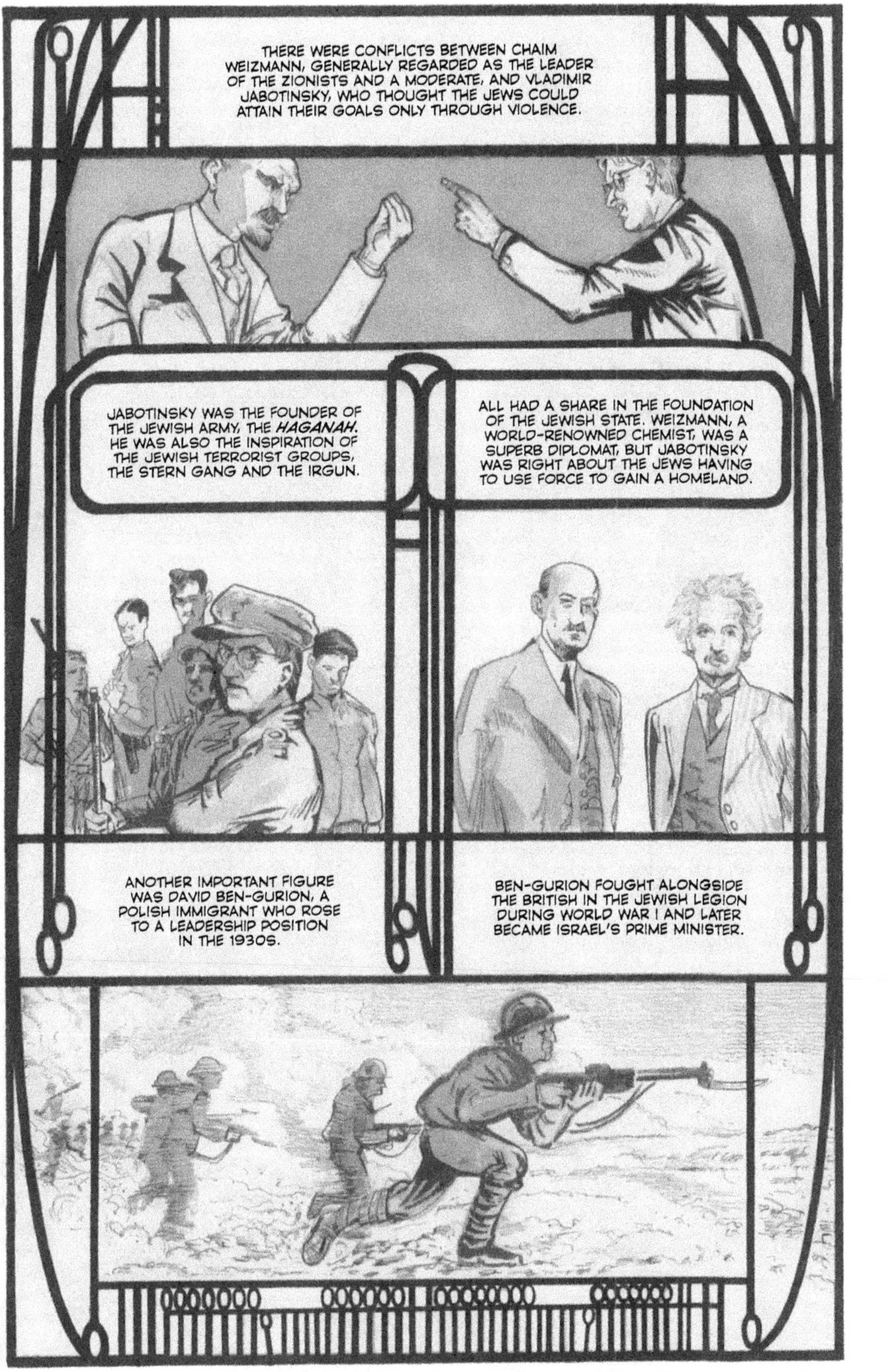
THERE WERE CONFLICTS BETWEEN CHAIM WEIZMANN, GENERALLY REGARDED AS THE LEADER OF THE ZIONISTS AND A MODERATE, AND VLADIMIR JABOTINSKY, WHO THOUGHT THE JEWS COULD ATTAIN THEIR GOALS ONLY THROUGH VIOLENCE.
JABOTINSKY WAS THE FOUNDER OF THE JEWISH ARMY, THE *HAGANAH*. HE WAS ALSO THE INSPIRATION OF THE JEWISH TERRORIST GROUPS, THE STERN GANG AND THE IRGUN.
ALL HAD A SHARE IN THE FOUNDATION OF THE JEWISH STATE. WEIZMANN, A WORLD-RENOWNED CHEMIST, WAS A SUPERB DIPLOMAT, BUT JABOTINSKY WAS RIGHT ABOUT THE JEWS HAVING TO USE FORCE TO GAIN A HOMELAND.
ANOTHER IMPORTANT FIGURE WAS DAVID BEN-GURION, A POLISH IMMIGRANT WHO ROSE TO A LEADERSHIP POSITION IN THE 1930S.
BEN-GURION FOUGHT ALONGSIDE THE BRITISH IN THE JEWISH LEGION DURING WORLD WAR I AND LATER BECAME ISRAEL'S PRIME MINISTER.

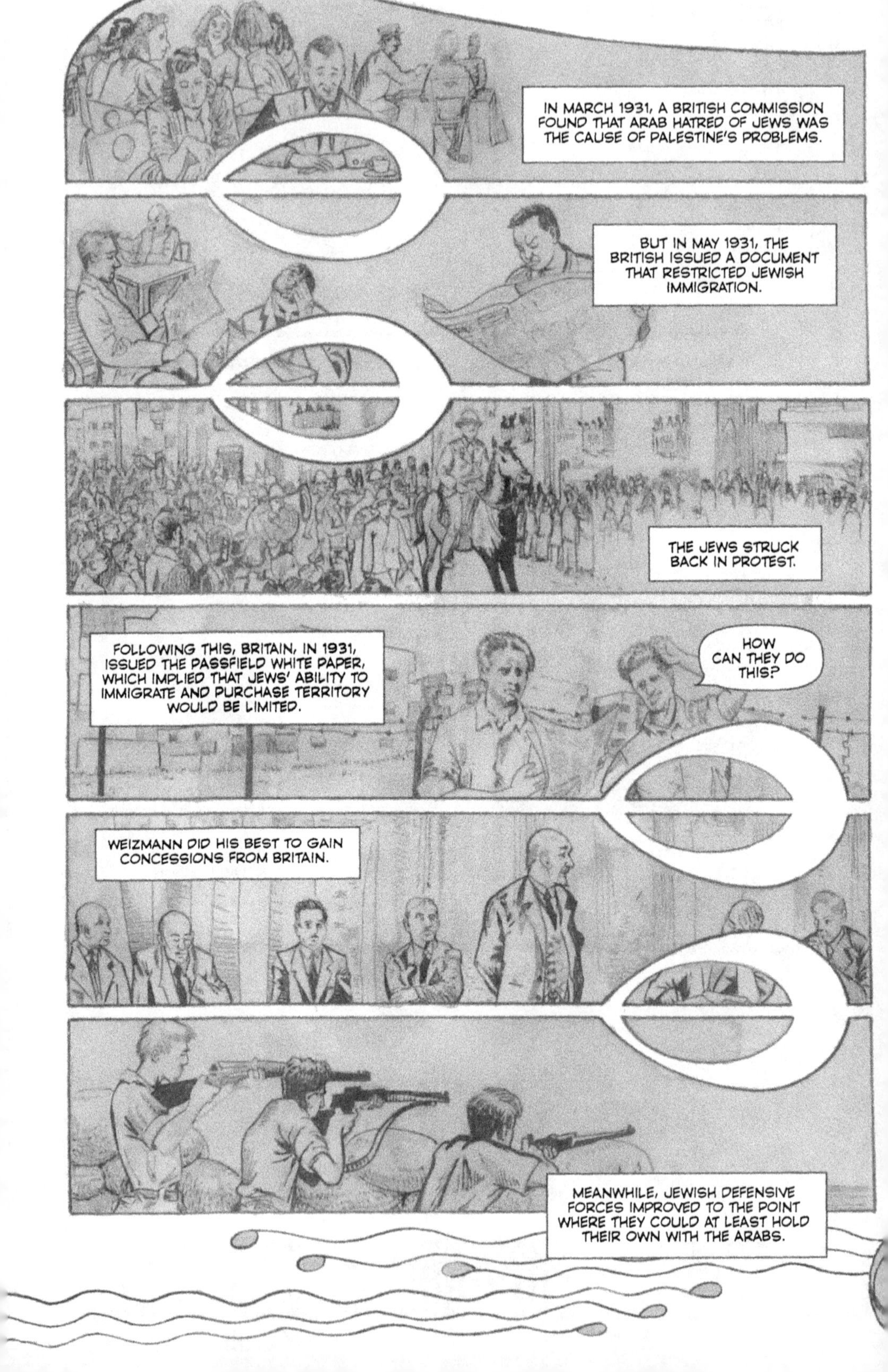
IN MARCH 1931, A BRITISH COMMISSION FOUND THAT ARAB HATRED OF JEWS WAS THE CAUSE OF PALESTINE'S PROBLEMS.
BUT IN MAY 1931, THE BRITISH ISSUED A DOCUMENT THAT RESTRICTED JEWISH IMMIGRATION.
THE JEWS STRUCK BACK IN PROTEST.
FOLLOWING THIS, BRITAIN, IN 1931, ISSUED THE PASSFIELD WHITE PAPER, WHICH IMPLIED THAT JEWS' ABILITY TO IMMIGRATE AND PURCHASE TERRITORY WOULD BE LIMITED.
HOW CAN THEY DO THIS?
WEIZMANN DID HIS BEST TO GAIN CONCESSIONS FROM BRITAIN.
MEANWHILE, JEWISH DEFENSIVE FORCES IMPROVED TO THE POINT WHERE THEY COULD AT LEAST HOLD THEIR OWN WITH THE ARABS.

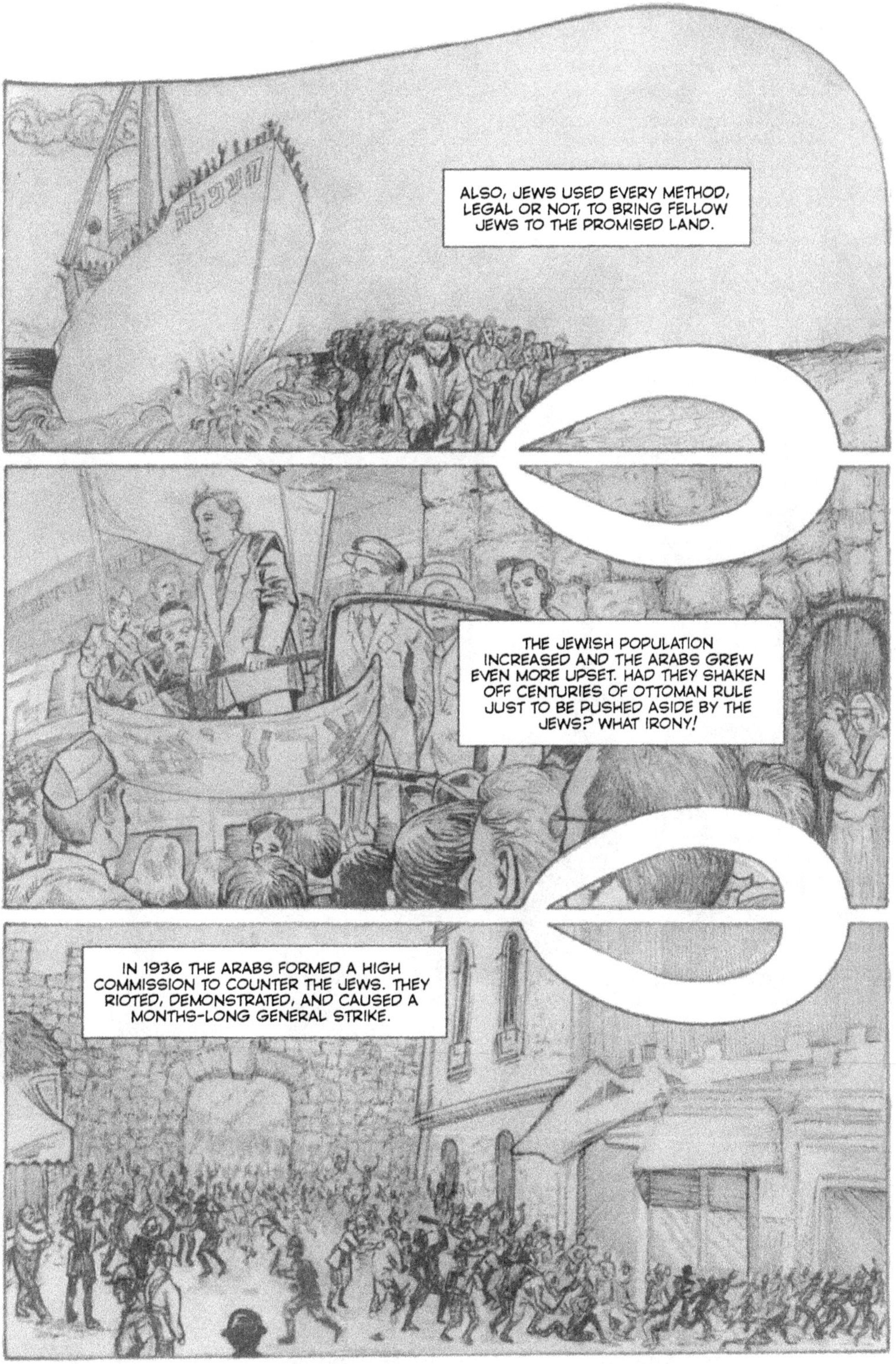
ALSO, JEWS USED EVERY METHOD, LEGAL OR NOT, TO BRING FELLOW JEWS TO THE PROMISED LAND.
THE JEWISH POPULATION INCREASED AND THE ARABS GREW EVEN MORE UPSET. HAD THEY SHAKEN OFF CENTURIES OF OTTOMAN RULE JUST TO BE PUSHED ASIDE BY THE JEWS? WHAT IRONY!
IN 1936 THE ARABS FORMED A HIGH COMMISSION TO COUNTER THE JEWS. THEY RIOTED, DEMONSTRATED, AND CAUSED A MONTHS-LONG GENERAL STRIKE.

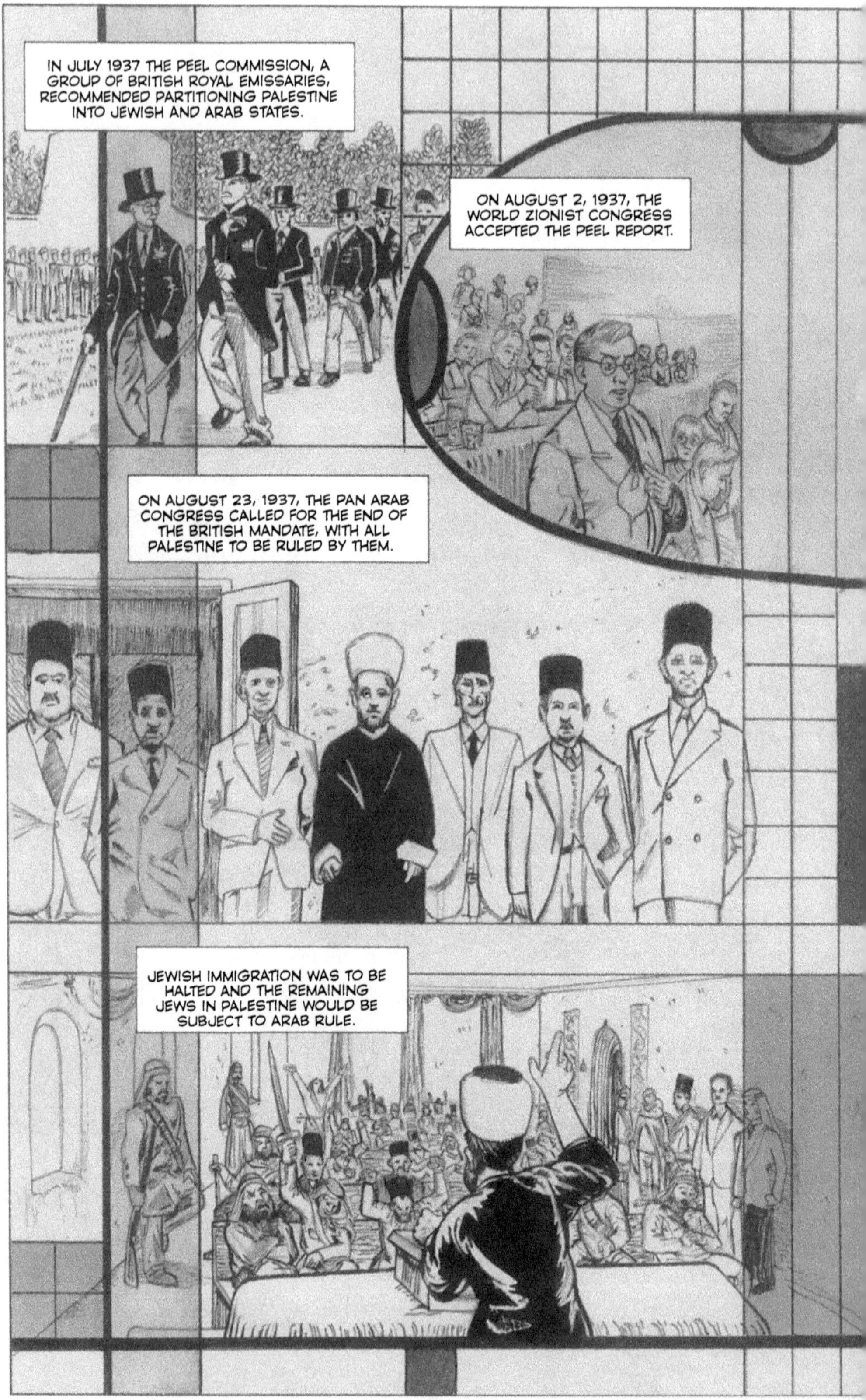
IN JULY 1937 THE PEEL COMMISSION, A GROUP OF BRITISH ROYAL EMISSARIES, RECOMMENDED PARTITIONING PALESTINE INTO JEWISH AND ARAB STATES.
ON AUGUST 2, 1937, THE WORLD ZIONIST CONGRESS ACCEPTED THE PEEL REPORT.
ON AUGUST 23, 1937, THE PAN ARAB CONGRESS CALLED FOR THE END OF THE BRITISH MANDATE, WITH ALL PALESTINE TO BE RULED BY THEM.
JEWISH IMMIGRATION WAS TO BE HALTED AND THE REMAINING JEWS IN PALESTINE WOULD BE SUBJECT TO ARAB RULE.

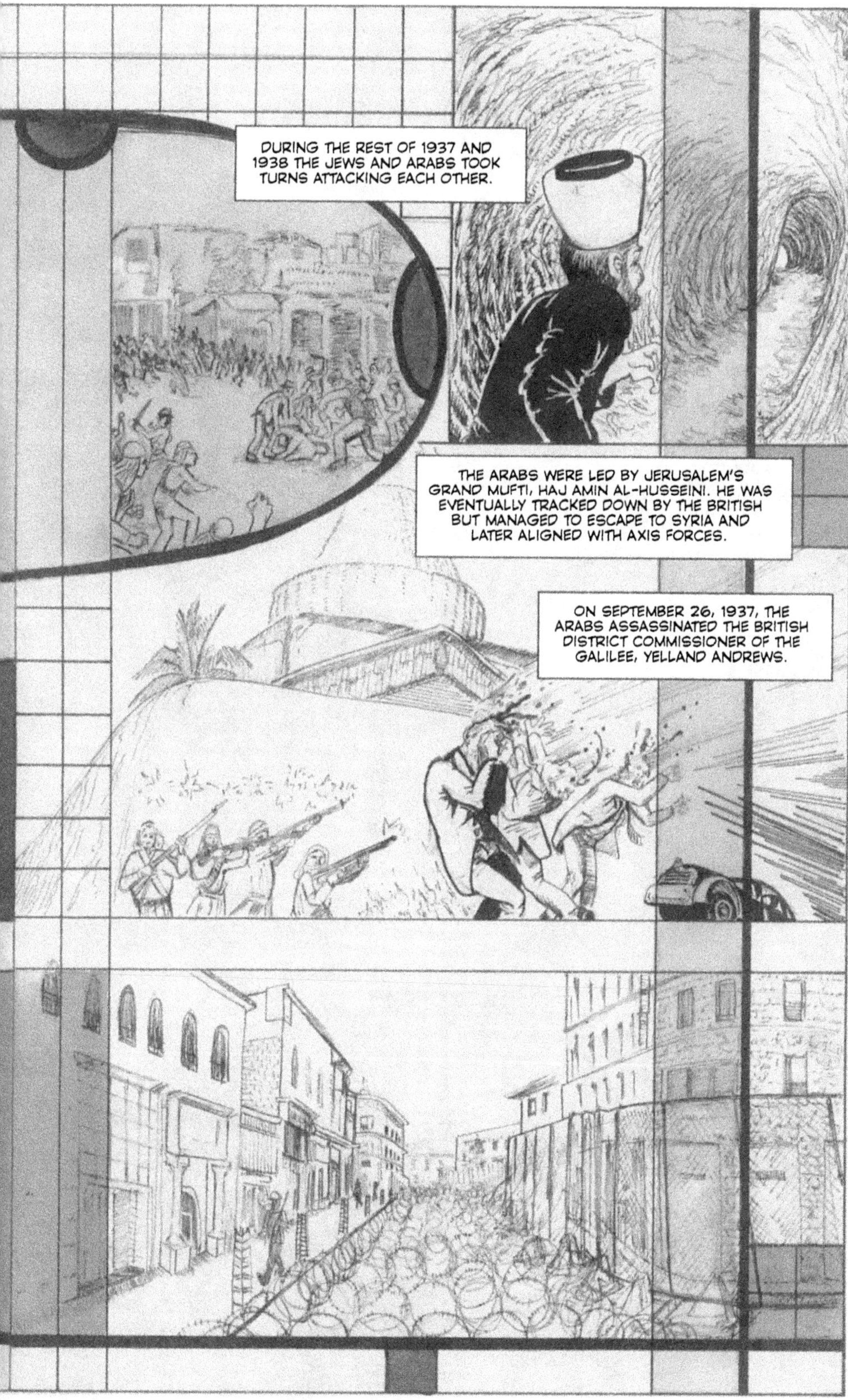
DURING THE REST OF 1937 AND 1938 THE JEWS AND ARABS TOOK TURNS ATTACKING EACH OTHER.
THE ARABS WERE LED BY JERUSALEM'S GRAND MUFTI, HAJ AMIN AL-HUSSEINI. HE WAS EVENTUALLY TRACKED DOWN BY THE BRITISH BUT MANAGED TO ESCAPE TO SYRIA AND LATER ALIGNED WITH AXIS FORCES.
ON SEPTEMBER 26, 1937, THE ARABS ASSASSINATED THE BRITISH DISTRICT COMMISSIONER OF THE GALILEE, YELLAND ANDREWS.

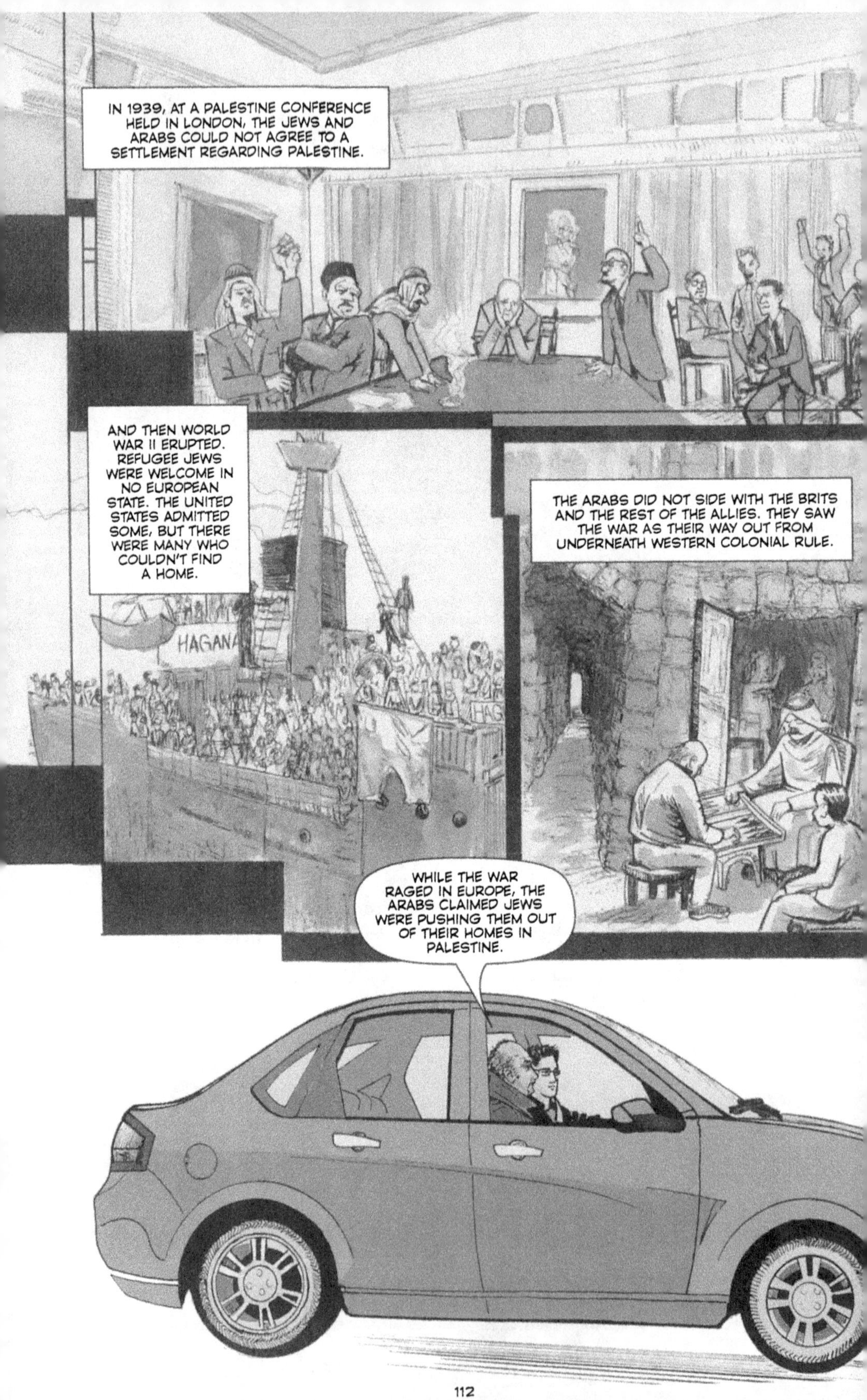
IN 1939, AT A PALESTINE CONFERENCE HELD IN LONDON, THE JEWS AND ARABS COULD NOT AGREE TO A SETTLEMENT REGARDING PALESTINE.
AND THEN WORLD WAR II ERUPTED. REFUGEE JEWS WERE WELCOME IN NO EUROPEAN STATE. THE UNITED STATES ADMITTED SOME, BUT THERE WERE MANY WHO COULDN'T FIND A HOME.
HAGANA
THE ARABS DID NOT SIDE WITH THE BRITS AND THE REST OF THE ALLIES. THEY SAW THE WAR AS THEIR WAY OUT FROM UNDERNEATH WESTERN COLONIAL RULE.
WHILE THE WAR RAGED IN EUROPE, THE ARABS CLAIMED JEWS WERE PUSHING THEM OUT OF THEIR HOMES IN PALESTINE.

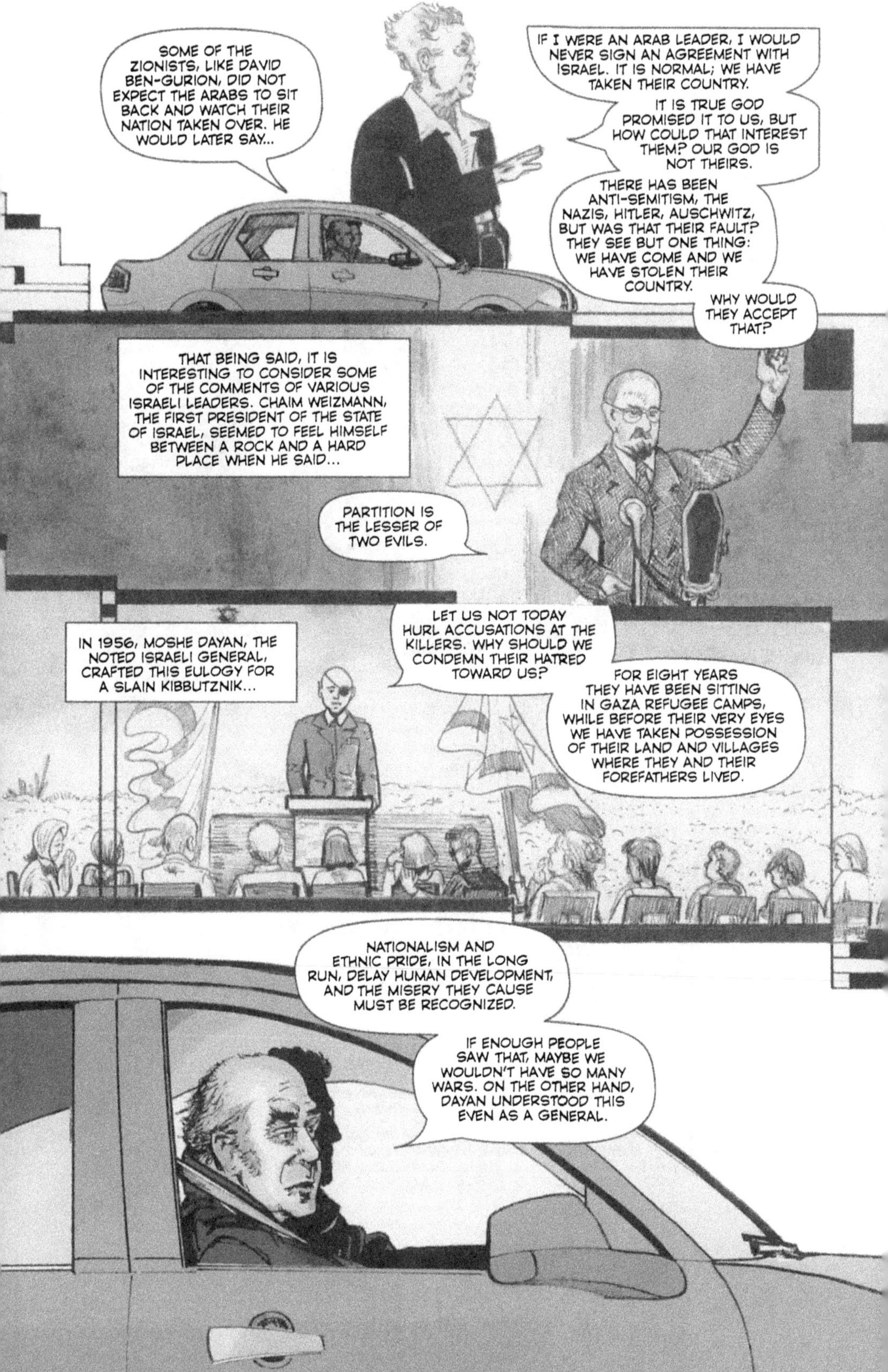
SOME OF THE ZIONISTS, LIKE DAVID BEN-GURION, DID NOT EXPECT THE ARABS TO SIT BACK AND WATCH THEIR NATION TAKEN OVER. HE WOULD LATER SAY...
IF I WERE AN ARAB LEADER, I WOULD NEVER SIGN AN AGREEMENT WITH ISRAEL. IT IS NORMAL; WE HAVE TAKEN THEIR COUNTRY.
IT IS TRUE GOD PROMISED IT TO US, BUT HOW COULD THAT INTEREST THEM? OUR GOD IS NOT THEIRS.
THERE HAS BEEN ANTI-SEMITISM, THE NAZIS, HITLER, AUSCHWITZ, BUT WAS THAT THEIR FAULT? THEY SEE BUT ONE THING: WE HAVE COME AND WE HAVE STOLEN THEIR COUNTRY.
WHY WOULD THEY ACCEPT THAT?
THAT BEING SAID, IT IS INTERESTING TO CONSIDER SOME OF THE COMMENTS OF VARIOUS ISRAELI LEADERS. CHAIM WEIZMANN, THE FIRST PRESIDENT OF THE STATE OF ISRAEL, SEEMED TO FEEL HIMSELF BETWEEN A ROCK AND A HARD PLACE WHEN HE SAID...
PARTITION IS THE LESSER OF TWO EVILS.
IN 1956, MOSHE DAYAN, THE NOTED ISRAELI GENERAL, CRAFTED THIS EULOGY FOR A SLAIN KIBBUTZNIK...
LET US NOT TODAY HURL ACCUSATIONS AT THE KILLERS. WHY SHOULD WE CONDEMN THEIR HATRED TOWARD US?
FOR EIGHT YEARS THEY HAVE BEEN SITTING IN GAZA REFUGEE CAMPS, WHILE BEFORE THEIR VERY EYES WE HAVE TAKEN POSSESSION OF THEIR LAND AND VILLAGES WHERE THEY AND THEIR FOREFATHERS LIVED.
NATIONALISM AND ETHNIC PRIDE, IN THE LONG RUN, DELAY HUMAN DEVELOPMENT, AND THE MISERY THEY CAUSE MUST BE RECOGNIZED.
IF ENOUGH PEOPLE SAW THAT, MAYBE WE WOULDN'T HAVE SO MANY WARS. ON THE OTHER HAND, DAYAN UNDERSTOOD THIS EVEN AS A GENERAL.

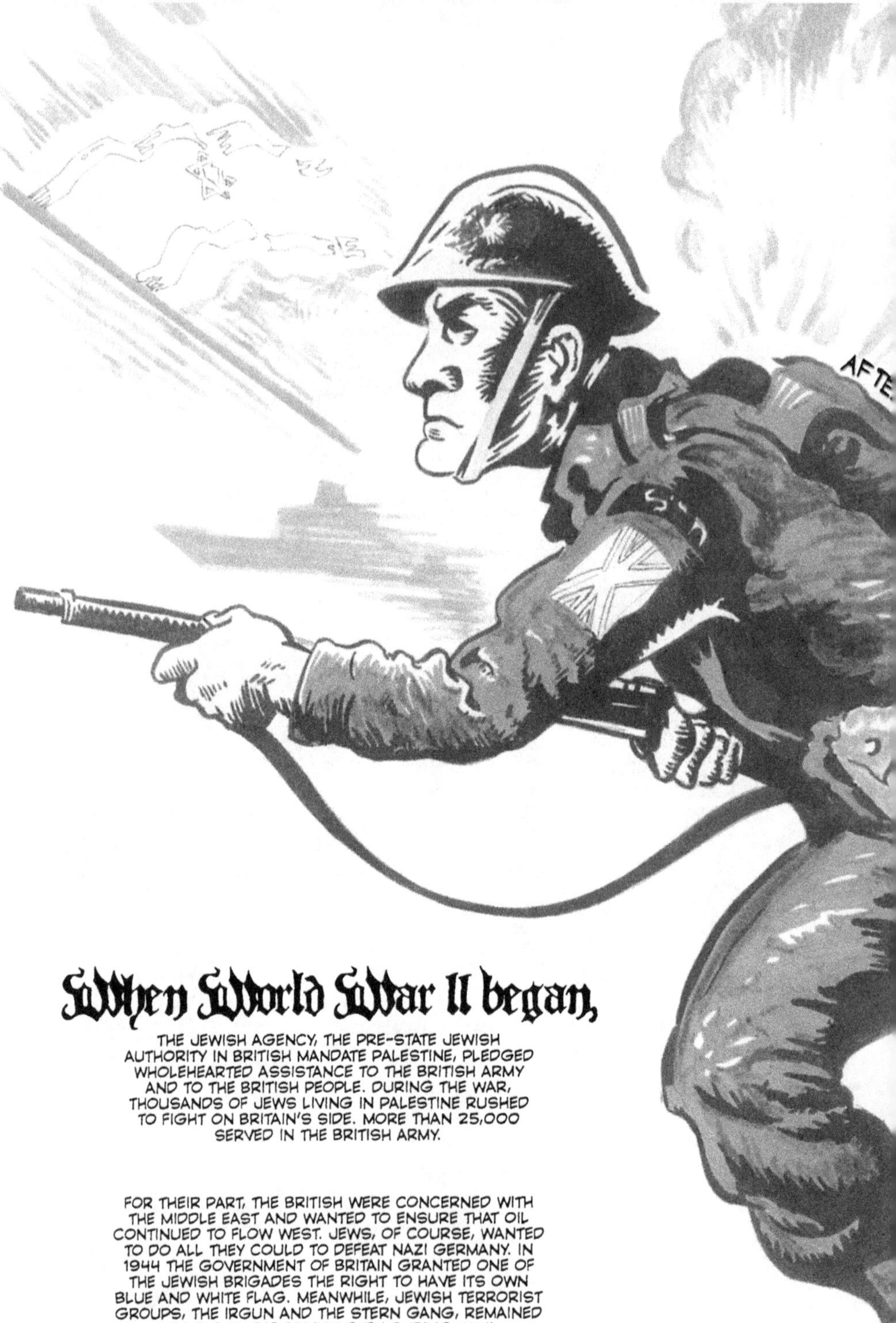

When World War II began,

THE JEWISH AGENCY, THE PRE-STATE JEWISH AUTHORITY IN BRITISH MANDATE PALESTINE, PLEDGED WHOLEHEARTED ASSISTANCE TO THE BRITISH ARMY AND TO THE BRITISH PEOPLE. DURING THE WAR, THOUSANDS OF JEWS LIVING IN PALESTINE RUSHED TO FIGHT ON BRITAIN'S SIDE. MORE THAN 25,000 SERVED IN THE BRITISH ARMY.

FOR THEIR PART, THE BRITISH WERE CONCERNED WITH THE MIDDLE EAST AND WANTED TO ENSURE THAT OIL CONTINUED TO FLOW WEST. JEWS, OF COURSE, WANTED TO DO ALL THEY COULD TO DEFEAT NAZI GERMANY. IN 1944 THE GOVERNMENT OF BRITAIN GRANTED ONE OF THE JEWISH BRIGADES THE RIGHT TO HAVE ITS OWN BLUE AND WHITE FLAG. MEANWHILE, JEWISH TERRORIST GROUPS, THE IRGUN AND THE STERN GANG, REMAINED HOSTILE TO THE BRITISH EVEN DURING WWII.

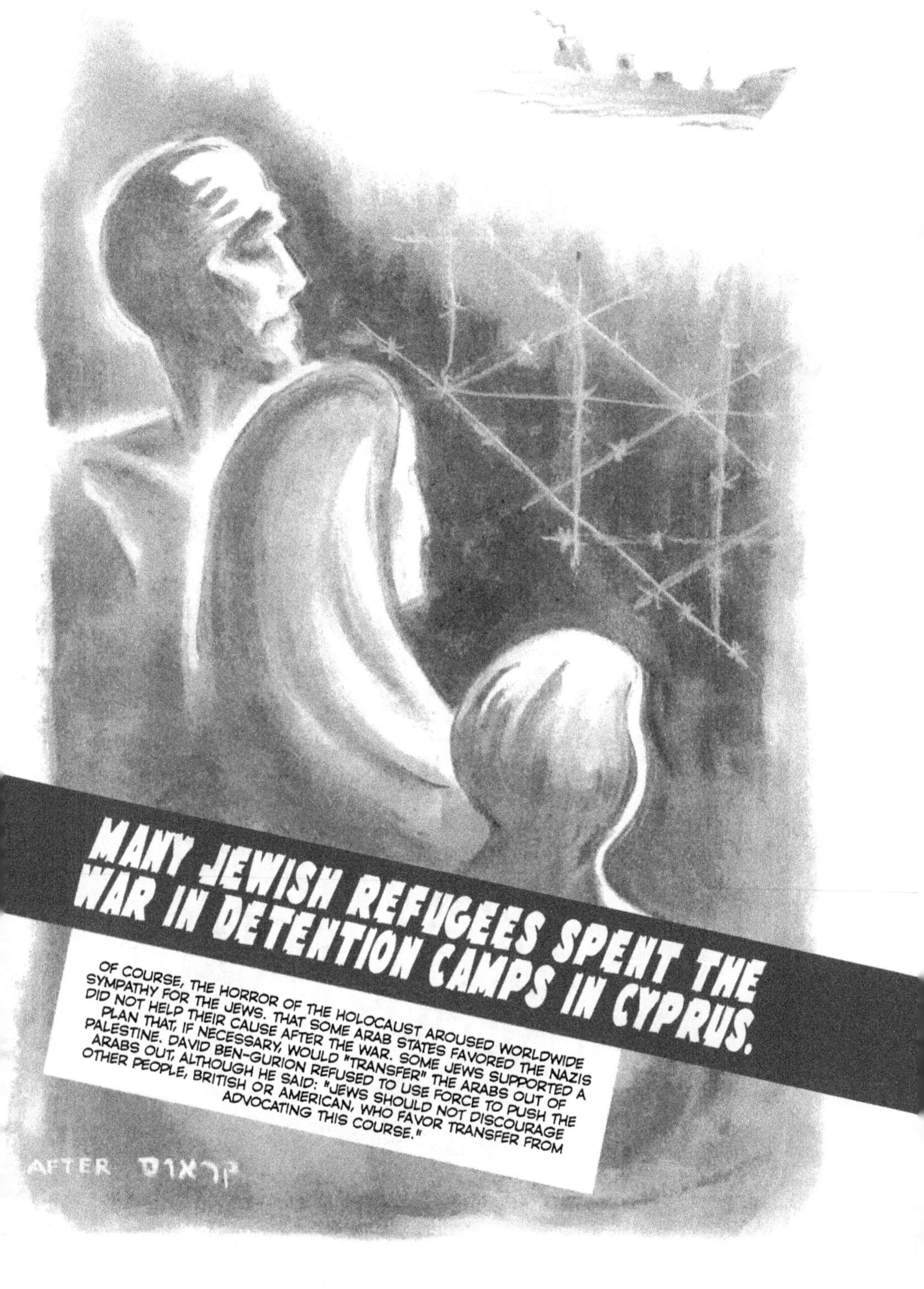
MANY JEWISH REFUGEES SPENT THE WAR IN DETENTION CAMPS IN CYPRUS.
OF COURSE, THE HORROR OF THE HOLOCAUST AROUSED WORLDWIDE SYMPATHY FOR THE JEWS. THAT SOME ARAB STATES FAVORED THE NAZIS DID NOT HELP THEIR CAUSE AFTER THE WAR. SOME JEWS SUPPORTED A PLAN THAT, IF NECESSARY, WOULD "TRANSFER" THE ARABS OUT OF PALESTINE. DAVID BEN-GURION REFUSED TO USE FORCE TO PUSH THE ARABS OUT, ALTHOUGH HE SAID: "JEWS SHOULD NOT DISCOURAGE OTHER PEOPLE, BRITISH OR AMERICAN, WHO FAVOR TRANSFER FROM ADVOCATING THIS COURSE."
AFTER קראוס

BY 1945 THE NAZIS' MASS MURDER OF JEWS WAS DISCOVERED BY THE ALLIES AND THE WORLD.

CONFIRMING WHAT MANY ALREADY KNEW.

THE IDEA OF A JEWISH SANCTUARY IN PALESTINE GAINED CREDENCE AND SUPPORTERS. THOUSANDS OF JEWS WANDERED AROUND EUROPE AFTER THE ALLIED VICTORY. THEY HAD LOST THEIR HOMES AND COULD NOT GO BACK TO THE COUNTRIES THEY CAME FROM.

A-26087

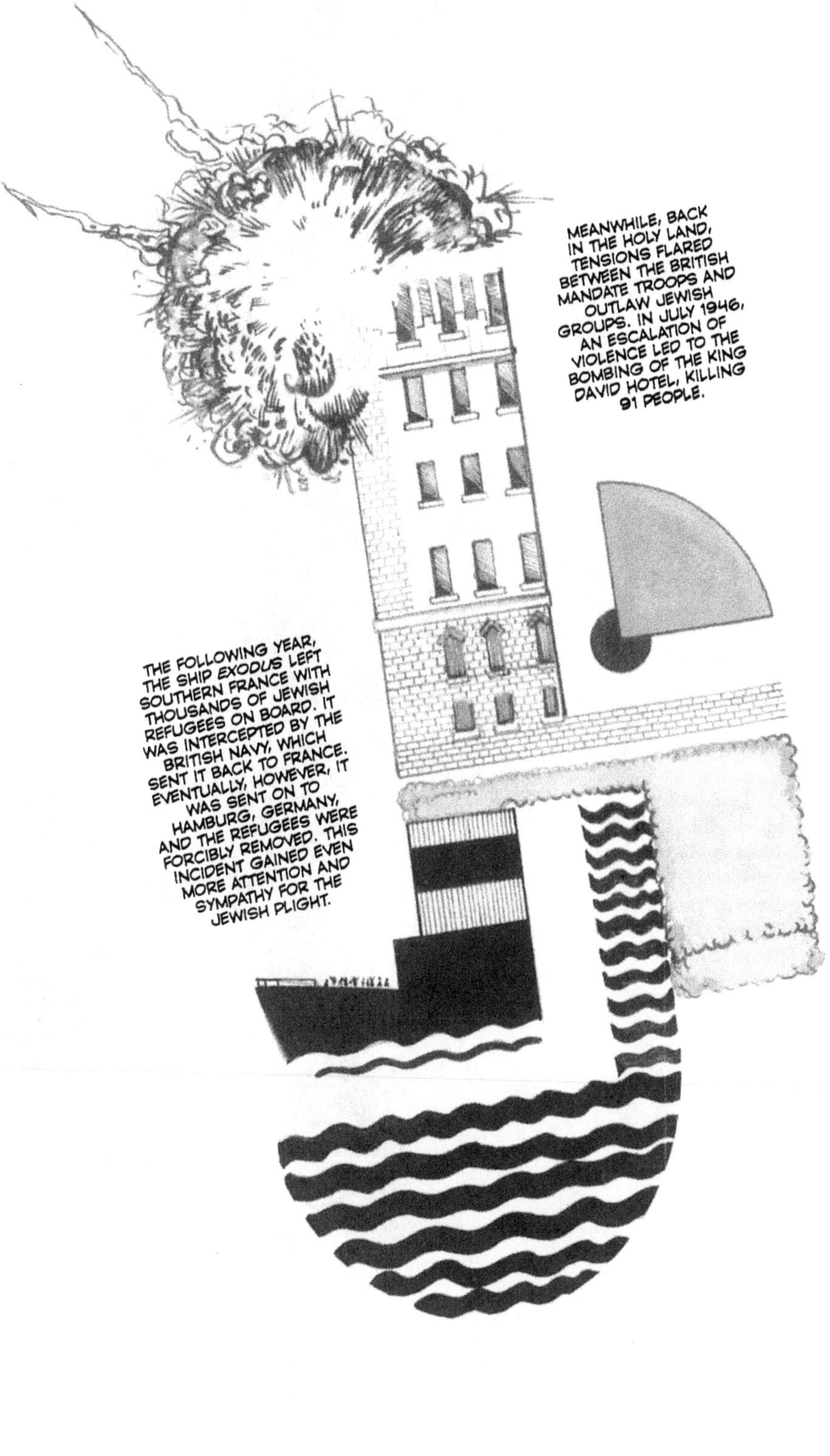
MEANWHILE, BACK IN THE HOLY LAND, TENSIONS FLARED BETWEEN THE BRITISH MANDATE TROOPS AND OUTLAW JEWISH GROUPS. IN JULY 1946, AN ESCALATION OF VIOLENCE LED TO THE BOMBING OF THE KING DAVID HOTEL, KILLING 91 PEOPLE.
THE FOLLOWING YEAR, THE SHIP *EXODUS* LEFT SOUTHERN FRANCE WITH THOUSANDS OF JEWISH REFUGEES ON BOARD. IT WAS INTERCEPTED BY THE BRITISH NAVY, WHICH SENT IT BACK TO FRANCE. EVENTUALLY, HOWEVER, IT WAS SENT ON TO HAMBURG, GERMANY, AND THE REFUGEES WERE FORCIBLY REMOVED. THIS INCIDENT GAINED EVEN MORE ATTENTION AND SYMPATHY FOR THE JEWISH PLIGHT.

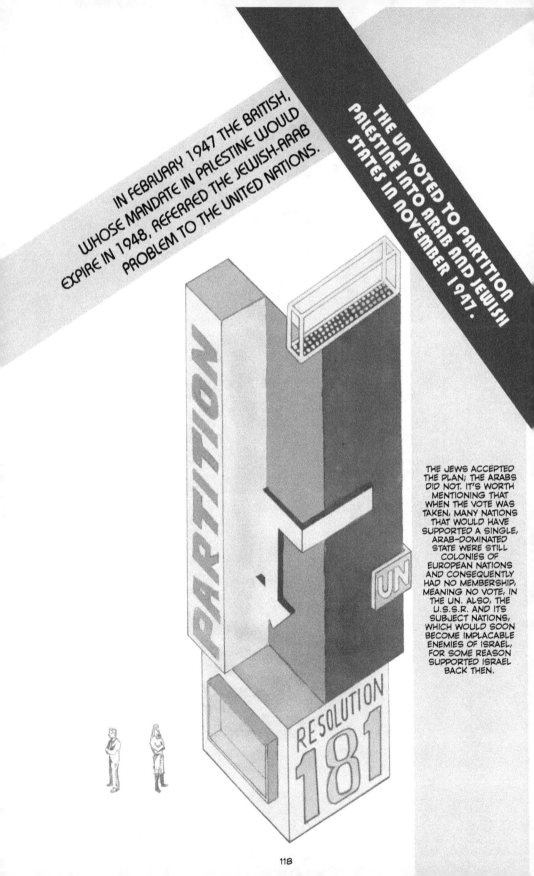

IN FEBRUARY 1947 THE BRITISH, WHOSE MANDATE IN PALESTINE WOULD EXPIRE IN 1948, REFERRED THE JEWISH-ARAB PROBLEM TO THE UNITED NATIONS.

THE UN VOTED TO PARTITION PALESTINE INTO ARAB AND JEWISH STATES IN NOVEMBER 1947.

PARTITION

UN

RESOLUTION 181

THE JEWS ACCEPTED THE PLAN; THE ARABS DID NOT. IT'S WORTH MENTIONING THAT WHEN THE VOTE WAS TAKEN, MANY NATIONS THAT WOULD HAVE SUPPORTED A SINGLE, ARAB-DOMINATED STATE WERE STILL COLONIES OF EUROPEAN NATIONS AND CONSEQUENTLY HAD NO MEMBERSHIP, MEANING NO VOTE, IN THE UN. ALSO, THE U.S.S.R. AND ITS SUBJECT NATIONS, WHICH WOULD SOON BECOME IMPLACABLE ENEMIES OF ISRAEL, FOR SOME REASON SUPPORTED ISRAEL BACK THEN.

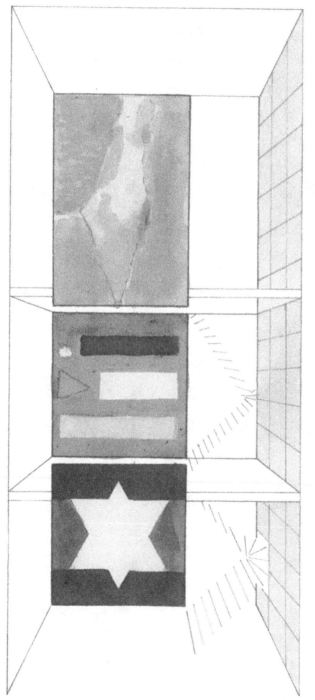

PARTLY BECAUSE OF THESE FACTORS, PALESTINE WAS DIVIDED INTO JEWISH AND ARAB TERRITORIES, THE ARAB TERRITORY BEING CONTROLLED BY JORDAN. BUT, LIKE I SAID, THE JEWS ACCEPTED THE IDEA AND THE ARABS REJECTED IT.

A JEWISH-ARAB WAR IN PALESTINE WAS INEVITABLE.

ON MAY 15, 1948, WITH BRITISH CONTROL OFFICIALLY OVER, THE JEWS DECLARED THEIR INDEPENDENCE AS THE STATE OF ISRAEL AND ALL-OUT WAR ERUPTED.

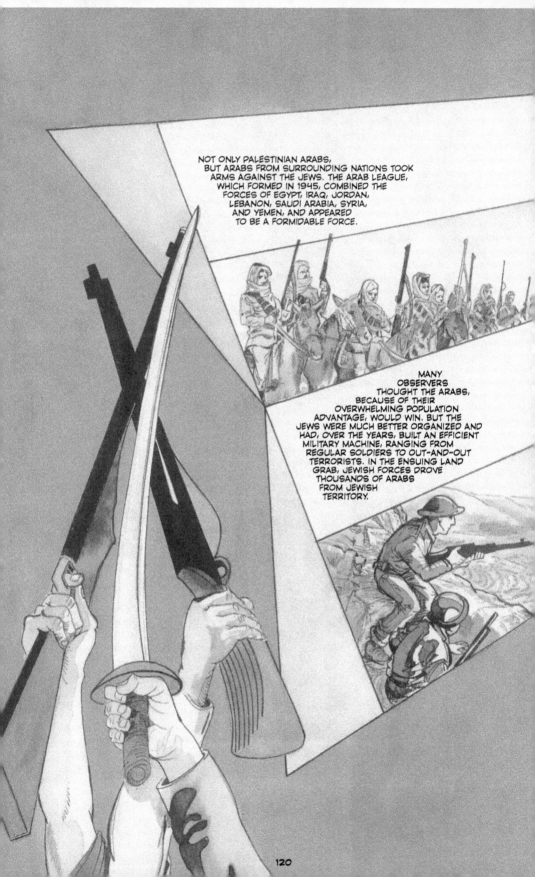

NOT ONLY PALESTINIAN ARABS, BUT ARABS FROM SURROUNDING NATIONS TOOK ARMS AGAINST THE JEWS. THE ARAB LEAGUE, WHICH FORMED IN 1945, COMBINED THE FORCES OF EGYPT, IRAQ, JORDAN, LEBANON, SAUDI ARABIA, SYRIA, AND YEMEN, AND APPEARED TO BE A FORMIDABLE FORCE.

MANY OBSERVERS THOUGHT THE ARABS, BECAUSE OF THEIR OVERWHELMING POPULATION ADVANTAGE, WOULD WIN. BUT THE JEWS WERE MUCH BETTER ORGANIZED AND HAD, OVER THE YEARS, BUILT AN EFFICIENT MILITARY MACHINE, RANGING FROM REGULAR SOLDIERS TO OUT-AND-OUT TERRORISTS. IN THE ENSUING LAND GRAB, JEWISH FORCES DROVE THOUSANDS OF ARABS FROM JEWISH TERRITORY.

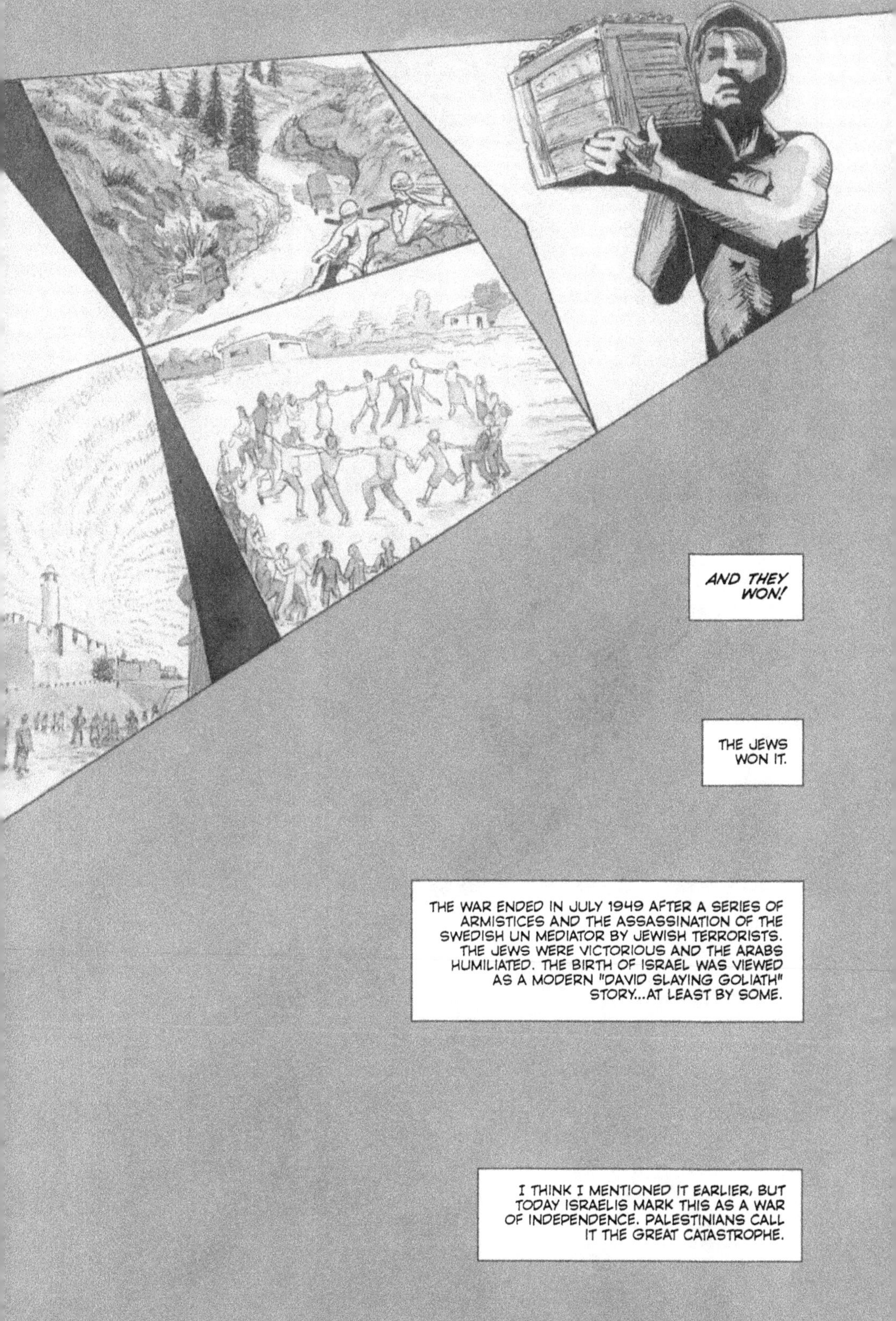
AND THEY WON!
THE JEWS WON IT.
THE WAR ENDED IN JULY 1949 AFTER A SERIES OF ARMISTICES AND THE ASSASSINATION OF THE SWEDISH UN MEDIATOR BY JEWISH TERRORISTS. THE JEWS WERE VICTORIOUS AND THE ARABS HUMILIATED. THE BIRTH OF ISRAEL WAS VIEWED AS A MODERN "DAVID SLAYING GOLIATH" STORY...AT LEAST BY SOME.
I THINK I MENTIONED IT EARLIER, BUT TODAY ISRAELIS MARK THIS AS A WAR OF INDEPENDENCE. PALESTINIANS CALL IT THE GREAT CATASTROPHE.

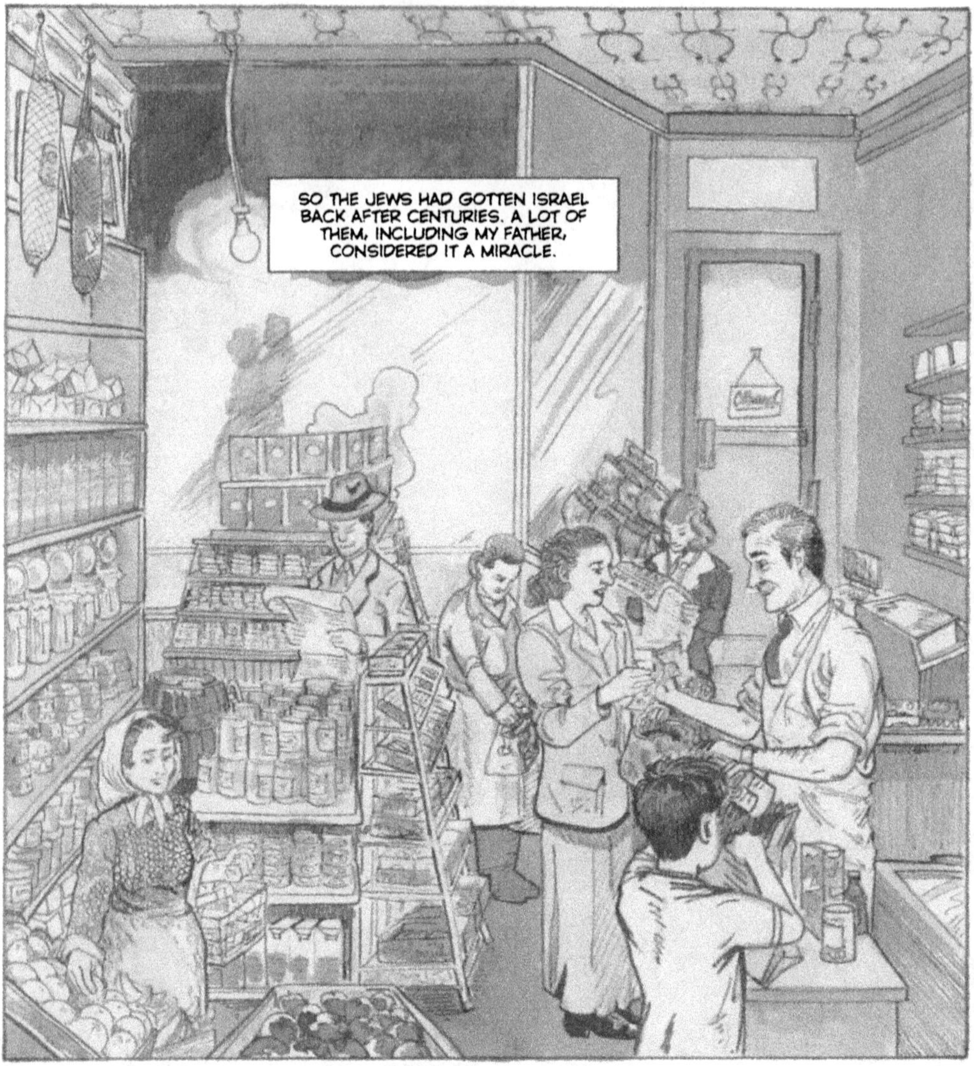
SO THE JEWS HAD GOTTEN ISRAEL BACK AFTER CENTURIES. A LOT OF THEM, INCLUDING MY FATHER, CONSIDERED IT A MIRACLE.

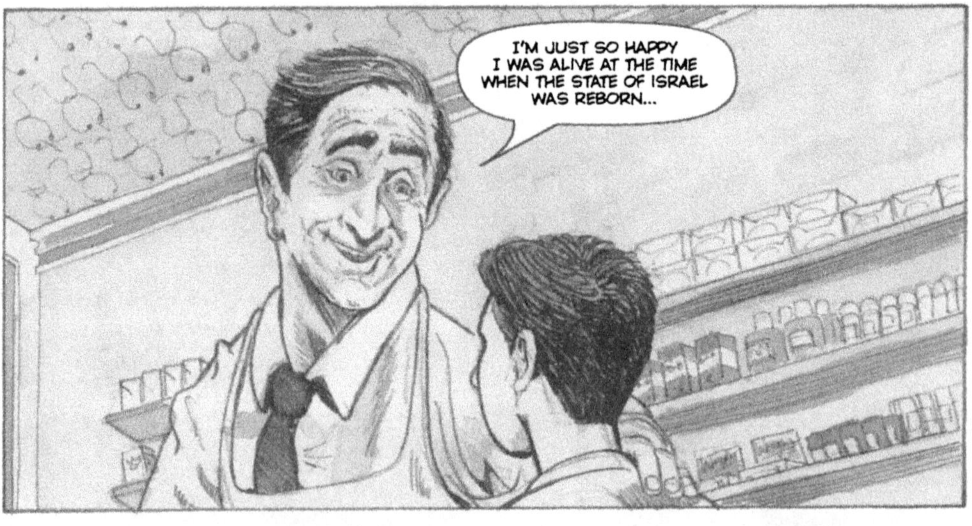
I'M JUST SO HAPPY I WAS ALIVE AT THE TIME WHEN THE STATE OF ISRAEL WAS REBORN...

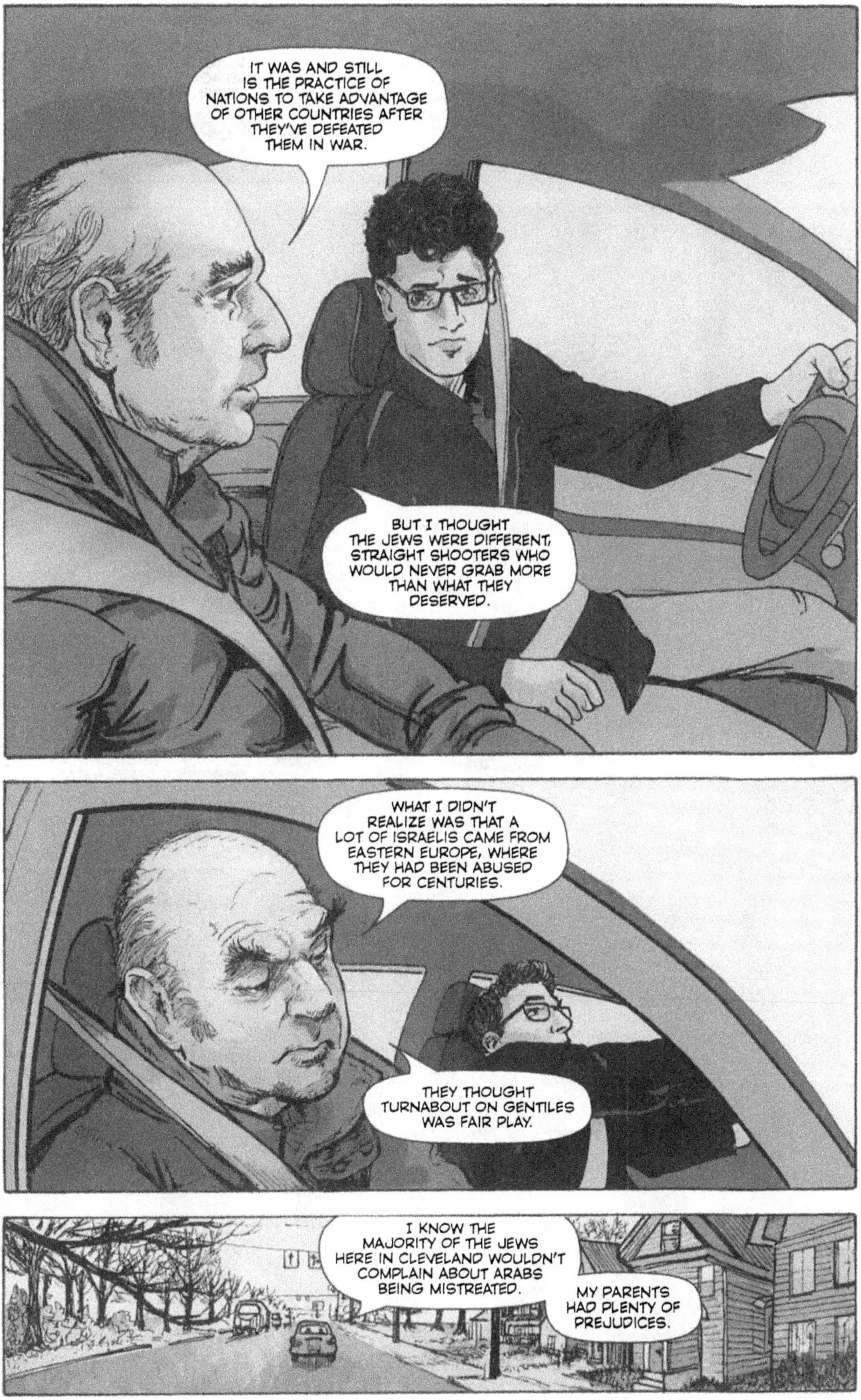
IT WAS AND STILL IS THE PRACTICE OF NATIONS TO TAKE ADVANTAGE OF OTHER COUNTRIES AFTER THEY'VE DEFEATED THEM IN WAR.
BUT I THOUGHT THE JEWS WERE DIFFERENT, STRAIGHT SHOOTERS WHO WOULD NEVER GRAB MORE THAN WHAT THEY DESERVED.
WHAT I DIDN'T REALIZE WAS THAT A LOT OF ISRAELIS CAME FROM EASTERN EUROPE, WHERE THEY HAD BEEN ABUSED FOR CENTURIES.
THEY THOUGHT TURNABOUT ON GENTILES WAS FAIR PLAY.
I KNOW THE MAJORITY OF THE JEWS HERE IN CLEVELAND WOULDN'T COMPLAIN ABOUT ARABS BEING MISTREATED.
MY PARENTS HAD PLENTY OF PREJUDICES.

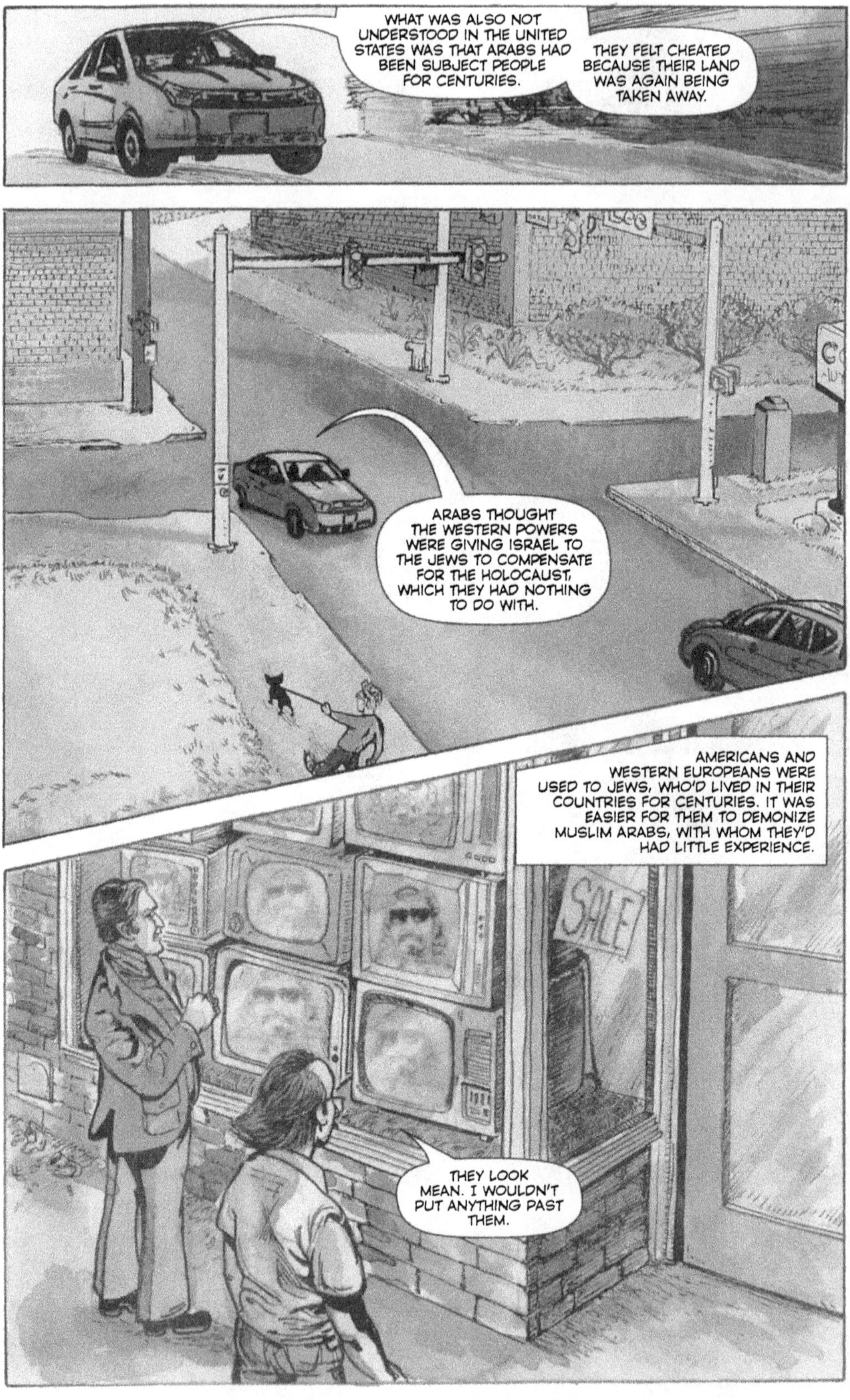
WHAT WAS ALSO NOT UNDERSTOOD IN THE UNITED STATES WAS THAT ARABS HAD BEEN SUBJECT PEOPLE FOR CENTURIES.
THEY FELT CHEATED BECAUSE THEIR LAND WAS AGAIN BEING TAKEN AWAY.
ARABS THOUGHT THE WESTERN POWERS WERE GIVING ISRAEL TO THE JEWS TO COMPENSATE FOR THE HOLOCAUST, WHICH THEY HAD NOTHING TO DO WITH.
AMERICANS AND WESTERN EUROPEANS WERE USED TO JEWS, WHO'D LIVED IN THEIR COUNTRIES FOR CENTURIES. IT WAS EASIER FOR THEM TO DEMONIZE MUSLIM ARABS, WITH WHOM THEY'D HAD LITTLE EXPERIENCE.
SALE
THEY LOOK MEAN. I WOULDN'T PUT ANYTHING PAST THEM.

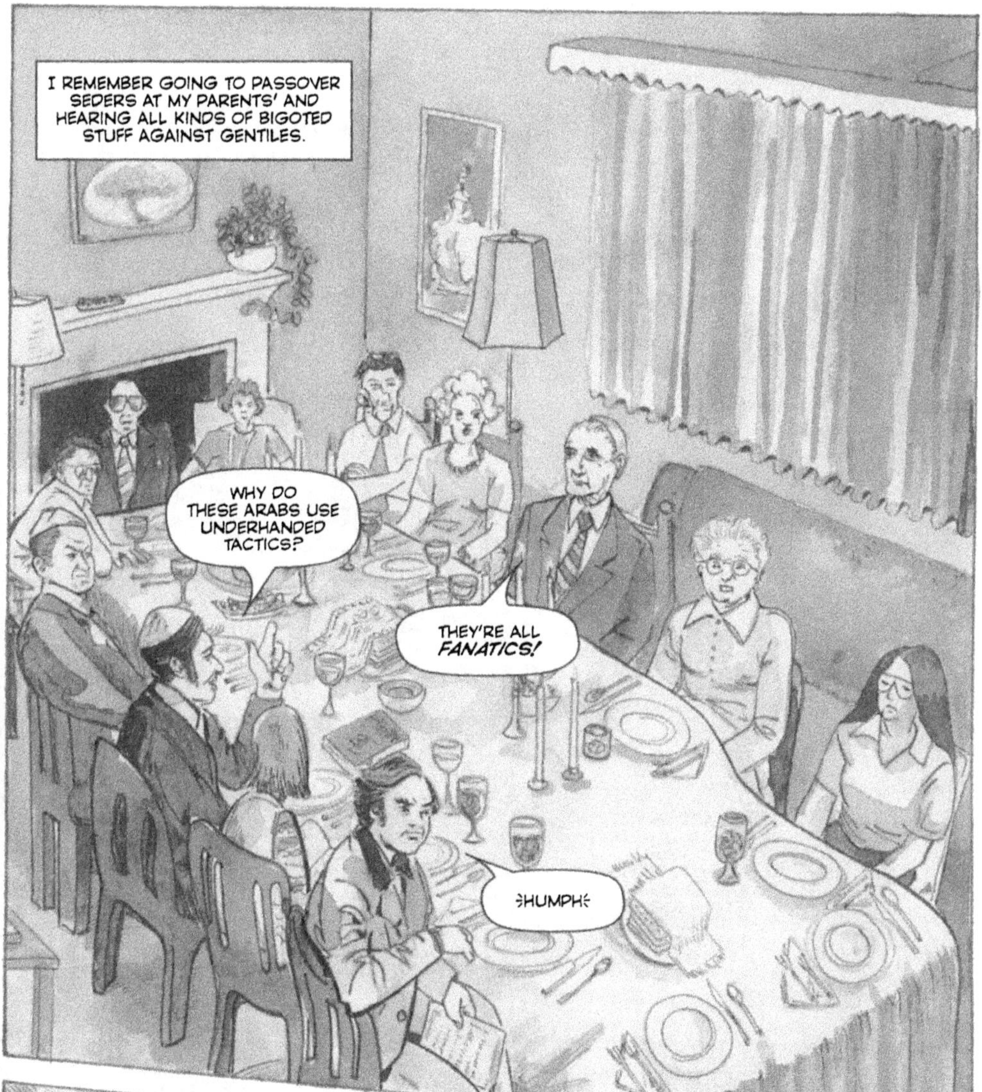
I REMEMBER GOING TO PASSOVER SEDERS AT MY PARENTS' AND HEARING ALL KINDS OF BIGOTED STUFF AGAINST GENTILES.
WHY DO THESE ARABS USE UNDERHANDED TACTICS?
THEY'RE ALL *FANATICS!*
HUMPH

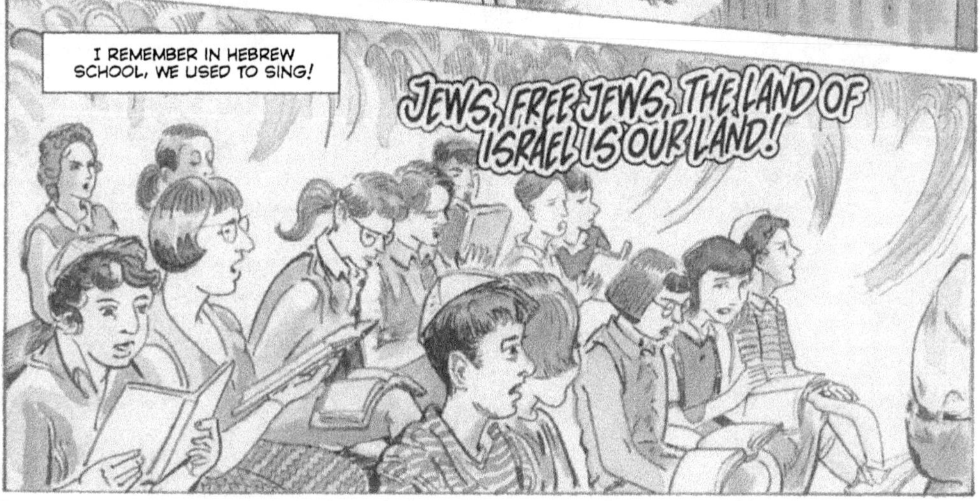
I REMEMBER IN HEBREW SCHOOL, WE USED TO SING!
JEWS, FREE JEWS, THE LAND OF ISRAEL IS OUR LAND!

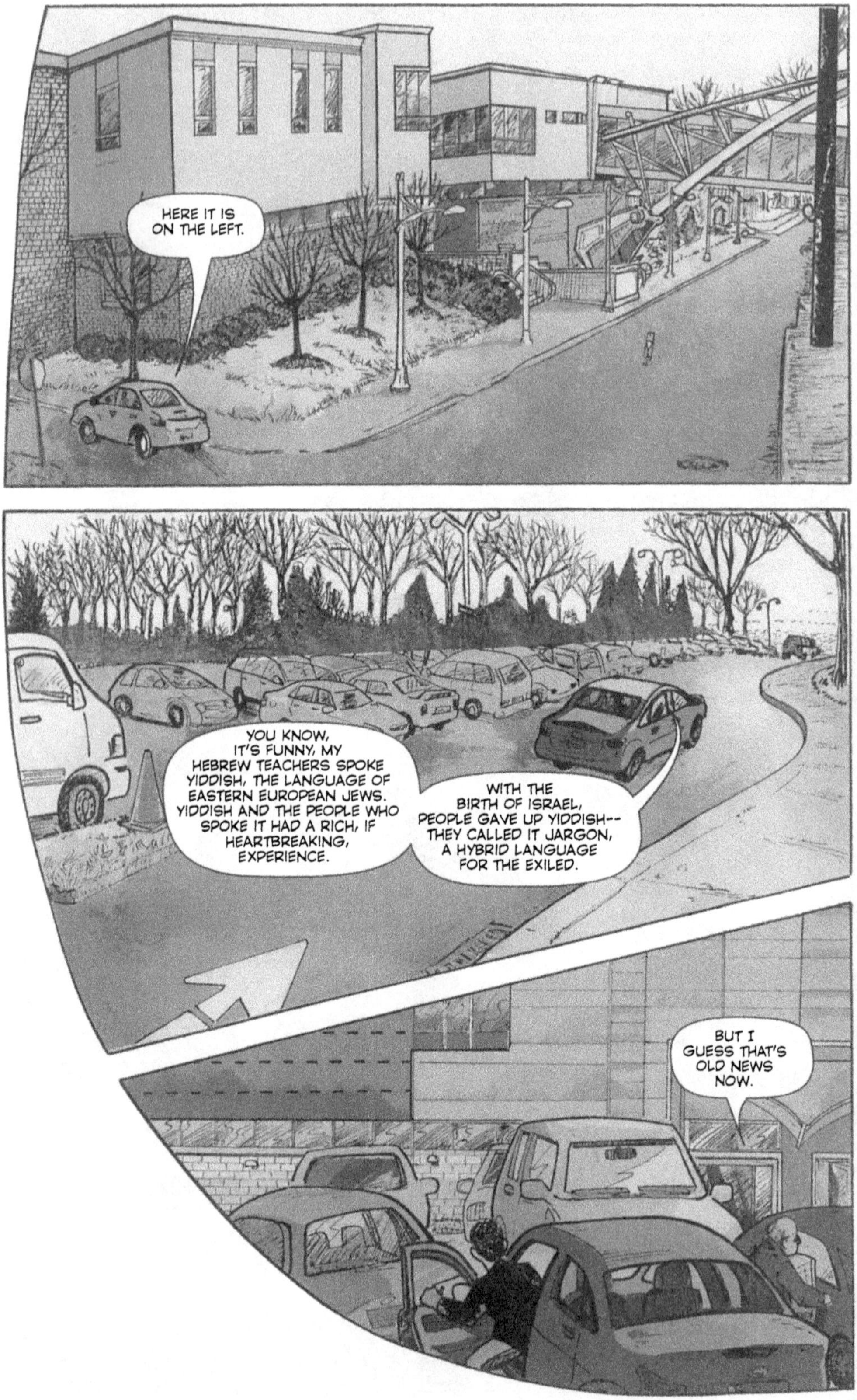
HERE IT IS ON THE LEFT.
YOU KNOW, IT'S FUNNY, MY HEBREW TEACHERS SPOKE YIDDISH, THE LANGUAGE OF EASTERN EUROPEAN JEWS. YIDDISH AND THE PEOPLE WHO SPOKE IT HAD A RICH, IF HEARTBREAKING, EXPERIENCE.
WITH THE BIRTH OF ISRAEL, PEOPLE GAVE UP YIDDISH-- THEY CALLED IT JARGON, A HYBRID LANGUAGE FOR THE EXILED.
BUT I GUESS THAT'S OLD NEWS NOW.

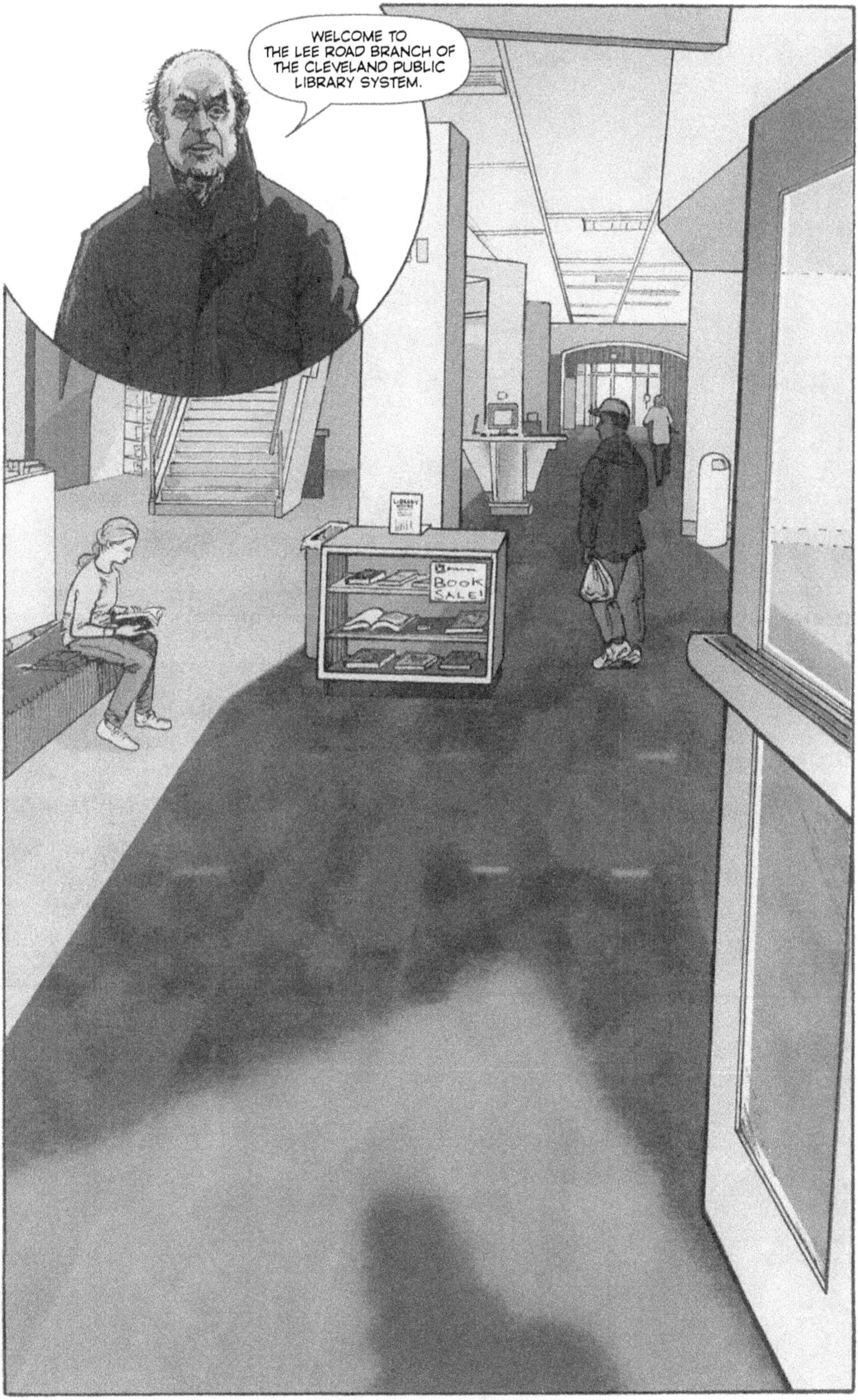
WELCOME TO THE LEE ROAD BRANCH OF THE CLEVELAND PUBLIC LIBRARY SYSTEM.
BOOK SALE!

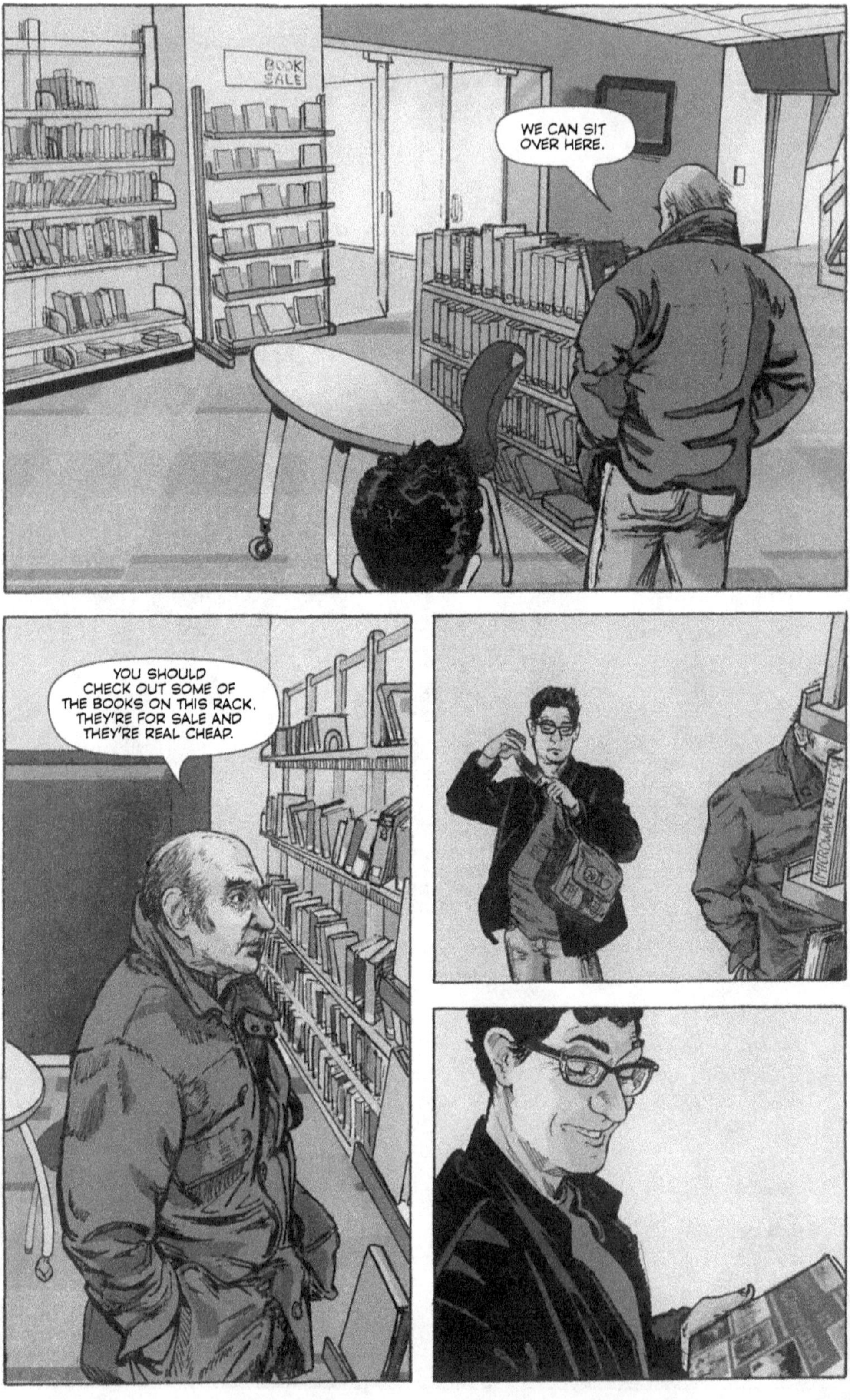
BOOK SALE
WE CAN SIT OVER HERE.
YOU SHOULD CHECK OUT SOME OF THE BOOKS ON THIS RACK. THEY'RE FOR SALE AND THEY'RE REAL CHEAP.

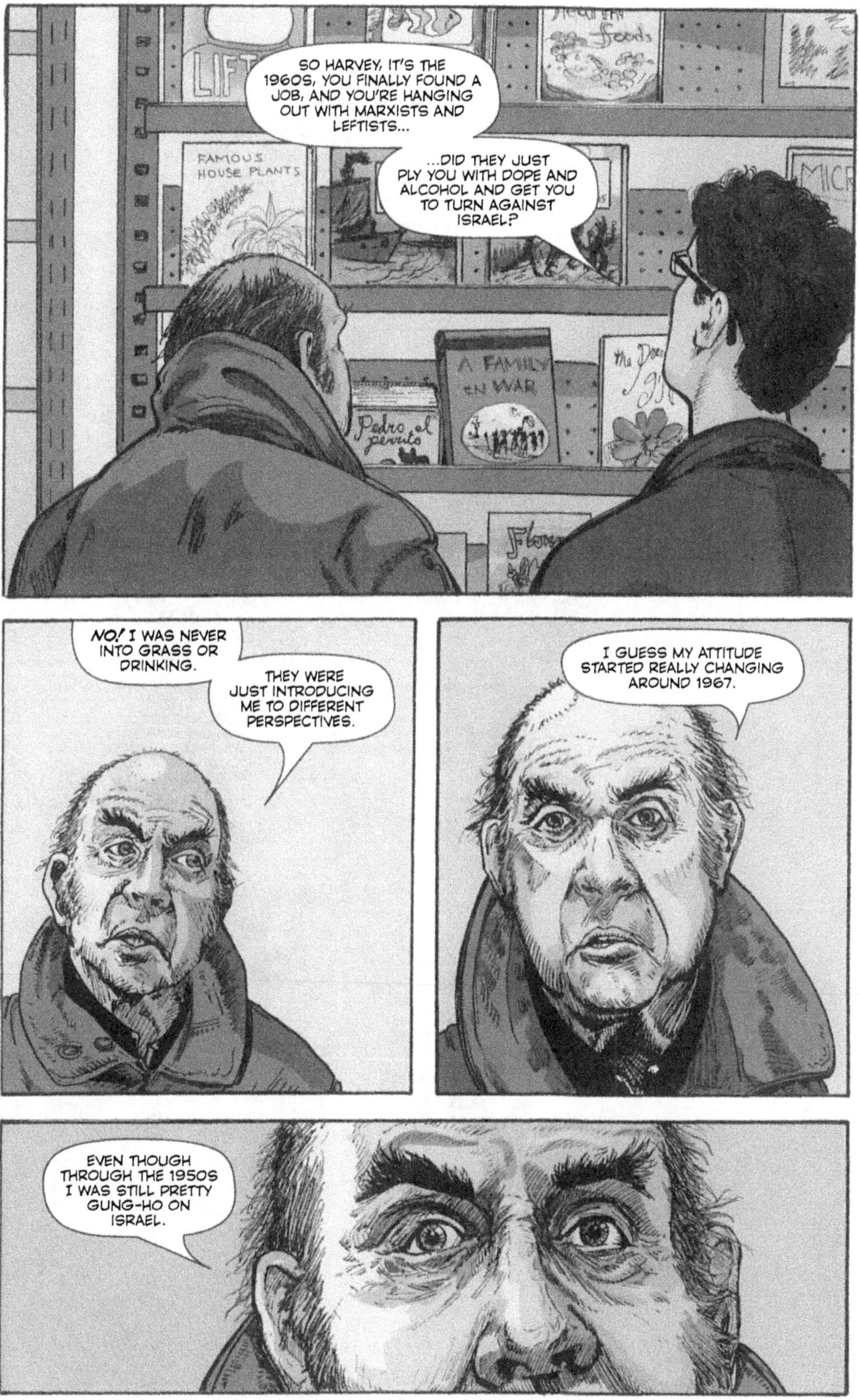
SO HARVEY, IT'S THE 1960S, YOU FINALLY FOUND A JOB, AND YOU'RE HANGING OUT WITH MARXISTS AND LEFTISTS...
...DID THEY JUST PLY YOU WITH DOPE AND ALCOHOL AND GET YOU TO TURN AGAINST ISRAEL?
FAMOUS HOUSE PLANTS
A FAMILY IN WAR
Pedro el perrito
NO! I WAS NEVER INTO GRASS OR DRINKING.
THEY WERE JUST INTRODUCING ME TO DIFFERENT PERSPECTIVES.
I GUESS MY ATTITUDE STARTED REALLY CHANGING AROUND 1967.
EVEN THOUGH THROUGH THE 1950S I WAS STILL PRETTY GUNG-HO ON ISRAEL.

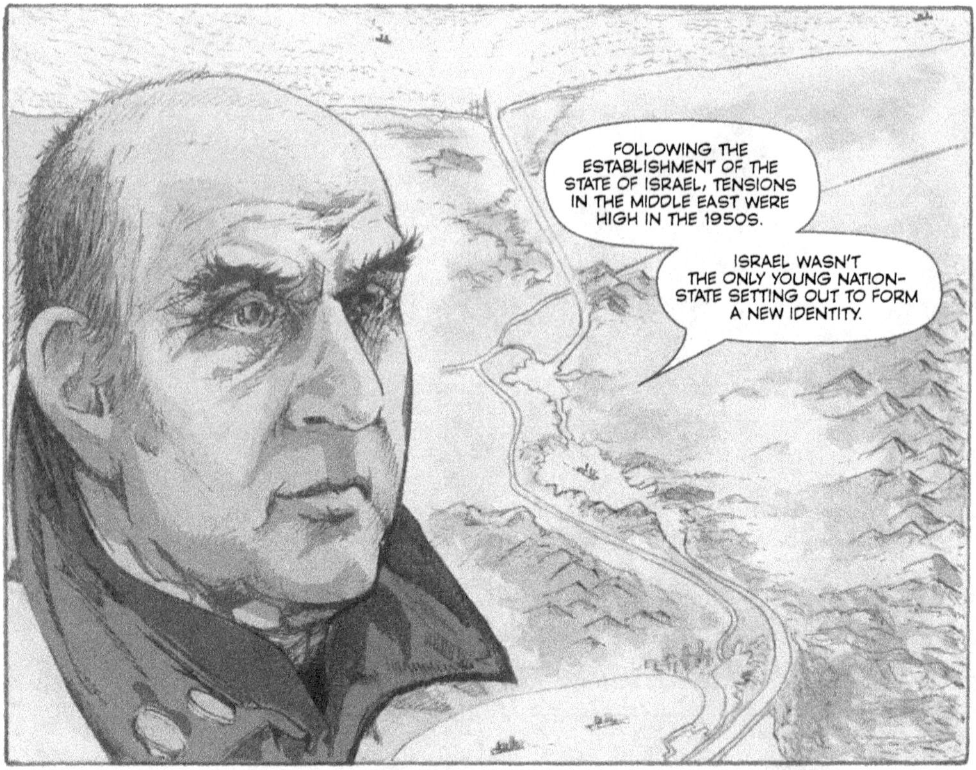
FOLLOWING THE ESTABLISHMENT OF THE STATE OF ISRAEL, TENSIONS IN THE MIDDLE EAST WERE HIGH IN THE 1950S.
ISRAEL WASN'T THE ONLY YOUNG NATION-STATE SETTING OUT TO FORM A NEW IDENTITY.

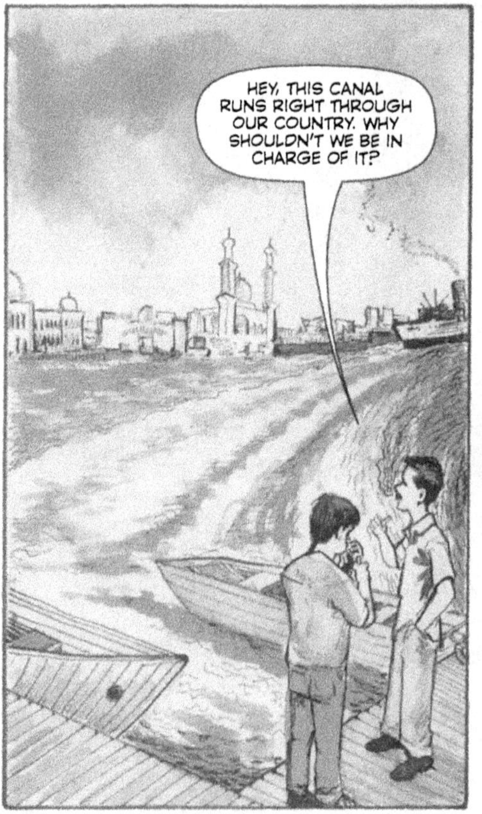
HEY, THIS CANAL RUNS RIGHT THROUGH OUR COUNTRY. WHY SHOULDN'T WE BE IN CHARGE OF IT?

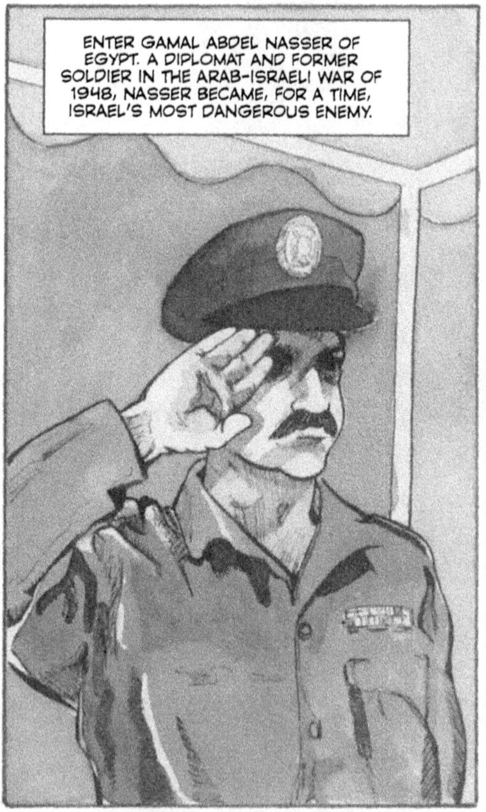
ENTER GAMAL ABDEL NASSER OF EGYPT. A DIPLOMAT AND FORMER SOLDIER IN THE ARAB-ISRAELI WAR OF 1948, NASSER BECAME, FOR A TIME, ISRAEL'S MOST DANGEROUS ENEMY.

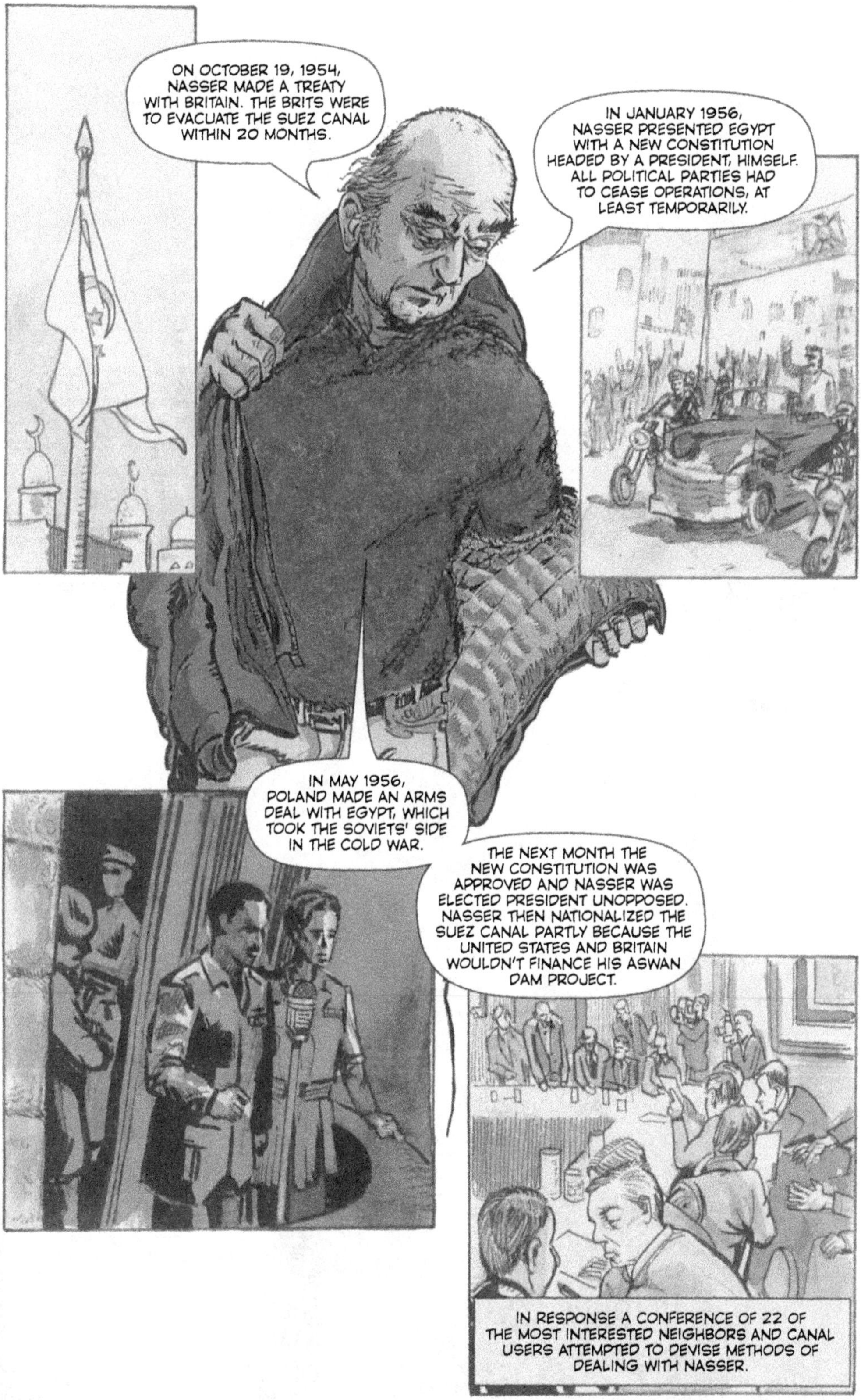
ON OCTOBER 19, 1954, NASSER MADE A TREATY WITH BRITAIN. THE BRITS WERE TO EVACUATE THE SUEZ CANAL WITHIN 20 MONTHS.
IN JANUARY 1956, NASSER PRESENTED EGYPT WITH A NEW CONSTITUTION HEADED BY A PRESIDENT, HIMSELF. ALL POLITICAL PARTIES HAD TO CEASE OPERATIONS, AT LEAST TEMPORARILY.
IN MAY 1956, POLAND MADE AN ARMS DEAL WITH EGYPT, WHICH TOOK THE SOVIETS' SIDE IN THE COLD WAR.
THE NEXT MONTH THE NEW CONSTITUTION WAS APPROVED AND NASSER WAS ELECTED PRESIDENT UNOPPOSED. NASSER THEN NATIONALIZED THE SUEZ CANAL PARTLY BECAUSE THE UNITED STATES AND BRITAIN WOULDN'T FINANCE HIS ASWAN DAM PROJECT.
IN RESPONSE A CONFERENCE OF 22 OF THE MOST INTERESTED NEIGHBORS AND CANAL USERS ATTEMPTED TO DEVISE METHODS OF DEALING WITH NASSER.

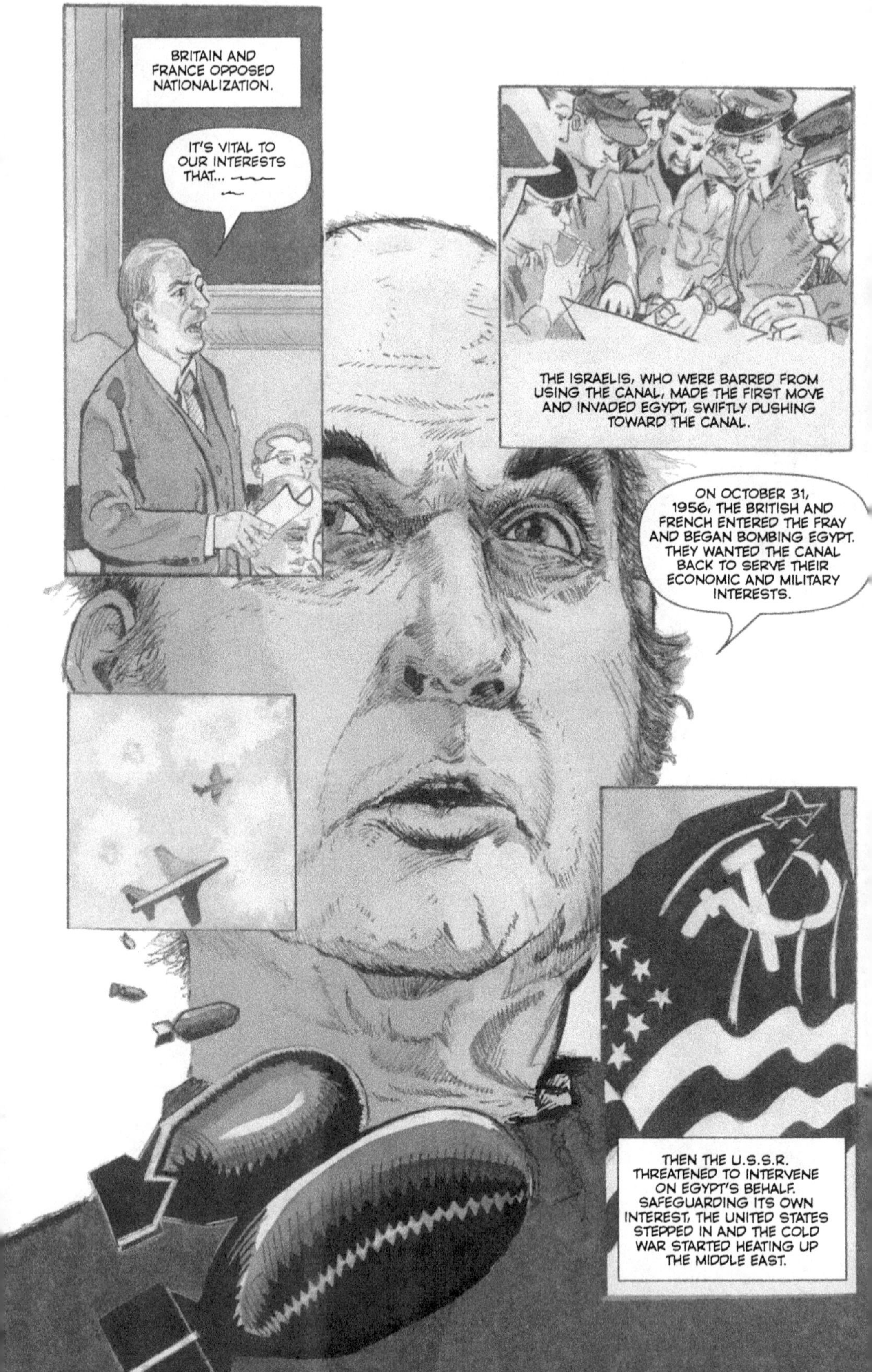
BRITAIN AND FRANCE OPPOSED NATIONALIZATION.
IT'S VITAL TO OUR INTERESTS THAT...
THE ISRAELIS, WHO WERE BARRED FROM USING THE CANAL, MADE THE FIRST MOVE AND INVADED EGYPT, SWIFTLY PUSHING TOWARD THE CANAL.
ON OCTOBER 31, 1956, THE BRITISH AND FRENCH ENTERED THE FRAY AND BEGAN BOMBING EGYPT. THEY WANTED THE CANAL BACK TO SERVE THEIR ECONOMIC AND MILITARY INTERESTS.
THEN THE U.S.S.R. THREATENED TO INTERVENE ON EGYPT'S BEHALF. SAFEGUARDING ITS OWN INTEREST, THE UNITED STATES STEPPED IN AND THE COLD WAR STARTED HEATING UP THE MIDDLE EAST.

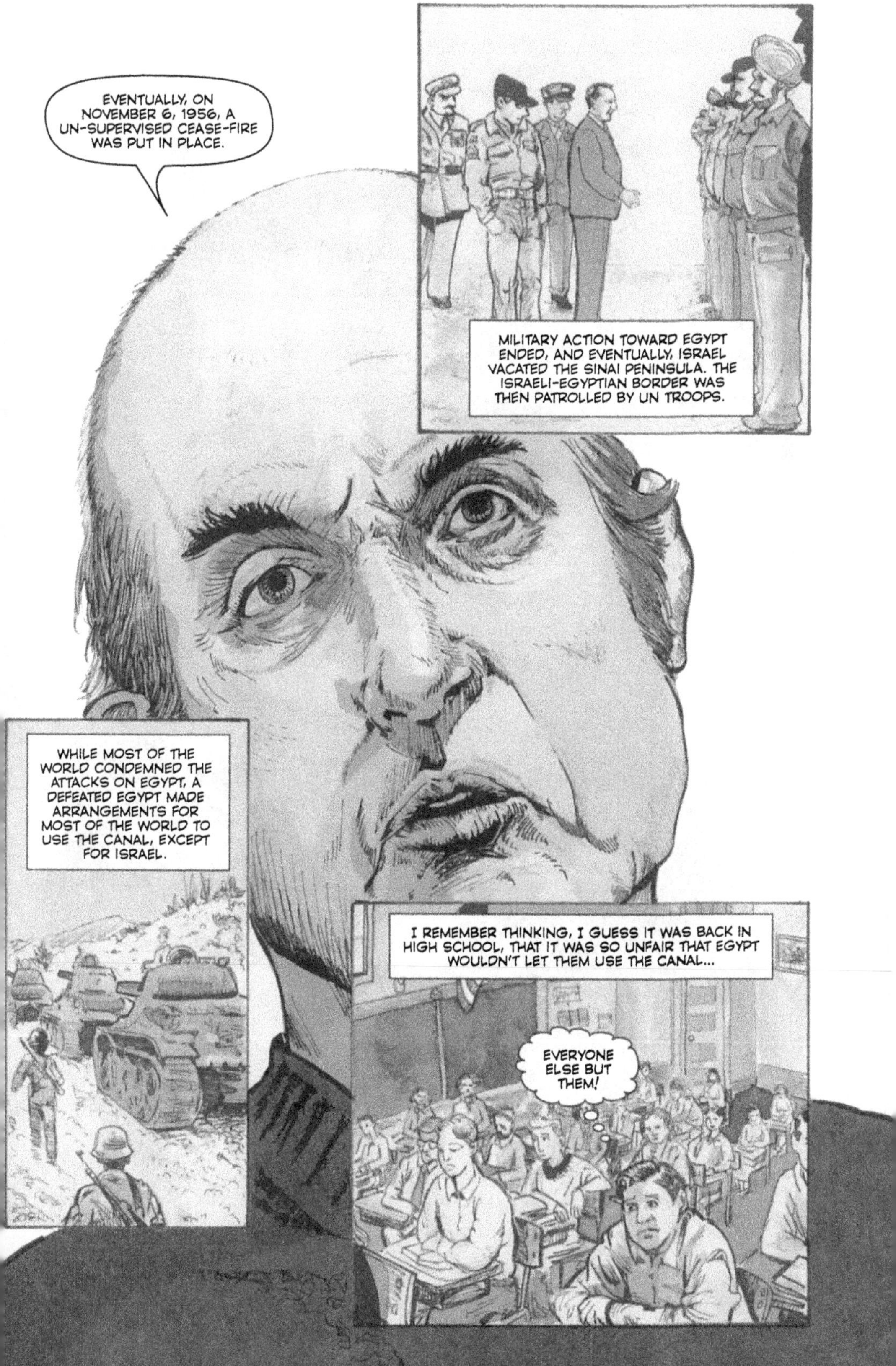
EVENTUALLY, ON NOVEMBER 6, 1956, A UN-SUPERVISED CEASE-FIRE WAS PUT IN PLACE.
MILITARY ACTION TOWARD EGYPT ENDED, AND EVENTUALLY, ISRAEL VACATED THE SINAI PENINSULA. THE ISRAELI-EGYPTIAN BORDER WAS THEN PATROLLED BY UN TROOPS.
WHILE MOST OF THE WORLD CONDEMNED THE ATTACKS ON EGYPT, A DEFEATED EGYPT MADE ARRANGEMENTS FOR MOST OF THE WORLD TO USE THE CANAL, EXCEPT FOR ISRAEL.
I REMEMBER THINKING, I GUESS IT WAS BACK IN HIGH SCHOOL, THAT IT WAS SO UNFAIR THAT EGYPT WOULDN'T LET THEM USE THE CANAL...
EVERYONE ELSE BUT THEM!

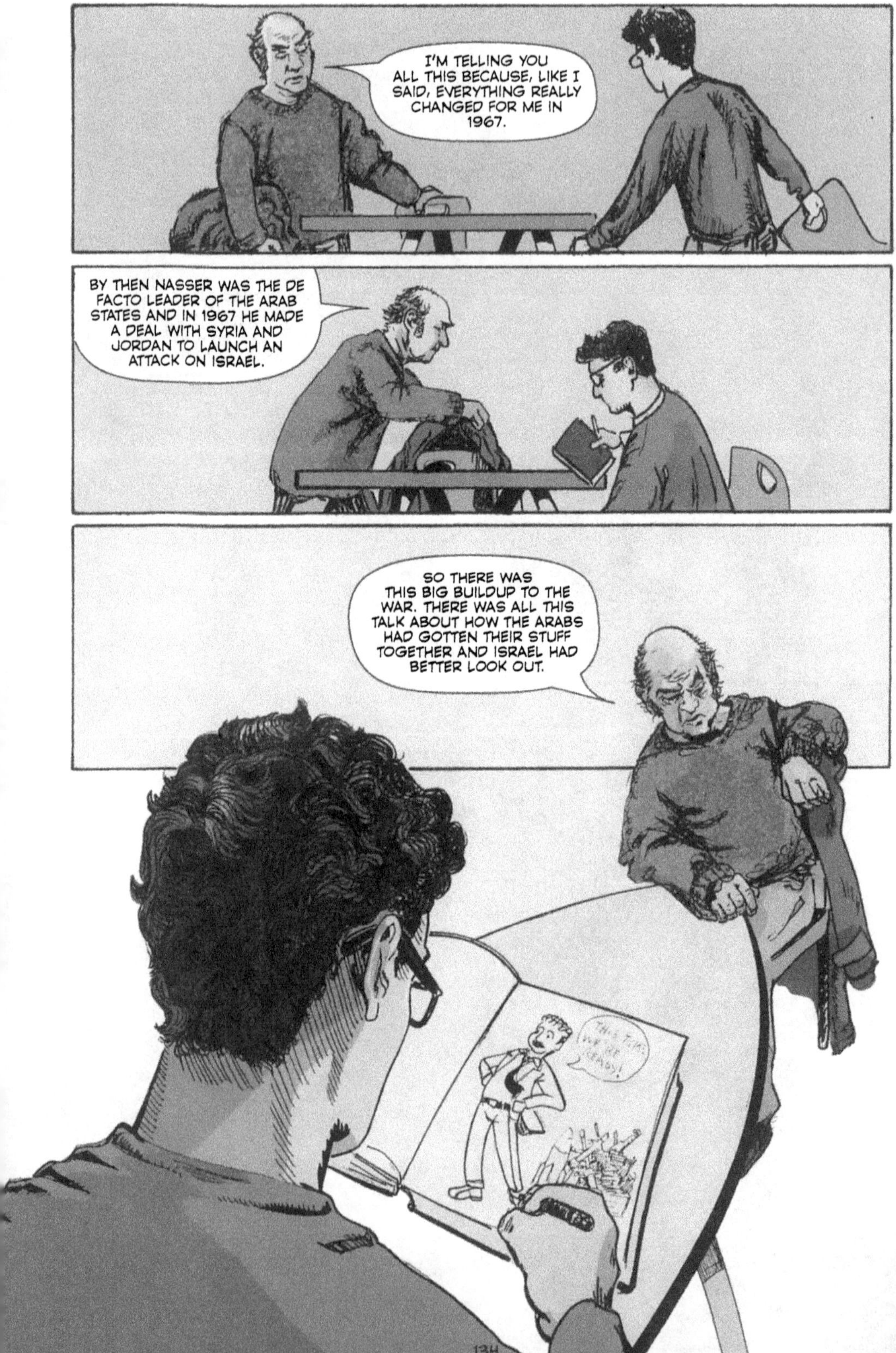
I'M TELLING YOU ALL THIS BECAUSE, LIKE I SAID, EVERYTHING REALLY CHANGED FOR ME IN 1967.
BY THEN NASSER WAS THE DE FACTO LEADER OF THE ARAB STATES AND IN 1967 HE MADE A DEAL WITH SYRIA AND JORDAN TO LAUNCH AN ATTACK ON ISRAEL.
SO THERE WAS THIS BIG BUILDUP TO THE WAR. THERE WAS ALL THIS TALK ABOUT HOW THE ARABS HAD GOTTEN THEIR STUFF TOGETHER AND ISRAEL HAD BETTER LOOK OUT.
THIS TIME WE'RE READY!

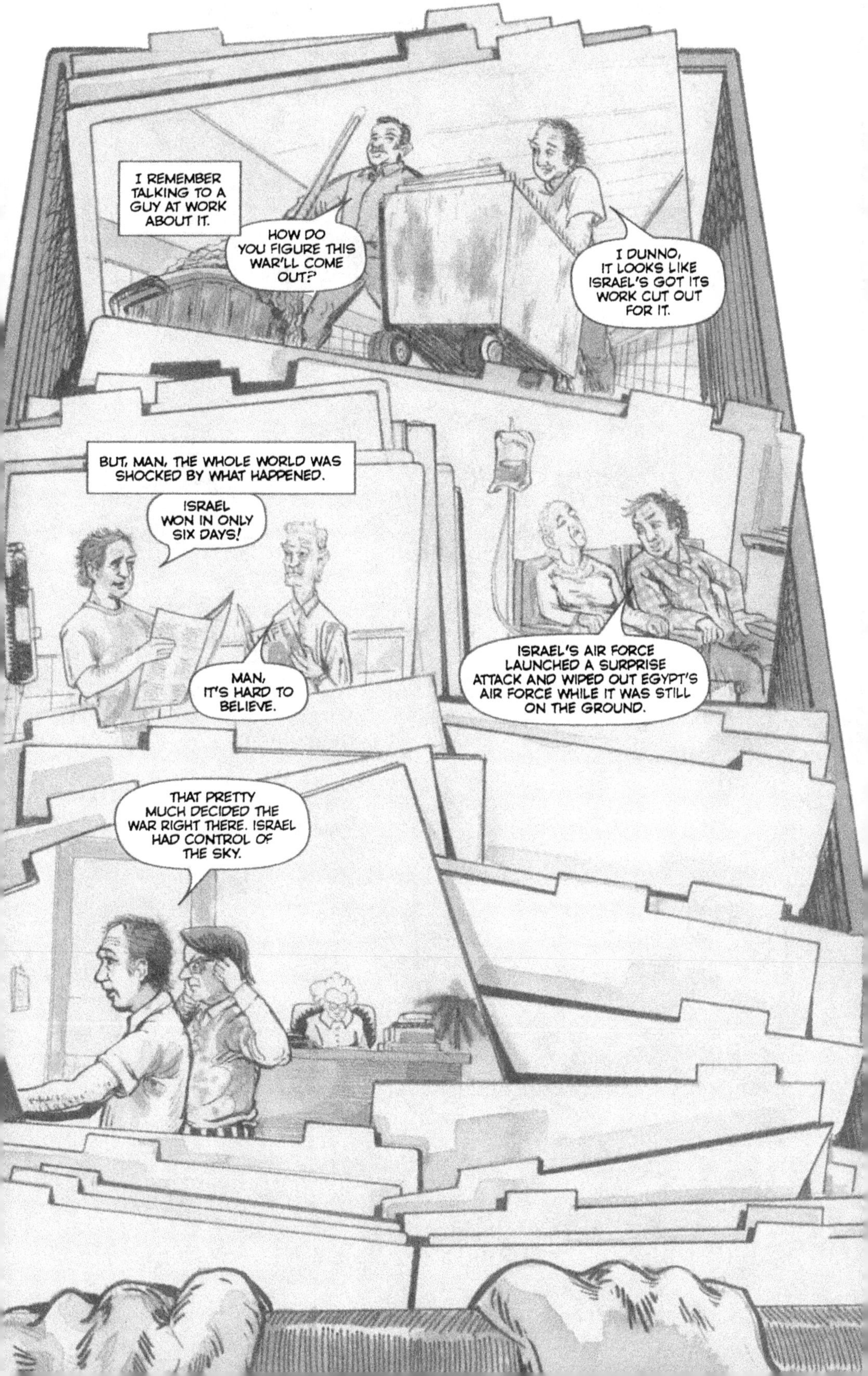
I REMEMBER TALKING TO A GUY AT WORK ABOUT IT.
HOW DO YOU FIGURE THIS WAR'LL COME OUT?
I DUNNO, IT LOOKS LIKE ISRAEL'S GOT ITS WORK CUT OUT FOR IT.
BUT, MAN, THE WHOLE WORLD WAS SHOCKED BY WHAT HAPPENED.
ISRAEL WON IN ONLY SIX DAYS!
MAN, IT'S HARD TO BELIEVE.
ISRAEL'S AIR FORCE LAUNCHED A SURPRISE ATTACK AND WIPED OUT EGYPT'S AIR FORCE WHILE IT WAS STILL ON THE GROUND.
THAT PRETTY MUCH DECIDED THE WAR RIGHT THERE. ISRAEL HAD CONTROL OF THE SKY.

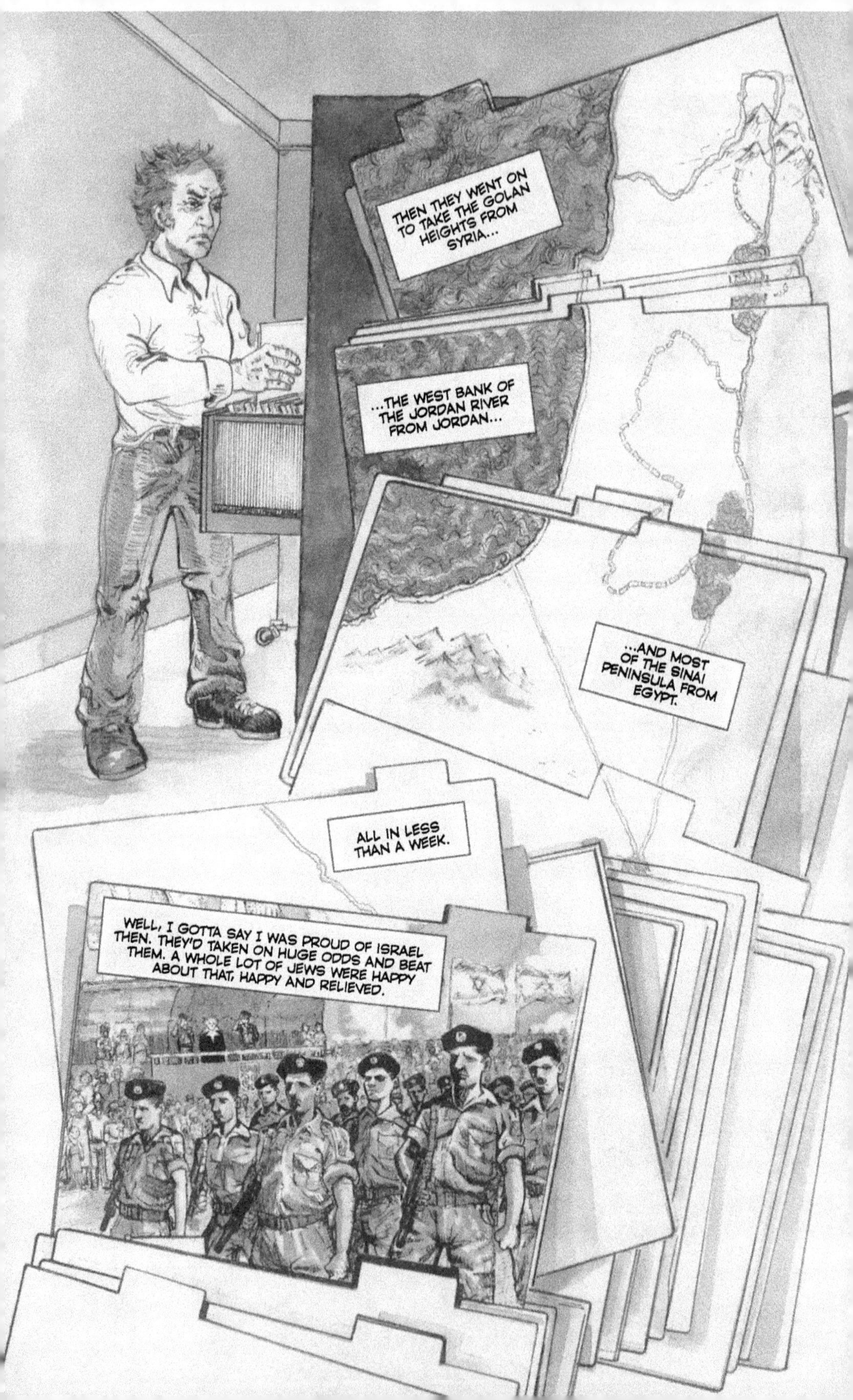
THEN THEY WENT ON TO TAKE THE GOLAN HEIGHTS FROM SYRIA...
...THE WEST BANK OF THE JORDAN RIVER FROM JORDAN...
...AND MOST OF THE SINAI PENINSULA FROM EGYPT.
ALL IN LESS THAN A WEEK.
WELL, I GOTTA SAY I WAS PROUD OF ISRAEL THEN. THEY'D TAKEN ON HUGE ODDS AND BEAT THEM. A WHOLE LOT OF JEWS WERE HAPPY ABOUT THAT, HAPPY AND RELIEVED.

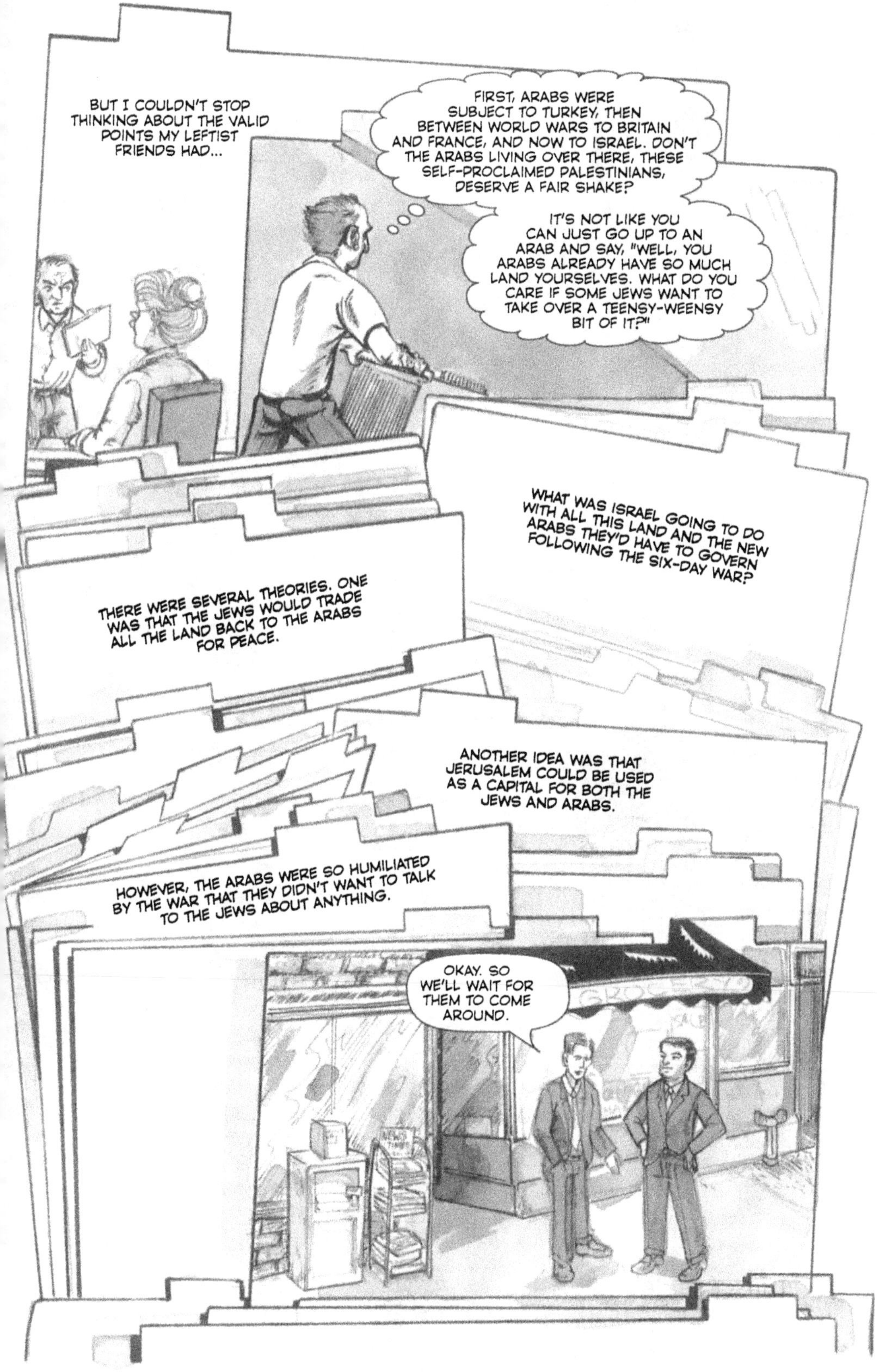
BUT I COULDN'T STOP THINKING ABOUT THE VALID POINTS MY LEFTIST FRIENDS HAD...
FIRST, ARABS WERE SUBJECT TO TURKEY, THEN BETWEEN WORLD WARS TO BRITAIN AND FRANCE, AND NOW TO ISRAEL. DON'T THE ARABS LIVING OVER THERE, THESE SELF-PROCLAIMED PALESTINIANS, DESERVE A FAIR SHAKE?
IT'S NOT LIKE YOU CAN JUST GO UP TO AN ARAB AND SAY, "WELL, YOU ARABS ALREADY HAVE SO MUCH LAND YOURSELVES. WHAT DO YOU CARE IF SOME JEWS WANT TO TAKE OVER A TEENSY-WEENSY BIT OF IT?"
WHAT WAS ISRAEL GOING TO DO WITH ALL THIS LAND AND THE NEW ARABS THEY'D HAVE TO GOVERN FOLLOWING THE SIX-DAY WAR?
THERE WERE SEVERAL THEORIES. ONE WAS THAT THE JEWS WOULD TRADE ALL THE LAND BACK TO THE ARABS FOR PEACE.
ANOTHER IDEA WAS THAT JERUSALEM COULD BE USED AS A CAPITAL FOR BOTH THE JEWS AND ARABS.
HOWEVER, THE ARABS WERE SO HUMILIATED BY THE WAR THAT THEY DIDN'T WANT TO TALK TO THE JEWS ABOUT ANYTHING.
OKAY. SO WE'LL WAIT FOR THEM TO COME AROUND.
GROCERY

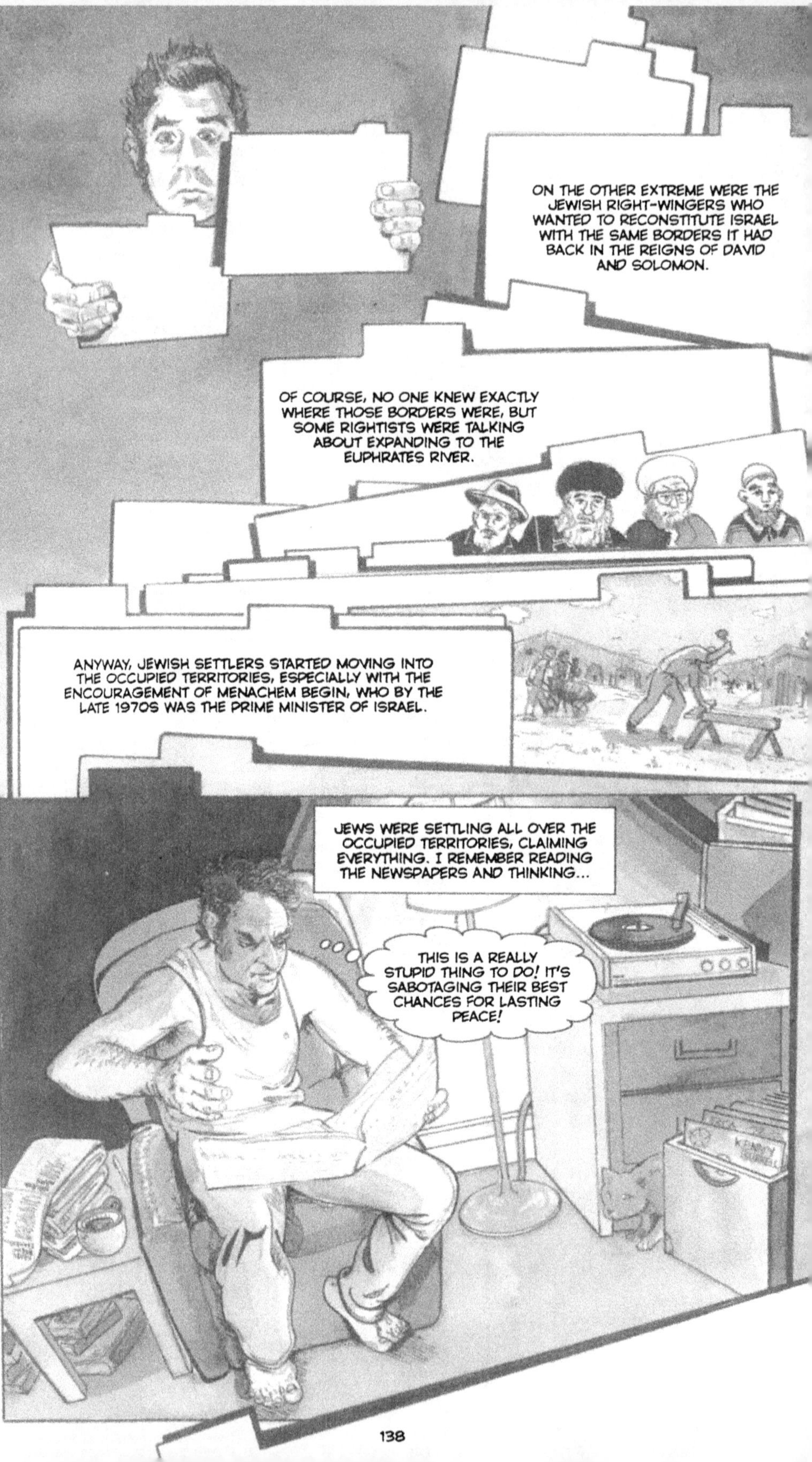
ON THE OTHER EXTREME WERE THE JEWISH RIGHT-WINGERS WHO WANTED TO RECONSTITUTE ISRAEL WITH THE SAME BORDERS IT HAD BACK IN THE REIGNS OF DAVID AND SOLOMON.
OF COURSE, NO ONE KNEW EXACTLY WHERE THOSE BORDERS WERE, BUT SOME RIGHTISTS WERE TALKING ABOUT EXPANDING TO THE EUPHRATES RIVER.
ANYWAY, JEWISH SETTLERS STARTED MOVING INTO THE OCCUPIED TERRITORIES, ESPECIALLY WITH THE ENCOURAGEMENT OF MENACHEM BEGIN, WHO BY THE LATE 1970S WAS THE PRIME MINISTER OF ISRAEL.
JEWS WERE SETTLING ALL OVER THE OCCUPIED TERRITORIES, CLAIMING EVERYTHING. I REMEMBER READING THE NEWSPAPERS AND THINKING...
THIS IS A REALLY STUPID THING TO DO! IT'S SABOTAGING THEIR BEST CHANCES FOR LASTING PEACE!

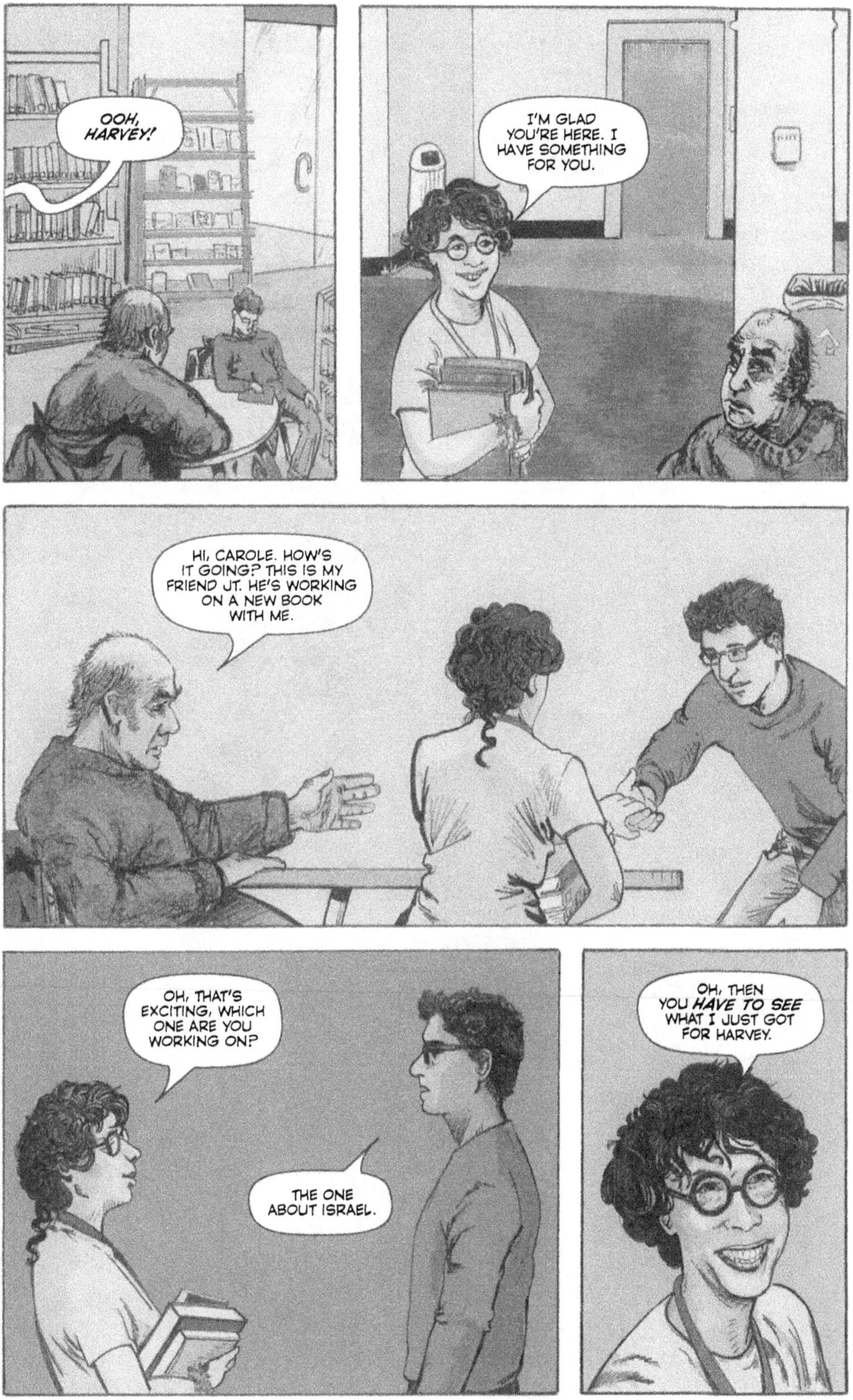
OOH, *HARVEY!*
I'M GLAD YOU'RE HERE. I HAVE SOMETHING FOR YOU.
HI, CAROLE. HOW'S IT GOING? THIS IS MY FRIEND JT. HE'S WORKING ON A NEW BOOK WITH ME.
OH, THAT'S EXCITING, WHICH ONE ARE YOU WORKING ON?
THE ONE ABOUT ISRAEL.
OH, THEN YOU *HAVE TO SEE* WHAT I JUST GOT FOR HARVEY.

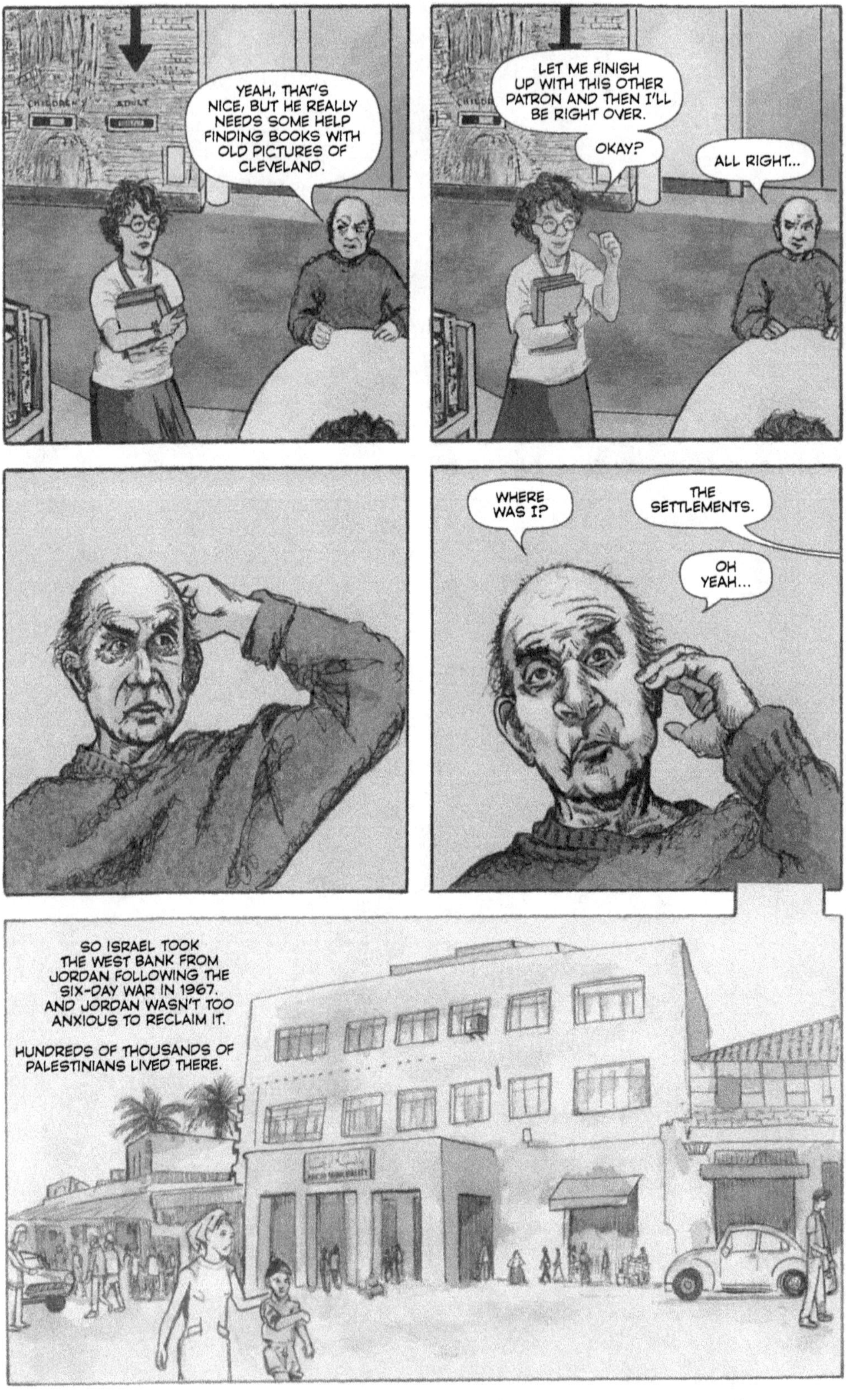
YEAH, THAT'S NICE, BUT HE REALLY NEEDS SOME HELP FINDING BOOKS WITH OLD PICTURES OF CLEVELAND.
LET ME FINISH UP WITH THIS OTHER PATRON AND THEN I'LL BE RIGHT OVER.
OKAY?
ALL RIGHT...
WHERE WAS I?
THE SETTLEMENTS.
OH YEAH...
SO ISRAEL TOOK THE WEST BANK FROM JORDAN FOLLOWING THE SIX-DAY WAR IN 1967. AND JORDAN WASN'T TOO ANXIOUS TO RECLAIM IT.
HUNDREDS OF THOUSANDS OF PALESTINIANS LIVED THERE.

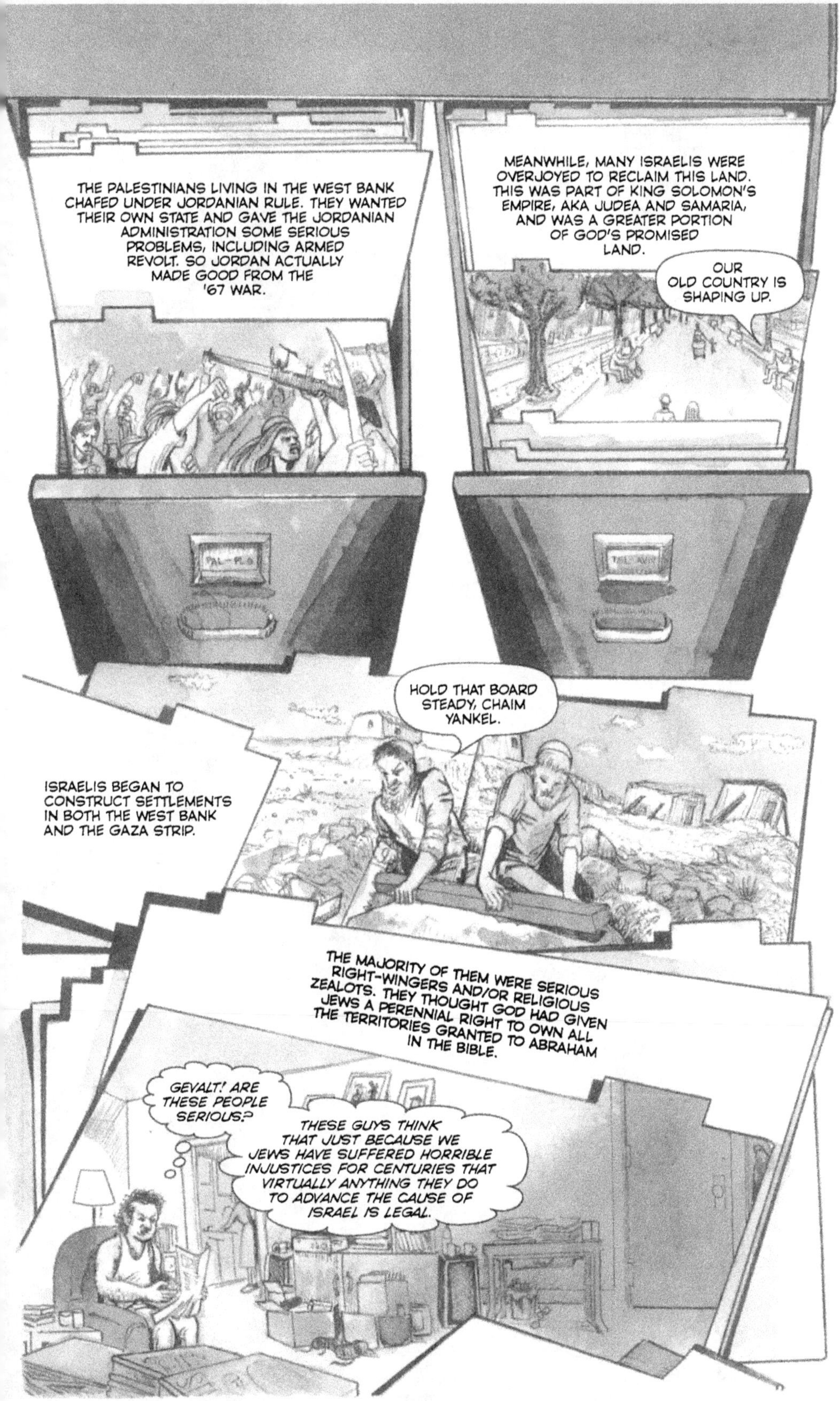
THE PALESTINIANS LIVING IN THE WEST BANK CHAFED UNDER JORDANIAN RULE. THEY WANTED THEIR OWN STATE AND GAVE THE JORDANIAN ADMINISTRATION SOME SERIOUS PROBLEMS, INCLUDING ARMED REVOLT. SO JORDAN ACTUALLY MADE GOOD FROM THE '67 WAR.
MEANWHILE, MANY ISRAELIS WERE OVERJOYED TO RECLAIM THIS LAND. THIS WAS PART OF KING SOLOMON'S EMPIRE, AKA JUDEA AND SAMARIA, AND WAS A GREATER PORTION OF GOD'S PROMISED LAND.
OUR OLD COUNTRY IS SHAPING UP.
ISRAELIS BEGAN TO CONSTRUCT SETTLEMENTS IN BOTH THE WEST BANK AND THE GAZA STRIP.
HOLD THAT BOARD STEADY, CHAIM YANKEL.
THE MAJORITY OF THEM WERE SERIOUS RIGHT-WINGERS AND/OR RELIGIOUS ZEALOTS. THEY THOUGHT GOD HAD GIVEN JEWS A PERENNIAL RIGHT TO OWN ALL THE TERRITORIES GRANTED TO ABRAHAM IN THE BIBLE.
GEVALT! ARE THESE PEOPLE SERIOUS?
THESE GUYS THINK THAT JUST BECAUSE WE JEWS HAVE SUFFERED HORRIBLE INJUSTICES FOR CENTURIES THAT VIRTUALLY ANYTHING THEY DO TO ADVANCE THE CAUSE OF ISRAEL IS LEGAL.

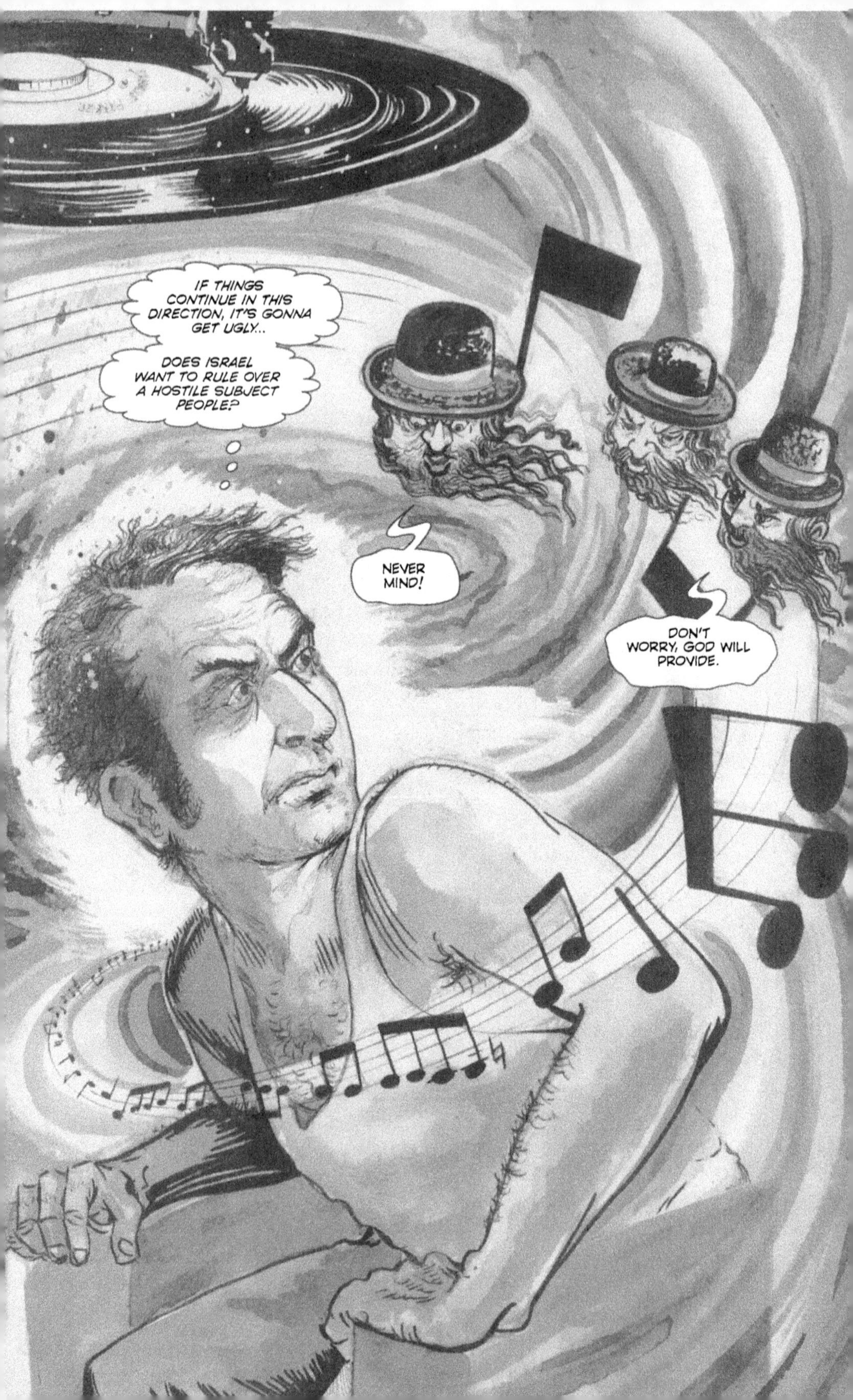
IF THINGS CONTINUE IN THIS DIRECTION, IT'S GONNA GET UGLY...
DOES ISRAEL WANT TO RULE OVER A HOSTILE SUBJECT PEOPLE?
NEVER MIND!
DON'T WORRY, GOD WILL PROVIDE.

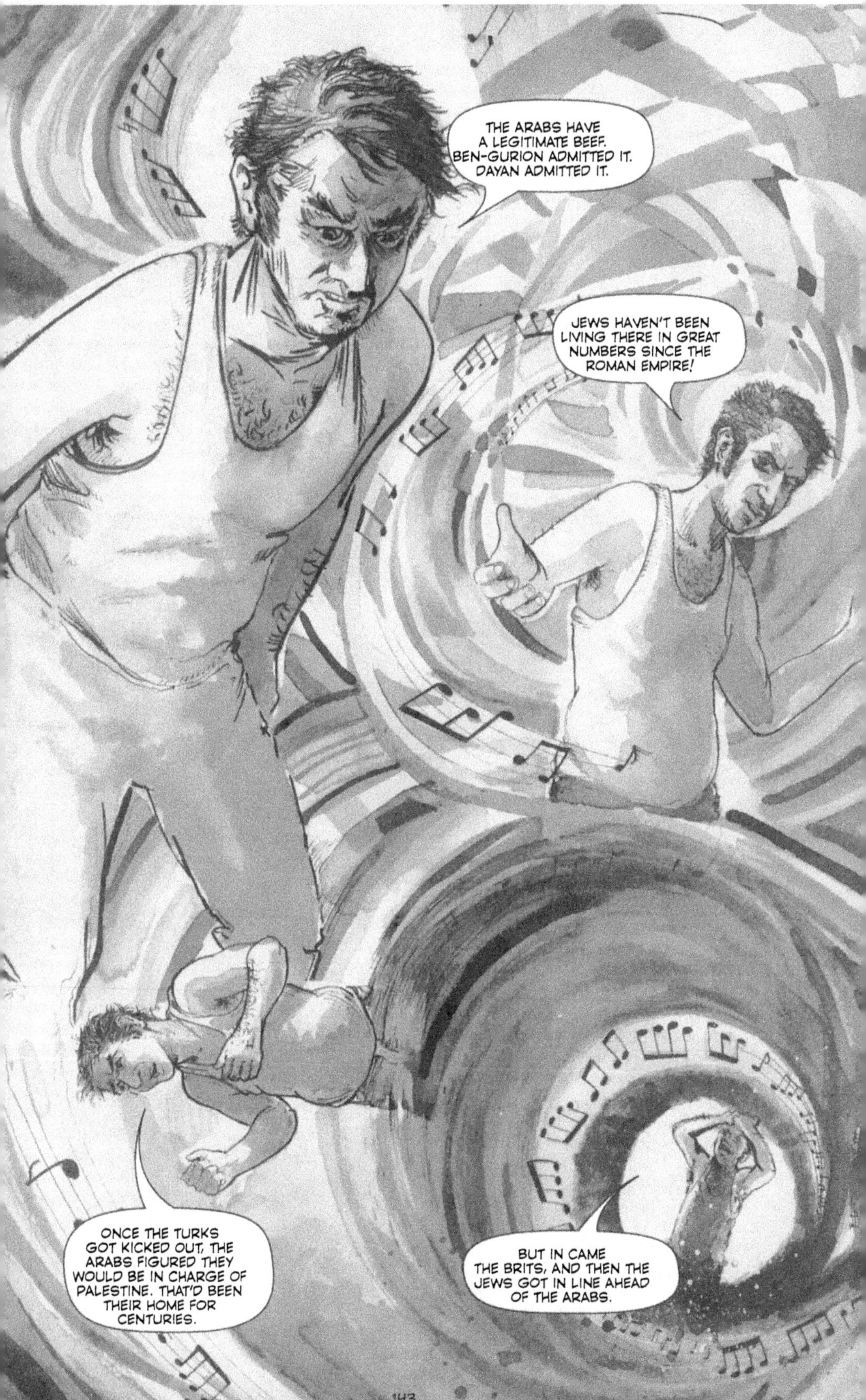
THE ARABS HAVE A LEGITIMATE BEEF. BEN-GURION ADMITTED IT. DAYAN ADMITTED IT.
JEWS HAVEN'T BEEN LIVING THERE IN GREAT NUMBERS SINCE THE ROMAN EMPIRE!
ONCE THE TURKS GOT KICKED OUT, THE ARABS FIGURED THEY WOULD BE IN CHARGE OF PALESTINE. THAT'D BEEN THEIR HOME FOR CENTURIES.
BUT IN CAME THE BRITS, AND THEN THE JEWS GOT IN LINE AHEAD OF THE ARABS.

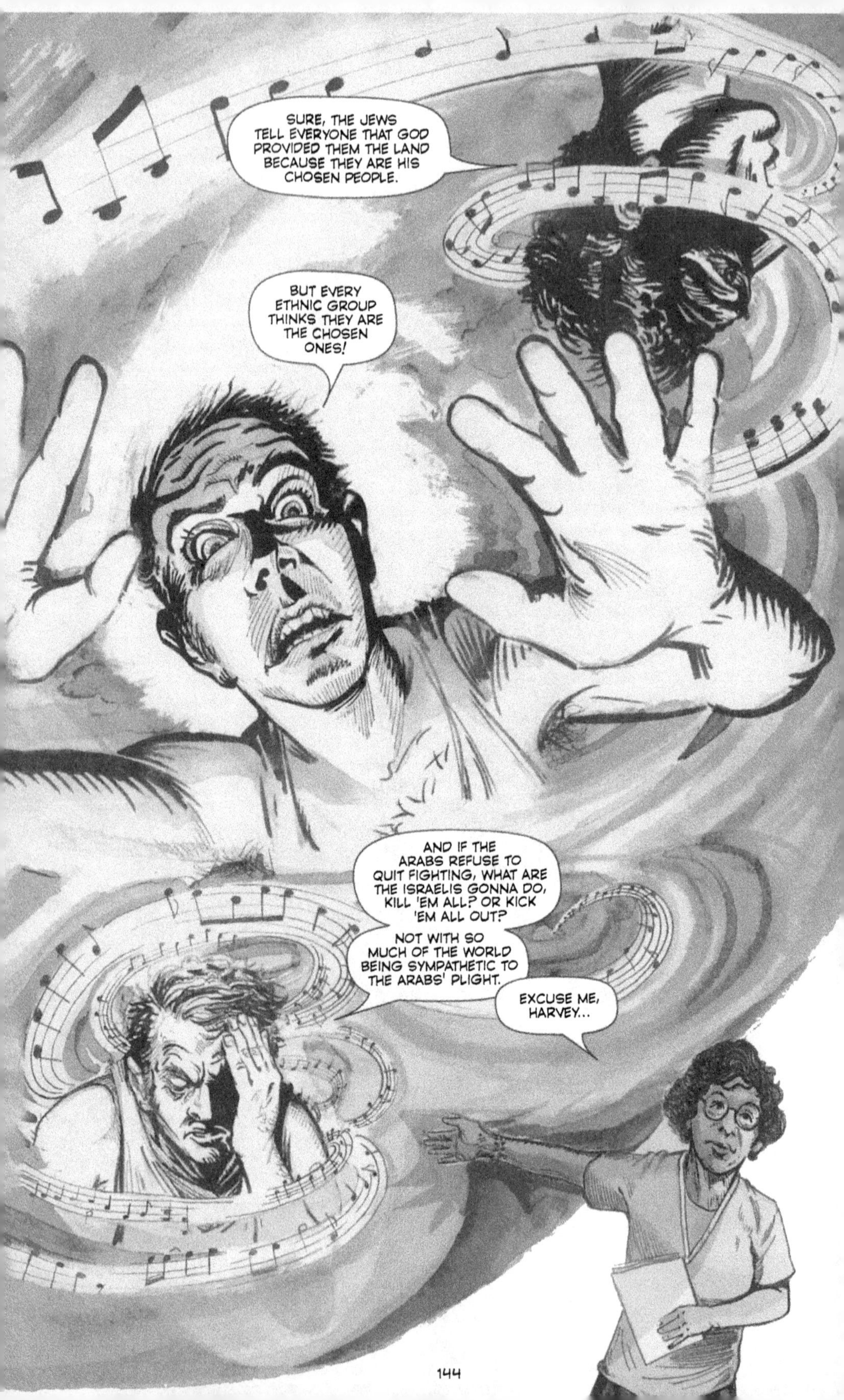
SURE, THE JEWS TELL EVERYONE THAT GOD PROVIDED THEM THE LAND BECAUSE THEY ARE HIS CHOSEN PEOPLE.
BUT EVERY ETHNIC GROUP THINKS THEY ARE THE CHOSEN ONES!
AND IF THE ARABS REFUSE TO QUIT FIGHTING, WHAT ARE THE ISRAELIS GONNA DO, KILL 'EM ALL? OR KICK 'EM ALL OUT?
NOT WITH SO MUCH OF THE WORLD BEING SYMPATHETIC TO THE ARABS' PLIGHT.
EXCUSE ME, HARVEY...

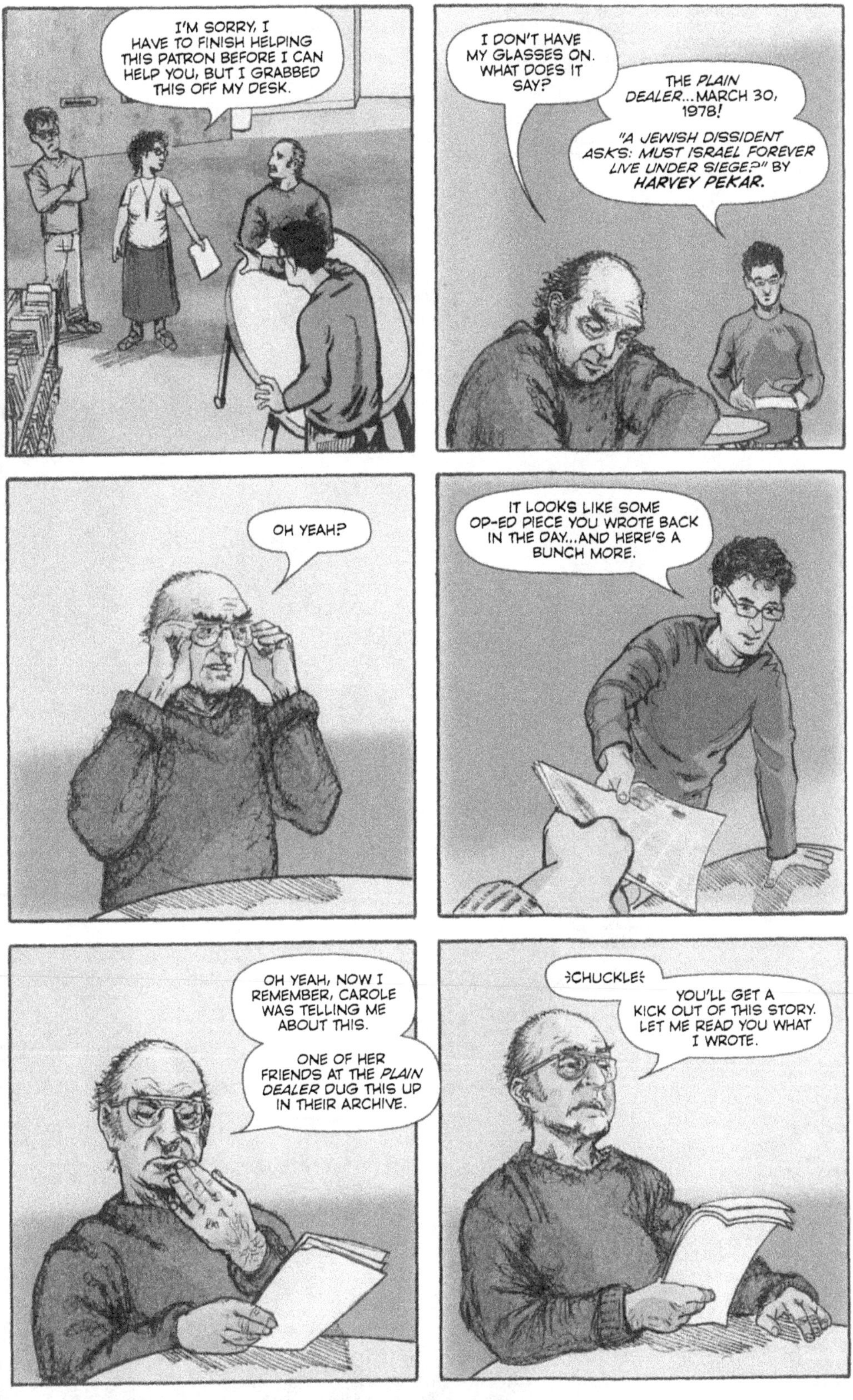
I'M SORRY, I HAVE TO FINISH HELPING THIS PATRON BEFORE I CAN HELP YOU, BUT I GRABBED THIS OFF MY DESK.
I DON'T HAVE MY GLASSES ON. WHAT DOES IT SAY?
THE *PLAIN DEALER*...MARCH 30, 1978!
"A JEWISH DISSIDENT ASKS: MUST ISRAEL FOREVER LIVE UNDER SIEGE?" BY **HARVEY PEKAR.**
OH YEAH?
IT LOOKS LIKE SOME OP-ED PIECE YOU WROTE BACK IN THE DAY...AND HERE'S A BUNCH MORE.
OH YEAH, NOW I REMEMBER, CAROLE WAS TELLING ME ABOUT THIS.
ONE OF HER FRIENDS AT THE *PLAIN DEALER* DUG THIS UP IN THEIR ARCHIVE.
CHUCKLE
YOU'LL GET A KICK OUT OF THIS STORY. LET ME READ YOU WHAT I WROTE.

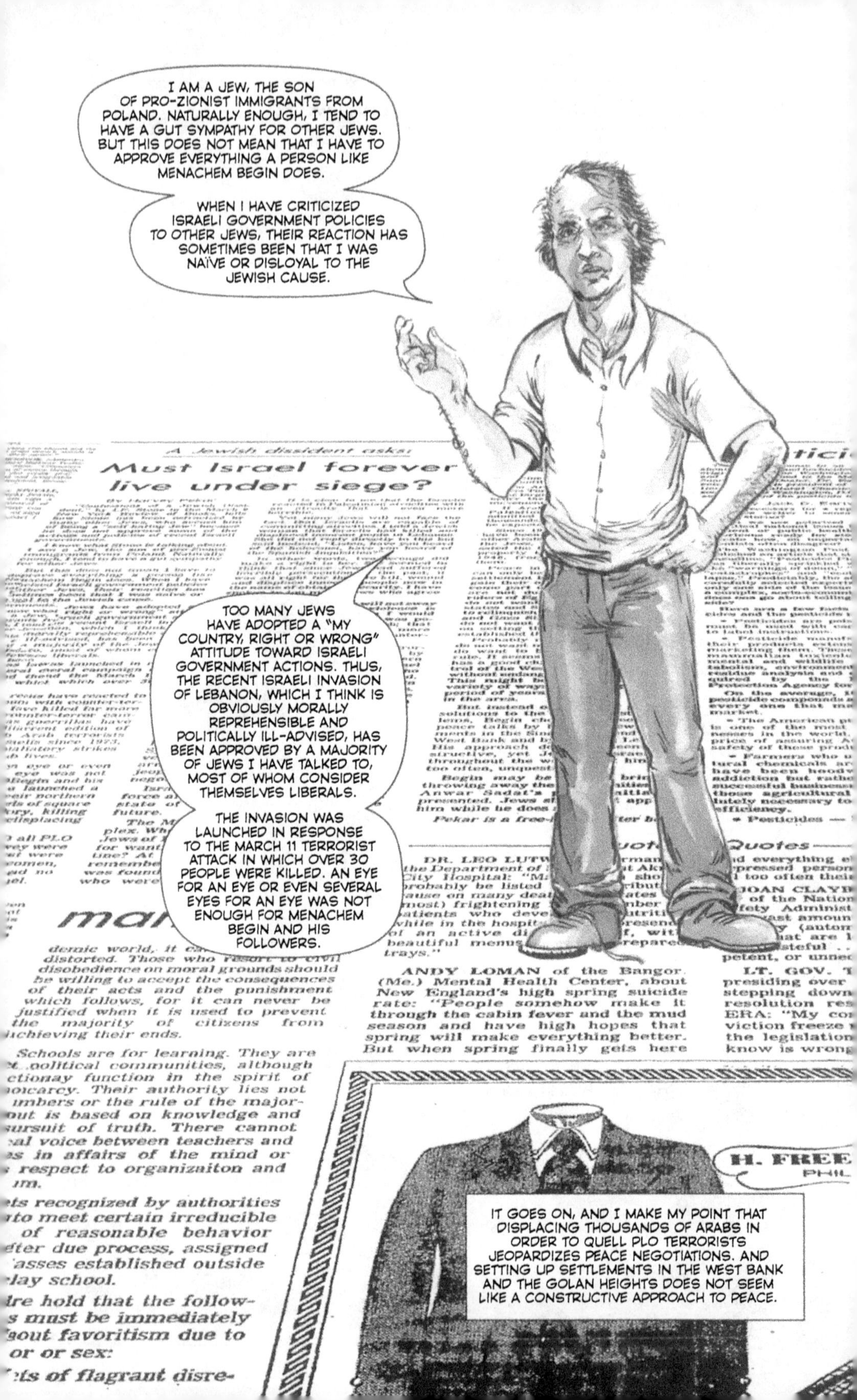
I AM A JEW, THE SON OF PRO-ZIONIST IMMIGRANTS FROM POLAND. NATURALLY ENOUGH, I TEND TO HAVE A GUT SYMPATHY FOR OTHER JEWS. BUT THIS DOES NOT MEAN THAT I HAVE TO APPROVE EVERYTHING A PERSON LIKE MENACHEM BEGIN DOES.
WHEN I HAVE CRITICIZED ISRAELI GOVERNMENT POLICIES TO OTHER JEWS, THEIR REACTION HAS SOMETIMES BEEN THAT I WAS NAÏVE OR DISLOYAL TO THE JEWISH CAUSE.
A Jewish dissident asks:
Must Israel forever live under siege?
TOO MANY JEWS HAVE ADOPTED A "MY COUNTRY, RIGHT OR WRONG" ATTITUDE TOWARD ISRAELI GOVERNMENT ACTIONS. THUS, THE RECENT ISRAELI INVASION OF LEBANON, WHICH I THINK IS OBVIOUSLY MORALLY REPREHENSIBLE AND POLITICALLY ILL-ADVISED, HAS BEEN APPROVED BY A MAJORITY OF JEWS I HAVE TALKED TO, MOST OF WHOM CONSIDER THEMSELVES LIBERALS.
THE INVASION WAS LAUNCHED IN RESPONSE TO THE MARCH 11 TERRORIST ATTACK IN WHICH OVER 30 PEOPLE WERE KILLED. AN EYE FOR AN EYE OR EVEN SEVERAL EYES FOR AN EYE WAS NOT ENOUGH FOR MENACHEM BEGIN AND HIS FOLLOWERS.
IT GOES ON, AND I MAKE MY POINT THAT DISPLACING THOUSANDS OF ARABS IN ORDER TO QUELL PLO TERRORISTS JEOPARDIZES PEACE NEGOTIATIONS. AND SETTING UP SETTLEMENTS IN THE WEST BANK AND THE GOLAN HEIGHTS DOES NOT SEEM LIKE A CONSTRUCTIVE APPROACH TO PEACE.

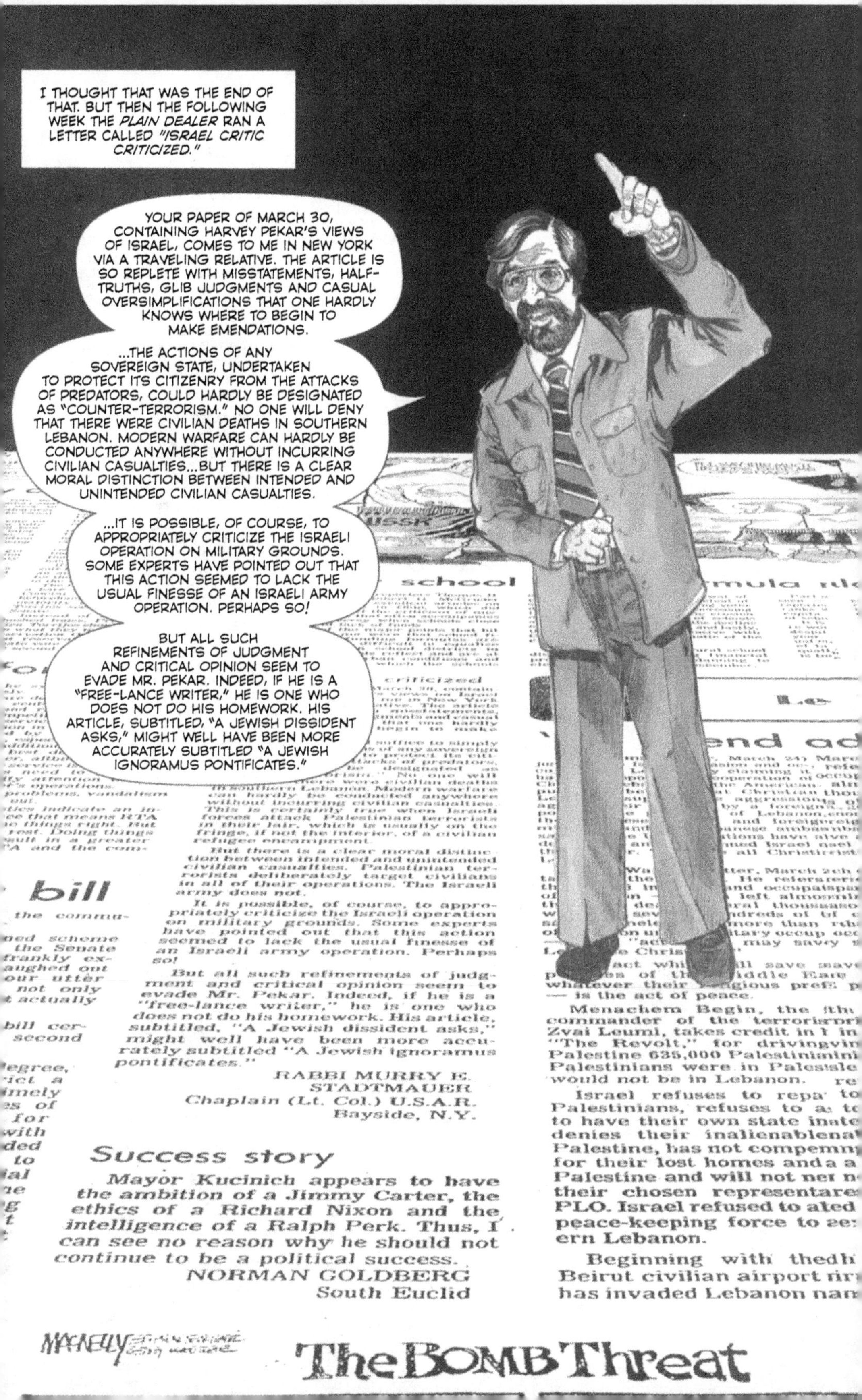

I THOUGHT THAT WAS THE END OF THAT. BUT THEN THE FOLLOWING WEEK THE *PLAIN DEALER* RAN A LETTER CALLED *"ISRAEL CRITIC CRITICIZED."*
YOUR PAPER OF MARCH 30, CONTAINING HARVEY PEKAR'S VIEWS OF ISRAEL, COMES TO ME IN NEW YORK VIA A TRAVELING RELATIVE. THE ARTICLE IS SO REPLETE WITH MISSTATEMENTS, HALF-TRUTHS, GLIB JUDGMENTS AND CASUAL OVERSIMPLIFICATIONS THAT ONE HARDLY KNOWS WHERE TO BEGIN TO MAKE EMENDATIONS.
...THE ACTIONS OF ANY SOVEREIGN STATE, UNDERTAKEN TO PROTECT ITS CITIZENRY FROM THE ATTACKS OF PREDATORS, COULD HARDLY BE DESIGNATED AS "COUNTER-TERRORISM." NO ONE WILL DENY THAT THERE WERE CIVILIAN DEATHS IN SOUTHERN LEBANON. MODERN WARFARE CAN HARDLY BE CONDUCTED ANYWHERE WITHOUT INCURRING CIVILIAN CASUALTIES...BUT THERE IS A CLEAR MORAL DISTINCTION BETWEEN INTENDED AND UNINTENDED CIVILIAN CASUALTIES.
...IT IS POSSIBLE, OF COURSE, TO APPROPRIATELY CRITICIZE THE ISRAELI OPERATION ON MILITARY GROUNDS. SOME EXPERTS HAVE POINTED OUT THAT THIS ACTION SEEMED TO LACK THE USUAL FINESSE OF AN ISRAELI ARMY OPERATION. PERHAPS SO!
BUT ALL SUCH REFINEMENTS OF JUDGMENT AND CRITICAL OPINION SEEM TO EVADE MR. PEKAR. INDEED, IF HE IS A "FREE-LANCE WRITER," HE IS ONE WHO DOES NOT DO HIS HOMEWORK. HIS ARTICLE, SUBTITLED, "A JEWISH DISSIDENT ASKS," MIGHT WELL HAVE BEEN MORE ACCURATELY SUBTITLED "A JEWISH IGNORAMUS PONTIFICATES."
school
criticized
bill
But there is a clear moral distinction between intended and unintended civilian casualties. Palestinian terrorists deliberately target civilians in all of their operations. The Israeli army does not.
It is possible, of course, to appropriately criticize the Israeli operation on military grounds. Some experts have pointed out that this action seemed to lack the usual finesse of an Israeli army operation. Perhaps so!
But all such refinements of judgment and critical opinion seem to evade Mr. Pekar. Indeed, if he is a "free-lance writer," he is one who does not do his homework. His article, subtitled, "A Jewish dissident asks," might well have been more accurately subtitled "A Jewish ignoramus pontificates."
RABBI MURRY E. STADTMAUER
Chaplain (Lt. Col.) U.S.A.R.
Bayside, N.Y.
Success story
Mayor Kucinich appears to have the ambition of a Jimmy Carter, the ethics of a Richard Nixon and the intelligence of a Ralph Perk. Thus, I can see no reason why he should not continue to be a political success.
NORMAN GOLDBERG
South Euclid
Menachem Begin, the
Israel refuses to repa
Beginning with the
MACNELLY
The BOMB Threat

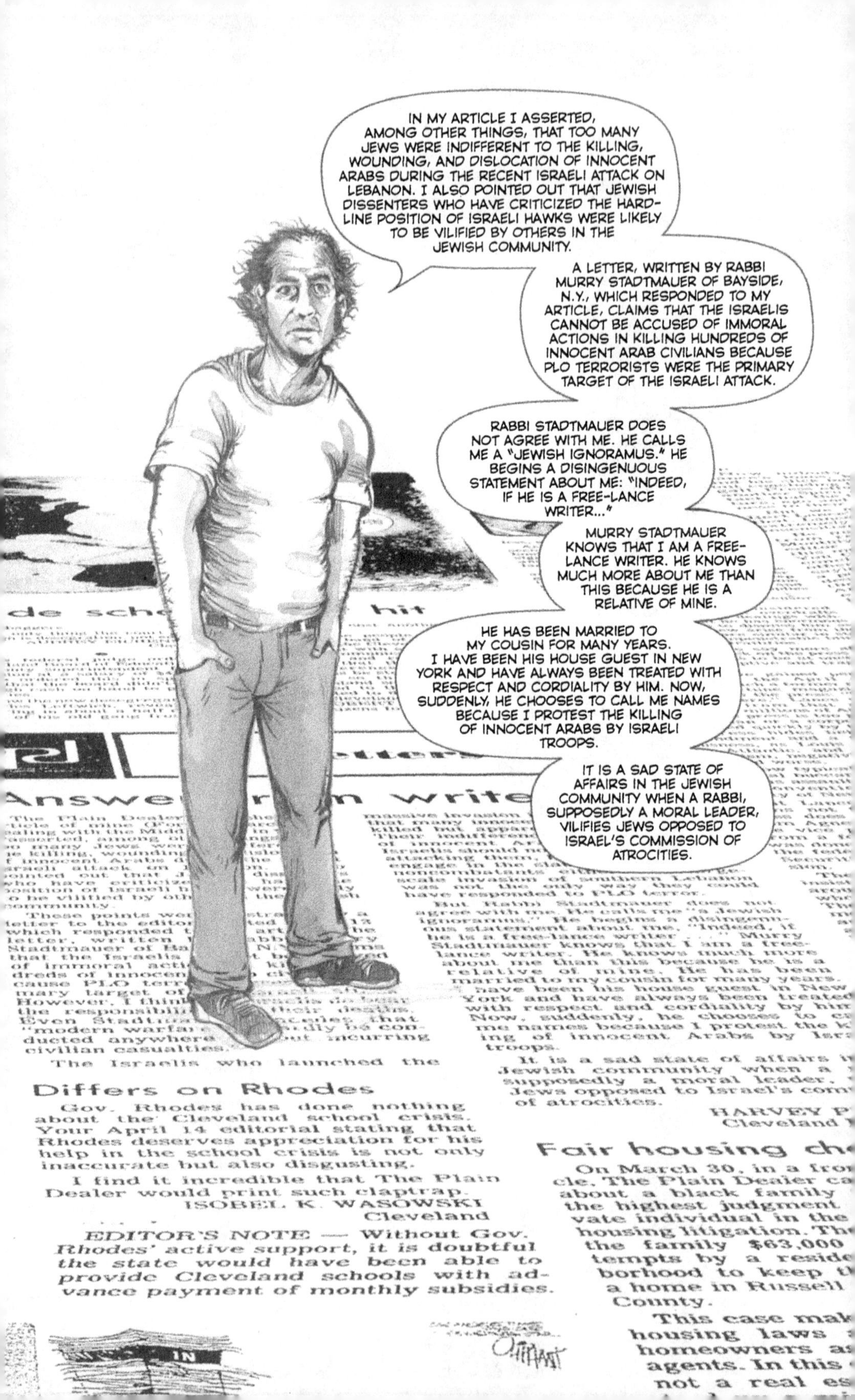
IN MY ARTICLE I ASSERTED, AMONG OTHER THINGS, THAT TOO MANY JEWS WERE INDIFFERENT TO THE KILLING, WOUNDING, AND DISLOCATION OF INNOCENT ARABS DURING THE RECENT ISRAELI ATTACK ON LEBANON. I ALSO POINTED OUT THAT JEWISH DISSENTERS WHO HAVE CRITICIZED THE HARD-LINE POSITION OF ISRAELI HAWKS WERE LIKELY TO BE VILIFIED BY OTHERS IN THE JEWISH COMMUNITY.
A LETTER, WRITTEN BY RABBI MURRY STADTMAUER OF BAYSIDE, N.Y., WHICH RESPONDED TO MY ARTICLE, CLAIMS THAT THE ISRAELIS CANNOT BE ACCUSED OF IMMORAL ACTIONS IN KILLING HUNDREDS OF INNOCENT ARAB CIVILIANS BECAUSE PLO TERRORISTS WERE THE PRIMARY TARGET OF THE ISRAELI ATTACK.
RABBI STADTMAUER DOES NOT AGREE WITH ME. HE CALLS ME A "JEWISH IGNORAMUS." HE BEGINS A DISINGENUOUS STATEMENT ABOUT ME: "INDEED, IF HE IS A FREE-LANCE WRITER..."
MURRY STADTMAUER KNOWS THAT I AM A FREE-LANCE WRITER. HE KNOWS MUCH MORE ABOUT ME THAN THIS BECAUSE HE IS A RELATIVE OF MINE.
HE HAS BEEN MARRIED TO MY COUSIN FOR MANY YEARS. I HAVE BEEN HIS HOUSE GUEST IN NEW YORK AND HAVE ALWAYS BEEN TREATED WITH RESPECT AND CORDIALITY BY HIM. NOW, SUDDENLY, HE CHOOSES TO CALL ME NAMES BECAUSE I PROTEST THE KILLING OF INNOCENT ARABS BY ISRAELI TROOPS.
IT IS A SAD STATE OF AFFAIRS IN THE JEWISH COMMUNITY WHEN A RABBI, SUPPOSEDLY A MORAL LEADER, VILIFIES JEWS OPPOSED TO ISRAEL'S COMMISSION OF ATROCITIES.
Differs on Rhodes
Gov. Rhodes has done nothing about the Cleveland school crisis. Your April 14 editorial stating that Rhodes deserves appreciation for his help in the school crisis is not only inaccurate but also disgusting.
I find it incredible that The Plain Dealer would print such claptrap.
ISOBEL K. WASOWSKI Cleveland
EDITOR'S NOTE — Without Gov. Rhodes' active support, it is doubtful the state would have been able to provide Cleveland schools with advance payment of monthly subsidies.
OLIPHANT

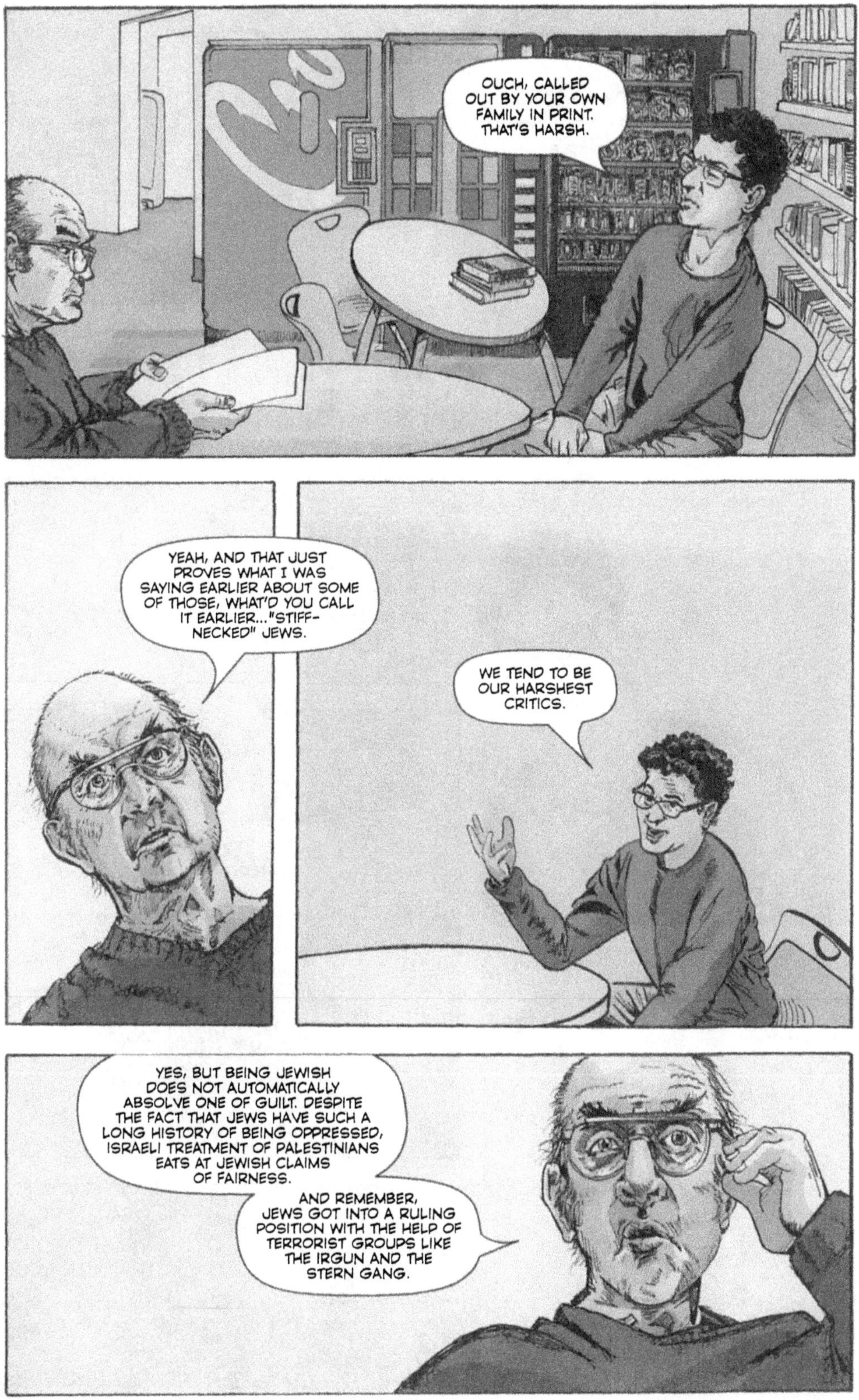
OUCH, CALLED OUT BY YOUR OWN FAMILY IN PRINT. THAT'S HARSH.
YEAH, AND THAT JUST PROVES WHAT I WAS SAYING EARLIER ABOUT SOME OF THOSE, WHAT'D YOU CALL IT EARLIER..."STIFF-NECKED" JEWS.
WE TEND TO BE OUR HARSHEST CRITICS.
YES, BUT BEING JEWISH DOES NOT AUTOMATICALLY ABSOLVE ONE OF GUILT. DESPITE THE FACT THAT JEWS HAVE SUCH A LONG HISTORY OF BEING OPPRESSED, ISRAELI TREATMENT OF PALESTINIANS EATS AT JEWISH CLAIMS OF FAIRNESS.
AND REMEMBER, JEWS GOT INTO A RULING POSITION WITH THE HELP OF TERRORIST GROUPS LIKE THE IRGUN AND THE STERN GANG.

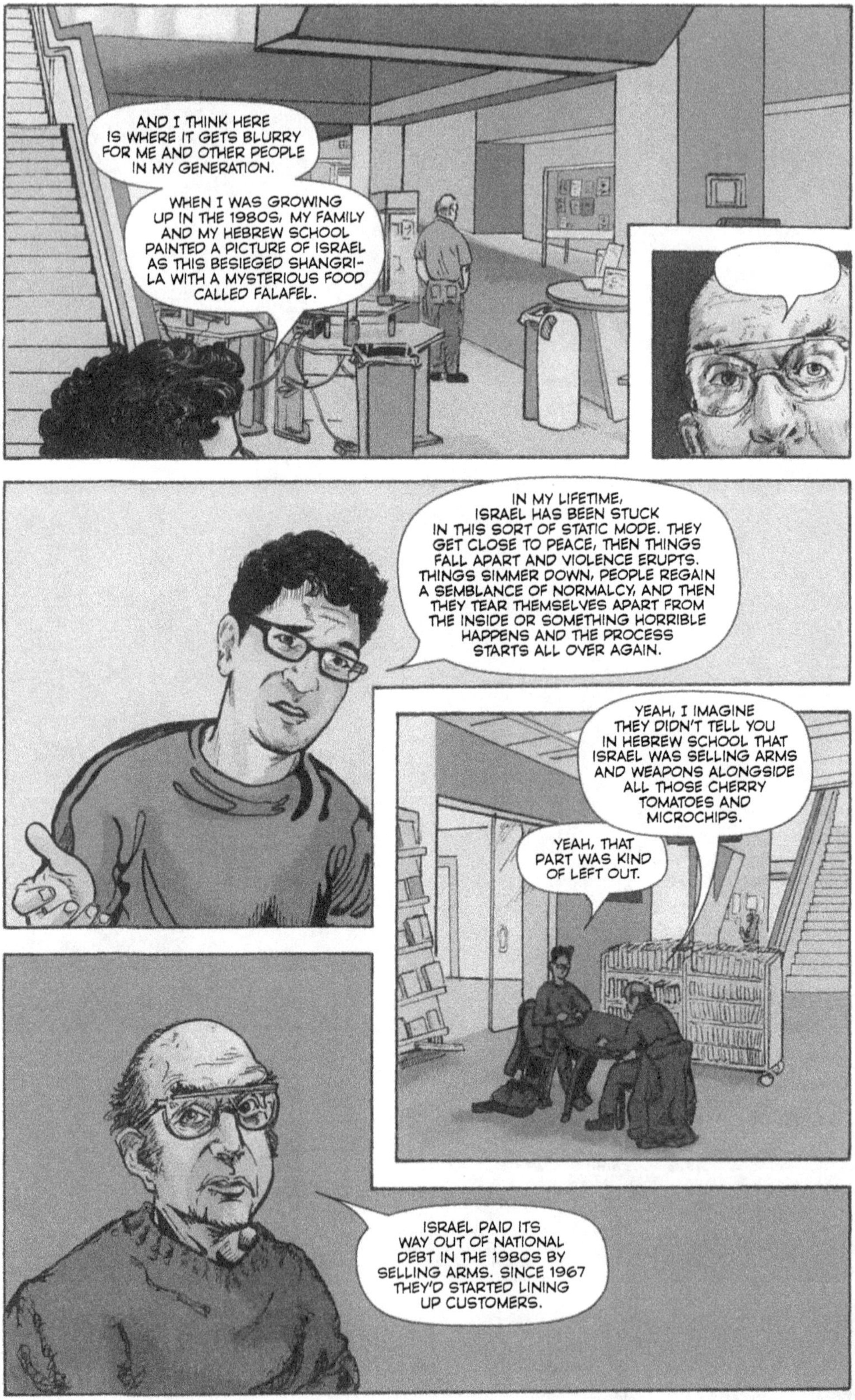
AND I THINK HERE IS WHERE IT GETS BLURRY FOR ME AND OTHER PEOPLE IN MY GENERATION.
WHEN I WAS GROWING UP IN THE 1980S, MY FAMILY AND MY HEBREW SCHOOL PAINTED A PICTURE OF ISRAEL AS THIS BESIEGED SHANGRI-LA WITH A MYSTERIOUS FOOD CALLED FALAFEL.
IN MY LIFETIME, ISRAEL HAS BEEN STUCK IN THIS SORT OF STATIC MODE. THEY GET CLOSE TO PEACE, THEN THINGS FALL APART AND VIOLENCE ERUPTS. THINGS SIMMER DOWN, PEOPLE REGAIN A SEMBLANCE OF NORMALCY, AND THEN THEY TEAR THEMSELVES APART FROM THE INSIDE OR SOMETHING HORRIBLE HAPPENS AND THE PROCESS STARTS ALL OVER AGAIN.
YEAH, I IMAGINE THEY DIDN'T TELL YOU IN HEBREW SCHOOL THAT ISRAEL WAS SELLING ARMS AND WEAPONS ALONGSIDE ALL THOSE CHERRY TOMATOES AND MICROCHIPS.
YEAH, THAT PART WAS KIND OF LEFT OUT.
ISRAEL PAID ITS WAY OUT OF NATIONAL DEBT IN THE 1980S BY SELLING ARMS. SINCE 1967 THEY'D STARTED LINING UP CUSTOMERS.

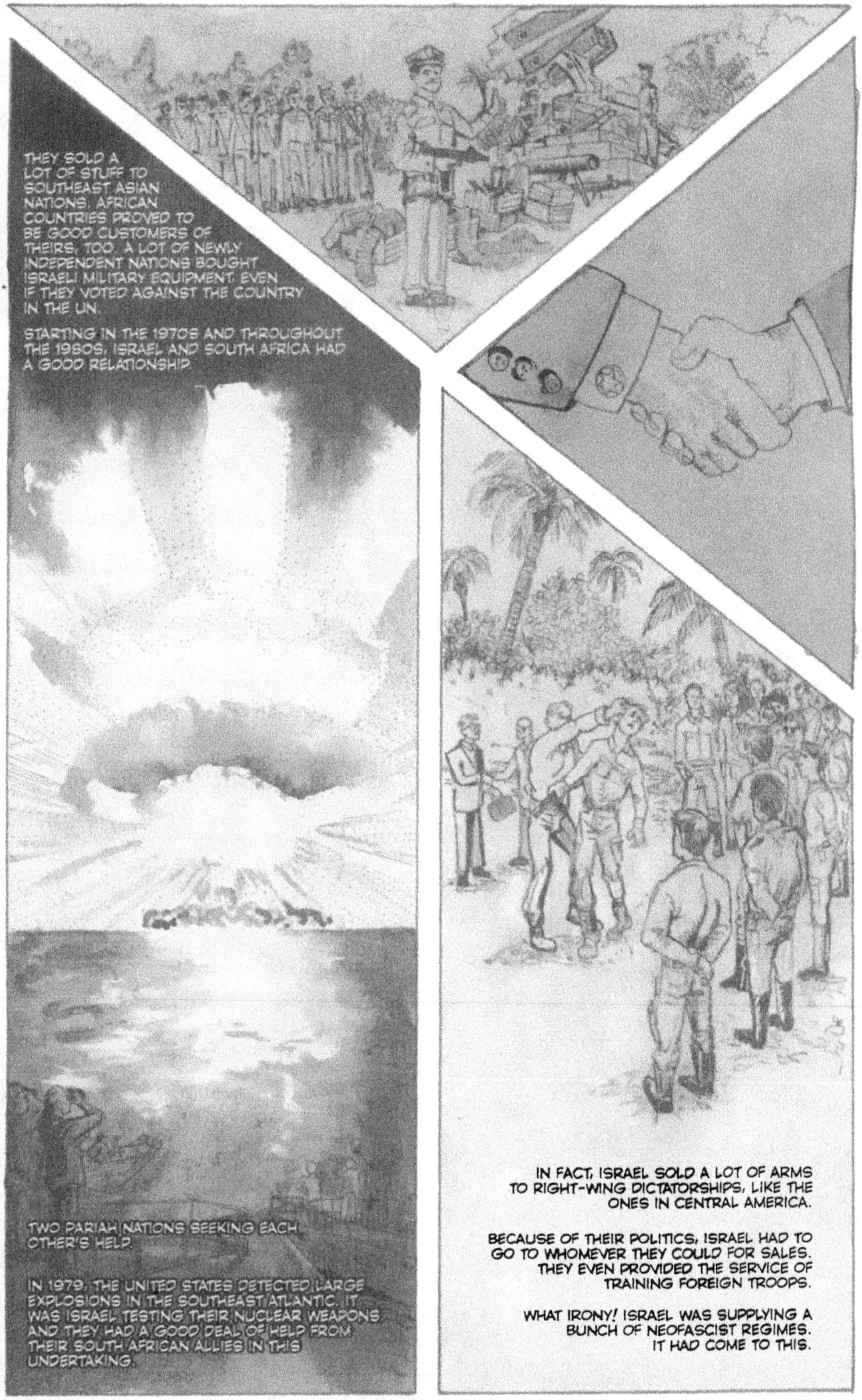
THEY SOLD A LOT OF STUFF TO SOUTHEAST ASIAN NATIONS. AFRICAN COUNTRIES PROVED TO BE GOOD CUSTOMERS OF THEIRS, TOO. A LOT OF NEWLY INDEPENDENT NATIONS BOUGHT ISRAELI MILITARY EQUIPMENT, EVEN IF THEY VOTED AGAINST THE COUNTRY IN THE UN.
STARTING IN THE 1970S AND THROUGHOUT THE 1980S, ISRAEL AND SOUTH AFRICA HAD A GOOD RELATIONSHIP.
TWO PARIAH NATIONS SEEKING EACH OTHER'S HELP.
IN 1979, THE UNITED STATES DETECTED LARGE EXPLOSIONS IN THE SOUTHEAST ATLANTIC. IT WAS ISRAEL TESTING THEIR NUCLEAR WEAPONS. AND THEY HAD A GOOD DEAL OF HELP FROM THEIR SOUTH AFRICAN ALLIES IN THIS UNDERTAKING.
IN FACT, ISRAEL SOLD A LOT OF ARMS TO RIGHT-WING DICTATORSHIPS, LIKE THE ONES IN CENTRAL AMERICA.
BECAUSE OF THEIR POLITICS, ISRAEL HAD TO GO TO WHOMEVER THEY COULD FOR SALES. THEY EVEN PROVIDED THE SERVICE OF TRAINING FOREIGN TROOPS.
WHAT IRONY! ISRAEL WAS SUPPLYING A BUNCH OF NEOFASCIST REGIMES. IT HAD COME TO THIS.

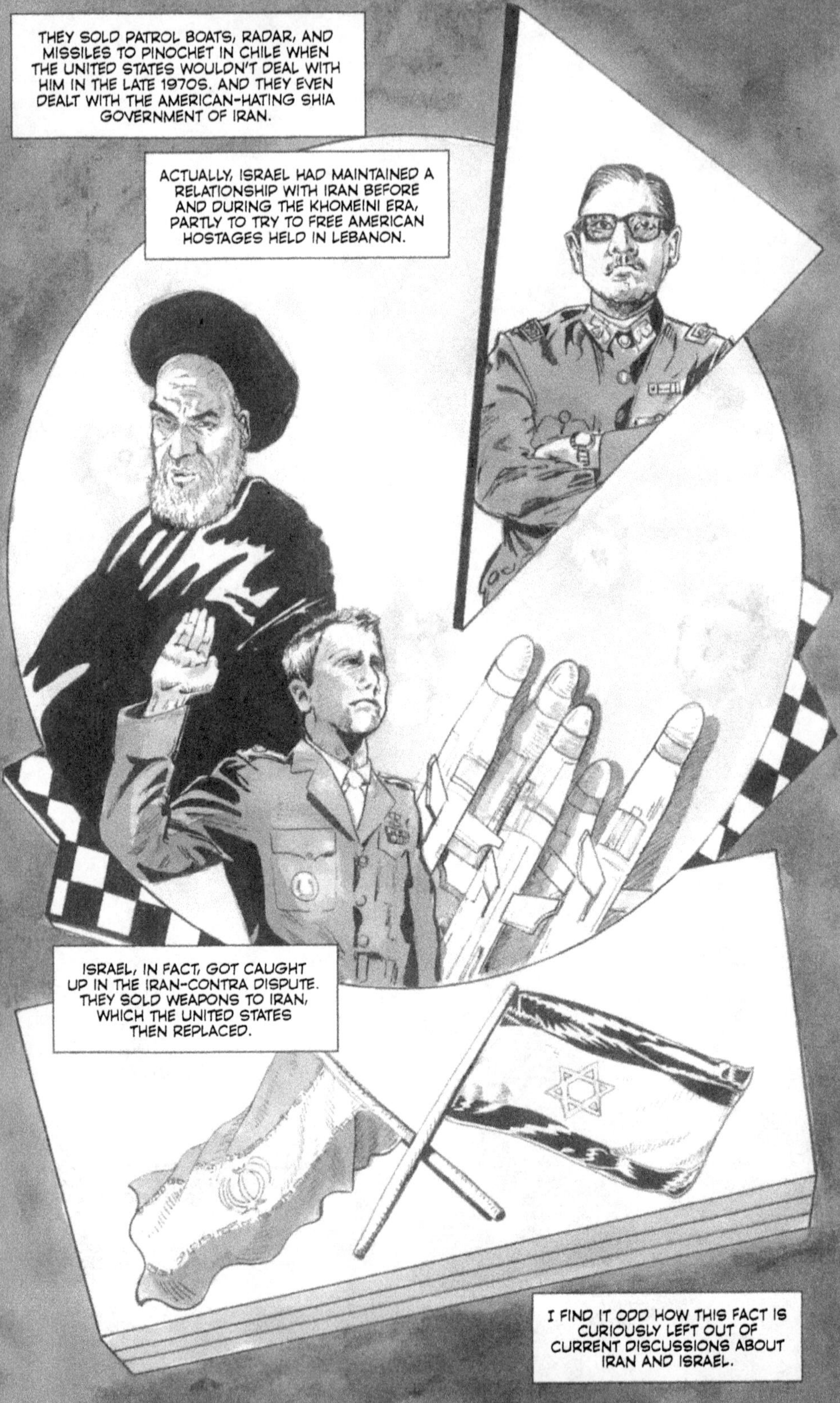
THEY SOLD PATROL BOATS, RADAR, AND MISSILES TO PINOCHET IN CHILE WHEN THE UNITED STATES WOULDN'T DEAL WITH HIM IN THE LATE 1970S. AND THEY EVEN DEALT WITH THE AMERICAN-HATING SHIA GOVERNMENT OF IRAN.
ACTUALLY, ISRAEL HAD MAINTAINED A RELATIONSHIP WITH IRAN BEFORE AND DURING THE KHOMEINI ERA, PARTLY TO TRY TO FREE AMERICAN HOSTAGES HELD IN LEBANON.
ISRAEL, IN FACT, GOT CAUGHT UP IN THE IRAN-CONTRA DISPUTE. THEY SOLD WEAPONS TO IRAN, WHICH THE UNITED STATES THEN REPLACED.
I FIND IT ODD HOW THIS FACT IS CURIOUSLY LEFT OUT OF CURRENT DISCUSSIONS ABOUT IRAN AND ISRAEL.

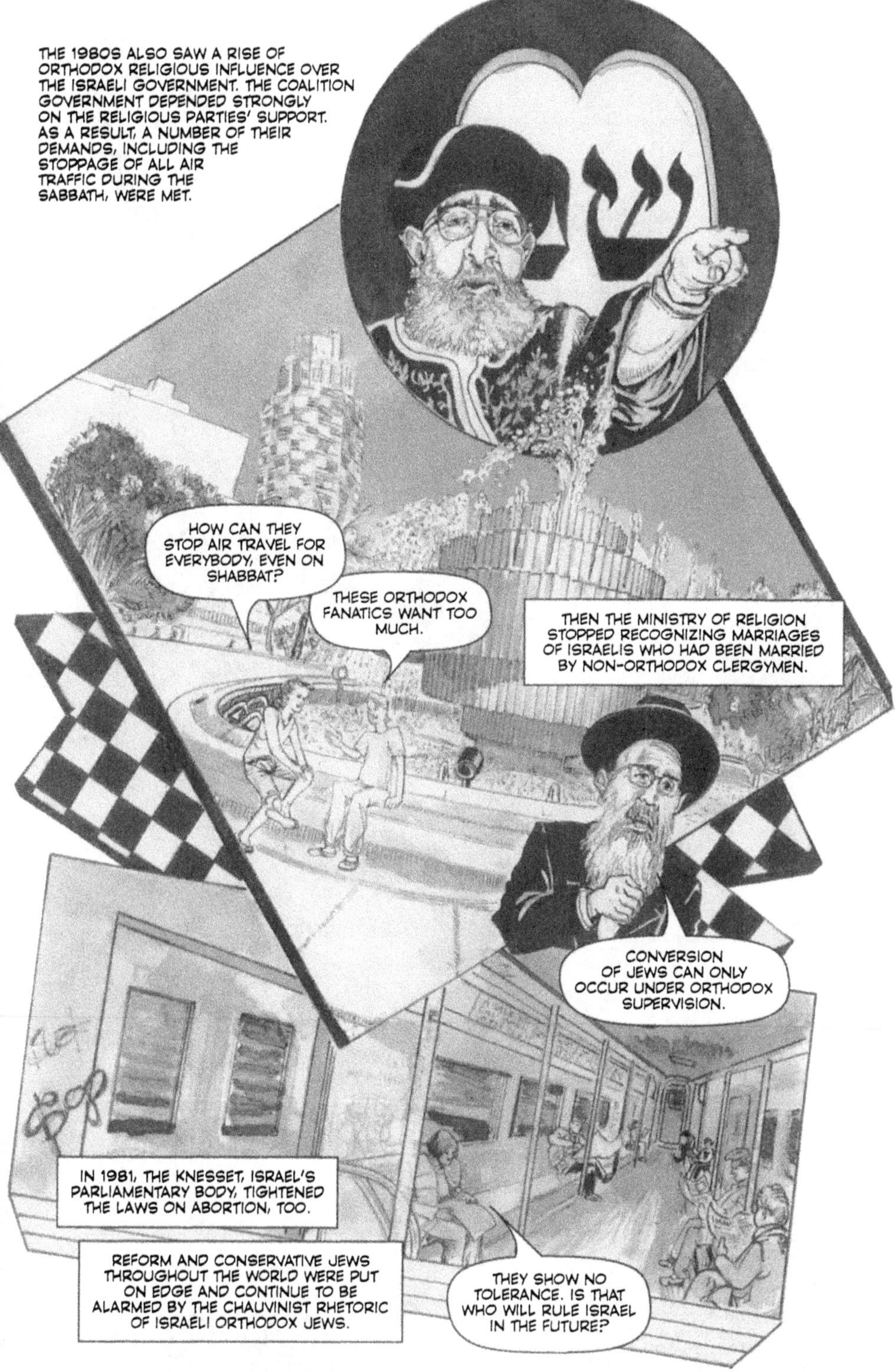
THE 1980S ALSO SAW A RISE OF ORTHODOX RELIGIOUS INFLUENCE OVER THE ISRAELI GOVERNMENT. THE COALITION GOVERNMENT DEPENDED STRONGLY ON THE RELIGIOUS PARTIES' SUPPORT. AS A RESULT, A NUMBER OF THEIR DEMANDS, INCLUDING THE STOPPAGE OF ALL AIR TRAFFIC DURING THE SABBATH, WERE MET.
HOW CAN THEY STOP AIR TRAVEL FOR EVERYBODY, EVEN ON SHABBAT?
THESE ORTHODOX FANATICS WANT TOO MUCH.
THEN THE MINISTRY OF RELIGION STOPPED RECOGNIZING MARRIAGES OF ISRAELIS WHO HAD BEEN MARRIED BY NON-ORTHODOX CLERGYMEN.
CONVERSION OF JEWS CAN ONLY OCCUR UNDER ORTHODOX SUPERVISION.
IN 1981, THE KNESSET, ISRAEL'S PARLIAMENTARY BODY, TIGHTENED THE LAWS ON ABORTION, TOO.
REFORM AND CONSERVATIVE JEWS THROUGHOUT THE WORLD WERE PUT ON EDGE AND CONTINUE TO BE ALARMED BY THE CHAUVINIST RHETORIC OF ISRAELI ORTHODOX JEWS.
THEY SHOW NO TOLERANCE. IS THAT WHO WILL RULE ISRAEL IN THE FUTURE?

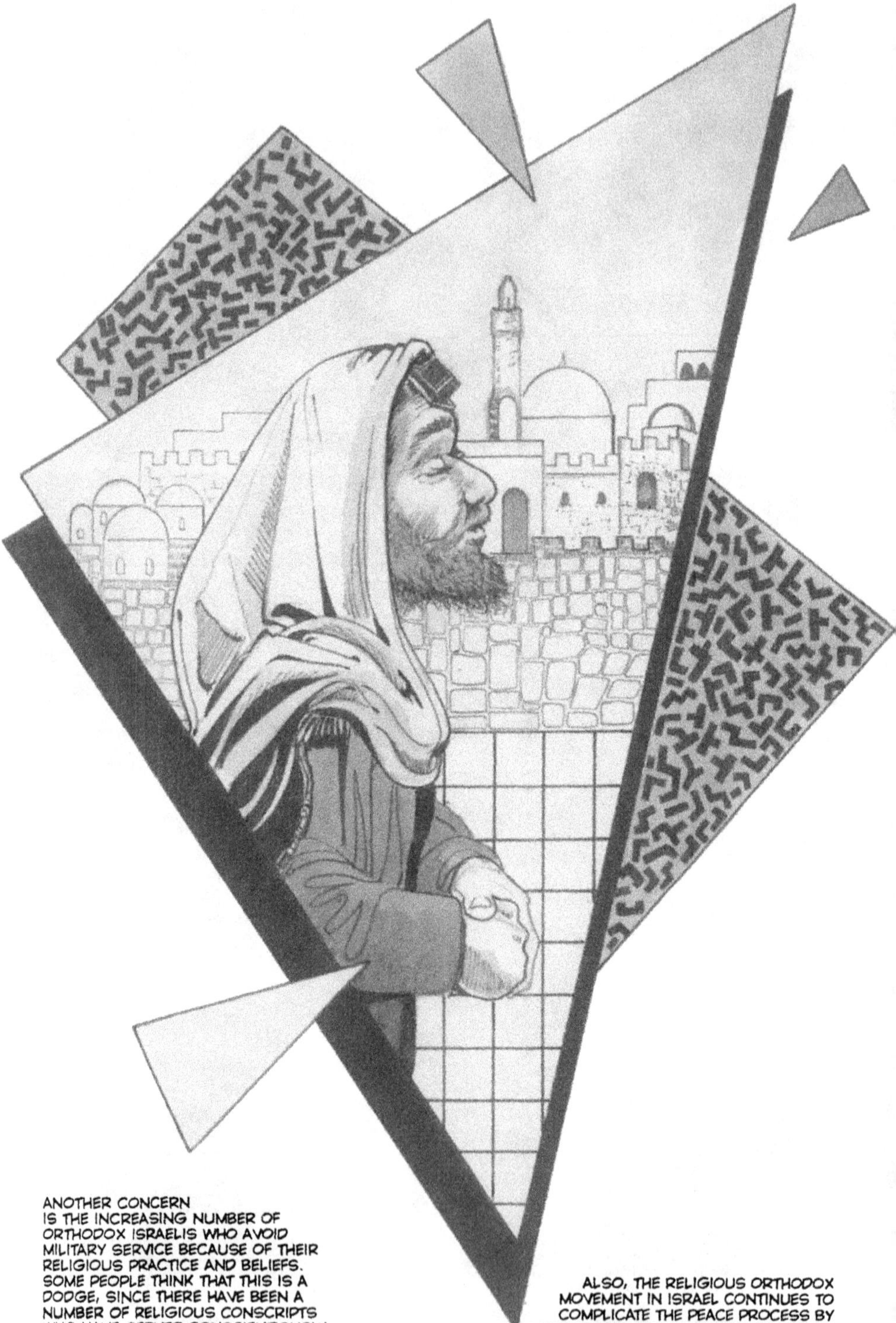

ANOTHER CONCERN
IS THE INCREASING NUMBER OF
ORTHODOX ISRAELIS WHO AVOID
MILITARY SERVICE BECAUSE OF THEIR
RELIGIOUS PRACTICE AND BELIEFS.
SOME PEOPLE THINK THAT THIS IS A
DODGE, SINCE THERE HAVE BEEN A
NUMBER OF RELIGIOUS CONSCRIPTS
WHO HAVE SERVED CONSCIENTIOUSLY,
AND WELL, IN THE PAST.

ALSO, THE RELIGIOUS ORTHODOX
MOVEMENT IN ISRAEL CONTINUES TO
COMPLICATE THE PEACE PROCESS BY
OPPOSING TERRITORIAL CONCESSIONS
OR AGREEMENTS WITH ARABS.

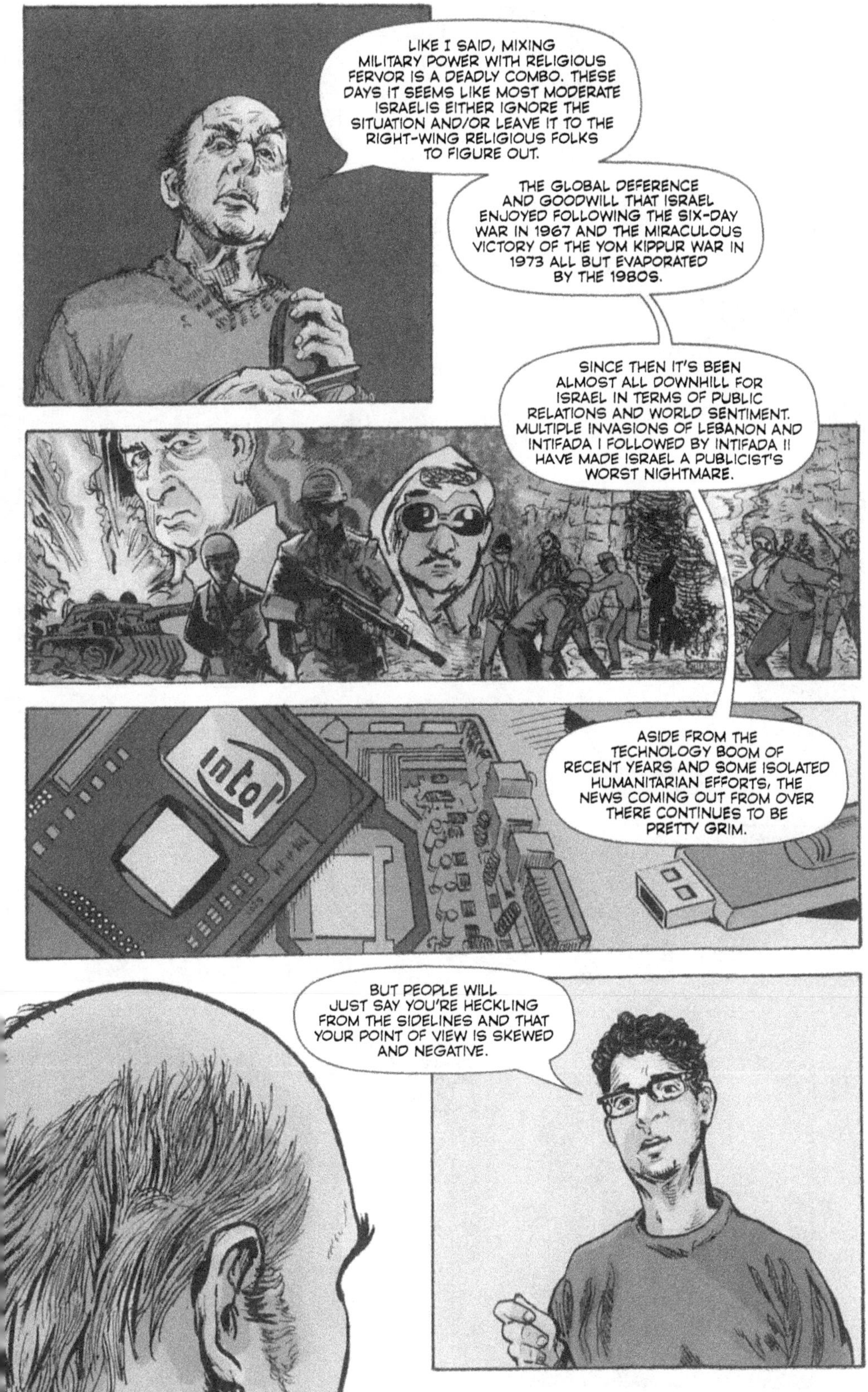
LIKE I SAID, MIXING MILITARY POWER WITH RELIGIOUS FERVOR IS A DEADLY COMBO. THESE DAYS IT SEEMS LIKE MOST MODERATE ISRAELIS EITHER IGNORE THE SITUATION AND/OR LEAVE IT TO THE RIGHT-WING RELIGIOUS FOLKS TO FIGURE OUT.
THE GLOBAL DEFERENCE AND GOODWILL THAT ISRAEL ENJOYED FOLLOWING THE SIX-DAY WAR IN 1967 AND THE MIRACULOUS VICTORY OF THE YOM KIPPUR WAR IN 1973 ALL BUT EVAPORATED BY THE 1980S.
SINCE THEN IT'S BEEN ALMOST ALL DOWNHILL FOR ISRAEL IN TERMS OF PUBLIC RELATIONS AND WORLD SENTIMENT. MULTIPLE INVASIONS OF LEBANON AND INTIFADA I FOLLOWED BY INTIFADA II HAVE MADE ISRAEL A PUBLICIST'S WORST NIGHTMARE.
ASIDE FROM THE TECHNOLOGY BOOM OF RECENT YEARS AND SOME ISOLATED HUMANITARIAN EFFORTS, THE NEWS COMING OUT FROM OVER THERE CONTINUES TO BE PRETTY GRIM.
BUT PEOPLE WILL JUST SAY YOU'RE HECKLING FROM THE SIDELINES AND THAT YOUR POINT OF VIEW IS SKEWED AND NEGATIVE.

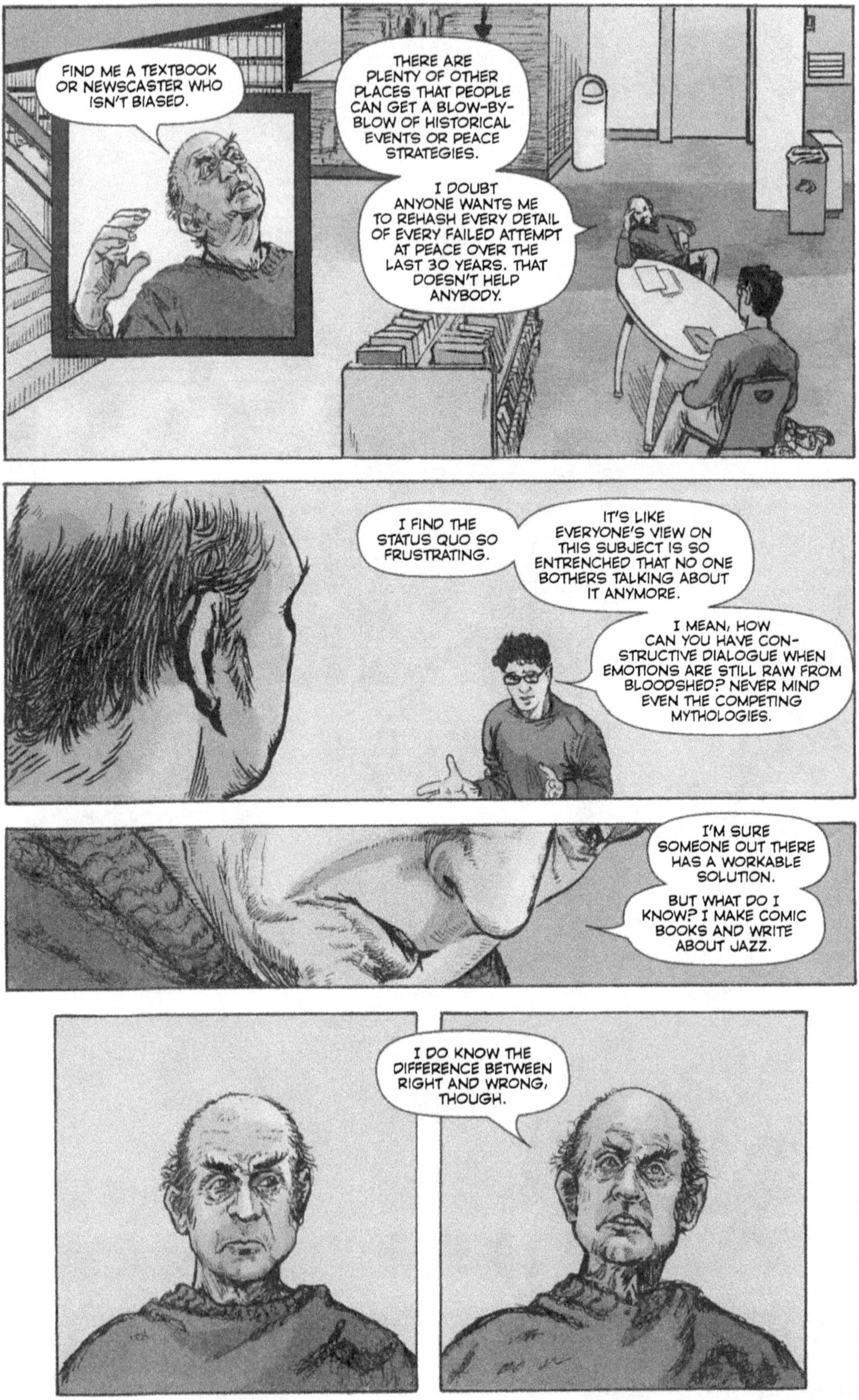
FIND ME A TEXTBOOK OR NEWSCASTER WHO ISN'T BIASED.
THERE ARE PLENTY OF OTHER PLACES THAT PEOPLE CAN GET A BLOW-BY-BLOW OF HISTORICAL EVENTS OR PEACE STRATEGIES.
I DOUBT ANYONE WANTS ME TO REHASH EVERY DETAIL OF EVERY FAILED ATTEMPT AT PEACE OVER THE LAST 30 YEARS. THAT DOESN'T HELP ANYBODY.
I FIND THE STATUS QUO SO FRUSTRATING.
IT'S LIKE EVERYONE'S VIEW ON THIS SUBJECT IS SO ENTRENCHED THAT NO ONE BOTHERS TALKING ABOUT IT ANYMORE.
I MEAN, HOW CAN YOU HAVE CONSTRUCTIVE DIALOGUE WHEN EMOTIONS ARE STILL RAW FROM BLOODSHED? NEVER MIND EVEN THE COMPETING MYTHOLOGIES.
I'M SURE SOMEONE OUT THERE HAS A WORKABLE SOLUTION.
BUT WHAT DO I KNOW? I MAKE COMIC BOOKS AND WRITE ABOUT JAZZ.
I DO KNOW THE DIFFERENCE BETWEEN RIGHT AND WRONG, THOUGH.

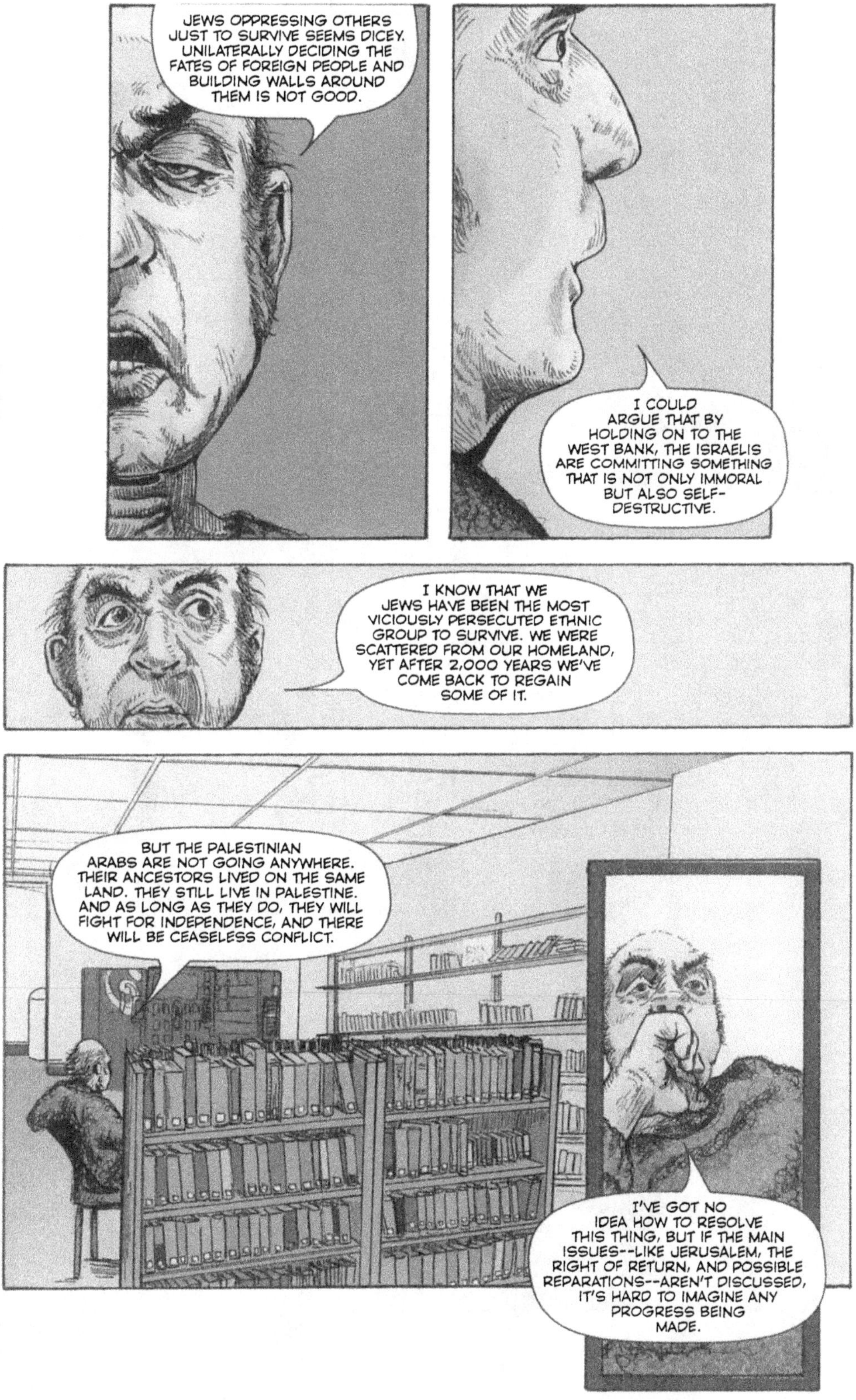
JEWS OPPRESSING OTHERS JUST TO SURVIVE SEEMS DICEY. UNILATERALLY DECIDING THE FATES OF FOREIGN PEOPLE AND BUILDING WALLS AROUND THEM IS NOT GOOD.
I COULD ARGUE THAT BY HOLDING ON TO THE WEST BANK, THE ISRAELIS ARE COMMITTING SOMETHING THAT IS NOT ONLY IMMORAL BUT ALSO SELF-DESTRUCTIVE.
I KNOW THAT WE JEWS HAVE BEEN THE MOST VICIOUSLY PERSECUTED ETHNIC GROUP TO SURVIVE. WE WERE SCATTERED FROM OUR HOMELAND, YET AFTER 2,000 YEARS WE'VE COME BACK TO REGAIN SOME OF IT.
BUT THE PALESTINIAN ARABS ARE NOT GOING ANYWHERE. THEIR ANCESTORS LIVED ON THE SAME LAND. THEY STILL LIVE IN PALESTINE. AND AS LONG AS THEY DO, THEY WILL FIGHT FOR INDEPENDENCE, AND THERE WILL BE CEASELESS CONFLICT.
I'VE GOT NO IDEA HOW TO RESOLVE THIS THING, BUT IF THE MAIN ISSUES--LIKE JERUSALEM, THE RIGHT OF RETURN, AND POSSIBLE REPARATIONS--AREN'T DISCUSSED, IT'S HARD TO IMAGINE ANY PROGRESS BEING MADE.

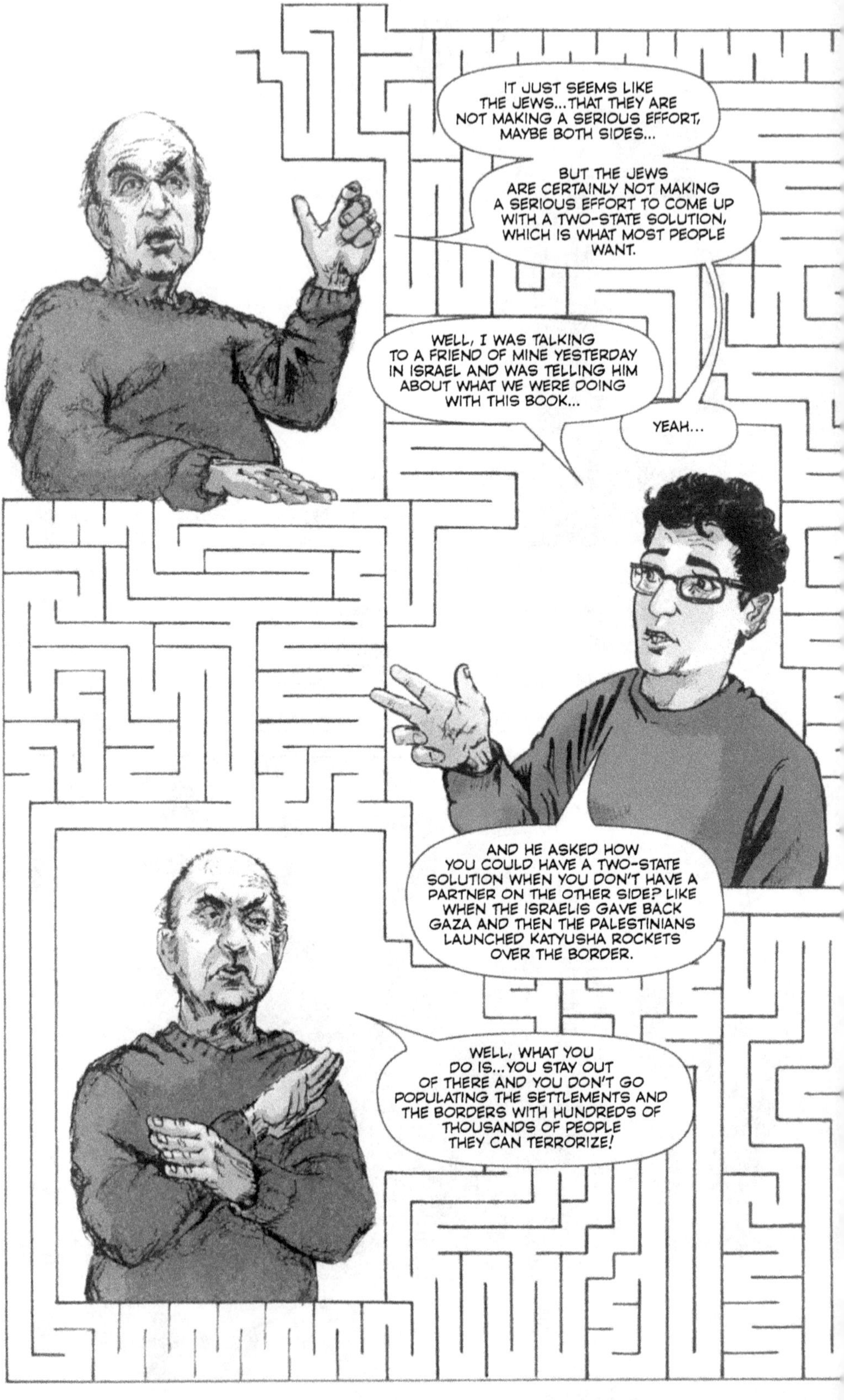
IT JUST SEEMS LIKE THE JEWS...THAT THEY ARE NOT MAKING A SERIOUS EFFORT, MAYBE BOTH SIDES...
BUT THE JEWS ARE CERTAINLY NOT MAKING A SERIOUS EFFORT TO COME UP WITH A TWO-STATE SOLUTION, WHICH IS WHAT MOST PEOPLE WANT.
WELL, I WAS TALKING TO A FRIEND OF MINE YESTERDAY IN ISRAEL AND WAS TELLING HIM ABOUT WHAT WE WERE DOING WITH THIS BOOK...
YEAH...
AND HE ASKED HOW YOU COULD HAVE A TWO-STATE SOLUTION WHEN YOU DON'T HAVE A PARTNER ON THE OTHER SIDE? LIKE WHEN THE ISRAELIS GAVE BACK GAZA AND THEN THE PALESTINIANS LAUNCHED KATYUSHA ROCKETS OVER THE BORDER.
WELL, WHAT YOU DO IS...YOU STAY OUT OF THERE AND YOU DON'T GO POPULATING THE SETTLEMENTS AND THE BORDERS WITH HUNDREDS OF THOUSANDS OF PEOPLE THEY CAN TERRORIZE!

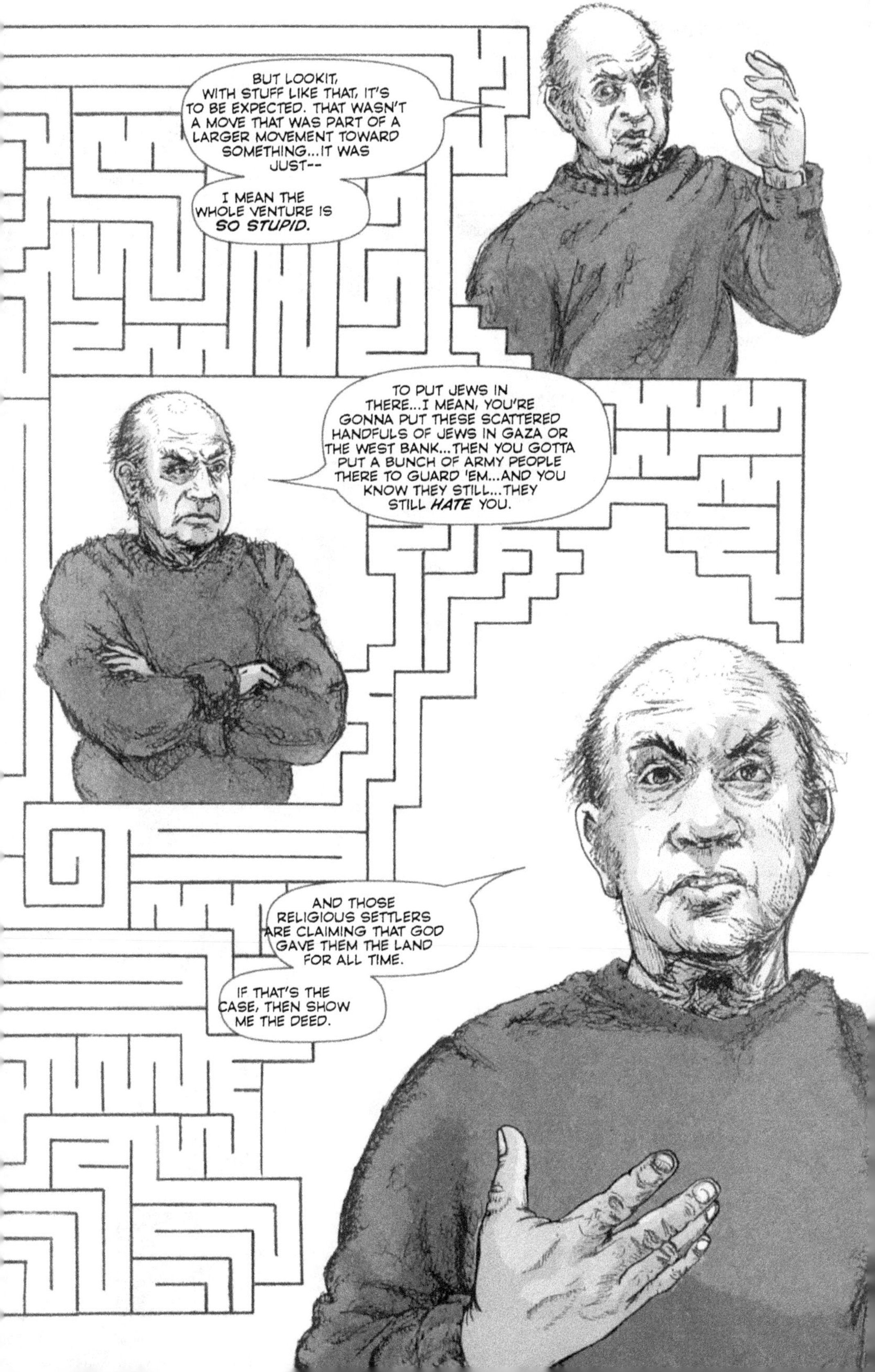
BUT LOOKIT, WITH STUFF LIKE THAT, IT'S TO BE EXPECTED. THAT WASN'T A MOVE THAT WAS PART OF A LARGER MOVEMENT TOWARD SOMETHING...IT WAS JUST--
I MEAN THE WHOLE VENTURE IS *SO STUPID.*
TO PUT JEWS IN THERE...I MEAN, YOU'RE GONNA PUT THESE SCATTERED HANDFULS OF JEWS IN GAZA OR THE WEST BANK...THEN YOU GOTTA PUT A BUNCH OF ARMY PEOPLE THERE TO GUARD 'EM...AND YOU KNOW THEY STILL...THEY STILL *HATE* YOU.
AND THOSE RELIGIOUS SETTLERS ARE CLAIMING THAT GOD GAVE THEM THE LAND FOR ALL TIME.
IF THAT'S THE CASE, THEN SHOW ME THE DEED.

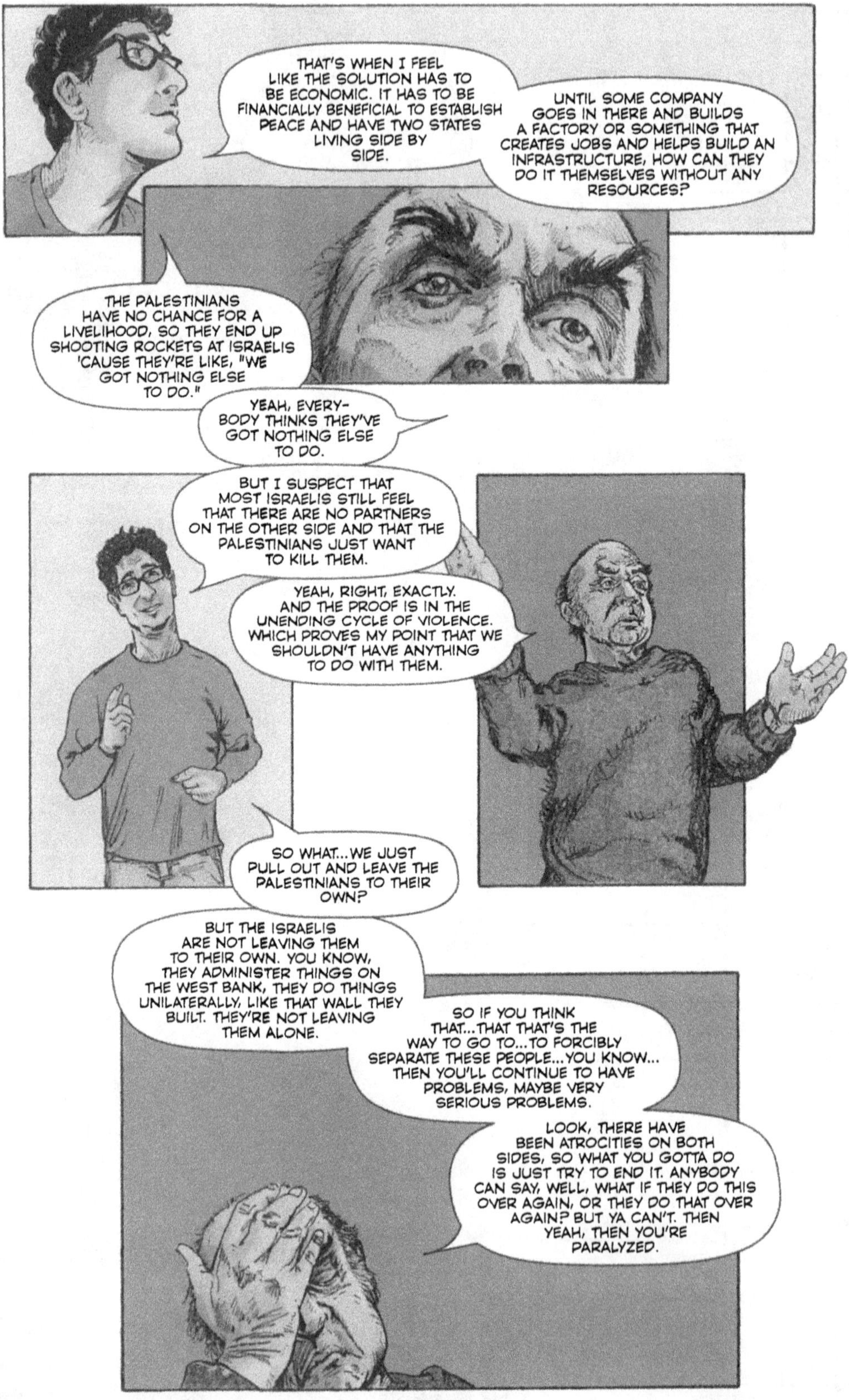
THAT'S WHEN I FEEL LIKE THE SOLUTION HAS TO BE ECONOMIC. IT HAS TO BE FINANCIALLY BENEFICIAL TO ESTABLISH PEACE AND HAVE TWO STATES LIVING SIDE BY SIDE.
UNTIL SOME COMPANY GOES IN THERE AND BUILDS A FACTORY OR SOMETHING THAT CREATES JOBS AND HELPS BUILD AN INFRASTRUCTURE, HOW CAN THEY DO IT THEMSELVES WITHOUT ANY RESOURCES?
THE PALESTINIANS HAVE NO CHANCE FOR A LIVELIHOOD, SO THEY END UP SHOOTING ROCKETS AT ISRAELIS 'CAUSE THEY'RE LIKE, "WE GOT NOTHING ELSE TO DO."
YEAH, EVERY-BODY THINKS THEY'VE GOT NOTHING ELSE TO DO.
BUT I SUSPECT THAT MOST ISRAELIS STILL FEEL THAT THERE ARE NO PARTNERS ON THE OTHER SIDE AND THAT THE PALESTINIANS JUST WANT TO KILL THEM.
YEAH, RIGHT, EXACTLY. AND THE PROOF IS IN THE UNENDING CYCLE OF VIOLENCE. WHICH PROVES MY POINT THAT WE SHOULDN'T HAVE ANYTHING TO DO WITH THEM.
SO WHAT...WE JUST PULL OUT AND LEAVE THE PALESTINIANS TO THEIR OWN?
BUT THE ISRAELIS ARE NOT LEAVING THEM TO THEIR OWN. YOU KNOW, THEY ADMINISTER THINGS ON THE WEST BANK, THEY DO THINGS UNILATERALLY, LIKE THAT WALL THEY BUILT. THEY'RE NOT LEAVING THEM ALONE.
SO IF YOU THINK THAT...THAT THAT'S THE WAY TO GO TO...TO FORCIBLY SEPARATE THESE PEOPLE...YOU KNOW... THEN YOU'LL CONTINUE TO HAVE PROBLEMS, MAYBE VERY SERIOUS PROBLEMS.
LOOK, THERE HAVE BEEN ATROCITIES ON BOTH SIDES, SO WHAT YOU GOTTA DO IS JUST TRY TO END IT. ANYBODY CAN SAY, WELL, WHAT IF THEY DO THIS OVER AGAIN, OR THEY DO THAT OVER AGAIN? BUT YA CAN'T. THEN YEAH, THEN YOU'RE PARALYZED.

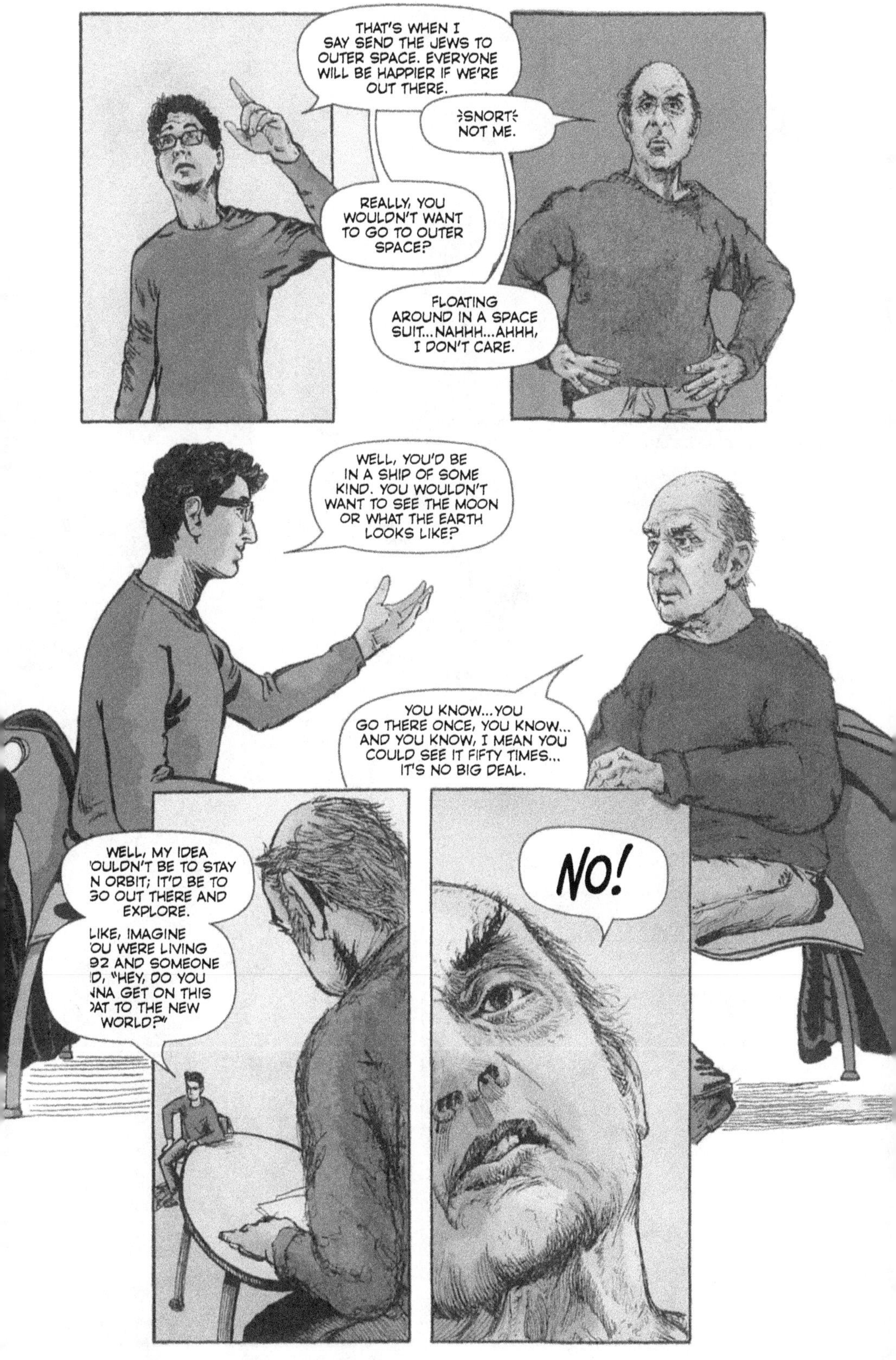
THAT'S WHEN I SAY SEND THE JEWS TO OUTER SPACE. EVERYONE WILL BE HAPPIER IF WE'RE OUT THERE.
SNORT NOT ME.
REALLY, YOU WOULDN'T WANT TO GO TO OUTER SPACE?
FLOATING AROUND IN A SPACE SUIT...NAHHH...AHHH, I DON'T CARE.
WELL, YOU'D BE IN A SHIP OF SOME KIND. YOU WOULDN'T WANT TO SEE THE MOON OR WHAT THE EARTH LOOKS LIKE?
YOU KNOW...YOU GO THERE ONCE, YOU KNOW... AND YOU KNOW, I MEAN YOU COULD SEE IT FIFTY TIMES... IT'S NO BIG DEAL.
WELL, MY IDEA OULDN'T BE TO STAY N ORBIT; IT'D BE TO O OUT THERE AND EXPLORE.
LIKE, IMAGINE OU WERE LIVING 92 AND SOMEONE D, "HEY, DO YOU NNA GET ON THIS AT TO THE NEW WORLD?"
NO!

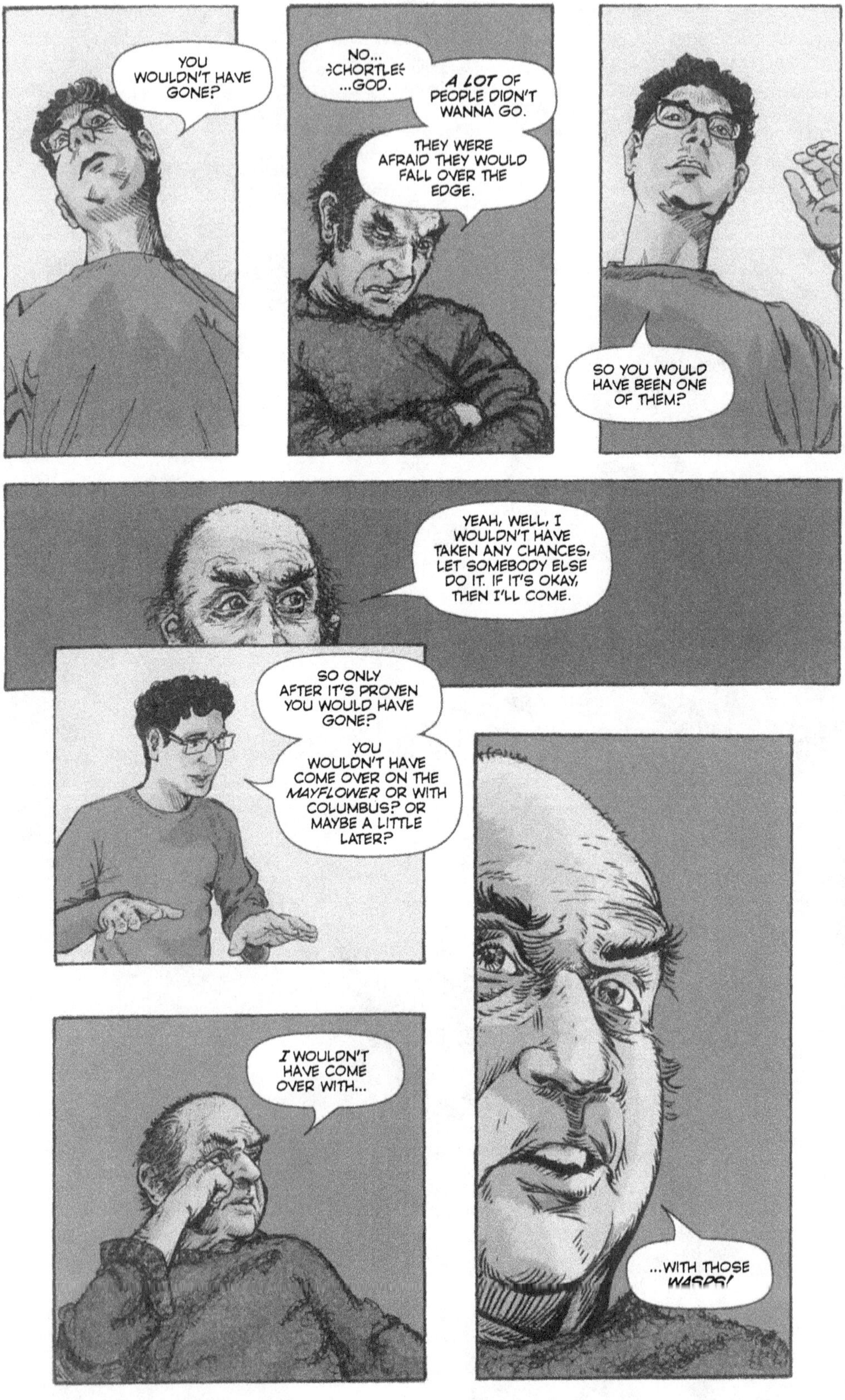
YOU WOULDN'T HAVE GONE?
NO... ≶CHORTLE≶ ...GOD.
A LOT OF PEOPLE DIDN'T WANNA GO.
THEY WERE AFRAID THEY WOULD FALL OVER THE EDGE.
SO YOU WOULD HAVE BEEN ONE OF THEM?
YEAH, WELL, I WOULDN'T HAVE TAKEN ANY CHANCES, LET SOMEBODY ELSE DO IT. IF IT'S OKAY, THEN I'LL COME.
SO ONLY AFTER IT'S PROVEN YOU WOULD HAVE GONE?
YOU WOULDN'T HAVE COME OVER ON THE *MAYFLOWER* OR WITH COLUMBUS? OR MAYBE A LITTLE LATER?
I WOULDN'T HAVE COME OVER WITH...
...WITH THOSE *WASPS!*

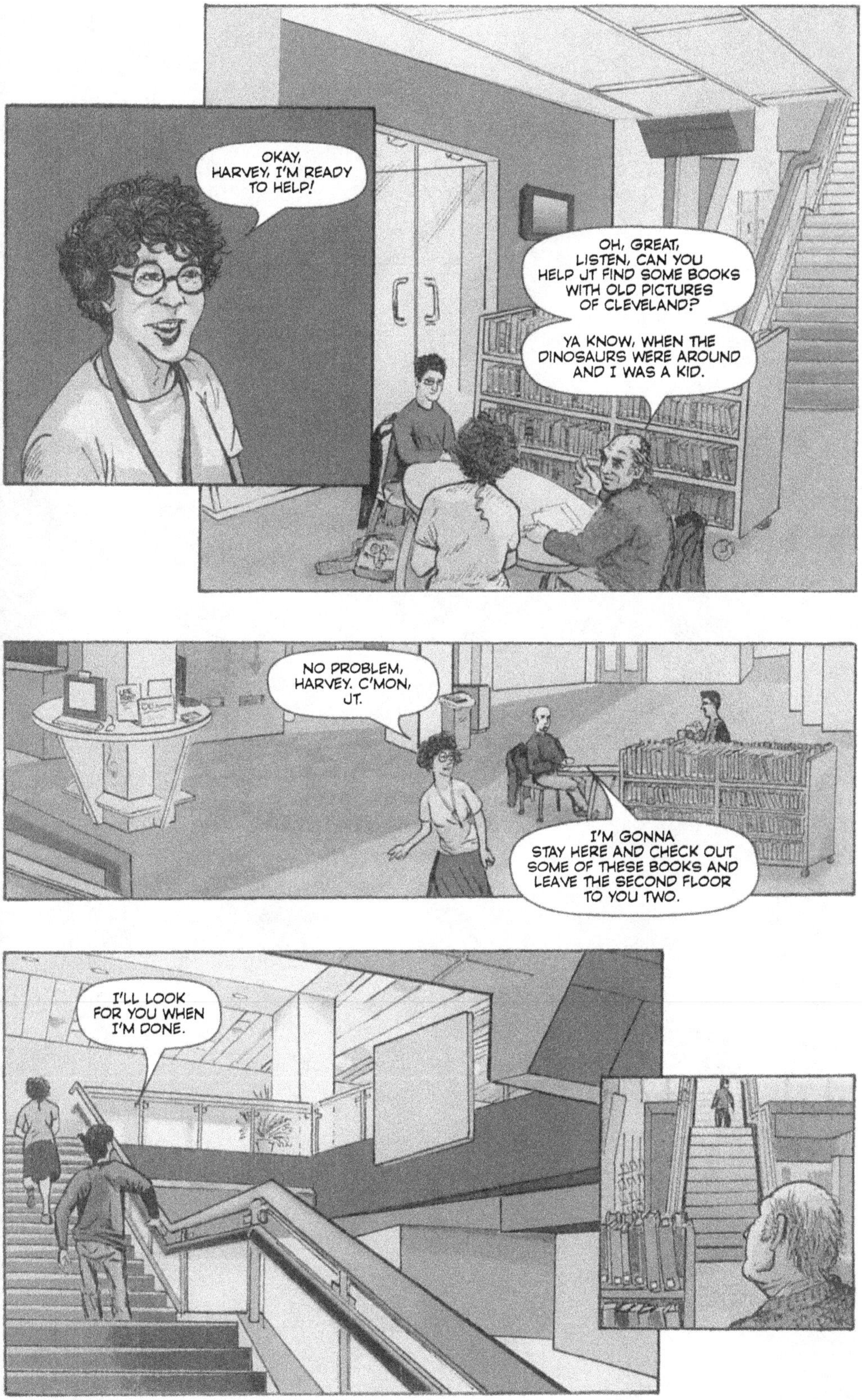
OKAY, HARVEY, I'M READY TO HELP!
OH, GREAT, LISTEN, CAN YOU HELP JT FIND SOME BOOKS WITH OLD PICTURES OF CLEVELAND?
YA KNOW, WHEN THE DINOSAURS WERE AROUND AND I WAS A KID.
NO PROBLEM, HARVEY. C'MON, JT.
I'M GONNA STAY HERE AND CHECK OUT SOME OF THESE BOOKS AND LEAVE THE SECOND FLOOR TO YOU TWO.
I'LL LOOK FOR YOU WHEN I'M DONE.

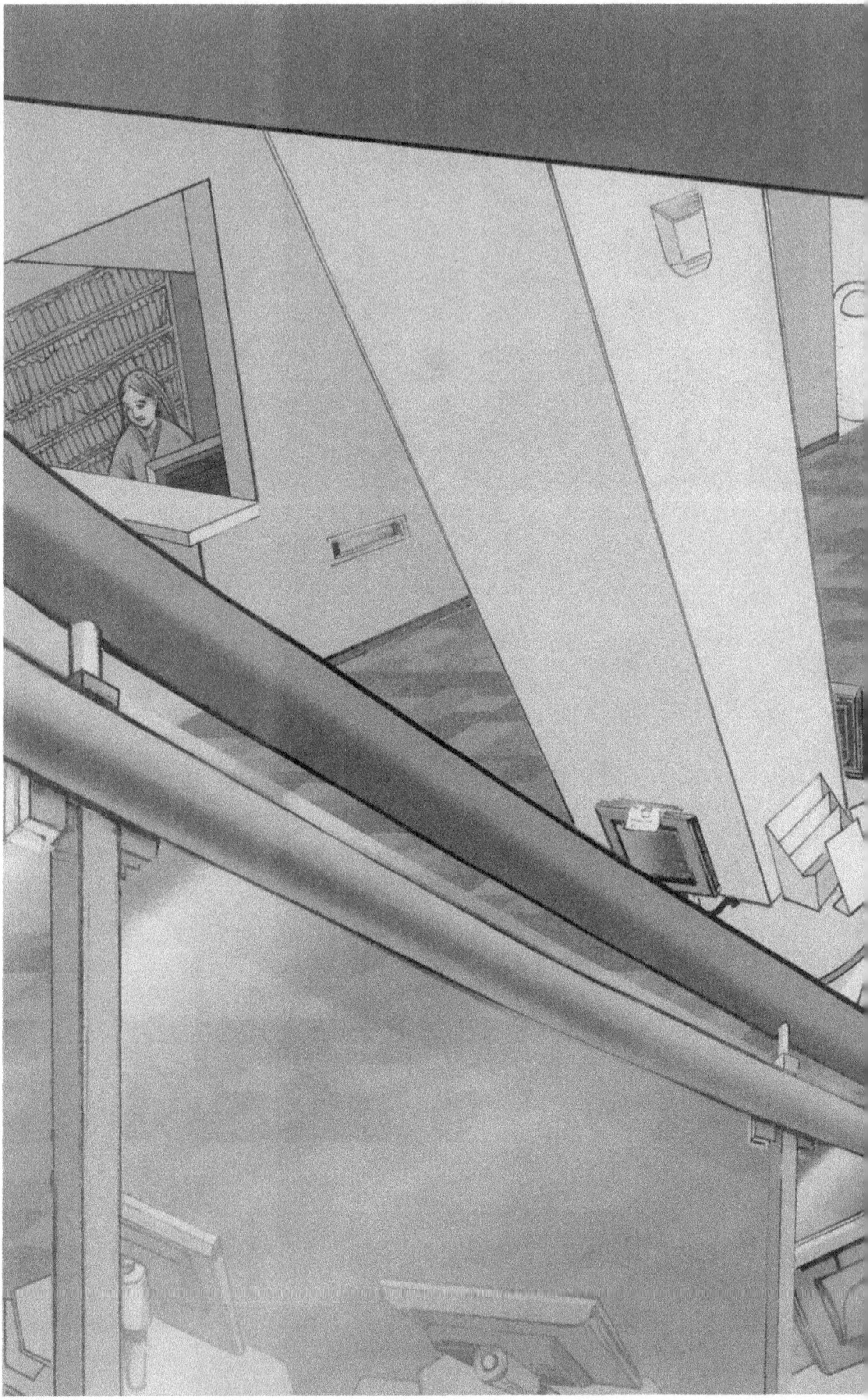

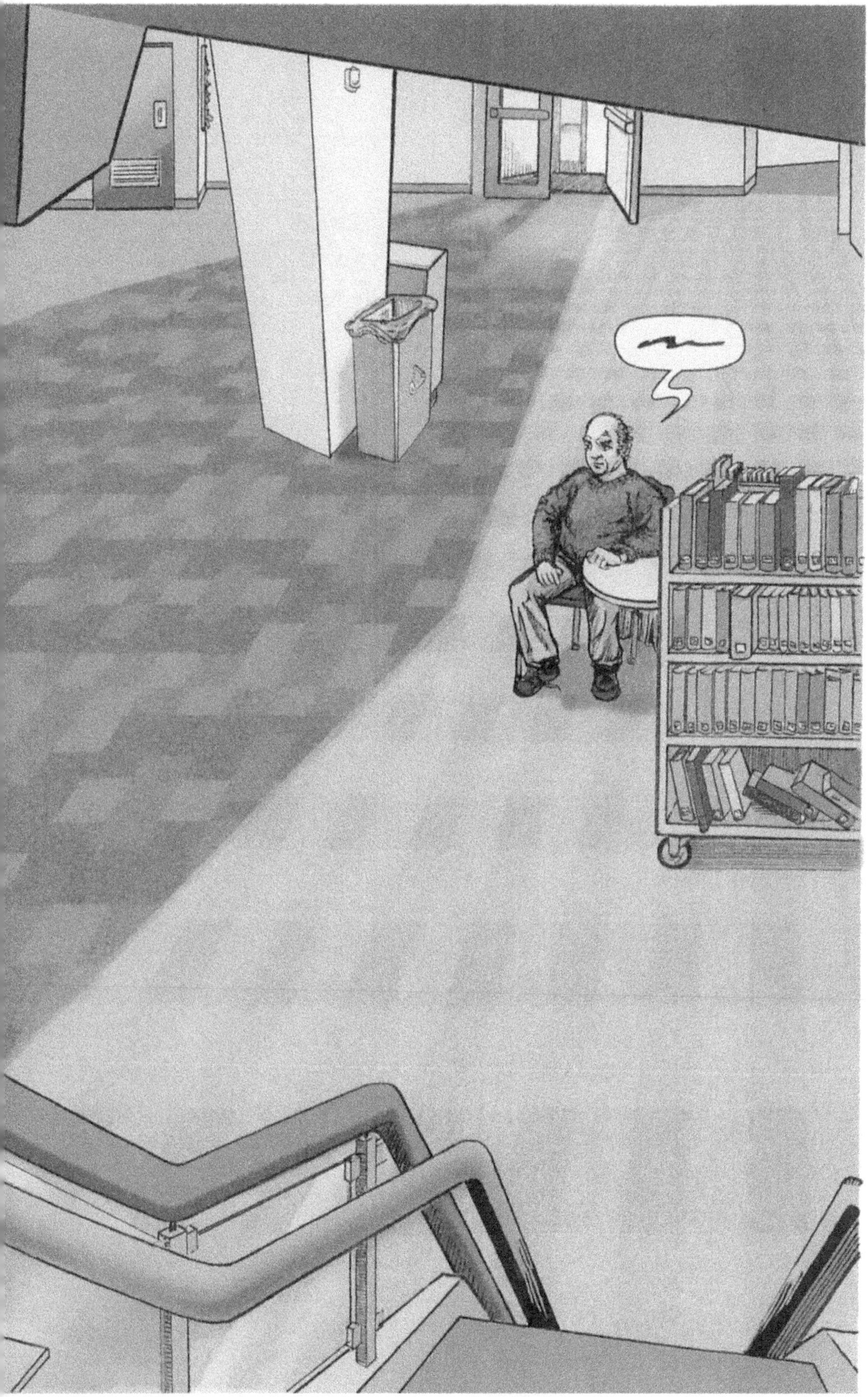

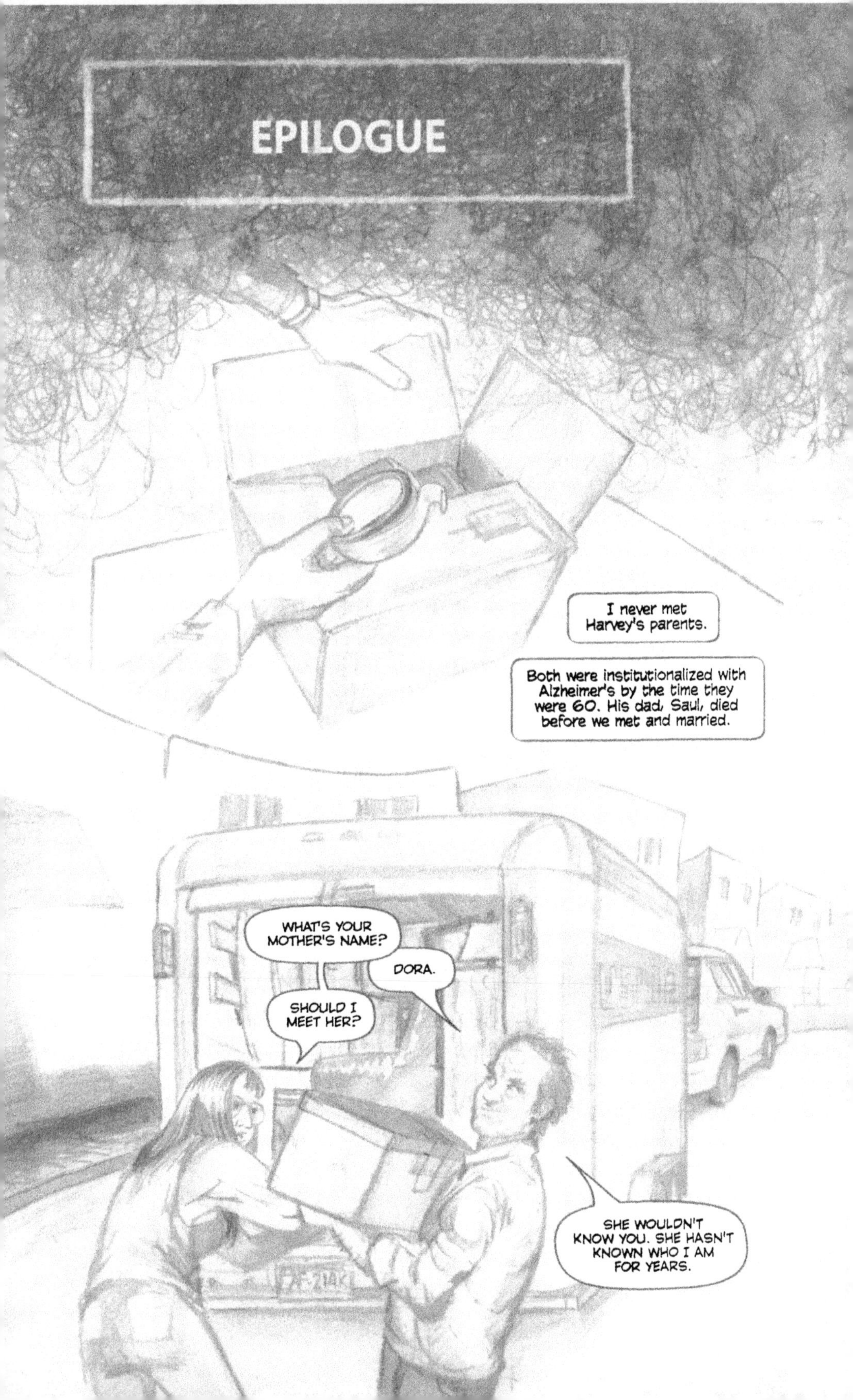
EPILOGUE
I never met Harvey's parents.
Both were institutionalized with Alzheimer's by the time they were 60. His dad, Saul, died before we met and married.
WHAT'S YOUR MOTHER'S NAME?
DORA.
SHOULD I MEET HER?
SHE WOULDN'T KNOW YOU. SHE HASN'T KNOWN WHO I AM FOR YEARS.

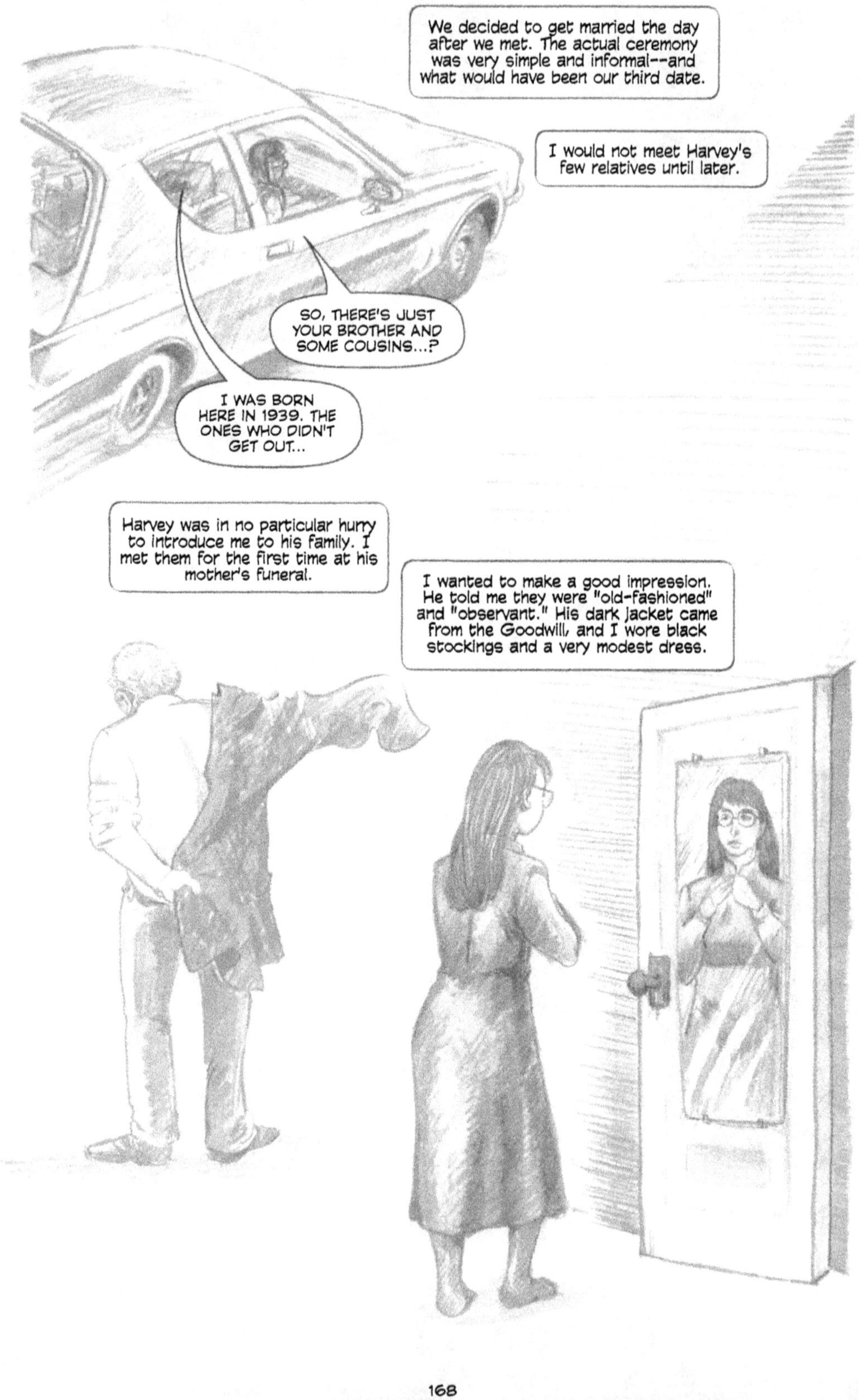
We decided to get married the day after we met. The actual ceremony was very simple and informal--and what would have been our third date.
I would not meet Harvey's few relatives until later.
SO, THERE'S JUST YOUR BROTHER AND SOME COUSINS...?
I WAS BORN HERE IN 1939. THE ONES WHO DIDN'T GET OUT...
Harvey was in no particular hurry to introduce me to his family. I met them for the first time at his mother's funeral.
I wanted to make a good impression. He told me they were "old-fashioned" and "observant." His dark jacket came from the Goodwill, and I wore black stockings and a very modest dress.

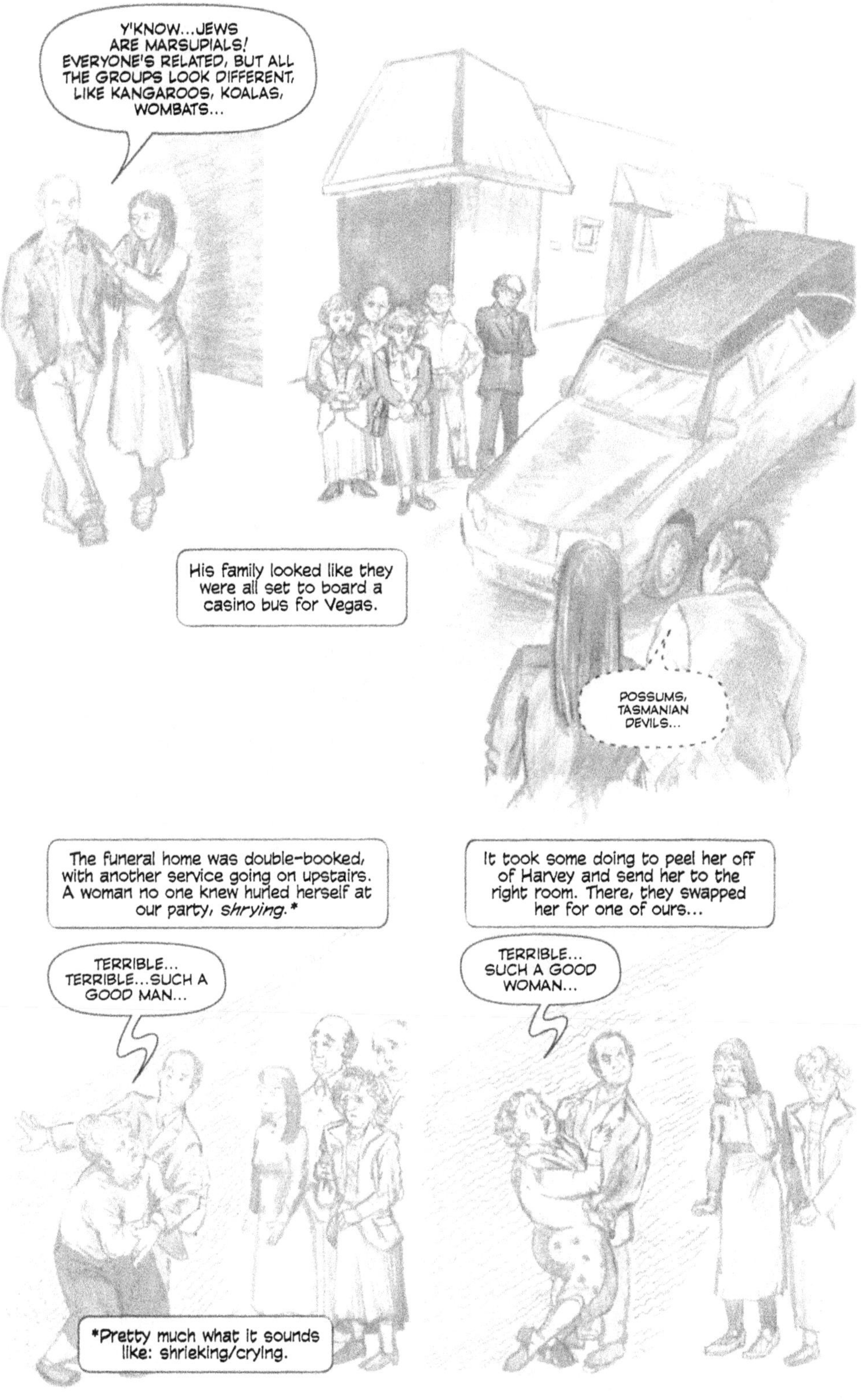
Y'KNOW...JEWS ARE MARSUPIALS! EVERYONE'S RELATED, BUT ALL THE GROUPS LOOK DIFFERENT, LIKE KANGAROOS, KOALAS, WOMBATS...
His family looked like they were all set to board a casino bus for Vegas.
POSSUMS, TASMANIAN DEVILS...
The funeral home was double-booked, with another service going on upstairs. A woman no one knew hurled herself at our party, *shrying.**
TERRIBLE... TERRIBLE...SUCH A GOOD MAN...
*Pretty much what it sounds like: shrieking/crying.
It took some doing to peel her off of Harvey and send her to the right room. There, they swapped her for one of ours...
TERRIBLE... SUCH A GOOD WOMAN...

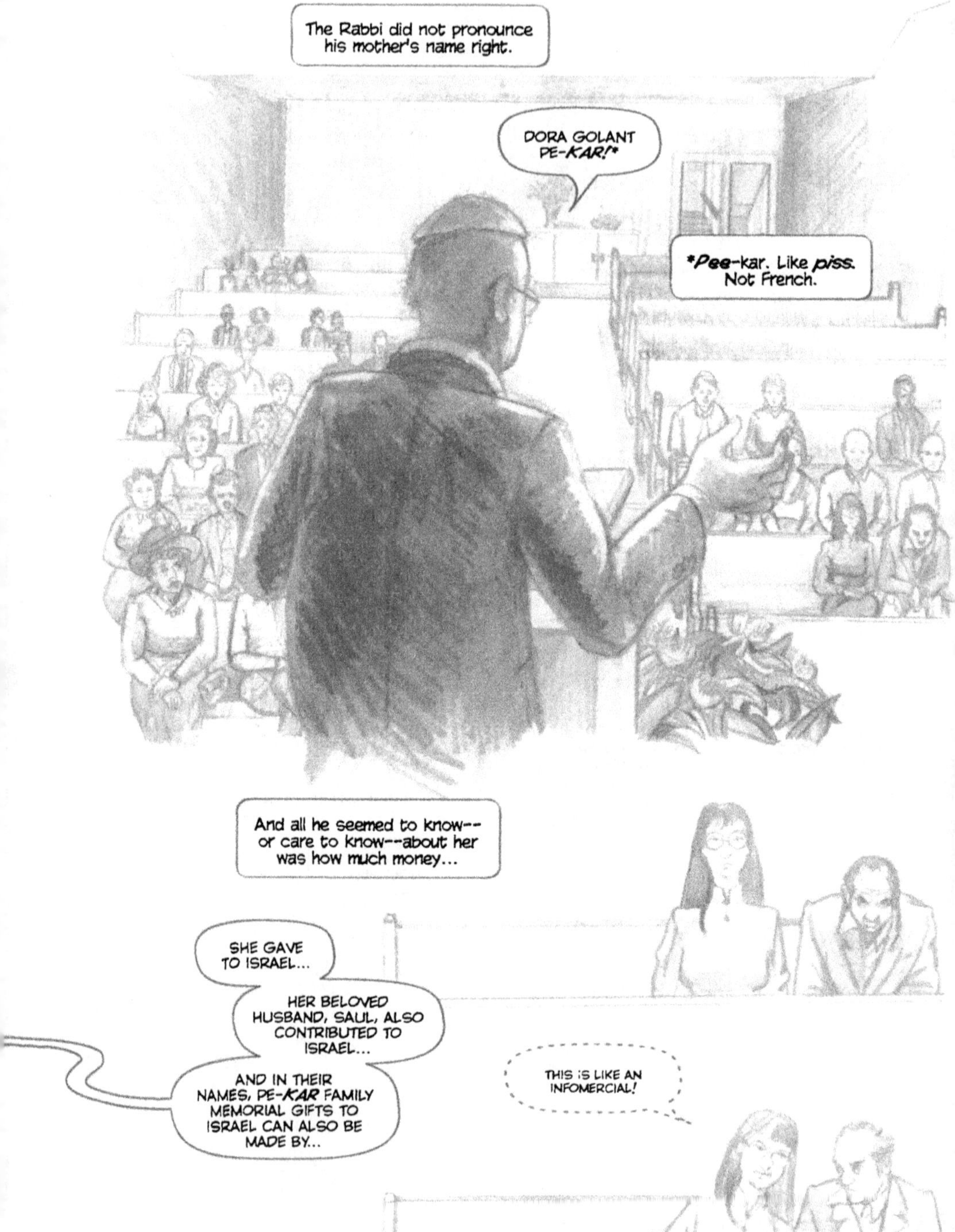
The Rabbi did not pronounce his mother's name right.
DORA GOLANT PE-KAR!*
*Pee-kar. Like piss. Not French.
And all he seemed to know--or care to know--about her was how much money...
SHE GAVE TO ISRAEL...
HER BELOVED HUSBAND, SAUL, ALSO CONTRIBUTED TO ISRAEL...
AND IN THEIR NAMES, PE-KAR FAMILY MEMORIAL GIFTS TO ISRAEL CAN ALSO BE MADE BY...
THIS IS LIKE AN INFOMERCIAL!

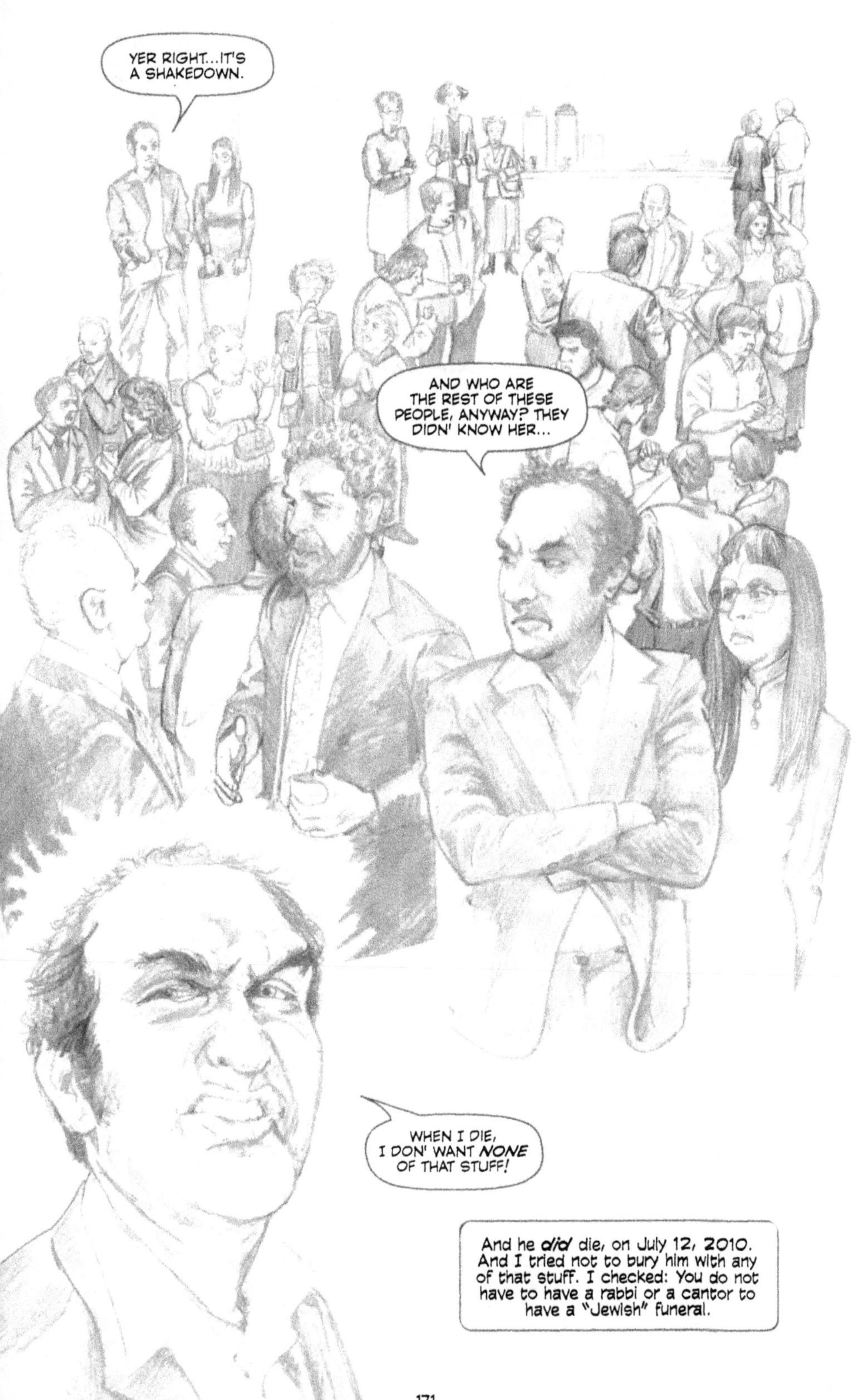
YER RIGHT...IT'S A SHAKEDOWN.
AND WHO ARE THE REST OF THESE PEOPLE, ANYWAY? THEY DIDN' KNOW HER...
WHEN I DIE, I DON' WANT *NONE* OF THAT STUFF!
And he *did* die, on July 12, 2010. And I tried not to bury him with any of that stuff. I checked: You do not have to have a rabbi or a cantor to have a "Jewish" funeral.

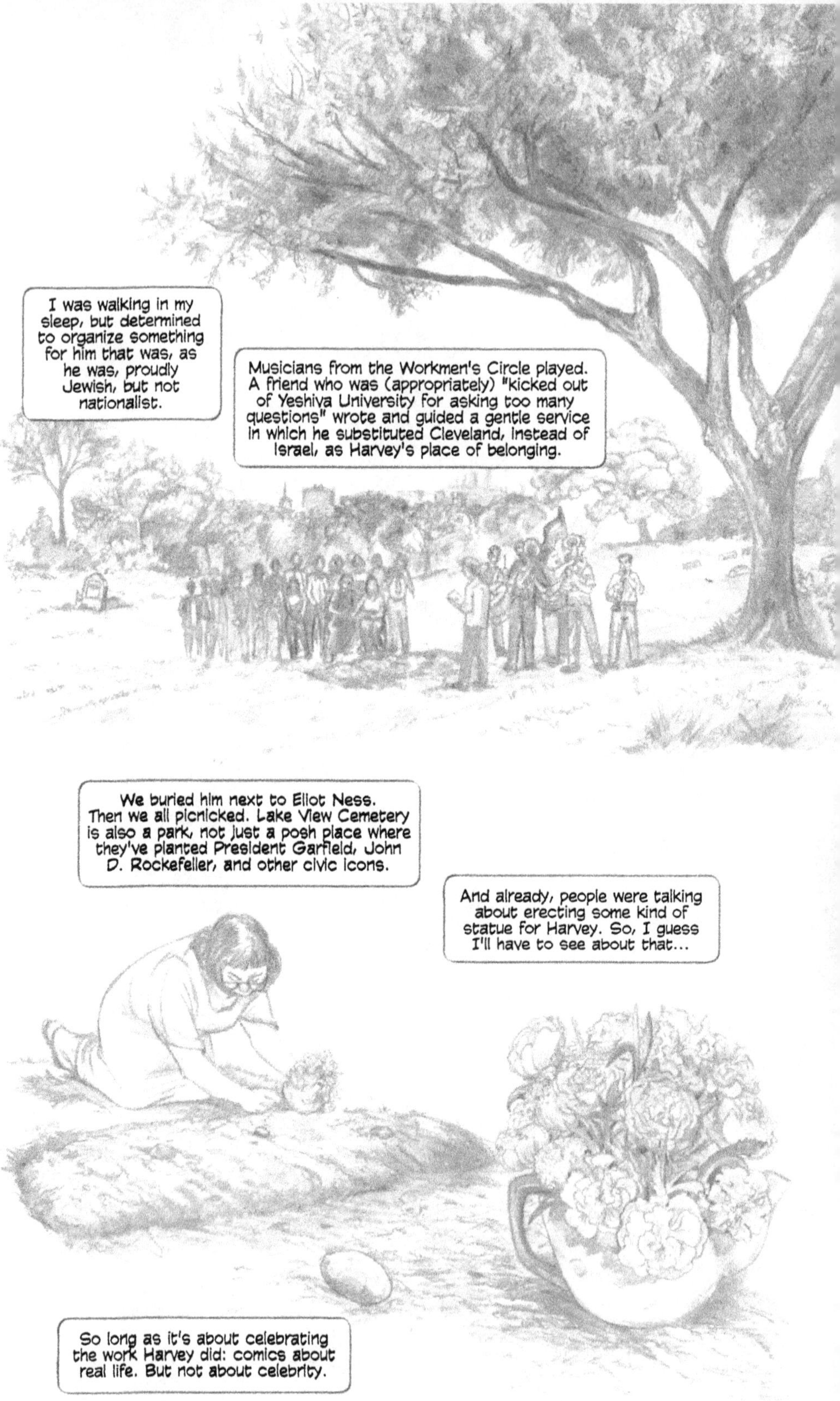
I was walking in my sleep, but determined to organize something for him that was, as he was, proudly Jewish, but not nationalist.
Musicians from the Workmen's Circle played. A friend who was (appropriately) "kicked out of Yeshiva University for asking too many questions" wrote and guided a gentle service in which he substituted Cleveland, instead of Israel, as Harvey's place of belonging.
We buried him next to Eliot Ness. Then we all picnicked. Lake View Cemetery is also a park, not just a posh place where they've planted President Garfield, John D. Rockefeller, and other civic icons.
And already, people were talking about erecting some kind of statue for Harvey. So, I guess I'll have to see about that...
So long as it's about celebrating the work Harvey did: comics about real life. But not about celebrity.

End.

Printed in the USA
CPSIA information can be obtained
at www.ICGtesting.com
LVHW091145150724
785511LV00005B/547

9 780809 074044